"Coming at a time when policing and police are in **great** turm
and Freedom in America advocates for police being 'guardi
authors present a model for achieving the guardian role."

James O. Finckenauer, *Distin*
Professional Fellow, Rutgers University

"A must-read for practitioners, educators, and students alike. The authors describe police training and educational practices in America and highlight high-profile current events to show that reform of police training and education practices is long overdue."

Jennifer Scroggins, *Associate Professor of Sociology and Criminal Justice, Montana State University Billings, USA*

"*Reframing Police Education and Freedom in America* promotes a collaboratively based adjustment to existing police academy training. This ground-breaking book offers a guide regarding a decentralized model of a need for higher-level thinking skills for police officers to achieve effective crime prevention and rebuild trust essential for community policing to flourish."

John B. Wilt, *Professor Emeritus of Administration of Justice, Danville Community College, USA*

"*Reframing Police Education and Freedom in America* offers a much-needed and timely, modern perspective on improving outdated methods of police education. Greenberg and Easterling promote the use of advanced technology and a renewed focus on critical thinking to transition away from policing's 'warrior mentality' of training for battle and toward building community trust in police."

D. Cygan, *Illinois State Police (Ret.), USA*

"Police education and training needs to evolve with the times. In this historically informed survey, Easterling and Greenberg grapple with the 'us–them,' problem in police enculturation, seeking ways to maintain the truism that police are civilians in uniform, not a breed apart."

John Kleinig, *Emeritus Professor of Philosophy, Department of Criminal Justice, John Jay College of Criminal Justice, USA*

"*Reframing Police Education and Freedom in America* is a captivating book that provides evidence-based recommendations for what law enforcement training and education should look like for the police to best-serve their communities, emphasizing the need for collaboration with the community in these transformative efforts. This is a must-read!"

Paige Reed, *Assistant Professor of Criminal Justice, Mary Baldwin University, USA*

"This meticulously researched volume should help inform police leaders and educators about the possibilities of police-citizen cooperation in the decades to come."

Beth J. Sanborn, *Police Officer and Educator*

REFRAMING POLICE EDUCATION AND FREEDOM IN AMERICA

This book untangles the components of police education and advocates a robust community-based training model with significant civilian oversight. The recommended approach recognizes that the citizenry needs to be included in the provision of basic police education, for it is they who must both support and be served by their police. The police must be role models for society, demonstrating that freedom and rights come with obligations, both to the community as a whole and to individuals in need within that community. Ultimately, the quality of police training and the public's safety depend not only on the leadership of police executives as well as the quality of educational institutions and police candidates but also on the building of a community's trust in its police.

The issues of police recruitment, education, and retention have greater consequence in an era when protests and other signs of negativity surround law enforcement. Several incidents, including, most notably, George Floyd's murder by police, have sparked new training initiatives regarding police de-escalation and community engagement. At the same time, the proliferation of gun violence and a contentious political climate have led some officers to refrain from undertaking proactive types of policing. In this context, reform of the police education system is urgent. This book examines police training at all levels of government—local, regional, state, and federal. In addition, citizen participation programs, including the role of the media and programs for furthering law-related education (LRE), are highlighted. The proposed police education model recognizes that ordinary members of the American public need to contribute to the provision of basic police education, for it is they who must both support and be served by their police. The focus is on teaching a "guardian style" of policing at the local level. Police education would combine higher education, necessary practical proficiencies, and intensive field experiences through a gradual level of greater responsibility—likely extending over a 2-plus-year period for trainees with less than a year of previous college credits.

This book will be of interest to a wide range of audiences such as law enforcement professionals and trainers, including those in executive development programs in police departments; community leaders, scholars, and policy experts who specialize in policing; concerned citizens; and students of criminal justice, especially those interested in police organization and management, criminal justice policy, and the historical development of police.

Martin Alan Greenberg is president of the Virginia Association of Criminal Justice Educators and chair of the Security and Crime Prevention Section within the Academy of Criminal Justice Sciences. He is also active in community activities concerning criminal justice reforms as well as humanitarian causes. He has authored six previous books and has served as a criminal justice program director at several universities in the USA. In New York City, he also served as a senior court officer and auxiliary police deputy inspector.

Beth Allen Easterling is a visiting associate professor of criminal justice at Roanoke College, USA. Her research on the criminal justice system has largely focused on the impact of incarceration on the family and has been published in a variety of criminological and sociological journals and books. She works to raise awareness of the strength and resilience of marginalized groups in society by highlighting their success stories through her roles as a researcher and teacher.

Routledge Series on Practical and Evidence-Based Policing

Books in the Routledge Series on Practical and Evidence-Based Policing disseminate knowledge and provide practical tools for law enforcement leaders and personnel to protect and serve the public and reduce crime. With an aim to bridge the "translation gap" between frontline policing and academic research, books in this series apply sound scientific methods as well as practical experience to make everyday police work safer and smarter. These books are an invaluable resource for police practitioners, academic researchers, public policymakers, and students in law enforcement and criminology programs to guide best practices in all aspects of policing.

Public Corruption in the United States
Analysis of a Destructive Phenomenon
Jeff Cortese

The Wicked Problems of Police Reform in Canada
Laura Huey, Lorna Ferguson & Jennifer L. Schulenberg

Human Rights Policing
Reimagining Law Enforcement in the 21st Century
Peter Marina & Pedro Marina

Interviewing Vulnerable Suspects
Safeguarding the Process
Edited by Dr Jane Tudor-Owen, Dr Celine van Golde, Dr Ray Bull & David Gee MBE

Reframing Police Education and Freedom in America
Martin Alan Greenberg & Beth Allen Easterling

For more information about this series, please visit: www.routledge.com

REFRAMING POLICE EDUCATION AND FREEDOM IN AMERICA

Martin Alan Greenberg and Beth Allen Easterling

Routledge
Taylor & Francis Group
NEW YORK AND LONDON

Designed cover image: Robert Knudsen. White House Photographs. John F. Kennedy Presidential Library and Museum, Boston

First published 2024
by Routledge
605 Third Avenue, New York, NY 10158

and by Routledge
4 Park Square, Milton Park, Abingdon, Oxon, OX14 4RN

Routledge is an imprint of the Taylor & Francis Group, an informa business

ISBN: 978-1-032-30947-7 (hbk)
ISBN: 978-1-032-30873-9 (pbk)
ISBN: 978-1-003-30739-6 (ebk)

DOI: 10.4324/9781003307396

Typeset in Sabon
by Apex CoVantage, LLC

This page is dedicated in honor of the legacy of Emmett Till and his mother, Mamie Till-Mobley. In 1955, Emmett Till, at age 14, was slain by white supremacists. After her son's death, Mamie Till-Mobley insisted on an open-casket funeral so viewers could see what happened to him. Before her death in 2003, she served as chair and co-founder of the Emmett Till Justice Campaign and worked to have her son's murder case reopened. Emmett Till's death shocked the nation and helped ignite the civil rights movement. In 2022, the US Congress awarded posthumously the Congressional Gold Medal to Emmett Till and Mamie Till-Mobley, the nation's highest civilian honor.

CONTENTS

FIGURES

WORDS OF INSPIRATION

The evident genius of the human spirit lies in the hard fact of life that we . . . [are] limited in all the important ways . . . We cannot do all that our powerful minds trick us into thinking we can. In a word, this is the mystery of being human. Our finest nature is not our ability to think and do. It is that we do and think as we do in spite of the obstacles . . . On average, the better ones among us continue to think and do what they can with no assurance that solutions will be found.

—Charles Lemert from *Thinking the Unthinkable* (2007)

ACKNOWLEDGMENTS

Thank you to the team at Taylor & Francis who have worked with us to make this idea come to life. In a time of such uncertainty in the field of criminal justice—and particularly policing—we appreciate the interest in this work and hope that this book will further the topics of discussion within its pages.

I would like to thank my colleagues and students from Mary Baldwin University who have been open to discussion on the topics of this book. These conversations have helped me ask bigger questions and have given me the inspiration to seek those answers, even when that pursuit is challenging. I am grateful beyond words for my husband, Major Joseph W. "Buzz" Easterling, USMC, Ret., and daughter, Kaitlyn Iris Easterling. Their patience and support mean the world to me and allow me to pursue the work I am passionate about. Most importantly, I am thankful for the collaboration with my co-author, whose mentorship, kindness, and grace have been invaluable in this project as well as in my personal and professional life more generally. Thank you for inviting me to work on this vision with you.

Beth Allen Easterling
Staunton, Virginia

I am very grateful for the spirit and collaborative efforts demonstrated by my coauthor. This book is only a reality because of her countless virtues. Throughout the project I have gained much knowledge during our discussions and periods of composing for greatest accuracy. I am more than ever convinced that an effective system of crime control is dependent on collaborative efforts.

I would like to especially acknowledge the scholars we have relied upon and whose work we have built upon. While the ultimate opinions expressed are our own, their scholarship and contributions to the field of police education have made this book project possible. In no particular order, they are Willard Oliver, Samuel Walker, John Kleinig, Joanna C. Schwartz, Rosa Brooks, Penny Harrington, Eric Foner, David H. Bayley, Peter K. Manning, Gary Cordner, Norm Stamper, and William Westley, each of whom has demonstrated a thorough dedication to civil liberties and constitutional guarantees. Much can be said about the contributions of each of these great educators and professionals. For example, Stamper's work is essential reading for understanding the intensely racist and anti-Black sentiments of police culture. William Westley was one of the very first researchers to identify how police subculture was reinforced by secrecy and violence.

In a world marked by the everyday emergence of new information technologies and overwhelming media scrutiny of all public behavior, it is exceedingly important to consider the work of such major academic figures in order to achieve the proper balance between safeguarding individual rights with the needs of public safety controls. For example, it would be wise to look at Peter K. Manning's *Policing Contingencies* (2003). His work draws on decades of fieldwork to investigate how law enforcement works on the ground and in the symbolic realm and why most efforts to reform the way police work have failed because of a failure to focus on crime prevention efforts. Similarly, John Kleinig's *The Ethics of Policing* (1996) provides invaluable information about the foundations and purpose of police authority and specific problems such as accountability, police discretion, and the use of force.

Finally, this work would never have been completed but for the remarkable efforts of my wife, Dr. Ellen C. Wertlieb, and son Dr. Edward W. Greenberg, who were always present to guide my stumbles.

Martin Alan Greenberg
Niskayuna, New York

PREFACE

"There is deep tension between community policing and the warrior identity that has become so prevalent in modern law enforcement. . . . Earning public trust will take decades and require rethinking how officers are trained as well as the legal and administrative standards used to review police violence" (Stoughton, 2015). Calls for reform are abundant, and the public is demanding sweeping changes to policing. Thus, any book on the status and future of police education may be somewhat out-of-date the day after it is submitted to its publisher since the field is constantly evolving. Both police academy curriculums and in-service courses are subject to alteration. Moreover, current training methods are under close scrutiny due to the notoriety of police responses to calls concerning people in crisis and what is needed to prevent more mass killings. The matter is also complicated by the existence of about 18,000 different police agencies in the United States, whose formats and renditions vary not only from state to state but often from agency to agency. Furthermore, as a "guardian" approach to policing comes to dominance in American society, significant changes will need to be made in existing police training curricula. In contrast to a paramilitary or "warrior" form of training emphasis, "the guardian model emphasizes the use of communication techniques instead of commands, equity instead of authority, and tactical restraint instead of forceful measures" (Helfgott et al., 2018). Significantly, the preservation of democratic values, including the protection of civil rights, is given prominence (see also Rahr & Rice, 2015; Miletich, 2013; Stoughton, 2015).

Police agencies may need to review the status of their existing training facilities so that officers can keep up not only with new models of law enforcement but also with new statutes (e.g., "red-flag" laws) and the latest technology, such as virtual and augmented reality training applications. On the other hand, the cost of such facilities might be staggering. In 2022, Steve McCraw, the director of the Texas Department of Public Safety, requested $1.2 billion to turn its existing training center north of Austin into a full-time statewide law enforcement academy—starting with a state-of-the-art active-shooter facility. Director McCraw told budget officials: "You need to practice in a real environment" (qtd. in Harper, 2022).

Driven by new forms of modern technology, the widespread availability of semiautomatic firearms, and global connectivity, the following types of crime have become more prevalent: cybercrime (especially, identity-related crimes); acts of terrorism; active shooters with mass casualties; the sexual exploitation of children; fraudulent medicine sales; human and organ trafficking; environmental crime; road rage shootings (see Deliso, 2021); and trafficking in cultural property, along with piracy, an old form of crime that has reemerged. People are "committing crimes in cyberspace that they would not otherwise commit. The anonymity of the Internet and the possibility of adopting flexible identities can be incentives for criminal behavior" (UN Congress on Crime, 2015). For example, illicit drugs and other products can be bought online and paid for with anonymous virtual currencies. Human trafficking activities can be covertly happening behind closed doors and computer screens. Moreover, a major new category of cybercrime appeared to intensify in 2021, having a catastrophic impact, namely, a widescale ransomware attack impacting gas pipelines and raising national gas prices overnight.

At the same time as the foregoing crimes have taken their toll of human life, everyday incidents of aggressive driving have increased. Incidents of road rage have increased steadily and overall, "roughly 30,000 people die in car accidents every year. Of those victims, 66% lose their lives due to dangerous driving" (Carsurance, 2022). The need for public services (such as helping citizens who are elderly or have disabilities navigate their surroundings) continues to require police intervention. These types of incidents give rise to the need for law enforcement to adapt its training and operations.

The problems associated with police work and the need to maintain law and order are compounded by other aspects of human behavior and the nature of the criminal justice system, such as what happens after a criminal conviction. If imprisonment is to be relied on for offenders—should there be an emphasis on its punitive or treatment aspects? According to Clear and Frost (2014), there has been an increasing pressure to downsize the scale of imprisonment and to find other less destructive ways of regulating offenders. Restorative justice and justice movements that center around victims produce research and programs aimed toward a goal of less punishment and lower incarceration rates (Heffner & FeldmanHall, 2019; Kelly, 2021). Furthermore, a number of scholars have questioned the role of traditional uniformed police (see Bayley, 1994; Vitale, 2017; Wilson & Kelling, 1982) for contending with modern-day crimes. Significantly, "a recurring feature of many of these 'new crimes' is that they involve protracted investigation and continuous monitoring" (Matthews, 2020, p. 322).

The police component of the criminal justice system most typically serves as the enforcement arm of the executive branch of government. However, in various localities, there are also special jurisdiction police officers who protect America's infrastructure, for example, transportation, harbor/port facilities, airports, public school districts etc. (see Census, 2011) or the other major branches of the government—judiciary and legislative. The US Capitol Police Force (USCP) is the special jurisdiction law enforcement agency created to protect life and property, prevent, detect, and investigate criminal acts, and enforce traffic regulations throughout a large complex of congressional buildings, parks, and thoroughfares. Additionally, USCP officers are responsible for protecting members and officers of Congress and their families. Oftentimes, these duties require that USCP officers serve throughout the United States and its territories and possessions. In early March 2021, when FBI Director Christopher Wray was first called before the Senate Judiciary Committee to explain the FBI's knowledge of any online foreshadowing regarding the January 6, 2021, riot or insurrection at the US Capitol while Congress certified Joe Biden as the winner of the 2020 presidential election, Director Wray warned that the January 6th attack was not an isolated event and that the problem of domestic terrorism was growing in the United States.

Over the years, there have been many hundreds of studies regarding the fundamental responsibilities of police agencies to maintain peace and enforce the law. In recent times, attention has focused on the death of George Floyd in May 2020 and the protests it generated. New community groups have arisen to address how police are funded and how to better hold officers accountable for abuse of force and racial bias. Some cities are pushing for police to no longer be the first responders for people in a mental health, homeless, or substance use crises. Recent studies show that nearly a quarter of fatal police encounters followed calls about "disruptive behavior" directly tied to a person's mental illness and/or substance abuse disorder.

The reform pressures have many cops leaving the job. At the same time, in July 2021, it was reported that ambush style attacks on police had nearly doubled since 2020 (Earles & Pazzona, 2021). In some areas, the police workforce was shrinking due to an unprecedented number of retirements and resignations. Retaining and recruiting police is proving to be difficult. Recruitment was already a serious challenge before the start of the COVID pandemic and the racial justice protests after Floyd's death. According to a Police Executive Research Forum (PERF) survey of about 200 police departments, police retirements were up by 45% and resignations by 18% in the period between April 2020 and April 2021, when compared with the preceding 12 months (MacFarquhar, 2021). Chief David Zack of the Asheville Police Department in North Carolina declared, "We have asked too much from police, and it has caught up with us nationally" (qtd. in MacFarquhar, 2021). Not counting the delays associated with advertising, testing, and performing background checks, it can take well over a year or longer to hire, train, and certify a new officer. On the other hand, this is not necessarily a negative aspect of policing and the authors are committed to an apprenticeship-type training model involving even longer time periods. The achievement of the "guardian style of policing" is well worth the effort. The instances of overly aggressive police tactics and outright cases of abuse of force have caused protestors to seek major police reforms and to assign some of their tasks to civilian agencies. Civilian oversight for basic training is non-existent. Many of the police reform plans put in place after the death of George Floyd have focused on banning chokeholds, requiring the use of body cameras, more detailed annual reports, holding monthly citizen-based council meetings on policing, the need for independent civilian review boards, calls for diversifying the makeup of police, ideas about creating police substations in neighborhoods with higher crime rates, and greater use of "community engagement officers," as well as additional training on implicit bias and de-escalation techniques. These recommendations do not fully embrace the important role in crime and terrorism prevention which average citizens can perform. The need for enhanced public support of the police is really the "elephant in the room"—so to speak. Calls for defunding the police are misguided, for they ignore the need for law enforcement officers to act as "guardians" and involve the citizenry in their work. Most crimes, incidents of domestic terrorism, and police violence result from individual action. Police and other types of organizations concerned with public safety need to offer opportunities for citizens to carry out greater crime prevention and oversight responsibilities. Ironically, the Floyd case involved an example of appropriate citizen action, but one that was not encouraged by the local police—the video recording of the incident by the steady hand and mind of 17-year-old Darnella Frazier. Her bravery and quick thinking in capturing the video of Officer Derek Chauvin pressing his knee on George Floyd's neck likely contributed to his convictions on state murder and manslaughter charges after a state trial and for using excessive force under color of law in a separate federal civil rights case in which Chauvin pleaded guilty (see Senter & Dewan, 2022).

In November 2022, the need to reform police education and training was placed front and center by the PERF when it released a new report—titled "Transforming Police Recruit Training: 40 Guiding Principles"—stating that the way in which new recruits are presently trained for their careers is in a state of crisis. The report recommends that law enforcement agencies in the United States should seriously rethink how they train new recruits for the job (Wyllie, 2022).

Ultimately, any type of police reform, including police education and training, will have its greatest impact if conducted at the local level, alongside an increase in public perception and support of policing more generally within individual neighborhoods. It is a well-established fact that most policing in the United States is done by law enforcement agencies at the local level and most Americans prefer that policing be controlled locally (Schwabe, 1999). According to Jon Meacham, a renowned presidential historian and Pulitzer Prize-winning author, "Democracy is not guaranteed. It is the hardest of human undertakings because it requires us to see each other not as rivals, but as neighbors" (qtd. in Kavathas, 2022). It is at the local level that good citizens are needed to work with their community's police to ensure a decent, just, and equitable society.

This book expands the discussion on police training. Understanding the history and current state of police training within the United States and beyond opens this conversation. By exploring various types of police academies (along with the social and educational opportunities that happen within their walls and the perception of police training by the general public), the conversation builds to offer suggestions for moving beyond some of the current models of police training. The concluding chapter of this book recommends a model for police recruiting, education, and training that can best be accomplished at the local level with the active support of the public. It is proposed as a model to help build the trust so necessary for "changing the very culture of policing by reaffirming that policing must be done with a community, not to a community" (Stoughton, 2015).

References

Bayley, D. (1994). *Police for the future*. Oxford University Press.

Carsurance. (2022). *29 road rage statistics for safe driving—2022 edition*. Retrieved February 12, 2022, from https://carsurance.net/insights/road-rage-statistics/

Census. (2011 July). *Census of state and local law enforcement agencies, 2008* (p. 8). US Department of Justice, Bureau of Justice Statistics Bulletin.

Clear, T., & Frost, N. (2014). *The punishment imperative: The rise and failure of mass incarceration in America*. New York University Press.

Deliso, M. (2021, June 12). 'Disconcerting' rise in road rage shootings resulting in death or injury, data shows. *ABC News*. Retrieved February 12, 2022, from https://abcnews.go.com/US/disconcerting-rise-road-rage-shootings-resulting-death- injury/story?id=78181165

Earles, J., & Pazzona, M. (2021, September 29). Law enforcement versus private security in the United States. *Security Magazine*. Retrieved February 12, 2022, from https://www.securitymagazine.com/blogs/14-security-blog/post/96189-law-enforcement- versus-private-security-in-the-united-states

Harper, B. K. (2022, November 23). Amid fallout from the Uvalde shooting, Texas DPS wants $1.2 billion for academy and active-shooter training facility. *Texas Tribune*. Retrieved November 24, 2022, from https://www.texastribune.org/2022/11/23/texas-dps-active- shooter-training/

Heffner, J., & FeldmanHall, O. (2019). Why we don't always punish: Preferences for non- punitive responses to moral violations. *Scientific Reports*, 9. Retrieved December 5, 2022, from https://www.nature.com/articles/s41598-019-49680-2

Helfgott, J. B., Strah, B. M., Pollock, J., Atherley, L. T., & Vinson, J. (2018). A qualitative approach to understanding guardian models of policing. *Journal of Qualitative Criminal Justice & Criminology*, *6*(1). https://doi.org/10.21428/88de04a1.ac7b66fa

Kavathas, C. (2022, July 21). *Jon Meacham shares message of hope for future of American democracy*. Retrieved November 27, 2022, from https://chqdaily.com/2022/07/jon-meacham-shares-message-of-hope-for-future-of-american-democracy./

Kelly, E. I. (2021). From retributive to restorative justice. *Criminal Law and Philosophy*, *15*, 237–247.

MacFarquhar, N. (2021, June 12). Police forces struggle to fill ranks in time of upheaval. *The New York Times*, Section A, p. 13.

Matthews, R. (2020, March). New times, new crimes: Notes on the depillarization of the criminal justice system. *Critical Criminology*, *28*, 309–326. https://doi.org/10.1007/s10612- 020-09489-2

Miletich, S. (2013, July 13). Police Academy 2.0: Less military training, more empathy. *The Seattle Times*. Retrieved December 3, 2022, from http://www.seattletimes.com/seattle- news/police-academy- 20-less-military-training-more-empathy

Rahr, S., & Rice, S. (2015). From warriors to guardians: Recommitting American police culture to democratic ideals. In *New perspectives in policing bulletin* (NCJ 248654). US Department of Justice, National Institute of Justice.

Schwabe, W. (1999). *Needs and prospects for crime-fighting technology: The federal role in assisting state and local law enforcement*. Rand Publishing.

Senter, J., & Dewan, S. (2022, July 8). Chauvin is sentenced to 21 Years in a case of civil rights violations. *New York Times*, p. A12.

Stoughton, S. (2015, April 10). Commentary: Law enforcement's "warrior" problem. *Harvard Law Review Forum. Harvard Law Review*, *128*(6), 225–234. https://harvardlawreview.org/2015/04/law-enforcements-warrior-problem/

UN Congress on Crime. (2015, April 12–19). *New and emerging forms of crime: Threats the world must reckon with*. 13th United Nations Congress on Crime Prevention and Criminal Justice, Doha [Fact sheet]. https://www.un.org/en/events/crimecongress2015/pdf/Factsheet_5_Emerging_forms_of_ crime_EN.pdf

Vitale, A. (2017). *The end of policing*. Verso.

Wilson, J., & Kelling, G. (1982, March). Broken windows: Police and neighborhood safety. *The Atlantic Monthly*, *12*, 29–38.

Wyllie, D. (2022, November 18). *Examining PERF's '40 Guiding Principles' to 'retool' police recruit training*. Retrieved November 27, 2022, from https://www.policemag.com/650038/examining-perfs-40-guiding-principles-to-retool- police-recruit-training

PART I

Police Training in the 20th and Early 21st Centuries

1

INTRODUCTION

Exploring Police Education

Democracy, which derives from the Greek word—*demos* or "people," is defined, basically, as government in which the supreme power is vested in the people. In some forms, democracy can be exercised directly by the people; in large societies, it is by the people who have been freely elected as their representatives. In the words of President Abraham Lincoln, delivered at Gettysburg, Pennsylvania, on November 19, 1863, democracy is government "of the people, by the people, and for the people." Over a half century later, Raymond B. Fosdick (1883–1972)[1] addressed the role that police have in a democracy in his studies of both European and American police systems. He was especially concerned with how police officers and their leaders should be selected. Fosdick noted how chiefs of police are often torn between the needs of rank-and-file officers on the one hand and the needs of the city's chief executive on the other. He appreciated how these issues are complicated by political considerations (Fosdick, 1920). During a yearlong visit to Europe, he observed that both in England and on the European Continent, police were well trained as compared to American police. He described how the members of European police forces were carefully selected, and took note of their character traits—"in all grades the character of the personnel is the essential, constant factor of efficiency" (Fosdick, 1915, p. 38).[2] However, Fosdick (1915) observed that with the exception of England, the Continental system was not inherently responsible to the people but rather to autocratic rulers and governments—whereas in "America power rests ultimately with the people, and there is no fixed authority to which the police system can be handed over" (p. 37). In England, the police have no powers not possessed by any other citizens, and they "are the servants of the community" (Fosdick, 1915, p. 28).

In contemporary America, given the intensifying questions, criticism, and protests about police activities, the idea that the police were at one time conceived to be "the servants of the community" might come as a surprise. Actually, the origins of policing in Colonial America began as a relatively informal affair; it was "based on a for-profit, privately funded system that employed people part-time" (Waxman, 2017). For nearly two centuries, colonists

> relied on a 'night watch' in which volunteers signed up for a certain day and time, mostly to look out for fellow colonists engaging in prostitution or gambling. . . . But that system

DOI: 10.4324/9781003307396-2

> wasn't very efficient because the watchmen often slept and drank while on duty, and there were people who were put on watch duty as a form of punishment.
>
> *(Waxman, 2017)*

It was only when the English model of policing was deemed successful after 1829 that American cities began to experiment with the employment of full-time police departments, and most of the 19th century was devoted to ironing out how best to administer them—the matter being complicated by the control and influence of local political organizations. In the South, beginning in the first decade of the 18th century, the creation of police forces centered on the preservation of the slavery system.

> . . . slave patrols [were] tasked with chasing down runaways and preventing slave revolts. . . . During the Civil War, the military became the primary form of law enforcement in the South, but during Reconstruction, many local sheriffs functioned in a way analogous to the earlier slave patrols, enforcing segregation and the disenfranchisement of freed slaves.
>
> *(Waxman, 2017)*

It appears that communities in the United States have been struggling to find an appropriate way to police themselves throughout their entire history. Much of this is due to the essential democratic feature of American policing. In the United States as a whole, law enforcement is primarily the responsibility of local police and sheriff's departments, whose operating budgets are totally dependent upon the elected members of town, city, or county legislative bodies. On the local level, there are more than 15,000 police departments. Sheriff offices comprise an additional group of about 3,000 agencies. One study indicated that

> nearly half of all local police departments have fewer than 10 officers. Three in 4 of the departments have no more than two dozen officers. And 9 in 10 employ fewer than 50 sworn officers. . . . These departments' often limited resources and the decentralized structure of American law enforcement complicate efforts to mandate widespread training and policy changes.
>
> *(Berman, 2021)*

Police budgets for statewide law enforcement agencies also depend on elected representatives and state governors. Moreover, federal agencies such as the Federal Bureau of Investigation (FBI) and the US Marshals Service, which have specialized duties, are subject to Congressional oversight and funding. Only during the second half of the 20th century have mandatory minimum selection and training standards been adopted on a state-by-state basis.

Furthermore, there seems to be a growing tendency "to relinquish some of our sacred constitutional rights in favor of the perception of improved safety and security. Constitutional rights are now viewed by some, including some police, as an impediment to the public safety mission. Sadly, many have forgotten that protecting constitutional rights is the mission of police in a democracy" (Rahr & Rice, 2015, pp. 1–2). Nationally, due to substantial increases in the passage of federal statutes, there has also been a vast increase in the number of federal agents and investigative divisions in the United States. This trend was noticed over 50 years ago by Reiss (1971), who found that the number of federal laws "to be enforced by federal agents in some department of the executive branch grows with each session of Congress. . . . Public stances notwithstanding, the Congress of the United States has developed a national police force of substantial proportions" (Reiss, 1971, p. 217). At the same time, there has been a vast growth in the development of private policing in the United States for the protection of corporate interests. In addition, since the conclusion of World War II and especially after the demise of the Soviet Union after 1989, democracy has widened on the European Continent. In particular, the "European Union [EU] has also become a major player in democracy and human rights work, particularly since the expansion of the EU to include former communist nations in central and eastern Europe" (Lloyd, 2010, p. 548).

Thus, there is work to be done if America is to ensure a future based on individual liberties and its historic trust in a governmental system based upon the checks and balances built into the Constitution's Bill of Rights. America's law enforcement establishment can play a significant role in rebuilding the community ties that once upon a time existed in some communities. Rahr and Rice (2015) recall that "the friendly neighborhood beat cop—community guardian—has been replaced with the urban warrior, trained for battle and equipped with the accouterments and weaponry of modern warfare" (p. 2). There is an imperative needed to restore public confidence in police work. One way to do this is to recognize a problem within many existing police training schools—"an academy environment that is modeled after military boot camp, a model designed to produce a warrior ready for battle and ready to follow orders and rules without question" (Rahr & Rice, 2015, p. 4). At the very least, "given the realities of policing, critical thinking and decision-making, not memorization, should be a top goal of any training strategy" (Rahr & Rice, 2015, p. 4). The availability of new virtual reality training technology can be used to support training exercises devoted to critical decision-making during crisis incidents. One example is the APEX officer virtual reality training simulator. The device, which requires wearing a headset and backpack, can create any type of environment, from an active shooter scenario to a mental health call (Scott-Smith, 2022).

An "enhanced community policing" effort is needed to serve as an updated philosophy for policing in order to better address crime control and the related needs of community members.[3] "Citizen participation in anti-crime activities is the foundation on which community policing programs were created and are perpetuated" (Flexon et al., 2009, p. 180). Police and citizen interactions need to be conducted with dignity and respect in order to elevate to reality the ideals of policing embodied in the phrase "to serve and protect." The authors recognize that the seeds of a guardian approach to policing may be sown during recruitment and subsequent field training. A police educational model should bolster a recruit's sense of compassion, pride, and self-esteem, as well as their physical, emotional, and spiritual health. It involves nothing less than changing the police culture that is associated with old-style warrior identities to one embracing democratic ideals.

According to Chuck Wexler, Executive Director of the PERF, although "there are pockets of innovation in recruit training, training as a whole has not kept pace with. . . . not only the training recruits receive in the academy, but also the field training they engage in when they exit the academy. . . . American policing needs to re-imagine and retool recruit training" (qtd. in PERF, 2022, p. 3). A new PERF report, partly based on a survey of hundreds of law enforcement leaders, found that "recruit training simply has not kept pace with the dramatic changes that have taken place in policing in recent decades or with the increasingly complex and challenging realities that today's police officers face. In too many instances, academies continue to train officers to be warriors, even though their agencies and communities expect them also to be guardians, social workers, and community partners" (PERF, 2022, p. 8). The PERF report did not present a "model curriculum" or specific details on what ought to be taught to new recruits, but rather a set of 40 "guiding principles that agencies and academies should adopt in order to begin the process of change . . ." (PERF, 2022, p. 9).

Any modification of the police culture must start during recruit training. This book's final chapter considers how to strengthen community policing and public safety through the establishment of "model precincts"—recommended as a new style of police academy and field training.[4] Four essential features of this new apprenticeship-style training proposal are (1) the inclusion of college-based educators and education in the model; (2) decentralization of the training process to the community level; (3) the introduction of community field-based experiences at early stages through service in auxiliary police and related capacities; and (4) hands-on experience using vital community social service resources. Significantly, the achievement of a guardian style of law enforcement can be augmented by the establishment of basic training apprenticeships involving recruit participation in cadet, auxiliary, and reserve police units. Civilians can assist in this goal by their willingness to serve in volunteer police roles and participate in various oversight committees and boards.

Volunteer Police Work

While community policing demands that citizens and police authorities work closely together in the coproduction and maintenance of public safety and order, unless a citizen decides to affiliate with his or her local police department in some occupational title, current opportunities for working alongside working police officers are actually quite limited. A good way for full-time college students and New York City residents who are 18 to 33 years of age to affiliate with the New York City Police Department (NYPD) is to become a member of its part-time Cadet Corps. Cadets also receive tuition assistance, police training, and work experience. Otherwise, in New York City, there are only a handful of meaningful roles for average citizens to participate in community policing efforts, such as serving as a member in its unsalaried auxiliary police program, participating in an adult or youth citizen's police academy course, and/or participating in monthly Community Council meetings at local precincts. Neighborhood Watch groups are also popular in some areas, but they only thrive if citizen leaders are available.

In New York City, the auxiliary role is quite substantial and relevant since it involves opportunities to receive police training in order to patrol neighborhood streets, housing projects, or transit facilities. The main responsibilities of auxiliaries are to observe and report conditions requiring the services of the regular police. The auxiliaries wear police uniforms but are only equipped with nightsticks and handcuffs. In addition, every New York City Police Precinct, Housing Police Service Area, and Transit District has a pool of "loaner" vests for auxiliary officers to use while on patrol. Although such volunteers are unsalaried and only engage in part-time patrol work, their duties and personal traits are not necessarily that much different from what regular officers do when engaged in nonenforcement duties. These types of duties and traits include (1) nurturing, caretaking, calming, and empathizing abilities for addressing crises; (2) skills to handle health emergencies as well as control traffic and crowds; (3) sufficient social maturity to cope with incidents of crime, juvenile delinquency, suicidal threats and gestures, substance abuse, and missing persons; and (4) undertaking special assignments involving parades and sporting events, weather emergencies, and search and rescue. Generally, auxiliaries are best used in crime prevention initiatives, such as routine patrols, traffic control, and various types of local crime prevention initiatives. Units of auxiliary police are common in many jurisdictions throughout the United States.

Another type of volunteer police officer is the "reservist." Reservists are typically trained to the same level as regular police and therefore engage in the full variety of crime calls. Many police jurisdictions, especially in western states, have part-time paid or unpaid reserve police units. These agencies sometimes deploy and train these volunteers to serve "in specialized units such as marine and dive-team units, search and rescue, mounted units, training units, community policing specialty programs, children's programs, driving under the influence checkpoints, and other various special events" (Wolf & Dobrin, 2021). "Reserve and auxiliary law enforcement volunteers are an understudied but potentially valuable asset to communities and criminal justice agencies. . . . With diminishing resources, shrinking budgets, and the demand for qualified personnel continuing to rise, many police agencies rely on volunteers to help offset their costs. But, beyond the need to do more with less, volunteering in police work can create a positive partnership between members of the community and their local government" (Wolf et al., 2015, p. 38). On the other hand, without the appropriate training neither volunteer police nor regular police will be able to perform well enough to earn the public's confidence and trust. Significantly, when citizens commit "to serve in roles within police agencies [it] allows for the ultimate transparency, enabling community members to provide input, understand the role and function of policing, and learn first-hand about the complexities of serving society in this role" (Wolf & Dobrin, 2021).[5] No matter the situation, the volunteer officers—auxiliaries or reserves—must command respect, demonstrate courage, and have self-control (see President's Commission, 1967, p. 121). These types of volunteer peace officer positions can also be used for the provision of basic training apprenticeships for individuals seeking a career in police work.

Law enforcement and criminal justice education did not arise in a vacuum. They arose due to the consequences of the grave social problems and imbalances in America's social fabric taking place at the start of the 20th century. At the beginning of the 20th century, there were perhaps a handful of schools for police training, but today there may be as many as 822 basic training academies in the United States, with about half administered by academic institutions, one-third by local agencies, and the remainder coordinated by regional and state entities (see PERF, 2022, pp. 11 and 13; Little Hoover Commission, 2021, p. 14). "Nine states centralize administration of all training through a single academy, which can help ensure greater consistency in the curriculum, instruction, and oversight that recruits receive. But the more typical model is Ohio, which has more than 80 police academies spread out among big-city departments; state, community and technical colleges; and career centers" (PERF, 2022, p. 13). A central issue with regard to police training may not concern the number of existing schools of police but rather their quality and ability to deliver personnel who will be better able to meet the challenges of today and tomorrow.

Police Training and Academic-Related Programs

According to Joseph Schafer and John Jarvis (2017) and others (e.g., Scott, 2010; Bykov, 2014), "the first U.S. police training academy was August Vollmer's Berkeley Police School, which opened in 1908. At the time, most agencies did not provide formal training to new officers, and the idea of providing new personnel with training on basic policing skills was, at the time, quite revolutionary. In 1935, the FBI initiated the National Police Academy (now the National Academy) as one of the first efforts to provide advanced training to veteran police personnel. The establishment of these two police education and training programs laid the foundation for the way in which modern officers are prepared to enter and advance in their careers in policing" (Schafer & Jarvis, 2017, p. 56). The date of 1908 is commonly used to identify the start of formal police training in the United States, but other programs were in existence in a few municipal police departments.

There were a variety of police training programs prior to Vollmer's school. For example, in New York City a police training course "came into existence in 1853. Police captains instructed officers in the 'school of soldier' and drill instructors were appointed to train and discipline officers in crowd and riot control" (NYPD, 1993, p. 4). But it was not until 1924 when "a course of comprehensive training for all members of the Department was introduced at the 'Police College' on Broome Street in Manhattan. New officers spent an arduous three months studying police doctrine" (NYPD, 1993, p. 6). On the other hand, it was not until 1959 that minimum police training for the entire State of New York was established. In so doing, New York became the first state in the nation to establish basic training for newly appointed police officers. This was accomplished by creating the Municipal Police Training Council (MPTC), as well as promulgating rules and regulations with respect to the content and presentation of required training. When the new rules became effective July 1, 1960, the Basic Course for Police Officers consisted of 80 hours of instruction in specified areas. Currently, an MPTC-approved Basic Course must consist of at least 639 hours of instruction in specified areas (Division of Criminal Justice Services, 2022).

Research indicates that one of the earliest schools for police instruction began on August 31, 1869, at the Saint Louis Police Department. The first school was located in police headquarters and then the schools operated out of the districts. In 1869, training guidelines were a part of the department's manual, stating, for example, that "All patrolmen hereafter appointed shall for the term of one month thereafter be formed into a class for instruction, which shall meet at the Central Station. They shall there be instructed for one hour each day by one of the Captains, concerning their powers, duties, and privileges, and also for the same length of time shall receive instruction from a Captain of the force. They shall be placed on beat for one tour of duty each night with a patrolman, so as to learn the practical mode of discharging patrol duty. They will receive full and systematic instruction and explanation in respect to the police law, the laws of the State, and the laws and ordinances of the City" (Brockelsby & Scheetz, 1987, p. 2). The next major change in the organization of the Saint Louis Academy did not come until December 1, 1911, when the Bureau of Efficiency was created. A lieutenant assigned to the bureau was placed in charge of the school. By 1913, all probationary patrolmen were required to attend the School of Instruction for a period of 30 days, with lectures delivered by the Department's medical staff on first aid to the injured and by "prominent attorneys" on state laws, city ordinances, the preparation of evidence, and other subjects. In addition, the new patrolmen were to be "thoroughly drilled in army tactics and target practice by the Drillmaster and given courses of physical training and exercises by one of the assistant surgeons and by a physical instructor, assigned to this work" (Brockelsby & Scheetz, 1987, p. 2). The city consolidated its police training when an academy complex opened in 1929 and police recruits at the new academy were trained in patrolling, target practice, first aid, calisthenics, geography, spelling, penmanship, boxing, and swimming, with the training lasting for four weeks. The school established a library in 1947 at its police academy, and it was considered to be the largest police department-owned library in the nation (Frie, 2022, p. 70).

According to the timeline provided by the Greater Cincinnati Police Museum (GCPM), the following events took place in the 1880s: in 1880, drill practice was introduced under the administration of Cincinnati Mayor Richard Moore Bishop (1812–1893), who said that the drill practices are "almost indispensable in dispersing a crowd or quelling riot"; in 1886, a police gymnasium was established and an instructor hired to provide physical training to members of the Cincinnati Police Force; and in 1888, a School of Instruction was established for formal training for all members at a station, presented by the district lieutenant (GCPM, 2022).

The early pioneers of police training not only included Berkeley Police Chief August Vollmer and Mayor Bishop of Cincinnati, but also Cincinnati's Police Chief William P. Penn. In his April 1, 1868 report to the Board of Police Commissioners, Chief Penn recommended "that a 'School of the Policeman' be established, and every person appointed on the force, as well as the present members thereof, be subject to at least one month's careful instruction in relation to the duties he will be required to perform" (qtd. in Brockelsby & Scheetz, 1987, p. 1).

However, it is quite obvious that a police academy is not the same as a college degree program. Notably, Schafer and Boyd (2007) distinguished between police training and higher education, indicating that police training is designed to impart an understanding of the "tools of the trade" whereas higher education is meant to provide the basis for problem solving and future learning. Yet, "there is clear value in mandatory time spent in a pre-service academy experience. Students potentially benefit through intangible processes related to socialization, acculturation, and the development of a professional esprit de corps and identity" (Schafer & Jarvis, 2017, p. 58). McCay (2011) indicates that police academies also serve "as socialization for the recruit into the police culture and its traditions . . . [but], this places an intense ethical burden on the police and those who train them. It is the trainers' responsibility to ensure that officers have been given the vast skill set needed, from cognitive to psychomotor, to perform in the manner in which the public expects" (p. 2).

Aside from the origins of the police academy with its numerous and various formats, higher education has played a major role in police career preparation for more than a hundred years. Criminal justice education had its beginnings in 1893 "when the University of Chicago School of Sociology was established with a component on crime and deviance in society" (Hale, 1998, p. 387). Chicago also became the venue for the first National Conference on Criminal Law and Criminology held by Northwestern University in 1909, which led to the founding of the American Institute of Criminology and Criminal Law. The Institute inaugurated the *Journal of Criminal Law and Criminology* in 1910.[6] Writing in the journal's inaugural issue, James W. Garner, its first editor-in-chief, commented that the conference was composed of about 150 delegates

> representing the various professions and occupations concerned directly or indirectly with the administration of the criminal law and the punishment of criminals, and included members of the bench and bar, professors of law in the universities, alienists, criminologists, penologists, superintendents of penal and reformatory institutions, psychologists, police officials, probation officers, and the like. . . . In character and purpose the conference was entirely without precedent in the history of the United States. . . . Although the idea of such a gathering was new to America it is an old one in Europe, where congresses of criminologists have frequently been held for the promotion of criminological science and the consideration of practical problems connected with the administration of criminal justice.
>
> *(Garner, 1910, pp. 2–3)*

However, "virtually all historical pieces on criminal justice education begin with Vollmer" (Southerland et al., 2007, p. 88). August Vollmer has been credited with not only the establishment in 1908 of the first educational program designed specifically for police personnel—the Berkeley Police School but also connecting it with an institution of higher education—the University of California. The relationship was formalized in 1916 when the University's Berkeley campus offered its first crime-related courses. Recognition of the new academic specialty came in 1923 when a Berkeley policeman earned a baccalaureate degree with a major in economics and a minor in criminology. From the late 1920s through the 1930s several institutions developed programs emphasizing the administrative aspects of policing and criminal justice. In addition to Vollmer, the pioneers in police education included O. W. Wilson and V. A. Leonard. As "farsighted police administrators, these leaders clearly recognized a need for 'professionalism' in policing and of the role of higher education in achieving it" (Finckenauer, 2005, p. 414). On the other hand, most of the early programs included a strong training component (Southerland et al., 2007). By 1965, there were 64 colleges and universities offering such educational programs in criminal justice. "The period 1965–1978 was one of uncontrolled, rampant growth of criminal justice higher education. By 1970, the number of degree programs had multiplied nearly eightfold with the total number reaching just under 500. . . . An additional 200 were added by 1973 and by 1978 the number had almost doubled again, reaching 1,200" (Southerland et al., 2007, p. 88).

According to Sloan (2018), "especially at the undergraduate level, this growth was driven by such factors as prime-time television offerings (e.g., the Law & Order and CSI franchises), increases in the number of entry-level positions available in criminal justice and related agencies (e.g., private security) as a result of new recruitment efforts and retirements of veteran practitioners, and the fact these positions offer reasonable salaries and benefits" (Sloan, 2018, pp. 193–194). Sloan (2018) further illustrates this growth by calculating that "in the United States between academic years 1970–1971 and 2014–2015 . . . the number of bachelor's degrees awarded in criminal justice increased . . . from 2,045 to 62,723" (p. 194). In particular, "the criminal justice share of total bachelor's degrees awarded increased from under 1% in 1970–1971 to 3.4% in 2014–2015 and that criminal justice bachelor's degrees went from 29th to 9th most awarded in the U.S." (Sloan, 2018, p. 194).

The huge growth of criminal justice related higher education programs was a product of the turbulent 1960s and millions of dollars in federal funding. The field was also able to draw upon its deep roots established in various parts of the country during the first half of the 20th century as well as the unique fabric of America's justice system, which is embedded in the US Constitution. The American criminal justice system holds that offenders should receive due process before being held accountable for any harm they may have committed. According to a 1934 decision of the US Supreme Court, due process is violated if a practice or rule "offends some principle of justice so rooted in the traditions and conscience of our people as to be ranked as fundamental" (see *Snyder v. Massachusetts*, 291 U.S. 97, 105).[7] A critical part of due process is ascertaining the mental state of offenders to determine whether particular crimes were committed intentionally, negligently, recklessly, or knowingly (see Robinson, 2002; Southerland et al., 2007). The rise of a 24-hour media news cycle has made reports about crime, law, courts, and corrections available to all, and many facets of the criminal justice system have become essential features of the nation's culture.

Criminal justice educational programs turn out tens of thousands of students each year, making criminal justice "one of a campus' relevant, contemporary, and highly marketable degree options" (Flanagan, 2000, p. 5). Students seek out the criminal justice major as a background for working in the criminal justice field as police officers, lawyers, probation officers, correctional officers, juvenile justice personnel, and other jobs that are perceived as exciting and with some ability to help others (Flanagan, 2000). Aside from these obvious career paths, a criminal justice major "can be a lead-in to law school" (Sloan, 2018, p. 194). By the start of the 21st century, there were more than 125,000 students majoring in criminal justice in the United States (Flanagan, 2000), at least half of whom were specifically interested in going into law enforcement (Krimmel, 1999).

The institutions and processes of the American justice system have been evolving at a quickened pace since the late 1960s and 1970s due to concerns about rising crime rates, social change, urban unrest, and the availability of significant federal funding for educating both pre-service and in-service peace officers. Moreover, the field has not been short of disagreements. Since many colleges and universities offer degrees in criminal justice, it is not surprising to discern curricula that vary among them. For example, despite voluminous research on victims of crime, only a small percentage has a required course on this topic (Bostaph et al., 2014). In addition, studies have shown that "only round 20 percent of four-year CCJ [Criminology and Criminal Justice] programs require coursework on race and gender. Some CCJ programs do not even offer these courses as an elective" (Abreu, 2020). Some criminal justice departments have programs that are more vocationally focused while others are more academic and theoretically focused. Especially, after the events of 9/11, finding the correct balance has become more complex (e.g., see Birzer & Palmiotto, 2002). Overall, according to James Finckenauer (2005, p. 415), "from 'cop shop' to certification, the evolution of criminal justice education has been characterized as a quest for 'credibility and legitimacy'." In a survey of 670 programs to assess the quality of bachelor's degree programs in criminal justice (BCJ) in the United States based on Academy of Criminal Justice Sciences (ACJS) standards relating to their curriculum, Sloan (2018) determined that BCJ programs met few curriculum standards and that departmental factors were especially significant influences on the number of standards met. The survey was limited by using ACJS standards for just one area—curriculum and programs in criminology were omitted.[8] Since 2018, the ACJS has stopped accepting new applications for certification under its standards.

As of that year only 11 universities had successfully participated in the organization's academic certification review process (see https://www.acjs.org/page/Cert_Programs).[9]

The ideal mix of career-related criminal justice curricula has yet to be determined. Nonetheless, this has and should not impede academic entrepreneurs and police training specialists from combining forces in order to find the best balance. Moreover, how these materials are delivered to interested students and/or police recruits need not be limited to any one format. "For example, there are now several means by which academic credits may be earned, including: (1) completing advanced placement courses and exams while still in high school; (2) completing training offered by employers [at training academies, the military, and occupationally related continuing education] and, (3) earning credits toward a degree simply by having been in the workforce for a number of years. The question is not necessarily whether these credit-earning experiences are valid, but rather how many credits are these experiences worth and will institutions perceive their value differently in the wake of ongoing police, court, and corrections reform initiatives?" (Hummer & Byrne, 2021, pp. 415–416). There has been an expanding trend for academic institutions to accept life experience credits (Klein-Collins et al., 2020). The diversity among college curricula and delivery formats is unlikely to abate any time soon since there are many views about what constitutes the most valuable core curricular courses for pursuing criminal justice careers. On other hand, there appears to be at least some consensus on the need for

> well-rounded, diverse experiences . . . for success in the field going forward. Such an education will include components of a liberal arts education, practical learning, and work and life experiences that produce justice system actors who look at deviant behavior–and justice-involved individuals–through a broader lens than simple punitiveness or deterrence.
>
> *(Hummer & Byrne, 2021, p. 436)*

Moreover, there appears to be little reason to believe that contemporary interest in undergraduate education in criminal justice will decline. Today, the need for qualified police officers has become particularly acute in several regions of the United States. Surely, the nation's lower unemployment rates and the sporadic reports of police violence have impacted general interest in this career field.[10] In such an environment, recruiters have to compete for the best qualified recruits. The police recruiters must deal with the hard facts involving lower salaries (especially in rural townships), tarnished image, and increasingly tougher standards for new recruits and limited job flexibility. One Chicago Police Department recruiter indicated "You don't move up in a police department the way you would in a dot-com" (qtd. in Libaw, 2017). The possession of college credits, let alone a degree in criminal justice, may assist students in their career search.

Trends in College Programs

An attempt to look into the future was made in July 2004 by various participants at the National Institute of Justice's Annual Research and Evaluation Conference. They agreed that "the world of 2040 will have a more shared culture due to such trends as globalization, mobility, and spreading diversity" and they recommended that in the interim that new policies and technologies would be needed to help leaders and "citizens realize a criminal justice system that is fair, equitable, and respectful" (Ritter, 2004). Speakers at the conference emphasized: the need to understand the co-evolution of crime and crime fighting; the influence of global and professional culture on the world's criminal justice systems; and how the field of justice administration will largely depend on developments in policies and technologies (Ritter, 2004).

Clearly, technological advances have and are having a great influence on crime fighting. Developments in surveillance, biometrics, DNA analysis, and radio frequency identification microchips have enhanced crime prevention and crime solving. Increasingly, sophisticated intelligence databases are being used not only by police officers and analysts but by the general public (e.g., sex offender registries). The occurrence of the events of September 11, 2001, has added an entirely new dimension to the importance and need for educating future leaders dealing with peacemaking and domestic security. New degree programs in homeland security, emergency preparedness, and cybersecurity are proliferating. Many such programs exist online including a short course from Harvard University where students can learn how to assess the vulnerabilities of an organization's critical business systems, networks, and data and have the ability to draft, strategize, and develop a cyber risk mitigation strategy, including the appropriate legal and compliance steps that need to be taken when responding to and reporting cyberattacks to law enforcement (Harvard, 2022).

Mercy College in Dobbs Ferry with New York City satellite campuses in Manhattan and the Bronx has established a Cybersecurity Education Center, offering a combined Cybersecurity undergraduate and master's degree program. The Center was designated as a "National Center of Academic Excellence in Information Assurance Education" by the National Security Agency and the Department of Homeland Security (Mercy College, 2022).

In Erie, Pennsylvania, Mercyhurst University has added to its Cybersecurity Program a cyber lab at the school's Hammermill Library. The lab is a high-security Network Operation Center established with a corporate partner employing the college's students. The strategic partnership between Mercyhurst's Ridge College of Intelligence Studies and Applied Sciences and Federal Resources Corporation (FRC) provides students with opportunities to work with real clients conducting virtual forensics, threat analysis, and more (Mercyhurst University, 2022).

The newest college at the State University of New York at Albany is the College of Emergency Preparedness, Homeland Security and Cybersecurity. Its degree programs prepare students to respond to and recover from natural and human-caused risks and threats around the world (UAlbany, 2017). Its baccalaureate degree programs emphasize leadership, public administration, management, risk analysis, ethics, policy making, planning, strategic communication, and systemic thinking.

The birth of the field of artificial intelligence (AI) presents both promises and pitfalls for balancing the need for public safety with concern for personal liberty. While

> a slew of new machine learning tools promise to help protect us—quickly and precisely tracking those who may commit a crime before it happens. . . . The data being used to 'teach' the software systems is embedded with bias, and only serves to reinforce inequality.
>
> *(Reese, 2022)*

In order to help address the use of AI by law enforcement agencies, the resources provided by major universities will be needed to provide the necessary training, support, and oversight.

There are also significant changes taking place to help transform the conduct of public safety professionals through more higher education courses in the humanities. For example, the John Jay College of Criminal Justice is addressing this need in a project that

> places the humanities and criminal justice in dialogue with one another by infusing the facts of our legal system with the historical, interpretive and analytical methods that are the hallmarks of humanistic inquiry. . . . The humanities perform a democratizing function by giving us access to a wide range of lived experiences and creating a common intellectual experience that fosters an enlarged sense of human community. For future law enforcement officers, engagement with the humanities is essential preparation for working together with people whose view of the world might be different than their own.
>
> *(Byrne & Bezbatchenko, 2021)*

Accordingly, John Jay's revised curriculum is covering topics such as racial justice, immigration, education, and the urban experience. Students are being asked to consider: who in our society is policed and who is protected?; when do an individual's rights matter more than a group's rights?; what is the role of police in a democratic society?; and what is the difference between law and justice? The new humanities core seeks to "ensure that future law enforcement officers educated at John Jay engage with challenging and inspiring works that raise questions students would otherwise probably not encounter through traditional criminal justice education" (Byrne & Bezbatchenko, 2021).

Another important trend is the merger of career training and academic coursework. According to Holly Zanville, Strategy Director at the Lumina Foundation, "People have always acquired learning from multiple sources—school, work, military, travel, self-study, and community and volunteer service. And long before learning was packaged into credentials awarded primarily by schools (K-12, colleges and universities, and specialty institutions), there were many ways of assessing, verifying, and even licensing that learning. Historically, that occurred for many skilled workers through guilds: Groups of workers set and maintained standards, and new entrants apprenticed to learn various crafts" (qtd. in Klein-Collins et al., 2020, p. iv). The merging of police training with the curriculums of colleges and universities degree programs appears to be a possible trend in the making, but it must be cautioned that "higher education can be quite an intransigent institution in its own right, so one should not approach it naively when looking for better models for police education and training" (Cordner & Shain, 2011, p. 283). Chapter 4 addresses this trend, providing particular references to specific programs. Hummer and Byrne (2021) provide a number of practical suggestions for colleges to award credit for courses based on their professional work and training experiences; for example, "as with the number of experience credits accepted toward degree completion, programs should have a specific template for where experiential-based learning activities fit into the major program, and, optimally, be a requirement for criminal justice majors" (p. 435).

Exploring Police Education

As was stated by the 1967 President's Commission on Law Enforcement and the Administration of Justice's assessment of justice issues during a period of civil unrest, "the struggle to maintain a proper balance between effective law enforcement and fairness to individuals pervades the entire criminal justice system. It is particularly crucial and apparent in police work because, as has been noted, every police action can impinge directly, and perhaps hurtfully, on a citizen's freedom of action" (President's Commission, 1967, p. 93).[11]

So too, "it is likely that criminal justice education is at an inflection point. A set of factors including changing demographics, technological innovation, a global pandemic, and a pervasive view of systemic bias in the justice system, are compelling the field to re-assess how to best educate both pre- and in-service students" (Hummer & Byrne, 2021, p. 436). In order to address systemic bias in programs designed to prepare potential candidates for criminal justice careers it is of critical importance to make sure there is sufficient access to the variety of delivery modes of instruction among adult students who have not traditionally had strong access to these programs. Institutions must make concerted efforts to encourage low-income adult students and adult students of color—particularly Black adult students—to take advantage of offerings. On the other hand, such referrals cannot be done in a void—all such programs need to be vetted in order to ensure their quality. Southerland and her associates (2007) addressed the general use of accreditation and standards as a means to ensure quality in higher education.

As standards for higher education in criminal justice need to be addressed, a similar effort is needed with regard to police training. Berman (2021) has indicated that "The latticework of law enforcement draped across the country doesn't just include departments of varying sizes, but forces with distinct procedures that often exist side by side in neighboring communities." According to Dennis Kenney,[12] a former Florida police officer and a professor at the John Jay College of Criminal Justice in New York who has more than 35 years of experience in varied aspects of criminal justice, that means "the rules of policing change depending on where you are. . . . Within a county, you can have one police department that has one set of policies and another that has another set of policies. And certainly the level of training varies greatly" (qtd. in Berman, 2021).

Notwithstanding the importance of professional and academic education in the field of law enforcement, all adults living in a democratic society or any society should serve as the ultimate guardians of their own freedom and forge their own path toward the ideals set forth in the preamble to the United Nations' Universal Declaration of Human Rights: "Recognition of the inherent dignity and of the equal and inalienable rights of all members of the human family is the foundation of freedom, justice, and peace in the world." According to Little (2020), "the rights enumerated in the declaration were controversial among the U.N.'s member nations, and remain so today." It proclaimed, among other rights, that "Everyone has the right to a standard of living adequate for the health and well-being of himself and of his family, including food, clothing, housing and medical care and necessary social services" (see Article 25).[13] A guardian philosophy of policing should take into consideration such a standard and seek to assure societal welfare through means suggested by "community policing." Community policing in its simplest form is the development and fostering of a working relationship and a cooperative spirit between the community and its law enforcement agency, so as to better serve the community's needs and service expectations. A realization of the full potential of community policing is possible provided all of the components and resources of the community are marshaled by police for the promotion of community safety and its general welfare.

The provision of welfare services cannot be underestimated. Economic factors have repeatedly been linked to family disruptions. Economic factors have been found to be an important predictor of conflict for both married and cohabiting couples, and research has suggested that financial strain increases couple-level violence for cohabiting and married couples (Hardie & Lucas, 2010). Luwig et al. (2001) studied whether crime can be linked to high poverty neighborhoods. They explored how criminal behaviors can spread throughout a community, tempting others to commit crimes. Their study used data from a randomized housing-mobility experiment, including juvenile arrest records, to study the effects of relocating families from high- to low-poverty neighborhoods on juvenile crime. Their findings suggested that providing families with the opportunity to move to lower-poverty neighborhoods reduces violent criminal behavior by teens. In addition, the health of a community, especially mental health, has become an essential part of planning for the protection of youth and family members. The problems associated with substance abuse are also matters where first responders are often called upon. While studies have repeatedly shown that the majority of individuals with mental illness are not violent and that the majority of violent acts are not committed by those with mental illness (Glied & Frank, 2014), reports also indicate that 3% to 5% of violent acts can be attributed to persons with serious mental illness (Mentalhealth.gov., 2022). In the United States, 24% of individuals who are incarcerated reported receiving a clinical diagnosis or treatment for a mental health disorder within the past year, and 49% reported experiencing symptoms of a mental health disorder (James & Glaze, 2006). One study estimated that about 1 in 10 arrested individuals with a mental health disorder are involved with the justice system due to mental health symptoms (Skeem et al., 2011).

The specific causes of crime have been long debated. Many efforts to address this issue have suffered from a lack of data about the amount and nature of crime occurrences in the United States. A new data-based system is being implemented. The new system, known as the National Incident-Based Reporting System (NIBRS), has been designed to provide information on a much larger number of crimes than has previously been calculated, as well as details such as the time of day, location, and types of weapons involved, if applicable. It also provides demographic data, such as the age, sex, race, and ethnicity of victims, known offenders, and arrestees. Researchers will now be able to learn about when and where crime takes place, what form it takes, and the characteristics of its victims and perpetrators. According to the FBI (2022), the database will collect data for 52 offenses plus 10 additional offenses for which only arrests are reported. The previous system counted only limited data for 10 offenses and 20 additional crimes for which only arrests were reported. The new system collects more detailed information, including incident date and time, whether reported offenses were attempted or completed, expanded victim types, relationships of victims to offenders and offenses, demographic details, location data, property descriptions, drug types and quantities, the offender's suspected use of drugs or alcohol, the involvement of gang activity, and whether a computer was used in the commission of the crime (FBI, 2022). All persons concerned with crime prevention as well as better practices in law enforcement should benefit from the new system, especially individuals who engage in criminal justice work. However, the system is totally dependent on reports from the field. In 2019, "NIBRS received violent and property crime data from 46% of law enforcement agencies, covering 44% of the U.S. population that year. Some researchers have warned that the transition to a new system could leave important data gaps if more law enforcement agencies do not submit the requested information to the FBI" (Gramlich, 2020). If we expect the police to act more like guardians than warriors, Americans everywhere need to encourage their local police to support this new database.

College students interested in police careers can engage in volunteer police activities to not only handle additional administrative tasks associated with agency participation in NIBRS, but also qualify for such tasks as: helping to coordinate neighborhood watch programs; conducting seminars on citizenship, law, and security; augmenting and/or revitalizing School Resource Officer programs; staffing storefront police mini-station locations; developing and contributing to programs to reduce identity theft; ensuring that new "Red Flag" laws are operational;[14] and organizing youth and family-oriented recreational activities. Qualified college students and other individuals would be especially valuable in sharing information about mental health and wellness matters. Such activities can readily be undertaken while serving in auxiliary or reserve police units. These opportunities are considered in the "Model Precinct" training program presented in Chapter 12. Walker (1993) states that a key rationale for greater citizen involvement in criminal justice "is solidly based on a substantial body of research indicating that traditional police crime-fighting tactics are extremely limited" (p. 59). The following section provides an overview of each of the book's chapters, beginning with Chapter 2.

Chapter Overviews

Chapter 2 explores the nature of local, regional, and state level police training academies. Regional, or decentralized, academies typically enable several smaller cities and towns to pool their resources and bring together their new recruits for pre-service training. A trend in various regions of the nation is to also include in regional academies qualified persons interested in police careers as well as some related peace officer positions. Enrollment by these civilian pre-service trainees is often only available on a space-available basis, and civilian trainees must often cover their own expenses. One way to refer to these types of academies is to refer to them as "hybrid academies" because of their inclusion of both non-employed civilian and recently hired personnel.

Chapter 3 considers the development of a variety of selected federal law enforcement academies. In particular, the Federal Law Enforcement Training Center (FLETC), the FBI Academy, the FBI National Academy, the US Border Patrol Academy, and the US Customs and Border Protection (CBP)—Field Operations Academy are prominent among the highlighted groups. FLETC provides law enforcement training for more than 90 federal agencies, several state, local, and tribal agencies, and it assists with training at several International Law Enforcement Academies (ILEAs). The FBI National Academy does not train FBI agents; rather law enforcement managers nominate candidates because of demonstrated leadership qualities. Participants are drawn from all parts of the nation as well as from foreign nations. Graduates of the National Academy have the opportunity to join the nonprofit FBI National Academy Associates, Inc. (FBINAA). Its 16,000 members represent all 50 states, 194 countries, and over 8,200 law enforcement agencies.

Chapter 4 explores the characteristics of pre-service, pre-employment, and college-based police training programs in the United States. Pre-service police academies are those police training institutions that provide basic training to students who have already been hired by their agencies and are therefore on that agency's payroll, and the cost of the training is paid by the employing agency. Pre-employment academies provide basic police training for individuals who have not yet been hired by any police agency, and the cost of the police training is borne by the individual. In some instance, as a cost-savings measure, pre-service academies will reserve some spaces for pre-employment students. Such a combined program is frequently found in college-based police training programs. These combined programs may be identified as hybrids. The college-based academy is typically located on or near the campus of the sponsoring college and oftentimes includes a college credit option. The mixed assortment of training programs has arisen in the United States because the nation's police system is highly decentralized, existing at the local, state, and federal levels.

Chapter 5 considers five different nations' (the UK, the Netherlands, Finland, Kenya, and India) police academies, exploring how each nation's culture influences policing. In addition, the trend toward transnational police training is addressed. The organizations of the INTERPOL Global Academy and the ILEAs are presented. The latter program was initiated by the United States in partnership with several host nations and 17 federal US law enforcement agencies. The ILEAs were established during the 1990s and are administered by the United States Department of State Bureau of Diplomatic Security and Bureau of International Narcotics and Law Enforcement.

Chapter 6 reflects on the long and unfinished march toward racial equality in the United States. It focuses on the need to build a sense of trust and legitimacy for police departments by seeking qualified police candidates who reflect a community's diversity. Problems associated with the recruitment and selection of qualified minority and female candidates are addressed. Additional matters relevant to the selection of police personnel as well as expanded activities to engage community members in the hiring process are discussed, such as the best practices for minority recruitment.

Chapter 7 addresses the critical need to reduce unnecessary violence by police. It is recommended that lessons involving higher-level thinking skills be offered at police academies to improve the abilities of officers to cope with stressful incidents without having to resort to the use of force. An emphasis is placed on the need to recognize learning differences among recruits as well as the cultural differences of the communities they will serve. A shift away from an overemphasis on behaviorist training is recommended with an expectation of reducing incidents of violence. Overall, the chapter emphasizes how a closer connection between police academies and academic institutions can more properly prepare future and current police officers for the realities of the job.

In Chapter 8 the current state of police training is viewed along with its limitations and opportunities. One opportunity is to present "bias-free" police training. The need for upgrading police training has become apparent given the complex nature of crime and the realities of every day police work. Incidents involving abject failures in police response are identified, including the history of the Lincoln assassination. In that national tragedy, Metropolitan Police Officer John Parker was temporarily named to the White House protective detail. Parker was the only one of the officers with a spotty record, so it was a tragic coincidence that he drew the assignment to guard the president that evening. In addition, the contemporary problem of assigning officers to mentor new recruits who may not be suitable is highlighted. With respect to carrying out actual police duties, the personal life crises faced by Abraham Lincoln are illustrated with the hope that their gravity may encourage police officers to address their own serious issues. Since police work may involve whether a person lives or dies, learning by doing and teaching by experience can produce either heartbreak or joy.

Chapter 9 provides an overview of the organization of several different types of citizen police academies. In all, 16 programs are highlighted and it is quickly revealed how the curriculums of most are remarkably similar. Their origins as well as advantages and disadvantages are discussed. It is recommended that auxiliary and reserve police officers become active participants in these civilian public safety courses by training them to become "Community Police Academy" instructors. By having qualified citizens' train other citizens, these programs can provide the means for more citizens to achieve safer living and working environments. Citizen academies are unique because they provide an opportunity for average citizens to obtain a first-hand look at the activities and operation of the law enforcement agency operating within their community.

The definition and origin of Law Related Education (LRE) are considered in Chapter 10. Emphasis is given to what the police need to know about the law beyond their initial academy training as well as how the police may extend knowledge about the law to others. One way for police to demonstrate their resolve to move from "warrior" to "guardian" status is by becoming qualified as LRE instructors. Already, thousands of police have become certified to act as school resource officers and/or D.A.R.E. (Drug Abuse Resistance Education) and G.R.E.A.T. (Gang Resistance Education and Training instructors. Typically, post-academy training has been available for such roles. Overall, police participation in LRE can uplift police professionalism and at the same time help in achieving a more civic-minded nation.

Chapter 11 explores features regarding the nature of policing in popular culture, including stereotypes and misinformation. Such perceptions along with the implications for widely held stereotypes are discussed as well as the potentials for educating citizens about how their police are actually trained. Special attention is given to the use of 21st century media outlets and how police trainees and officers are portrayed in the news, podcasts, television, and feature films.

Chapter 12 concludes the book and addresses the benefits and limitations of a recommended decentralized precinct apprenticeship training model. The authors are advocates for a grassroots innovative approach for qualifying candidates for local police work—under the title of "The Model Precinct." The steps to be undertaken begin with existing or updated screening processes involving intellectual, physical, mental, and legal selection considerations. However, instead of new recruits reporting to a local, zone, or municipal police academy for a generally uninterrupted four to six–month program of instruction, they immediately report to a police precinct or other location where police are routinely assigned to patrol areas in their home jurisdiction. In some small towns or other types of municipalities, this location may be a central police headquarters building or office. The locations become the focal point of all basic training instruction and activities. Whenever possible, this instruction is supplemented by an academic educational program conducted at a nearby campus. The lack of a nearby college campus is compensated for through Zoom and other hybrid computer assisted methods of instruction. The need to have expert instruction in such fields as self-defense, firearms, crisis intervention/de-escalation techniques, substance abuse, emergency vehicle operation, and related areas is addressed by intermittent course attendance at state police and/or correctional academies.

New recruits who already possess significant academic credentials may have parts of their training program waived through appropriate testing. If new recruits possess prior experience as a volunteer or peace officer, they would also have the opportunity to have portions of their training waived through testing procedures. Volunteer police are members of authorized permanent organizations of a public agency who perform one or more police functions in an overt manner for little or no compensation.

The new trainees will be provided with supervisory instructor/mentors for the length of their training program. Such mentor/instructors must be qualified through the relevant peace officer and training (POST) state agency or board as well as vetted by a community civilian oversight panel. Their qualifications and supervisory performance will be reviewed on a quarterly schedule by the local panel. During daily assignments, the new trainees will engage in a progressive series of field exercises, from basic traffic enforcement and the delivery of mental health first aid to responding to the crises and other emergencies expected of sworn officers. Significantly, at each stage of the program, trainees will be expected to work closely with community members and organizations in order to become familiar with the resources and needs of their jurisdictions. Appropriate orientations and other guidance are to be provided by supervisory instructor/mentors. Program curriculums are also to be evaluated periodically by the civilian oversight panel, and all recruit performance records will be similarly evaluated before a new recruit can be fully sworn in as a police officer. In this way, basic training may be enhanced beyond the scope of the minimum state standards of traditional training academies. It permits a unique collaboration between police agency, the community, and college for the purpose of designing an appropriate curriculum that fulfills public safety objectives.

"The challenges of the 21st century—violence, intercultural conflict, social and economic injustice, resource shortages, substance abuse—require us to think broadly and even more creatively about the future" (Nicholl, 1999, p. viii). The police not only have a critical role to play in supporting change by taking stock of the current situation, but they must always be seen as accountable to individual citizens, to the law, and to the courts. Above all, in order to maintain the integrity, meaning, and purpose of law in a democratic society, the police must serve not only to preserve order but also to serve and protect the rule of law as an instrument for guaranteeing individual freedom.

Notes

1 Fosdick authored 14 books during his lifetime. He was "born in Buffalo to a long line of clergymen, Raymond B. Fosdick (1883–1972) admired Woodrow Wilson so much that he transferred from Colgate College to Princeton where he received his M.A. in 1906. As a student, Fosdick visited New York's Lower East Side where the living conditions of immigrant families so appalled him that after graduation and during his law studies he worked at the Henry Street Settlement, which provided social services to poor families" (Plunkett Lake Press, 2022). After graduating from New York Law School in 1908, Fosdick began working for the City of New York. He rose to become a chief investigator in his post of Commissioner of Accounts. "While investigating white slavery, he met John D. Rockefeller, Jr. (JDR Jr.) who was working with a special grand jury investigating the same issue. JDR Jr. hired Fosdick in 1913 to head up a study for the newly created Bureau of Social Hygiene, a Rockefeller philanthropy working to prevent social ills among the urban poor, including prostitution, venereal disease and crime" (Plunkett Lake Press, 2022). In 1913, Fosdick spent nearly a year in Europe. The cities he visited included London, Liverpool, Manchester, Birmingham, Glasgow, Edinburgh, Paris, Lyons, Berlin, Hamburg, Bremen, Dresden, Munich, Stuttgart, Cologne, Vienna, Budapest, Rome, Brussels, Amsterdam, and Rotterdam (Fosdick, 2015). "Fosdick's study of European law enforcement was published as *European Police Systems* in 1916. In 1917 Fosdick studied military training for the US Army and Navy and then

served as special representative of the War Department in France and as a civilian aide to General Pershing. After World War I Fosdick became Under-Secretary General of the League of Nations, a position he left in 1920 when the United States did not ratify its membership in the organization. In 1920 Fosdick returned to the Bureau of Social Hygiene and was a close associate of JDR Jr., serving as his attorney and advisor, and in prominent roles in Rockefeller philanthropies. . . . As a trustee of the Rockefeller Foundation, Fosdick played a key role in the Foundation's reorganization in 1928, and in 1936 was named president of the Rockefeller Foundation and of the General Education Board . . . Fosdick's contributions to public service and philanthropy were recognized by many awards, including the Distinguished Service Medal for his war work, and the titles of Commander in the French Legion of Honor and Fellow of the American Academy of Arts and Sciences" (Plunkett Lake Press, 2022).

2 According to Fosdick (2015), "Europe insists also upon a thoroughly trained policeman in the rank and file of her force. The training school is one of the important activities of every well-organized police department in England and on the Continent. Some of the schools are elaborate organizations, with separately constructed buildings and complete equipment. London's course lasts for eight weeks; Manchester's for three months. The term of the Paris school is four months; Berlin's, five weeks; Dresden's, six weeks. The course in Hamburg extends over two periods of six weeks each, separated by practical service on the streets for a term of six weeks. Vienna's school term extends over an entire year. The Carabinieri and City Guards of Italy have six months' training" (pp. 32–33).

3 In July 1994, the highly regarded journal of *Crime and Delinquency* devoted an entire 170-page journal issue to an examination of the various facets of community policing (see volume 40, issue 3). The topics covered included: community policing reform; community policing in Chicago and Brooklyn; the impact of community policing on police personnel; community policing management styles; community crime prevention measures; and problems associated with stimulating community involvement in community policing. The special journal issue was edited by Dennis Rosenbaum and Arthur Lurigio (1994) who contended that "Community policing is the latest reform in law enforcement and is quite popular among politicians, citizens, and police managers" (p. 299). On the other hand, they observed that the "concept of community policing is rather nebulous, and in the field, it assumes many forms, including foot patrol, ministations, and community organizing. Both internal and external factors have limited the success of its implementation, and so far, it has never become fully operational on a large scale" (Rosenbaum & Lurigio, 1994, p. 299). The journal issue was especially timely because it appeared when a major federal initiative for local policing was underway. The greatest portion of these funds was to be dedicated to putting officers on the street to engage in community policing. Currently, community policing is considered "the prevailing organizational strategy of police departments in the United States . . . [focusing] on neighborhood challenges while relying on a joint, formal problem-solving process" (Flexon et al., 2009, p. 180). For definitions of "community policing" see: Weisel and Eck (1994, p. 51); Wilkinson and Rosenbaum (1994, p. 110); and Oliver and Armstrong (1998, p. 51).

4 The "Model Precinct" is envisioned as a way to harness "the energies and talents of experienced law enforcement officers, as well as college educators, in order to prepare candidates for police officer work. In this preservice approach to police training, local police facilities serve as an extension of the college campus, and police personnel and college faculty collaborate on the implementation and design of the program. The Model Precinct would combine intensive fieldwork experience, a college degree course of study, and the completion of basic police school requirements into a single program. It also would permit a unique collaboration between police officials and college professors for the purpose of designing an appropriate curriculum that fulfills these objectives" (Greenberg, 1998).

5 The history of volunteer police can be divided into five epochs having some degree of overlap, including from earliest to latest: the lay justice period featuring the Native American military societies, the militia, etc.; the vigilant era consisting of the detective societies and posses; the spy era during the Progressive Era and World War I; the transformation era between 1920 to 1970; and the assimilation era (beginning about 1970 to present time) when civil defense and other varieties of volunteer police become an integrated part of the community policing strategy of many police departments (Greenberg, 2005).

6 The *Journal of Criminal Law and Criminology* is a student-run publication at Northwestern University School of Law that prints four issues annually and rests upon a century of scholarship

devoted to the scientific study of criminal law and criminology. Since its inception in 1910, the *Journal* has tried to cover the broad field of legal scholarship on crime through the publication of legal articles, criminological research, book reviews, and symposia. The *Journal* is consistently ranked among the most influential legal and criminology publications and is widely read and cited. All issues of the *Journal* are available free online at: https://scholarlycommons.law.northwestern.edu/jclc/).

7 In a later case, the US Supreme Court in 1950 stated: "It is now the settled doctrine of this Court that the Due Process Clause embodies a system of rights based on moral principles so deeply imbedded in the traditions and feelings of our people as to be deemed fundamental to a civilized society as conceived by our whole history. Due Process is that which comports with the deepest notions of what is fair and right and just" (Solesbee v. Balkcom, 339 U.S. 9, 16).

8 Sloan (2018) concluded, "If 'quality' is measured by the number of standards met by the entity under scrutiny, curricula in bachelor's programs in criminal justice must be deemed as being inferior at best. They routinely lack mission statements or stated goals/objectives; they fail to cover core, required areas of the discipline such as policing or corrections; they do not require students to take courses on diversity issues nor ethics; they do not make enough electives available to students pursuing the major; and they do not make concentrations available in the major for students to pursue."

9 The ACJS standards were adopted in 2005. To be certified by the Academy of Criminal Justice Sciences (ACJS) an institution of higher education needed to provide evidence demonstrating that its program was in compliance with all requirements of the certification standards. For example, Standard D. 3 of the "Certification Standards for College/University Criminal Justice Baccalaureate Degree Programs" states: "Only credit from institutions that are accredited by their regional higher education accrediting body is accepted for transfer into an undergraduate criminal justice program. No academic credit is awarded by the criminal justice program for life experience or for military, police academy, or other professional training."

10 "The dynamics underpinning the shortages vary by department, but there are national trends making it harder for police forces to attract applicants. The first is a strong economy. Nelson Lim, a researcher at the RAND Corporation, a think-tank, says this is nothing new. When plenty of jobs are available, people are usually less motivated to enter dangerous professions. Police forces as well as the armed forces tend to field less interest in boom times. . . . Philadelphia had 350 vacancies, largely due to a spate of retirements. Last spring, Dallas cancelled two academy classes for lack of applicants; its preliminary applications dropped by over 30% between 2010 and 2015. In 2012, the ratio of police officers to population hit its lowest level since 1997" (Force, 2017).

11 "America's form of government, its laws and its Constitution, all express the desire to maintain the maximum degree of individual liberty consistent with maintenance of social order. The process of striking this balance is complex and delicate. An example is the 'probable cause' standard that governs arrest. Probable cause does not insure that no innocent man ever will be arrested, but it does restrict police actions that are arbitrary or discriminatory or intuitive. At the same time, it is far less restrictive than the standard that governs conviction in court-'proof beyond a reasonable doubt.' If the police had to abide by that standard before making an arrest, law enforcement would be an all but impossible job" (President's Commission, 1967, p. 93).

12 Dr. Kenney holds a Ph.D. degree in criminal justice from Rutgers University. He is the author or co-author of numerous articles and books including *Police Pursuits: What We Know* (2000), *A Conflict of Rights* (1999), *Crime in the Schools* (1998), *Organized Crime in America* (1995), and *Crime, Fear and the New York City Subways* (1986). He "recently completed complex projects including nationwide surveys of citizens and police in both Yemen and Albania, an evaluation of U.S. sponsored training of police in Ukraine, and a multi-year, multi-city study of abortion-related conflict and violence from the public safety perspective (Kaiser Family Foundation). In addition, he recently completed an evaluation of the Houston Police "Investigative First Responder" effort as well as a multi-city study of police diversity issues. . . . Most recently, he has received funding to develop methods of professional transformation for police managers in Colombia as well as the newly formed national police in Mexico" (John Jay College, 2022).

13 The Universal Declaration of Human Rights (UDHR) is a milestone document in the history of human rights. Drafted by representatives with different legal and cultural backgrounds from all regions of the world, the Declaration was proclaimed by the United Nations General Assembly in Paris December 10, 1948 (General Assembly resolution 217 A) as a common standard of

achievements for all peoples and all nations. It sets out, for the first time, fundamental human rights to be universally protected and it has been translated into over 500 languages. The UDHR is widely recognized as having inspired, and paved the way for, the adoption of more than 70 human rights treaties, applied today on a permanent basis at global and regional levels (all containing references to it in their preambles). "By calling for an end to discrimination on the basis of race, sex, religion, national origin, or ideology, the Declaration foreshadowed struggles for civil and political rights that were yet to come. Articles calling for equal pay for equal work and universal health care were among those on which the United States itself still falls short. . . . Eleanor Roosevelt [helped to craft the Declaration], in her role as chair of the U.N. commission responsible for writing it. The creation of an organization that would unite the nations of the world had been a dream of her late husband, President Franklin Roosevelt, and she saw the elaboration of an international bill of rights as crucial to that work" (Gjelten, 2018). The Declaration can be found online at: https://www.un.org/en/about-us/universal-declaration-of-human-rights.

14 "Red Flag" laws involve petitioning civil courts to temporarily take away the firearms of a family member who is experiencing a mental health crisis and has access to firearms. The petition may involve a family or household member who is making threats or is experiencing suicidal thoughts. These laws, also known as "extreme risk protection order laws" have become an increasingly popular tool to prevent mass shootings, suicides and deadly domestic violence. By October 2021, "nineteen states and the District of Columbia [had] . . . adopted them, sometimes with bipartisan support. Fourteen of those laws came after the 2018 school shooting in Parkland, Florida—a catalyzing event that led to a wave of gun restrictions nationwide. . . . Most states allow only law enforcement and family or household members to petition the courts to temporarily seize or prevent the purchase of firearms, while some states also offer the option to medical professionals, school officials, coworkers and current or former partners" (Vasilogambros, 2021). However, one of the biggest barriers to their use to help prevent mass shootings and potential suicides appears to be the lack of awareness about these laws (Public Affairs, 2023).

References

Abreu, J. (2020, August 25). Why U.S. colleges are failing at justice education. *The Crime Report.* Retrieved November 17, 2022, from https://thecrimereport.org/2020/08/25/why-u-s-colleges-are-failing-at-justice-education/

Berman, M. (2021, May 8). Most police departments in America are small. That's partly why changing policing is difficult, experts say. *The Washington Post.* Retrieved November 19, 2022, from https://www.washingtonpost.com/nation/2021/05/08/most-police-departments-america-are-small-thats-partly-why-changing-policing-is-difficult-experts-say/

Birzer, M. L., & Palmiotto, M. J. (2002). Criminal justice education: Where have we been? And where are we heading? *The Justice Professional*, *15*(3), 203–211.

Bostaph, L. G., Brady, P., & Giacomazz, A. (2014). Criminal justice education: Are we missing one-third of the crime triangle? *Journal of Criminal Justice Education*, *25*(4), 468–485.

Brockelsby, L. L., & Scheetz, R. E. (1987, April). St. Louis police training: A long and proud history and today's regional concept. *FBI Law Enforcement Bulletin*, *56*(4), 1–5. https://www.ojp.gov/pdffiles1/Digitization/105097NCJRS.pdf

Bykov, O. (2014). Police academy training: An evaluation of the strengths and weaknesses of police academies. *Themis: Research Journal of Justice Studies and Forensic Science*, 2, Article 9. https://doi.org/10.31979/THEMIS.2014.0209. https://scholarworks.sjsu.edu/themis/vol2/iss1/9

Byrne, D. N., & Bezbatchenko, A. W. (2021, January 25). Educating future law enforcement officers. *Inside Higher Ed.* Retrieved May 20, 2023, from https://www.insidehighered.com/views/2021/01/26/criminal-justice-education-needs-change-and-humanities-must-play-role-opinion

Cordner, G., & Shain, C. (2011, August). Editorial: The changing landscape of police education and training. *Police Practice & Research*, *12*(4), 281–285.

Division of Criminal Justice Services. (2022). *History of the basic course for police officers.* Retrieved November 16, 2022, from https://www.criminaljustice.ny.gov/ops/training/bcpo/index.htm

FBI. (2022). *National incident-based reporting system (NIBRS).* Retrieved November 20, 2022, from https://www.fbi.gov/how-we-can-help-you/need-an-fbi-service-or-more- information/ucr/nibrs

Finckenauer, J. O. (2005). The quest for quality in criminal justice education. *Justice Quarterly*, *22*(4), 413–426.

Flanagan, T. (2000). Liberal education and the criminal justice major. *Journal of Criminal Justice Education*, *11*(1), 1–13.

Flexon, J. L., Lurigio, A. J., & Greenleaf, R. G. (2009, March–April). Exploring the dimensions of trust in the police among Chicago juveniles. *Journal of Criminal Justice*, *37*(2), 180–189. https://doi.org/10.1016/j.jcrimjus.2009.02.006

Force. (2017, January 5). *The force is weak: Police departments struggle to recruit enough officers*. Retrieved May 2, 2018, from https://www.economist.com/news/united- states/21713898-stronger-economy-partly-blame-police-departments-struggle-recruit- enough

Fosdick, R. B. (1915). European police systems. *Journal of Criminal Law & Criminology*, *6*(1), 28–38.

Fosdick, R. B. (1920). *American police systems*. The Century Company.

Frie, L. (2022). *City of Saint Louis Metropolitan police department: Historical photos and illustrations*. St. Louis Police Veterans' Association. Retrieved November 17, 2022, from http://slpva.com/HISTORICAL%20SAINT%20LOUIS%20POLICE%20PHOTOS.pdf

Garner, J. W. (1910). Editorial. *Journal of American Institute Criminal Law and Criminology*, *1*(1), 2–5.

GCPM. (2022). *Cincinnati police department history—1875 to 1899*. Retrieved November 17, 2022, from https://police-museum.org/greater-cincinnati-police-history/chronological- history-of-the-cincinnati-police-department/cincinnati-police-department-history-1875- to-1899/

Gjelten, T. (2018, December 10). *Boundlessly idealistic, universal declaration of human rights is still resisted*. NPR. Retrieved November 21, 2022, from https://www.npr.org/2018/12/10/675210421/its-human-rights-day-however-its-not- universally-accepted

Glied, S., & Frank, R. G. (2014). Mental illness and violence: Lessons from the evidence. *American Journal of Public Health*, *104*(2), e5–e6.

Gramlich, J. (2020, November 20). What the data says (and doesn't say) about crime in the United States. *Pew Research Center*. Retrieved November 20, 2022, from https://www.pewresearch.org/fact-tank/2020/11/20/facts-about-crime-in-the-u-s/

Greenberg, M. A. (1998). The model precinct: Issues involving police training. *FBI Law Enforcement Bulletin*, *9*(98), 14–16. https://www.thefreelibrary.com/The+model+precinct%3A+issues+involving+police+trai ning.-a021202919

Greenberg, M. A. (2005). *Citizens defending America: From colonial times to the age of terrorism*. University of Pittsburgh Press.

Hale, D. C. (1998). Criminal justice education: Traditions in transition. *Justice Quarterly*, *15*(3), 385–394.

Hardie, J. H., & Lucas, A. (2010, October). Economic factors and relationship quality among young couples: Comparing cohabitation and marriage. *Journal of Marriage and Family*, *72*(5), 1141–1154. doi:10.1111/j.1741-3737.2010.00755

Harvard. (2022). *Cybersecurity: Managing risk in the information age: Online short course*. Retrieved November 18, 2022, from https://pll.harvard.edu/course/cybersecurity-managing-risk-information-age

Hummer, D., & Byrne, J. (2021). Rethinking criminal justice education: Applying experience credits towards CJ degree completion—generates dollars, but does it make sense? *Journal of Criminal Justice Education*, *32*(4), 415–445.

James, D. J., & Glaze, L. E. (2006, December 12). *Mental health problems of prison and jail inmates*. US Department of Justice, Office of Justice Programs, Bureau of Justice Statistics. Report NCJ-213600). https://www.bjs.gov/content/pub/pdf/mhppji.pdf

John Jay College. (2022). *Dennis Kenney*. Retrieved November 20, 2022, from https://www.jjay.cuny.edu/faculty/dennis-kenney

Klein-Collins, R., Taylor, J., Bishop, C., Bransberger, P., Lane, P., & Leibrandt, S. (2020, December). *The PLA boost: Results from a 72-institution targeted study of prior learning assessment and adult student outcomes. Revised*. Council for Adult and Experiential Learning (CAEL) and Western Interstate Commission for Higher Education (WICHE). https://files.eric.ed.gov/fulltext/ED609770.pdf

Krimmel, J. (1999). Career choice and characteristics of criminal justice undergraduates. *Journal of Criminal Justice Education*, *10*(2), 277–289.

Libaw, O. W. (2017, July 10). *Police face severe shortage of recruits*. Retrieved May 2, 2018, from http://abcnews.go.com/US/story?id=96570&page=1

Little, B. (2020, December 8). *How Eleanor Roosevelt pushed for a universal declaration of human rights*. Retrieved November 20, 2022, from https://www.history.com/news/eleanor-roosevelt-universal-declaration-human-rights

Little Hoover Commission. (2021, November). *Issue brief: Comparing law enforcement basic training academies*. Retrieved November 16, 2022, from https://lhc.ca.gov/sites/lhc.ca.gov/files/Reports/264/Report264.pdf

Lloyd, L. (2010, Summer). European approaches to democracy promotion. *International Journal: Canada's Journal of Global Policy Analysis*, *65*(3), 547–559. https://doi.org/10.1177/002070201006500302

Luwig, J., Duncan, G., & Hirschfeld, P. (2001, May). Urban poverty and juvenile crime: Evidence from a randomized housing-mobility experiment. *The Quarterly Journal of Economics*, *116*(2), 655–679. https://doi.org/10.1162/00335530151144122200 1

McCay, D. A. (2011, August). *They are old enough to carry guns, should we teach them like children? The application of adult learning strategies in police training* (Purdue University, PhD Dissertation). Purdue University, Graduate School. https://www.proquest.com/openview/11c56b6ece3c5b16e0c13448a7f218a4/1?pq- origsite=gscholar&cbl=18750

Mentalhealth.gov. (2022, February 28). *Mental health myths and facts*. Retrieved November 22, 2022, from https://www.mentalhealth.gov/basics/mental-health-myths-facts

Mercy College. (2022). *Cybersecurity education center*. Retrieved November 18, 2022, from https://www.mercy.edu/academics/school-liberal-arts/department-mathematics-and-computer-sciences/cybersecurity-education

Mercyhurst University. (2022, April 12). *Area legislators to tour FRC network operations center at Mercyhurst*. Retrieved November 18, 2022, from https://www.mercyhurst.edu/news/area-legislators-to-tour-frc-network-operations-center- at-mercyhurst

Nicholl, C. G. (1999). *Community policing, community justice, and restorative justice: Exploring the links for the delivery of a balanced approach to public safety*. US Department of Justice, Office of Community Oriented Policing Services.

NYPD. (1993). *History of New York City police department*. New York City Police Department. https://www.ojp.gov/pdffiles1/Digitization/145539NCJRS.pdf

Oliver, M. B., & Armstrong, G. B. (1998). The color of crime: Perceptions of Caucasians' and African-Americans' involvement in crime. In M. Fishman & G. Cavender (Eds.), *Entertaining crime: Television reality programs* (pp. 19–35). Aldine de Gruyter.

PERF. (2022, November). *Transforming police recruit training: 40 guiding principles*. Police Executive Research Forum. https://www.policeforum.org/assets/TransformingRecruitTraining.pdf

Plunkett Lake Press. (2022). *Raymond B. Fosdick*. Retrieved November 13, 2022, from https://plunkettlakepress.com/rfo.html

President's Commission. (1967). *The president's commission on law enforcement and administration of justice, task force report: The police*. U.S. Government Printing Office.

Public Affairs. (2023, January 11). What are 'red flag' laws and how can they prevent gun violence? *UC Davis Health*. Retrieved May 21, 2023, from https://health.ucdavis.edu/news/headlines/what-are-red-flag-laws-and-how-can-they-prevent-gun-violence/2023/01

Rahr, S., & Rice, S. K. (2015, April). From warriors to guardians: Recommitting American police culture to democratic ideals. In *New perspectives in policing bulletin*. US Department of Justice, National Institute of Justice. NCJ 248654. Retrieved November 14, 2022, from https://www.ojp.gov/pdffiles1/nij/248654.pdf

Reese, H. (2022, February 23). What happens when police use AI to predict and prevent crime? *JSTOR Daily*. Retrieved May 19, 2023, from https://daily.jstor.org/what-happens-when-police-use-ai-to-predict-and-prevent-crime/

Reiss, Jr., A. J. (1971). *The police and the public*. Yale University Press.

Ritter, N. M. (2004). *Preparing for the future: Criminal justice in 2040*. Retrieved May 1, 2018, from https://www.nij.gov/journals/255/pages/2040.aspx

Robinson, M. (2002). *Justice blind? Ideals and realities of American criminal justice*. Prentice Hall.

Rosenbaum, D. P., & Lurigio, A. J. (1994). An inside look at community policing reform: Definitions, organizational changes, and evaluation findings. *Crime and Delinquency*, *40*(3), 299–314. https://doi.org/10.1177/0011128794040003001

Schafer, J. A., & Boyd, S. (2007). The future of education and training for policing. In J. A. Schafer (Ed.), *Policing 2020: Exploring the future of crime, communities, and policing* (pp. 372–413). Federal Bureau of Investigation.

Schafer, J. A., & Jarvis, J. P. (2017). The landscape of police education and training 2037. *The Police Chief*, *84*(10), 56, 58.

Scott, M. S. (2010). Policing and police research: Learning to listen, with a Wisconsin case study. *Police Practice & Research*, *11*(2), 95–104.

Scott-Smith, B. (2022, November 17). *New London police department extends public outreach efforts with new initiatives*. WSHU Public Radio. Retrieved November 18, 2022, from https://www.wshu.org/connecticut-news/2022-11-17/new-london-police-department-extends-public-outreach-efforts-with-new-initiatives

Skeem, J. L., Manchak, S., & Peterson, J. K. (2011). Correctional policy for offenders with mental illness: Creating a new paradigm for recidivism reduction. *Law and Human Behavior*, *35*(2), 110–126.

Sloan, J. J, III. (2019). The state of criminal justice educational programs in the United States: Bachelors' degrees, curriculum standards, and the ongoing quest for quality. *Journal of Criminal Justice Education*, *30*(2), 193–222. doi:10.1080/10511253.2018.1457701

Southerland, M. O., Merlo, A. V., Robinson, L., Benekos, P. J., & Albanese, J. S. (2007). Ensuring quality in criminal justice education: Academic standards and the reemergence of accreditation. *Journal of Criminal Justice Education*, *18*(1), 87–105.

UAlbany. (2017, January 26). *Senior homeland security official named UAlbany dean*. Retrieved May 2, 2018, from https://www.timesunion.com/local/article/Senior- Homeland-Security-official-named-UAlbany-10887383.php

Vasilogambros, M. (2021, October 5). *Red flag laws are saving lives. They could save more*. Retrieved November 21, 2022, from https://www.pewtrusts.org/en/research-and- analysis/blogs/stateline/2021/10/05/red-flag-laws-are-saving-lives-they-could-save-more

Walker, S. (1993). Involving citizens in violence prevention: A reply to Rosenfeld, Decker, and givens. *American Journal of Police*, *12*(3), 59–64.

Waxman, O. B. (2017, May 18). How the U.S. Got its police force. *Time*. Retrieved November 19, 2022, from https://time.com/4779112/police-history-origins/

Weisel, D. L., & Eck, J. E. (1994). Toward a practical approach to organizational change: Community policing initiatives in six cities. In D. P. Rosenbaum (Ed.), *The challenge of community policing: Testing the promises* (pp. 53–72). Sage.

Wilkinson, D. L., & Rosenbaum, D. P. (1994). The effects of organizational structure on community policing: A comparison of two cities. In D. P. Rosenbaum (Ed.), *The challenge of community policing: Testing the promises* (pp. 110–126). Sage.

Wolf, R., Albrecht, J. F., & Dobrin, A. (2015, October). Reserve policing in the United States: Citizens volunteering for public service. *The Police Chief*, *82*, 38–47.

Wolf, R., & Dobrin, A. (2021, December 31). The benefits of reserve officers in modern policing: Utilizing the strengths and expertise of volunteers for ultimate agency transparency. *Police1.com*. https://www.police1.com/police-jobs-and-careers/articles/the-benefits-of-reserve-officers-in-modern-policing-PuOKPUUc1pEYkRdT/

PART II

Types of Police Academies and Training

2

BIG CITY, REGIONAL, HYBRID, AND STATE POLICE ACADEMIES

Building safer, less violent communities is a major challenge all states and local communities are facing. A critical role in this effort is the nature and conduct of contemporary police academies. At its most basic level, the completion of a police academy is the first step police officers must take in their career journeys, learning the basic policies and skills needed to perform in a law enforcement role. While little published academic research has been done on specific local and state police academies, scholars still recognize the importance of what happens in these institutions, particularly for community-police relations once trainees graduate and hit the streets in their locales (Skogan et al., 2015). This chapter provides an overview of the most common types of academies: big city, state, and regional police academies. Academies will range in scope/content of training and education as well as length, often dependent on the type of academy (local, regional, hybrid, state, or federal) and geographic location. However, no matter the type, academies like police departments are often required to do more with fewer resources. Generally speaking, police academies will involve both classroom education and physical and tactical field training. Students at any academy, often referred to as recruits, cadets, or trainees, will have to pass a series of written and physical tests over the course of their time in training, before beginning on-the-job-training in the police department of their (often conditional) hire. Conditional employment is a common practice among professions involving such necessities as background checks, drug screenings, physical exams, and psychological exams or tests (PoliceApp, 2019). As such, police officers often fall into this category. The process of just getting a spot in a police academy (when many trainees often, but not always, begin receiving a paycheck) can be long and tedious–and then trainees must attend and pass the academy before being hired into a full-time position with an agency.

The duration of academies vary, but on average, a police academy in the United States involves around 833 hours of training (Buehler, 2021), which equates to approximately 6 months of time in an academy (American Police Officers Alliance, 2019). This number varies depending on source and who is surveyed. The Police Executive Research Forum (PERF), an independent research organization that focuses on critical issues in policing and founded in 1976, has indicated that most academies are approximately 807 hours, or

DOI: 10.4324/9781003307396-4

20 weeks (PERF, 2022), which is relatively the same as what the Bureau of Justice Statistics (Buehler, 2021) has reported. North Carolina has the longest training averages for their academies, with over 900 hours required on average, while Mississippi has the least average hours required, at 400 hours (Hendricks, 2020). Police academies in the United States tend to be shorter; by comparison, other Western democracies devote more time to police training (PERF, 2022). With recruiting being difficult for many agencies in the United States,[1] some departments are choosing to shorten the time spent in the police academy in hopes of attracting more candidates. For example, Virginia has experienced a shortage of officers in various agencies across the state. To attract out-of-state applicants with experience, some jurisdictions in Virginia are shortening the police academy training period to eight weeks, specifically for applicants who have at least three years of experience in law enforcement in other states. For those who qualify for Governor Youngkin's "Option 5," incoming officers attend a shorter academy where they are trained on Virginia-specific laws and policies as well as in "high-liability" areas, such as use of force and DUI (Burchett, 2022). Over 80% of police academy graduates across the United States are also required to complete a period of accompanied training in the field following graduation from the academy (Buehler, 2021).

A minimum age is a universal requirement to become a police recruit. Depending on the hiring agency, recruits typically have to be at least 18–23 years old (and in some cases, such as with the Federal Bureau of Investigation, there is also a maximum age) to begin academy training. (In many cases, however, the application process can begin before the recruit-to-be's minimum age birthday.) In terms of education, most often only a high school diploma or GED is required to enter a police academy. This also varies by locale, and federal jobs often have higher education standards. For example, the FBI requires a four-year college degree and at least two years of full-time professional work experience, or it requires that recruits have an advanced degree and at least one year of full-time professional work experience (FBI Jobs, 2022). Psychological, written, and physical testing are also generally required to be passed during the recruitment and application phases before a conditional hire to a potential recruit is made, prior to entering a police academy (American Police Officers Alliance, 2019).

Recruits entering police academies can expect to have a rigorous and regimented schedule, which typically mirrors a paramilitary structure. While at the academy, recruits will wake early, exercise regularly, participate in team-building activities, take classes in a variety of subjects, and be required to maintain a strict dress code. If the academy has a dormitory, room organizational and cleanliness standards must be kept. The socialization of future officers is an important latent function of police academies across the nation. Each cohort of new recruit trainees will face, together, a continuing series of daily challenges, and the collective stress serves to bond police officers to each other and their profession. Friendships made during their training experience often continue for a lifetime. Survival tips are frequently presented and the socialization that begins in police academies drives the subculture of policing. The perception of the dangers of the job as well as its occupational isolation further enhances and strengthens the socialization process and bonds built through that process (McCartney & Parent, 2015).

When Rosa Brooks, a law professor at Georgetown University's School of Law, was undergoing her basic training to become a volunteer reserve police in Washington, DC, her instructors told her, "There's no such thing as a routine call." They said: "You had to approach every situation 'tactically,' which meant you had to always be thinking about the numerous ways in which you could be killed, and act in a manner calibrated to keep you from becoming a dead hero" (Brooks, 2021, p. 81).

Other characteristics of the socialization process taking place at police academies and throughout field training supervision programs place a heavy emphasis on demonstrating: "bravery, [a command presence,] and physical courage to back up other officers in times of danger; character and moral courage to do the right thing, even if it is not the easiest course of action; loyalty to the department and to their fellow officers; willingness to use force, even deadly force, if the situation warrants such a response; and ability to hold their ego in check in the face of verbal abuse or other mistreatment from the public" (O'Keefe, 2004, p. 184). Above all, new recruits are expected to look and act like a police officer. They will need to acquire a "healthy cynicism toward people" in situations that may potentially cause a danger to the officer or the public's safety. While at other times, situations may call for "sensitivity and caring" (see O'Keefe, 2004, pp. 68 and 184). In these ways, the new officers become part of the police subculture and its "accompanying mind-set early in their careers" (Malmin, 2012). However, conflicts regarding appropriate behavior may begin to arise after academy completion and once employed in an agency if some field training officers (FTOs) tell new recruits "that they should forget everything they learned in the academy because their FTO will teach them about 'real' police work—including the subculture" (Malmin, 2012).

Regional, hybrid, and individual city police-run academies follow similar protocols. Regional and hybrid academies, generally speaking, are run by organizations other than the police departments the recruits will actually join. They are often less specific in terms of policies and training because graduates will go on to a variety of departments. They have a more academic focus, sometimes even being run by or in close association with academic institutions. In fact, community colleges or technical schools run approximately 46% of academies in the country, while law enforcement (agency-run) academies make up about 54% of training for police recruits (Buehler, 2021). The independent police-run academies are directed and can be taught by current law enforcement officers (LEOs) from the same agencies the recruits will be joining upon graduation. These academies are often more paramilitary in structure, offering training specific to the locale they serve as compared to decentralized training centers (Indeed Editorial Team, 2021).

While academies will vary from city-to-city and state-to-state, there are some consistent characteristics across locations. The United States (a federal system) has local, state, and federal level law enforcement agencies operating largely independently of each other. With approximately 18,000 separate agencies, it is cumbersome to compose an accurate, exhaustive list of every police academy in the nation. In 2002, an estimated 626 state and local police academies were reported to be operating in the United States (Hickman, 2007). By 2018, that number had risen to 861, training 59,511 recruits during the year, of which over 80% were male. Sixty-four percent of these recruits who began training were White, 17% were Hispanic, and 14% were Black. Just over 80% of recruits who began training finished the academy in 2018 (Buehler, 2021). Despite some differences, a number of general observations can be made and a "big picture" of police training can be drawn about police academies in the United States.[2] The sections below provide a few examples of big city, regional, hybrid, and state academies, profiling what "typical" large city, regional, hybrid, and state academies look like. These sections also explore the socialization process of police recruits and their concerns about the mental health services available to them.

The chapter concludes with a discussion of goals and reform efforts for big city, regional, and state police academies.

Big City Academies

According to its website,

> The Major Cities Chiefs Association (MCCA) is a professional organization of police executives representing the largest cities in the United States and Canada. The MCCA provides a unique forum for urban chiefs, sheriffs and other law enforcement executives to share ideas, experiences and strategies. MCCA provides a collaborative forum for the advancement of public safety through innovation, research, policy development, government engagement, community outreach, and leadership development.
>
> *(MCCA, 2023)*

This organization has about 100 members with regional representation from the eastern, central, and western sections of the United States. Contrary to popular opinion, very few large urban police forces actually resembled a paramilitary model until recent decades. Throughout much of the 20th century the focus of police reform centered on professionalism (e.g., see Stone & Travis, 2011; Griffin, 1998; Walker, 1976). However, with respect to race relations, the police have been found seriously wanting in this aspect of professionalism since the organization of the police during the time of slavery in the US. In the South, the development of slave patrols served as the forerunner for many police departments.

The definition of what constitutes a big or major city is open for interpretation. Both geographic size and population could be considered. For the purposes of this discussion, the definition provided by the National Center for Education Statistics (NCES) will be used, which offers a comprehensive typology of cities for education purposes (NCES, 2022a) that can assist in exploring city characteristics. The NCES defines a large city as a geographic location that is in both an urbanized area and principal city with a population of at least 250,000 (NCES, 2022b). The three largest US cities are New York, NY (population over 8.6 million), Los Angeles, CA (population over 4 million), and Chicago, IL (population over 2.6 million) (World Population Review, 2022). The discussion on big city academies focuses on these largest cities in order to offer a few insights into police academy education and training as they have sometimes served as a model for other academies (and police departments). Any changes in police training will likely have their greatest impact if they are first initiated in these large cities.

One of the defining features of big city versus small town police departments from a training perspective is the centralization of training in large cities. Large metropolitan areas tend to have their own police academies that feed into their own police departments. They are more likely to have formalized, longer academies with higher application/entry requirements. For example, the New York, Los Angeles, and Chicago police academies require applicants to be at least 20 years of age to apply and at least 21 to begin their academy programs. All three academies also have maximum age requirements (35–40) for entry. New York and Chicago require at least 60 hours of college credit and Chicago will waive this requirement with a minimum number of months of military or other related experience. Los Angeles only requires a high school diploma, GED, or equivalent. These three academies also require background checks, medical, physical, and psychological evaluations, and a written test among other qualifying factors, which are typical requirements of most academies regardless of locale. These "big three" academies also have residency and citizenship requirements; academy training and education last about six months, in-keeping with the national average. New police recruits are provided education and training in the following areas: relevant state laws, physical conditioning, tactical training, driver education, school safety, and traffic enforcement. The academies in the largest cities serve hundreds of recruits each year, though numbers fluctuate with each class (Chicago Police Department, 2022; Los Angeles Police Department, 2022; New York Police Department, 2022).

The recruiting activities of big city police departments involve targeted recruiting and outreach, with recruiters being active on social media, with updated websites and personnel available to go to job fairs and other types of recruiting events. The Los Angeles Police Department's website makes a concerted effort to note the importance of future police officers having "interpersonal skills, sensitivity, and respect for others; decision making and judgment; maturity and discipline; honesty, integrity, and personal ethics" (Los Angeles Police Department, 2022). Notably, such characteristics seem to extend beyond the stereotypical tactical and physical skills of police academy recruits, instead recognizing some of the roles attributed to social work. The online description, however, has avoided using these words. In an era of rising concern about police violence, police academies (particularly in large cities) are becoming more attuned to the needs of their recruits and the demands of society. It is now common practice in many large cities for police candidates to be advised to follow social media pages for up-to-date information on workshops and test prep events.

Regional Academies

While large cities have the resources to run their own, individualized police academies, smaller cities, towns, and rural areas tend to hold decentralized or regional academies. These regional academies are independent of law enforcement agencies and are not run by a specific police department. Multiple police (and sheriffs') departments send recruits to these regional training schools. Smaller police departments have fewer resources than larger ones, with less funding and fewer staff members when compared to their metropolitan counterparts. Running a police academy for individual, smaller departments is not cost-effective, so pooling recruits (and resources) from multiple agencies within a region allows for formal training in a more cost-effective manner. Further, recruits from these regional schools do not typically live as residents of the academy but rather keep their homes in the community and come to class, generally five days per week, during their training period.

Many examples and variations of regional academies exist, and looking at individual examples can help draw a picture of what a regional academy looks like. One such example of a regional academy is the Johnson County Regional Police Academy in Overland, KS, on the campus of Johnson County Community College.[3] This academy provides education and training for 18 agencies within the larger county. Prospective applicants are required to apply through individual departments who, upon an offer for hire, will send them to the Johnson County Regional Police Academy. Recruits in the academy are also enrolled into the local community college and are eligible to earn up to 12 credit hours toward an associate degree in the Administration of Justice program. The curriculum consists of classroom, physical, and tactical training. Faculty members have law enforcement experience.

This academy is 18 weeks long and graduates will hold the certification to become a Kansas LEO, allowing them to begin work with their agency of hire (Johnson County Community College, 2022).

Other regional, decentralized academies encompass an even broader spectrum of training for different agencies. For example, the Central Shenandoah Criminal Justice Academy (a nationally accredited criminal justice training academy)[4] in Weyers Cave, VA hosts LEO, jail officer, animal control officer, and communications officer programs. The basic law enforcement program hosts many of the rural region's police recruits. It is 20 weeks long and covers legal topics, first aid training, as well as other tactical and investigative topics. Students spend most of the time in classroom settings but also receive tactical, firearms, and physical training (Central Shenandoah Criminal Justice Academy, 2022). One regional academy in upstate New York has hosted as many as 18 different police agencies in one recent basic academy session.[5] Another example of a regional academy hosting a variety of courses other than only a basic academy is the State Center Regional Training Facility at Fresno City College. In addition to a basic police academy course, this training center has courses for probation officers, advanced officer training, recertification courses, out-of-state waver testing, criminal investigation courses, dispatcher courses, and others (Fresno City College, 2022).

There are many organizational types and different locations of regional academies. Consequently, it is difficult to describe in detail what a "typical" regional academy looks like. It is important to recognize that, though there is so much variation, these academies are generally more academic in nature and do not focus on a specific department. They may also be sharing space with other types of criminal justice professionals and college students, not just police officers and recruits. After completing these academies, new police officers will arrive at their departments of hire for more specific on-the-job training with officers from the agency where they will be working.

There is some debate on whether or not decentralized police training is "good enough" for future police officers. Those who are in favor of such academies can tout its cost effectiveness, academic rigor, and adaptability to adequately train police officers in a variety of jurisdictions. Critics note that they do not offer specific training for the agencies in which trainees will be working. In Ohio, despite negative media coverage, an officer in the Salisbury Police Department wrote to the *Columbus Dispatch* in 2015 praising the state's decentralized training model for being less costly to taxpayers and fulfilling the state-level direction for academy training, with field training occurring in specific jurisdictions once training had been completed. The letter writer stated that although it may have become commonplace to criticize police in the state as not being sufficiently trained, it does not mean that the training system is inadequate of fulfilling its mandate (Brooks, 2015).

Hybrid Regional Academies

In recent years, primarily due to budget limitations, various states such as Missouri, New York, Florida, Vermont, and others have established regional academies where persons interested in police careers as well as some related peace officer positions, including corrections, may enroll at their own expense. In some states, enrollment for civilian pre-employment trainees (independent, non-sponsored students who must pay their own tuition) may attend such "hybrid academies" only on a space-available basis. For example, this is true for the Collin College Law Enforcement Academy located at the new Public Safety Training Center in McKinney, Texas, as well as at the Orange County Sheriff's Basic Police Academy program in Tustin, California. Admission into the latter program is granted upon completion of all prerequisites and requirements and with the approval of the Criminal Justice Academies coordinator at Santa Ana College. A similar policy exists at the Senator John J. Shumaker Public Safety Center (PSC) located at the Harrisburg Area Community College (HACC), the largest and oldest community college in Pennsylvania. Its workforce training programs are focused on police, fire, healthcare, and emergency-service personnel. In addition, the Public Safety Center offers response and safety training for private industry and other organizations (PSC, 2022).

The Eastern Missouri Law Enforcement Training Center is located in Lake St. Louis, about 43 miles from the city of St. Louis. It offers a challenging 1,000-hour police training program, which far exceeds the established 600 minimum hours of training needed to obtain a Missouri Class A Peace Officer License. The Academy was first chartered in 1979 when various law enforcement agencies in St. Charles County came together to form the St. Charles County Law Enforcement Training Center, Inc. This name remains today as the academy's official title, but it also has several registered "doing business as" titles. These include the Eastern Missouri Law Enforcement Training Center; the Eastern Missouri Police Academy (EMPA); and the Police Academy. When the Academy was first formed, it occupied space in the then Sheriff's Department located in downtown St. Charles. Today, the mission of the Academy has three areas of concentration: to train civilians to become licensed peace officers in Missouri; to provide continuing education for working peace officers, both in resident classes offered at the Academy and certification of individual department in-service programs; and to provide the licensing and training of security guards and watchmen for St. Charles County. The Academy has a permanent staff that coordinate the daily activities of the Academy, including an Executive Director responsible for overall operations and an Executive Assistant who handles all financial matters. The Academy is a private not-for-profit organization chartered under the laws of Missouri (EMPA, 2023).

Most police applicants in Missouri traditionally pay their way through an academy. The exceptions include the Missouri State Highway Patrol, St. Louis Metropolitan Police Department, and St. Louis County Police Department. New recruits in these departments attend the in-house academies provided for their training. In recent years, the hybrid academies and their trainees have benefitted as a result of police agencies "sponsoring recruits, essentially paying their way and paying them while they are attending" (Leasor, 2022). According to Thomas Leasor (2022), Eastern Missouri Police Academy's executive director, "other agencies have different incentives, such as paying off a recruits Academy after they are off probation with their specific agency. Recruits in this region have figured out that they are much like free agents in baseball so they will come into our academy looking for the best offer. They are recruited heavily by agencies from across our region, and other states. . . . St. Louis County Police Department also recruits from us but seldom do my recruits go there. Because of this, I have agencies that are from prominent areas of the region that pay really well, and will sponsor a recruit through the Academy, not get applicants to sponsor because they will enter the Academy searching for the best offer it seems" (Leasor, 2022). Missouri now has a scholarship program for police academy applicants that will pay up to $5,000 for that recruit to attend an academy. The new scholarship program was introduced in order to increase the number of police officers (LakeExpo.com, 2022).

The new Missouri scholarship program was launched at the start of November 2022. It consisted of a one million dollar budget known as the "Missouri Blue Scholarship" fund to address officer shortages in law enforcement agencies across the state. Applicants must be US citizens and Missouri residents attending or planning to enter a law enforcement academy. The scholarship pays $5,000 toward the cost of attending a law enforcement academy in the state. The amount of the award is paid directly to the law enforcement academy after completion of eight weeks of training. The scholarships are available to non-sponsored law enforcement training academy recruits (those whose tuition is not being paid by a law enforcement agency). They were to be awarded on a first come, first served basis (Lake-Expo.com, 2022).

Additional information about hybrid regional academies is covered in Chapter 4 dealing with pre-service, pre-employment, and college-based academies.

State Academies

Nowhere in the world of policing have the features representative of a paramilitary model of policing been more prominent than in the development of the many corps of troopers and highway patrols established by the states. The New York State Police and the Pennsylvania State Police are excellent examples. State police academies prepare state-level LEOs (often referred to as state troopers) for careers as sworn state police officers. While academies vary based on location, they often have higher requirements to enter as compared to smaller, local/regional academies. In the United States, every state trooper must be a US citizen or lawful permanent resident. Candidates must not have any felonies or DUIs, must have a valid driver's license, and be able to pass screening tests (background, written, psychological, physical) similar to those required in other types of academies (Policeofficer.org, 2022). In 2001, 49 states required prospective state troopers to be high school graduates.[6] Twenty states required additional college education or prior military or law enforcement service (or a combination education and service) as requirements (Burriesci & Melley, 2001). Most state police academies are over 20 weeks long, require over 700 hours of training, and many have residency components. Again, states will vary in their specific requirements. Brief summaries of the Virginia, Massachusetts, and Texas academies are explored below in order to illustrate various state police academy procedures and policies.

The Commonwealth of Virginia's State Police Academy is 27 weeks long and includes a residency component. To apply, individuals must be 21 years of age by the time training begins, have a high school diploma, and hold a valid driver's license. Having a felony conviction, some misdemeanor offenses and illicit drug use are automatic disqualifiers. To begin the academy, individuals must pass visual, hearing, physical, and written tests as well as successfully undergo a background investigation, polygraph test, and psychological evaluation. Trainees live at the academy in Richmond, Virginia, during the workweek and return to their homes on the weekends. The academy places an important focus on teamwork. The academy's curriculum includes police tactics as well as driving and physical skills (Virginia State Police, 2022).

In Virginia, troopers in recruiter teams spend time on college campuses (though no college degree is required) and attend job fairs throughout the state. The hiring process alone can take three to six months, so potential applicants are encouraged to apply as early as possible.[7] There are options for new troopers to work across the state for their initial assignment upon academy graduation. After two or more years, new troopers become eligible to

of community policing as a primary philosophy in policing, often taught in the academy.[9] Looking at job satisfaction among police officers, Yüksel and Tosum (2015) examined a small sample of interviews with American police officers at a university[10] and found that the socialization of police officers is a varied and evolving process.

Many individuals choose policing because they want to give back to society. In addition, the advent of community policing has led to higher levels of job satisfaction. For example, 68% of a sample of sworn police officers attending in-service training cited wanting "to help people or serve society" as a reason for becoming a police officer (Dolan Consulting Group, 2019). In contrast to older policing philosophies, community policing explicitly opens the door for recognition of policing as a helping profession beyond just enforcing the law. Yüksel and Tosum (2015) found that the focus on community policing itself is crucial in the socialization of police officers. This focus shift from a crime-fighting perspective to a problem solving one is still evolving. The creation of partnerships with public agencies and organizations has also helped increase job satisfaction. Clearly, the adoption of community policing practices is providing intrinsic rewards for police officers throughout their careers (Yüksel & Tosum, 2015). Yüksel and Tosum (2015) reflect on the work of Van Maanen (1975) and note that these more recent findings provide a more positive view of the way police officers view their jobs and communities. Police academy directors are well advised to emphasize such training (see Rahr & Rice, 2015). While individual differences occur based on individual characteristics, socialization within a community policing framework stands out as an important factor contributing to greater job satisfaction (Yüksel & Tosum, 2015). Studies suggest that what drives public perception of police officers in the community policing era is how citizens believe they are treated by police officers (Rahr & Rice, 2015). As police academies turn more and more toward a community policing focus at all levels, the public's safety should be enhanced.

The Importance of Mental Health Training

In recent years, a number of the larger city police academies have incorporated mental health services for recruits and crisis intervention training. It has been a problem of long-standing significance that some officers fail to seek out necessary resources to cope with stress, dealing instead with emotional turmoil in a state of solitude. Mark Malmin (2012), who served as a peace officer in California for 28 years with experience as a detective, hostage negotiator, and field trainer argues that "officers need to treat themselves with greater humanity and stop perpetuating" a tough guy subculture (p. 19). Oftentimes, the training process itself includes "in your face" experiences that provoke stress. This can result in physical and mental responses that can be personally damaging and also impact performance. Police training should recognize the toll that unnecessary stress can play on recruits and find better ways to address their training goals. New recruits should not be expected to handle more imposed stress than they might encounter on patrol (Malmin, 2012).

As training continues to evolve in terms of education and training, the mental health of future officers should be at the forefront of the evolution of police training. In 2012, Hulse and McDermott explored the need for police officers to have skills to be counselors on many calls, though they rarely receive training on such topics. They called for those in counseling professions to reach out and volunteer with police departments to help with such training. The recognition that police are often called to be social workers, but without the appropriate training, continues to grow. With this realization comes the acknowledgement that police officers are often carrying stress beyond the violent and gruesome aspects of the job. These job hazards have long been known and discussed. As police are called upon to perform social services rather than law enforcement, new training methods need development.

The Law Enforcement Mental Health and Wellness Act of 2017 spurred research and development for programs within police agencies that specifically address the well-being of officers. Arlington County Police Department in Virginia is an example of an agency that promotes the mental health of its officers. With the assistance of the Cummings Foundation for Behavioral Health (2022) police program, the physical and mental health of Arlington County officers is being addressed throughout their careers and into retirement.

Other police departments are also concerned about and facilitate the long-term mental health and wellness of their officers. A report for the Department of Justice (Copple et al., 2019) on 11 case studies on the topic of mental health and wellness of LEOs found that eight of the studied departments had included resiliency and self-care topics in training academies. The departments in this study included Dallas; Indianapolis; Las Vegas, the Los Angeles County Sheriff's Office, Milwaukee, Nashville, San Antonio, and Tucson. Large police departments, especially, continue to recognize the importance of and need for mental health support of officers for personal well-being and in order to keep departments adequately staffed to serve their communities. A recent PERF report cites and commends the San Diego and New York City Police Departments for also including wellness training within their academies. The PERF report notes, "A culture of wellness should be established within the academy beginning on the first day" (PERF, 2022, p. 38). Hopefully, as policing evolves and research expands on the importance of mental and physical well-being of first responders, other police academies will follow suit.

The Big Picture of Academies and Calls for Reform

With police officers under more scrutiny than ever, police training continues to remain under a microscope. Many organizations (and citizens) have devised various ways to "rate" police departments across the nation, often related to use of force. The Institute for Criminal Justice Reform's mission is to make the lives of citizens and police officers safer through training reform. This organization discovered that 37 states allowed police officers without academy training to perform police work and has called for increased field and in-service training both before and after becoming a sworn officer. It has also cited the disproportionate number of civilians killed each year, as compared to officers killed in the line of duty (Institute for Criminal Justice Reform, 2022).

Police Scorecard is an organization that operates a website exploring police shootings and use of force. Looking at use of force, number of arrests, closed cases, and accountability (based on their definitions) the number one "best" police department was Woodbury, MN–but the department's score was only 67% (Police Scorecard, 2022). The public, and pundits, continue to call for changes to policing and police training. The publicity after the tragic death of George Floyd and the calls to "defund the police" by enraged citizen groups have directly contributed to the widespread institution of reforms concerned with greater police accountability.

The criminal justice system is foundational to our society, with local police serving as the primary means for enforcing laws in the United States. Relevant, meaningful reforms should be welcomed to improve public safety. In 2018, over 80% of police academy recruits had training on intervening when there is excessive use of force by other police officers (Buehler, 2021), which indicates police departments and academies are aware of the need for change. While most positive interactions and activities of police officers are often not reported or otherwise made known to the public, negative encounters will continue to receive the public's attention. Citizens' trust in police work needs to be restored. Police academies can be the starting point for positive change in the profession as a while. While police academies differ in size, philosophy, length, etc., the socialization of police officers remains an important function of the academy experience. The process of socialization is a key factor for developing a "guardian" or a "warrior" style of policing. Clearly, if appropriate citizen partnerships can be developed the "guardian" model should have a better chance to succeed. Chapter 12 offers a localized and decentralized police training model in order to further enhance the likelihood of achieving this goal.

At the very least, police training schools must step-up to the temper of our times. "Gun sales in the U.S. hit historic highs as the coronavirus pandemic took hold, the economy stalled and people took to the streets to protest police brutality and racial injustice" (Dale, 2023). At the start of 2021, a mob attacked the US Capitol, leading to the deaths of a rioter who was shot and three others who died during the rampage. Later, four police officers who responded to the scene or were assigned there committed suicide. A fifth officer perished the day after the riot from natural causes. He had two strokes, according to the medical examiner (McCarthy, 2022). According to the Rev. Jonathan Lee Walton, the president of Princeton Theological Seminary, "The pandemic has amplified and accelerated so many dangerous trends. We are experiencing a social recession that's literally bankrupting our souls. . . . We are normalizing diseases of despair like loneliness, addiction, and gun violence" (qtd. in Dale, 2023).

Police academies have great potential for making the "guardian" approach of policing the dominant style for the delivery of police services in America. All police academies at the local and state levels function as gatekeepers and pathways for the newest members of the police profession. Accordingly, issues such as gender inequalities, ethical concerns, and bias among local and state police agencies should be addressed at the earliest stages of police training.

In addition, it should be altogether feasible for community participation opportunities to be created as an integral part of police academy programs. This is essential for achieving the guardian model of police work. As affirmed by Rahr and Rice (2015) "guardian education is humanistic. It takes shape through criminal justice education that is not only vocational but also stresses ethics, theory and the nature of virtue" (p. 1). Moreover, despite decades "of aspiring to effective community policing, American law enforcement seems to have drifted off the course of building close community ties toward creating a safe distance from community members, in some cases substituting equipment and technology as the preferred means of gathering information about crime and addressing threats to public safety" (Rahr & Rice, 2015, p. 2). In order to counter this trend, it will be necessary for an informed electorate to take steps to change its current direction in order to better serve the interests of the public.

Is More Training Really the Answer to Curtail Police Violence?

It is not the amount of training or the location of the training, but rather the overall mindset of a police force and its individual officers that has to change for less violent police responses that are so widely publicized in the media.

> The role of police in maintaining public safety has broadened over the years, well beyond law enforcement, to include responding to incidents involving drug addiction, mental health crises and domestic violence. But as that role has changed, education and training have not kept pace. Too few future police officers are prepared to respond to such new challenges thoughtfully, safely and effectively.
>
> *(Byrne & Bezbatchenko, 2021)*

Surely, more insightfulness and input by members of the community may help. A short review of the similarities and differences among police academies may lead to a better understanding of how contemporary basic police training schools function. In turn, new directions and guidance might be offered to improve upon the existing modes of police training.

Big city, regional, hybrid, and state police academies have a number of differences. Big cities are more likely to host their own academies within their agencies, with a focus on department-specific and local policies. Smaller cities and towns tend to send their recruits to regional, decentralized academies, where they will be in classes with recruits from various departments and maybe even share space with college students or professionals training to work in specific settings (e.g., schools, hospitals, airports, parks, forests). States have their own academies to become state police officers or troopers where they concentrate on state-level policies and prepare for work across a state's more rural areas. Educational or prior-service requirements may vary greatly across academies. Based on the type and location of the academy, trainees will spend their time doing a variety of activities to learn policy; improve physical fitness; increase technical skills; and create an *esprit de corps*. Statewide or large regional academies are more likely to provide dormitories, while city and countywide academies are more likely to send their trainees home at the end of each day.

Despite such variations, many similarities allow for some generalizations to be made across these different types of academies. Entry requirements tend to be similar, often (but not universally) requiring recruits to be at 21 years old; have residency/citizenship; pass background checks; meet literacy standards; and satisfy psychological, medical, and fitness standards. The goals across these different types of academies also parallel each other. Academies educate and train individuals to serve the public and uphold the law. Trainees in and outside of the classroom learn the basics of police work. The US Supreme Court held in the case of *Canton v. Harris*, 489 U.S. 378 (1989) that police departments have an affirmative duty to train officers on core tasks. Police academies, however, are limited in what they can teach and prepare future officers for in a closed or narrow campus setting with time constraints. Therefore, after academy graduation new officers typically enter into probationary and on-the-job training periods (i.e., field training), working alongside veteran officers in their agencies before going out on their own. As the George Floyd and Tyre Nichols cases and so many others have illustrated, poor field training can lead to tragic incidents of police misconduct. Even if these tragedies do not happen on a daily basis, their negative impacts on individual lives as well as the profession of policing cannot be understated. Most departments require a minimum amount of time working the streets or as a "beat cop" before becoming eligible for transfer, promotion, or assignment to a specialty unit. There is no substitute for field experience for grasping the realities of police work. As officers proceed from one call to the next, they learn more and more about the communities they serve. Sometimes, particularly at the state level, veteran officers will return to the academy to complete additional training in a new specialty area. Police academies at local levels do not always utilize their facilities for the ongoing training of current officers, though the potential exists to reopen academies for future educational reform efforts.[11]

According to the Rev. Dr. Jonathan Lee Walton, the president of Princeton Theological Seminary, "Social media, Zoom church, remote work, and virtual reality may be 'convenient,' but they are morally anemic substitutes for human connection" (qtd. in Dale, 2023). A community-based approach to basic police training is recommended in Chapter 12 for local police training. The authors believe that placing recruits in community settings at the earliest stages of their socialization into the world of policing will enhance opportunities for creating stronger human connections and help foster the necessary community engagement that may improve public safety. Surely, "positive police contact facilitates public confidence. People tell good cops what is going on in their neighborhoods and work with them to keep it safe. They view good cops as part of their community—one of the key distinguishing characteristics between cops with a guardian mindset and cops who operate with a warrior mindset" (Rahr & Rice, 2015, p. 3).

The following chapter considers a sample of the training programs currently preparing federal officers and agents for their respective career positions. In particular, the Federal Law Enforcement Training Center (FLETC), the FBI Academy, the FBI National Academy, the US Border Patrol Academy, and the US Customs and Border Protection Field Operations Academy are featured.

Notes

1 Not all police agencies across the country are having trouble with recruiting. For example, despite a policing shortage across the United States, Chicago actually experienced an increase in applications in 2022 through a number of significant initiatives (Fry, 2022).
2 See Buehler, 2021 for an extensive summary of police academies in the United States.
3 See Chapter 4 for additional descriptions of college-based academies.
4 Accreditation is offered by the Commission on Accreditation for Law Enforcement Agencies, CAELA. (CAELA, 2022)
5 See the list of agencies with recruits assigned to Session 72 of the Zone 5 Law Enforcement Training Center at: https://www.zone5academy.org/current_session.html.
6 Hawaii has no state police, but rather three county-wide police departments and one consolidated city-county department—the Honolulu Police Department (HPD). In addition, a Sheriff Division within the Hawaii Department of Public Safety carries out law enforcement responsibilities at state facilities and is the lead agency of the State Law Enforcement Coalition, which was formed to meet the mandates of the federal *Homeland Security Act*; for details see: https://dps.hawaii.gov/about/divisions/law-enforcement-division/sheriff-division/.
7 A few state police agencies may conduct short seminars for applicants or potential applicants looking to obtain additional information about the hiring process. For example, the Delaware State Police Recruiting Unit has held "How to Succeed in the Hiring Process" three-hour seminars. These events provide useful information to navigate the process as well as one-on-one Q & A time with Trooper Recruiters and recently hired Troopers (Delaware State Police, 2022).
8 See Chapter 6 for a more detailed discussion of the issues faced by women in police academies.
9 Scholars have criticized academies for not adequately adapting training to incorporate the philosophies and practices of community policing. Though the philosophy became popularized in the 1980s, little changed in academy training in the decades that followed (Bradford & Pynes, 1999).

10 Colleges and universities tend to have different application and training requirements, as compared to the city, regional, and state-level agencies discussed in this chapter. Even greater variation in policing and, thus, training, exists in such institutions. Some colleges and universities have sworn officers as well as actual police departments while others do not. The police department explored in Yüksel and Tosun (2015) was the Rutgers University Police Department, which is a relatively large university department in an urban area. Findings drawn from this study parallel the ideas regarding training and overlapping with socialization, as discussed in this chapter. It is worth noting, however, that little research has focused on police or security departments at colleges and universities in the United States and deserves more research.

11 This chapter has only provided an overview of different types of local and state-level police academies as well as the socialization process that can be generalized across these academy structures. Due to the division of jurisdictional authorities throughout the US under a system of federalism, there are thousands of police departments across the nation, making it impossible to provide a more comprehensive discussion of the many academies and their nuances.

References

American Police Officers Alliance. (2019). *Police academy training: What you need to know*. Retrieved August 3, 2022, from https://americanpoliceofficersalliance.com/police-academy-training-what-you-need-to-know/

Bradford, D., & Pynes, J. E. (1999). Police academy training: Why hasn't it kept up with practice? *Police Quarterly*, *2*(3), 283–301. doi:10.1177/109861119900200302

Brooks, J. (2015, June 5). Ohio's decentralized police training is working just fine. *The Columbus Dispatch*. Retrieved August 14, 2022, from https://www.dispatch.com/story/opinion/editorials/2015/06/05/ohio-s-decentralized-police-training/24211230007/

Brooks, R. (2021). *Tangled up in blue: Policing the American city*. Penguin Press.

Buehler, E. D. (2021). State and local law enforcement training academies, 2019–Statistical tables. In *Bureau of Justice Statistics*. NCJ 255915. Retrieved August 11, 2022, from https://bjs.ojp.gov/sites/g/files/xyckuh236/files/media/document/slleta18st.pdf

Burchett, C. (2022, December 10). Va. police departments offering shorter academies to entice out-of-state officers. *Police 1*. Retrieved December 12, 2022, from https://www.police1.com/police-recruiting/articles/va-police-departments-offering-shorter-academies-to-entice-out-of-state-officers-JHjYW22UDkItg6DC/

Burriesci, J. J., & Melley, M. (2001). *State police educational requirements and incentives*. OLR Research Report. Retrieved August 14, 2022, from https://www.cga.ct.gov/2001/rpt/2001-r-0092.htm

Bykov, O. (2014). Police academy training: An evaluation of the strengths and weaknesses of police academies. *Themis: Research Journal of Justice Studies and Forensic Science*, *2*(9), 142–159. https://doi.org/10.31979/THEMIS.2014.0209

Byrne, D. N., & Bezbatchensko, A. W. (2021, January 26). Educating future law enforcement officers. *Inside Higher Ed*. https://www.insidehighered.com/views/2021/01/26/criminal-justice-education-needs-change-and-humanities-must-play-role-opinion

CAELA. (2022). Retrieved August 11, 2022, from https://www.calea.org/

Central Shenandoah Criminal Justice Academy. (2022). Retrieved August 11, 2022, from https://www.cscjta.org/

Chicago Police Department. (2002). *Chicago police officer recruitment*. Retrieved August 10, 2022, from https://home.chicagopolice.org/bethechange/chicago-police-officer-recruitment/

Copple, C., Copple, J., Drake, J., Joyce, N., Robinson, M., Smoot, S., Stephens, D., & Villaseñor, R. (2019). *Law enforcement mental health and wellness programs: Eleven case studies*. Department of Justice, Office of Community Oriented Policing Services.

Cummings Foundation for Behavioral Health. (2022). *Police wellness*. Retrieved November 11, 2022, from https://cummingscfbh.org/police-wellness/

Dale, M. (2023, January 25). 'When does this stop?' For 2023, an alarmingly bloody start. *AP News*. Retrieved January 26, 2023, from https://apnews.com/article/crime-homicide-california-shootings-d93ba0560147cbbee3cff9c45fbbc523

Delaware State Police. (2022). *'How to succeed: In the hiring process' seminars*. Retrieved August 20, 2022, from https://dsp.delaware.gov/become-a-trooper/

Dolan Consulting Group. (2019, July). *Why do people become cops?* Retrieved November 12, 2022, from https://www.dolanconsultinggroup.com/news/why-do-people-become-cops/

EMPA. (2023). *Police academy; Eastern Missouri law enforcement training center*. Retrieved February 13, 2023, from https://empa.us/history.html

FBI Jobs. (2022). *Eligibility requirements*. Retrieved November 5, 2022, from https://www.fbijobs.gov/special-agents

Fresno City College. (2022). *State center regional training facility (SCRTF)*. Retrieved August 19, 2022, from https://www.fresnocitycollege.edu/academics/career-and-technical-education/police-academy/index.html

Fry, P. (2022, December 1). Chicago police leaders say applications have increased in 2022 despite national cop staffing shortage. *Chicago Tribune*. Retrieved December 14, 2022, from https://www.chicagotribune.com/news/criminal-justice/ct-chicago-police-recruitment-update-20221201-ccelca2ojrfofocl4udh52wara-story.html

Griffin, N. C. (1998). Five I's of police professionalism: A model for front-line leadership. *Crime Prevention and Community Safety: An International Journal*, *1*(2), 7–24.

Hendricks, C. (2020, June). *Documents show length of Georgia police training half the national average*. Retrieved August 11, 2022, from https://wgxa.tv/news/local/documents-show-length-of-georgia-police-training-half-the-national-average

Hickman, M. J. (2007). Academies, police. In J. R. Greene (Ed.), *The encyclopedia of police science* (3rd ed., Vol. 1). Taylor and Francis.

Hulse, D., & McDermott, P. J. (2012, September). Counselors: Support local police by sharing your skills. *Counseling Today*. Retrieved November 11, 2022, from https://ct.counseling.org/2012/09/counselors-support-local-police-by-sharing-your-skills/

Indeed Editorial Team. (2021, February). *FAQ: What do you do in the police academy?* Retrieved August 3, 2022, from https://www.indeed.com/career-advice/career-development/what-do-you-do-in-the-police-academy

Institute for Criminal Justice Reform. (2022). *The crisis we face*. Retrieved August 14, 2022, from https://www.trainingreform.org/

Johnson County Community College. (2022). *Johnson county regional police academy*. Retrieved August 11, 2022, from https://www.jccc.edu/academics/credit/police-academy/

LakeExpo.com. (2022, October 31). *Amid cop shortage, Missouri sets $1 million in scholarships for law enforcement recruits*. Retrieved November 5, 2022, from https://www.lakeexpo.com/news/lake_news/amid-cop-shortage-missouri-sets-1-million- in-scholarships-for-law-enforcement-recruits/article_bbe19dee-56f4–11ed-a390- 3f7958caaa29.html

Leasor, T. (2022, November 3). Personal communication from Thomas Leasor.

Los Angeles Police Department. (2022). *LAPD qualifications*. Retrieved August 10, 2022, from https://www.joinlapd.com/qualifications

Malmin, M. (2012). Changing police subculture. *FBI Law Enforcement Bulletin*, *81*(4), 14–19.

Mass.gov. (2022). *Recruit training at the state police academy*. Retrieved August 20, 2022, from https://www.mass.gov/info-details/recruit-training-at-the-state-police-academy.

MCCA. (2023). *Major cities chief association: About*. Retrieved January 24, 2023, from https://majorcitieschiefs.com/about/

McCarthy, A. C. (2022, March 11). No cops died 'in the Line of Duty' during the Capitol riot. *National Review*. Retrieved January 26, 2023, from https://www.nationalreview.com/2022/03/no-cops-died-in-the-line-of-duty-during-the- capitol-riot/

McCartney, S., & Parent, R. (2015). *Ethics in law enforcement*. BCcampus. Retrieved August 11, 2022, from https://ecampusontario.pressbooks.pub/ethicslawenforcement/

MHP. (2009). *Montana highway patrol: Applicant overview & study guide for the national police officer selection test*. Retrieved January 25, 2023, from https://dojmt.gov/wp-content/uploads/2011/06/Stanard-Online-Study-Guide_-revised- 2011–2.pdf

NCES. (2022a). *About us*. Retrieved August 10, 2022, from https://nces.ed.gov/about/

NCES. (2022b). *NCES locale classification and criteria*. Retrieved August 10, 2022, from https://nces.ed.gov/programs/edge/docs/locale_classifications.pdf

New York Police Department. (2022). *Hiring process*. Retrieved August 10, 2022, from https://www1.nyc.gov/site/nypd/careers/police-officers/po-hiring.page

NYSP. (2022). *Study guide: New York State Police Trooper examination*. Retrieved January 25, 2023, from https://joinstatepolice.ny.gov/system/files/documents/2022/10/study-guide- practice-test-for-the-nysp-trooper-examination-updated-for-pv-testing.pdf

O'Keefe, J. (2004). *Protecting the republic: The education and training of American police officers*. Pearson.

PERF. (2022, November). *Transforming police recruit training: 40 guiding principles*. Police Executive Research Forum. Retrieved December 14, 2022, from https://www.policeforum.org/assets/TransformingRecruitTraining.pdf

Police Scorecard. (2022). *Nationwide police scorecard*. Retrieved August 11, 2022, from https://policescorecard.org/

PoliceApp. (2019, February). *What to expect when you're applying to be a police officer*. Retrieved November 12, 2019, from https://www.policeapp.com/Blog/blogView.asp?BlogID=12

Policeofficer.org. (2022). *State trooper*. Retrieved August 14, 2022, from https://policeofficer.org/careers/state-trooper

Prokos, A., & Padavic, I. (2002). 'There oughtta be a law against bitches': Masculinity lessons in police academy training. *Gender, Work and Organization*, *9*(4), 439–459.

PSC. (2022). *Senator John J. Shumaker public safety center history*. Retrieved November 5, 2022, from https://www.hacc.edu/PublicSafetyCenter/History.cfm

Rahr, S., & Rice, S. K. (2015, April). From warriors to guardians: Recommitting American police culture to democratic ideals. In *New perspectives in policing bulletin*. US Department of Justice, National Institute of Justice. https://www.ojp.gov/pdffiles1/nij/248654.pdf

Skogan, W. G., Van Craen, M., & Hennesy, C. (2015). Training police for procedural justice. *Journal of Experimental Criminology*, *11*, 319–334. doi:10.1007/s11292-014-9223-6

Stone, C., & Travis, J. (2011, March). *Toward a new professionalism in policing. New perspectives in policing* (pp. 1–26). U.S. Department of Justice, Office of Justice Programs, National Institute of Justice, and Harvard University, John F. Kennedy School of Government, Program in Criminal Justice Policy and Management. file:///C:/Users/HP- User/Downloads/NewProfessionalism.pdf

Texas Department of Public Safety. (2022). *Become a Texas state trooper*. Retrieved August 14, 2022, from https://www.dps.texas.gov/section/training-operations-tod/become-texas-state-trooper

UN Women. (2021, August 11). *Racial bias must be addressed to create real change in police responses to gender-based violence*. Retrieved January 25, 2023, from https://www.unwomen.org/en/news/stories/2021/8/news-racial-bias-must-be-addressed- to-create-change-in-police-response-to-gender-based-violence

Van Maanen, J. (1975). Police socialization: A longitudinal examination of job attitudes in an urban police department. *Administrative Science Quarterly*, *20*(2), 207–228.

Virginia State Police. (2022). *Careers*. Retrieved August 14, 2022, from https://vatrooper.com/careers

Walker, S. (1976). Police professionalism: Another look at the issues. *The Journal of Sociology & Social Welfare*, *3*(6), 701–711. https://scholarworks.wmich.edu/jssw/vol3/iss6/10

World Population Review. (2022). *The 200 largest cities in the United States by population 2022*. Retrieved August 10, 2022, from https://worldpopulationreview.com/us-cities

Yüksel, Y., & Tosum, H. (2015). Understanding organizational socialization process of police officers and job satisfaction. *Electronic Journal of Social Sciences*, *14*(52), 170–182. Retrieved August 14, 2022, from https://dergipark.org.tr/en/download/article-file/70599

3

FEDERAL LAW ENFORCEMENT ACADEMIES

When there is no other news of the day affecting the United States, reporters for the mass media can simply pivot their attention to the US-Mexican border, where they are likely to find many stories of immigrants interacting with federal authorities regarding their legal status to enter into the country. Most often such individuals, many of whom are children, will first encounter members of the US Border Patrol. According to Vanessa Yurkevich (2018), a CNN reporter, who had the chance to meet trainees at the Border Patrol Academy, located in Artesia, New Mexico, some 150 miles northeast of El Paso, Texas, it is a tradition on the first day of training to become a Border Patrol agent for all new recruits to be "given a card with a photo of a fallen agent on it. . . . All new recruits get a different card—a 'silent partner,' they're called—as a way of honoring the 127 agents who have died in the line of duty while reminding them of the dangers of the job. The agents-in-training will carry the cards throughout their career." This chapter considers the historical development of federal law enforcement and highlights a small sample of the training programs currently preparing federal officers and agents for their respective career positions.

In particular, the FLETC, the FBI Academy, the FBI National Academy, the US Border Patrol Academy, and the US CBP—Field Operations Academy are prominent among the highlighted group. FLETC provides law enforcement training for more than 90 federal agencies, several state, local, and tribal agencies, and it assists with training at several ILEAs. The 10-week FBI National Academy program "is a professional course of study for U.S. and international law enforcement managers nominated by their agency heads because of demonstrated leadership qualities. . . . Participation is by invitation only, through a nomination process. Participants are drawn from every U.S. state and territory and from international partner nations" (FBI, 2022a).

As is the case with policing in the various states, the calculation of the exact number of federal law enforcement agencies is subject to change due to new legislation and occasional consolidation initiatives. The 2016 Census of Federal Law Enforcement Officers (CFLEO) was compiled by the Bureau of Justice Statistics (BJS), US Department of Justice. Its survey included agencies that employed full-time officers with federal arrest authority who were authorized to carry firearms while on duty. The CFLEO included supervisory and

DOI: 10.4324/9781003307396-5

non-supervisory personnel. It excluded officers in the Armed Forces, and it did not collect data on officers stationed in foreign countries. Due to restrictions on classified information, the CFLEO did not include the Central Intelligence Agency or the Transportation Security Administration's Federal Air Marshal Service. BJS determined that 86 agencies fell within their eligibility and were able to include data for a total of 83 agencies in their survey report. There were 132,110 full-time federal LEOs in 2016, representing an 8.4% increase in personnel since 2008 (Brooks et al., 2019, pp. 3 & 10).

Partial federal agency lists of varying significance can be found at the websites of the Metropolitan Police Department (MPD) of the District of Columbia and the International Association of Chiefs of Police (IACP). The *District of Columbia's Police Coordination Act of 1997* covers 32 separate federal law enforcement agencies, such as United States Capitol Police (USCP), United States Marshals Service, Library of Congress Police, Bureau of Engraving and Printing Police Force, Supreme Court Police, etc. (see https://mpdc.dc.gov/page/covered-federal-law-enforcement-agencies). The *Act* directed certain federal law enforcement agencies to enter into cooperative agreements with the MPD to assist the department in crime prevention and law enforcement activities in the District of Columbia.[1] According to the law enforcement career information website administered by the IACP entitled "Discover Policing" (a project that was supported by a grant from the US Department of Justice, Office of Community Oriented Policing Services) and last updated based on BJS 2008 statistics, there were

> 65 federal law enforcement agencies and 27 offices of inspector general that employed full time personnel authorized to make arrests and carry firearms. . . . Federal officers' duties include police response and patrol, criminal investigation and enforcement, inspections, security and protection, court operations, and corrections.
>
> *(IACP, 2018)*

In 2016, a government survey determined there were 13 federal law enforcement agencies with over 1,000 full-time officers, not including the Metropolitan Police Department in Washington, DC. The top eight agencies were: Customs and Border Protection (CBP) with 43,724 officers; the Federal Bureau of Prisons with 19,093 officers; the Federal Bureau of Investigation (FBI) with 13,799 officers; Immigration and Customs Enforcement (ICE) with 12,400; Secret Service with 4,729 officers; the Drug Enforcement Administration (DEA) with 4,181; the Department of Veterans Affairs Police Department with 3,839 officers; and the US Marshals Service with 3,788 officers (Brooks et al., 2019, p. 7).[2] Only a limited selection of several federal law enforcement agencies was made for inclusion in this chapter due to space limitations. Thus, only information highlighting a few of the largest agencies as well as a few others is included in this chapter. One jurisdiction, the Metropolitan Police Department (MPD), was selected in view of the fact that a recent *Washington Post* poll, found that 30% of Washingtonians felt unsafe from crime in 2022, the highest in more than two decades of *Post* polls. The finding comes as the city experienced continued gun violence and a surge in carjackings. Most residents said more police would reduce crime, but the share of those who rate police positively had dropped (Hermann et al., 2022). The information presented about the selected agencies focuses on their various tasks and training activities. The MPD was not included in the federal agency 2016 Bureau of Justice Statistics report, despite the fact of the District of Columbia's strategic importance as the nation's capital and its coordination agreements with many federal agencies. The federal agency 2016 BJS report did, however, include a total of 1,871 full-time federal LEOs serving in US Territories and Commonwealths (Brooks et al., 2019, p. 4, note b). Significantly, another BJS report covering local and 49 state police agencies in United States did list the MPD as the sixth largest local police department with 3,712 full-time officers in 2016 (Hyland & Davis, 2019, p. 14).

This chapter also addresses the important role of accreditation for the enhancement of federal law enforcement academies and training programs. "The accreditation of a federal law enforcement academy or training program provides assurance to the citizens they serve that the agency has voluntarily submitted to a process of self-regulation and successfully achieved compliance with a set of standards that has been collectively established by their peers within their professional community" (FLETC, 2022a). "Accreditation is a process that has been used within the United States for more than 200 years as a proven method for assisting hospitals, schools, and other institutions in the evaluation and improvement of their overall performance and effectiveness" (FLETA, 2005). It became a common practice for state and local law enforcement agencies after the establishment of the Commission on Accreditation for Law Enforcement Agencies, Inc. (CALEA) in 1979. Several tragic instances involving the ability of certain federal law enforcement agencies to carry out their respective missions contributed to the creation in 2002 of a separate entity for federal law enforcement agency training accreditation.

The Development of Federal Law Enforcement

Law enforcement arrangements vary across the world. In the United Kingdom and the United States, police agencies are authorized and defined by written statutes. "The development of policing in the United States closely followed the development of policing in England. In the early colonies policing took two forms. It was both informal and communal, which is referred to as the 'Watch,' or private-for-profit policing. . . . The watch system was composed of community volunteers whose primary duty was to warn of impending danger" (Potter, 2013). Later, after the War of 1812 with England, there was an expansion of commerce by internal water routes. These "natural travel routes were joined by canals and served to increase trade between cities on the coast and the interior. The goods so moved needed protection" (Lipson, 1975, pp. 20–21). In the absence of any organized police system, the owners of the barges, canal docks, and wharfs employed watchmen. In the South, "the southern colonies and their successor states, with their plantation systems, had special security problems connected with the capital investment in slavery" (Lipson, 1975, p. 19). In these areas, overseers were entrusted to watch over slaves on individual plantations and in order to guard against runaway slaves, contiguous plantation owners established slave patrols. "These patrols, and their leaders, were later given official or quasi-official status by deputization" (Lipson, 1975, p. 19). In the West, during America's westward movement, the United States also borrowed from the British tradition of having a *posse comitatus*, "a group of people who are mobilized by the sheriff to suppress lawlessness in the county. In any classic Western film, when a lawman gathers a 'posse' to pursue the outlaws, they are forming a posse comitatus" (Nunn, 2021).

As previous chapters have shown, the United States has developed a rather intricate system of policing and law enforcement agencies. By the end of the 19th century, the rise in crime accompanied by population growth in the cities due to the advent of industrialization and waves of immigrants inevitably led most states and local jurisdictions to create specific requirements and regulations for the establishment of publicly funded police forces. This arrangement has resulted in much duplication of services and the creation of a fragmented system of law enforcement, resulting in the establishment of thousands of separate agencies, some more specialized than others. Highway patrol and corrections officers fall in the category of law enforcement but are engaged in specialized functions. In addition, a variety of voluntary organizations and units, such as auxiliary or reserve police, have also been tasked with such specific roles as traffic and crowd control at special events.

Federal law enforcement agencies are also authorized and defined by written statutes, but they traditionally have emanated from one specific source—the US Congress. For example, the US Marshals Services was formed by the Judiciary Act of September 24, 1789. A great deal of the many federal law enforcement agencies also has specialized functions, especially in the field of investigations. One of the earliest federal government investigative agencies was the formation of the Office of Instructions and Mail Depredations to be the investigative and inspection branch of the US Post Office Department in 1830 (USPIS, 2022). Today, the United States Postal Service (USPS) has two law enforcement agencies: United States Postal Inspection Service and USPS Office of Inspector General (USPS, 2018).[3]

Federal law enforcement is largely a function of the Executive Branch of government, which includes US military forces. Dating back to the Revolutionary War, "military police have come to be recognized as an important element of the Army in both peace and war. The Military Police Corps traces its beginnings to the formation of a provost unit, the *Marechaussee* Corps, in the Continental Army. Authorized by Congress on 27 May 1778 with a name borrowed from the French term for provost troops, the special unit was assigned by General George Washington to perform those necessary police functions required in camp and in the field" (Wright Jr., 1992). Throughout the 19th century and beginning in its early decades, Army personnel "serving essentially as military police . . . played a vital role throughout the settlement of the trans-Appalachian West. Because of the proximity of Army outposts and the general scarcity of civil law enforcement authority, settlers looked to the military as the primary source of law and order" (Wright Jr., 1992). The Military Police Corps achieved permanent status in the U.S. Army in September 1941 (Wright Jr., 1992). The French military police known as the *marechaussee* were established by the middle of the 14th century and served as the model for the forces known as the *gendarmerie* by the middle of the 18th century. This was a national police force in all respects, "carefully organized down to a block or small sectional level. . . . Many of the principalities of Europe set up police systems which followed the pattern of the French" (Lipson, 1975 pp. 14–15).

On the other hand, the United States has never seriously contemplated the establishment of a national police force and by the *Posse Comitatus Act of 1878* specifically restricted the use of most military forces for the carrying out of everyday domestic law enforcement.[4] According to Lipson (1975), several of America's founding fathers and others had first-hand experiences with the French national police system during the periods in which they lived in France. "Like their English counterparts, they never indicated any desire to install a similar system. The drive for local autonomy, implicit in the separate colonies and carried over into their successor states, also mitigated any consideration of a national police" (p. 19). In addition, America's colonists also had experienced the nature of military rule when British military troops policed the colonies. This sentiment found "expression in the Constitution's division of power over the military between Congress and the president, and in the guarantees of the Third, Fourth, Fifth, and Sixth Amendments, which were in part reactions to abuses committed by the British army against American colonists" (Nunn, 2021). For these reasons, there has been a continuing unwillingness to permit any military interference in the affairs of civilian government. Nunn (2021) has characterized this reluctance as an American core value.

The US Marshals Service has claimed that since it was formed by the *Judiciary Act of 1789* and that the *Act* specifically determined that law enforcement was to be the US Marshals' primary function, it is the oldest or first federal law enforcement agency. Their website declares: "Other federal agencies have mistakenly believed they were the first. However, their claims fall short when researched in proper context. Although they had equally important functions, they were not conceived on the model of law enforcement at the same time" (US Marshals, 2022a). Whether or not this is an historic fact, the current missions of the Marshals Service as well as its federal agency "cousins" are more important matters.

Federal law enforcement also has deep historic roots with the establishment of the US Coast Guard (USCG), one of the oldest organizations of the federal government. The organization was established in 1790 along with construction of ten vessels, referred to as "cutters." The vessels and their crews were tasked with the enforcement of federal tariff and trade laws and to prevent smuggling; hence, its original name—the US Revenue Marine. When the Revenue Cutter Service merged with the US Life-Saving Service, it was officially renamed the Coast Guard, making it the only maritime service dedicated to saving life at sea and enforcing the nation's maritime laws. In 2003, along with more than 20 other agencies, the Coast Guard became a subdivision of the US Department of Homeland Security. "It is both a federal law enforcement agency and a military force. . . . In times of war, or at the direction of the President, the Coast Guard serves under the Department of the Navy, defending the nation against terrorism and foreign threats" (USCG, 2021). The type and extent of training members of the Coast Guard receive depends on a recruit's specialty as either active-duty enlisted, reserve enlisted, active-duty officer, or reserve officer (see below for details).

In addition, as we have seen already federal law enforcement's ancestry also included Postal Service agents and federal marshals who played important roles in the western territories. Their roles expanded during and after the period of westward expansion as the nation grew not only in size, but in commerce and population. By the beginning of the 20th century, the need for additional agencies and federal law enforcement personnel was spurred on by a series of new laws. The passage of the *Harrison Act of 1914* involved an attempt to regulate the use of narcotic drugs. Because taxes were supposed to be paid on legal narcotics, the enforcement of the *Harrison Act* was undertaken by the Bureau of Internal Revenue, within the Treasury Department. Thereafter, federal law enforcement accelerated as a direct result of the prohibition of alcohol, which began in 1920 with the passage of the 18th Amendment and its enforcement lasted until repeal by the 21st Amendment in 1933. The Department of Justice enforced prohibition, along with the Customs Service, Coast Guard, and the Bureau of Internal Revenue. The Bureau of Internal Revenue was involved because while alcoholic beverages were illegal, nonbeverage alcohol was to be taxed (Holcombe, 1996). In addition, the Department of Justice began its role in the enforcement of antitrust laws with the passage of the *Sherman Act of 1890*. Despite a general belief that the federal government was friendly to business during the Harding,

Coolidge, and Hoover administrations, by the 1920s antitrust case activity had become a routine function of the department (McCraw, 1984).

The various federal laws regarding narcotics, alcohol prohibition, anti-trust, and World Wars I and II helped spur the growth of federal law enforcement. The zeal of J. Edgar Hoover as the FBI's longest serving director also greatly contributed to this enlargement. From 1909 until 1935, the FBI was known as the Bureau of Investigation (BOI), a division of the Justice Department. One of the first major federal statutes requiring the use of this agency was the *White Slave Traffic Act of 1910*, also known as the *Mann Act*. The new law significantly increased the BOI's jurisdiction over interstate crime. Additional responsibilities for the BOI came with the advent of World War I in Europe. On April 6, 1917, Congress declared war on Germany and President Woodrow Wilson authorized the BOI to detain enemy aliens. On June 15, 1917, Congress passed the *Espionage Act of 1917*. The *Act* forbade espionage, interference with the draft, or attempts to discourage loyalty. It greatly increased the BOI's ability to deal with espionage and subversion during the war, but a lack of personnel hampered its efforts in enforcing the law. On May 16, 1918, the US Congress passed the *Sedition Act*, a piece of legislation designed to protect America's participation in World War I. Along with the *Espionage Act* of the previous year, the *Sedition Act* was orchestrated largely by A. Mitchell Palmer, the US attorney general under President Woodrow Wilson. The *Espionage Act* passed shortly after the US entrance into the war made it a crime for any person to convey information intended to interfere with the US armed forces' prosecution of the war effort or to promote the success of the country's enemies. On October 28, 1919, Congress passed the *National Motor Vehicle Theft Act*, also known as the *Dyer Act*. The *Dyer Act* authorized the BOI to investigate auto thefts that crossed state lines. Prior to its passage, jurisdictional boundaries between states hampered the ability of law enforcement officials to thwart interstate auto theft rings. Next came the "crime of the century." In response to the Lindbergh baby kidnapping case and other high-profile kidnappings, Congress passed the *Federal Kidnapping Act* in 1932. The act gave the BOI authority to investigate kidnappings that were perpetrated across state borders. Meanwhile, the period of prohibition had greatly contributed to a rise in organized crime, and the role of FBI was again expanded throughout the 1930s (FBI, 2022a).

Since the FBI's existence, a variety of other federal law enforcement and safety-related agencies have been created, such as the independent Civil Aeronautics Authority (CAA) in 1938, with its original three-member Air Safety Board for conducting accident investigations and recommending ways of preventing accidents. This board became the Civil Aeronautics Board (CAB) in 1940 and its responsibilities included safety rulemaking, accident investigation, and economic regulation of the airlines. By virtue of new legislation, in 1958, the functions of the CAA were transferred to a new independent Federal Aviation Agency responsible for civil aviation safety. In 1966, Congress authorized the creation of a cabinet department that would combine major federal transportation responsibilities. This new Department of Transportation (DOT) began full operations the following year and the Federal Aviation Agency was moved within DOT and received a new name, the Federal Aviation Administration (FAA). At the same time, CAB's accident investigation function was transferred to the new National Transportation Safety Board (NTSB). The NTSB maintains a database of major aviation, highway, marine, pipeline, and railroad investigations, both ongoing and completed, on its website: https://www.ntsb.gov/investigations/Pages/AllInvestigations.aspx. "Since its inception, the NTSB has investigated more than 149,000 aviation accidents and thousands of surface transportation accidents. On call 24 hours a day, 365 days a year, NTSB investigators travel throughout the country and to every corner of the world to investigate significant accidents and develop factual records and safety recommendations with one aim—to ensure that such accidents never happen again" (NTSB, 2022).[5] While the FAA does not conduct criminal investigations, it "does investigate airmen and employee or contractor employee involvement in criminal activity as it applies to employment or certification" (FAA, 2022a). All evidence of criminal acts discovered by the FAA are referred to the FBI, Department of Transportation, or the Office of Inspector General (FAA, 2022a). In the United States, the FBI undertakes the greatest share of federal criminal investigative work.

Congress enacted a series of anti-crime legislation over the months of May and June 1934 in response to crimes like the June 1933 "Kansas City Massacre," where gangsters killed Agent Raymond Caffrey, Jr., and other law enforcement officials. These new laws gave special agents the power of arrest and the authority to carry firearms. Previously, special agents could only make a "citizen's arrest," otherwise the agent had to call on a US marshal or local police officer to take custody of a suspect. In 1939, two years before the United States entered World War II, President Roosevelt assigned responsibility for investigating espionage, sabotage, and other subversive activities jointly to the FBI, the Military Intelligence Service of the War Department (MID), and the Office of Naval Intelligence (ONI). In November 1963, Lee Harvey Oswald assassinated President John F. Kennedy in Dallas, Texas. President Lyndon B. Johnson ordered the FBI to investigate the murder. At that time the FBI had no statutory authority to investigate presidential assassinations. Jurisdictional conflict between federal, state, and local authorities created confusion in the investigation of the case. The passage of the *Organized Crime Control Act of 1970* included a section known as the "Racketeer Influenced and Corrupt Organization Act" or RICO. RICO has become a very effective tool in convicting members of organized criminal enterprises. Cases arising under civil rights statutes in the 1960s and succeeding decades have also contributed to role of federal law enforcement (FBI, 2022a).

September 11, 2001, was the deadliest day in law enforcement history when 72 officers were killed while responding to the terrorist attacks on America. Following the massive terrorist attacks against New York and Washington, the FBI dedicated 7,000 of its 11,000 special agents and thousands of FBI support personnel to the PENTTBOM investigation. "PENTTBOM" is short for Pentagon, Twin Towers Bombing. The following month, all FBI field offices were ordered to create joint terrorism task forces/regional terrorism task forces to coordinate counterterrorism efforts across the United States (FBI, 2022a). In 2002, the US Department of Homeland Security was formed to lead the unified national effort to secure America, combining 22 different federal departments and agencies into a unified, integrated Cabinet agency.

FBI National Academy

In 1917, J. (John) Edgar Hoover (1895–1972) graduated with two law degrees from George Washington University. In 1924, after successive promotions in the Department of Justice, Attorney General Harlan Fiske Stone appointed the 29-year-old Hoover acting director of the Bureau of Investigation and by the end of the year he became director. Two years earlier, Hoover had also become an officer in the US Army Reserve, specializing in military intelligence. For a period of 55 years (1965–2020), the J. Edgar Hoover Foundation provided scholarships to needy college and university students without regard to race, creed, or religion who were pursuing degrees in law, enforcement studies, or forensic sciences. The National Law Enforcement Museum in Washington, DC, opened in 2018. The J. Edgar Hoover Foundation funded the J. Edgar Hoover Research Center within the Museum. The National Law Enforcement Officers Memorial Fund (NLEOMF), begun in 1984, built the National Law Enforcement Museum, adjacent to the Memorial in Washington, DC. The names of all the known line-of-duty deaths of LEOs are engraved on the walls of the National Law Enforcement Officers Memorial. At the end of 2021, there were 22,611 names of fallen officers so inscribed (NLEOMF, 2022). The Museum tells the story of American law enforcement through exhibits, collections, research, and education. Admission to the museum is free for children 12 and under not in a group of ten or more, and on Saturdays, admission is free for active or retired law enforcement officers (see https://nleomf.org/museum/visiting-information/).

In 1930, a study by the National Commission on Law Observance and Enforcement (the Wickersham Commission) recommended the standardization and professionalization of law enforcement departments across the United States through centralized training (FBI, 2022a). By the mid-1930s, the Federal Bureau of Investigation had instituted a rigorous training program for its own special agents and undertook an unprecedented step in police education and training by offering many aspects of its in-house training to selected law enforcement leaders throughout the United States. In order to increase the effectiveness of local law enforcement, in 1935, Hoover established the FBI National Academy (initially known as the "FBI Police Training School") to train selected personnel from state and local law enforcement agencies throughout the country. It adopted for this training program the same delivery model that has now become routine throughout the field of law enforcement training—the convening of groups of students to receive training as a cohort. The success of this model was due in large part to the benefits it provided, including: helping to overcome limitations on agency time, access to an appropriate venue, and the availability of capable instructors. Moreover, the experience has provided students with the benefits of certain "intangible processes related to socialization, acculturation, and the development of a professional esprit de corps and identity. . . . In addition, basic academies serve several functions. While providing personnel with threshold competencies and skills is important, academies also allow agencies to get a better sense of the temperament and aptitude of new personnel. In this way, the academy can compensate for or partially correct for deficiencies that personnel selection processes do not adequately filter out" (Schafer & Jarvis, 2017, p. 58). Of course, the FBI's new academy also helped cement ties between local police leaders and the FBI. In subsequent years, students from other countries were included in each session.

"The idea of a national training academy was first raised in late 1934 as part of U.S. Attorney General Homer Cummings' 'war on crime.' FBI Director J. Edgar Hoover then fleshed out an idea for professional education for law enforcement officers at the annual meeting of the International Association of Chiefs of Police (IACP) held in early July 1935. An IACP committee on police training had urged Director Hoover, who spoke at the conference on the value of professional police training, to consider offering such training under FBI auspices. Hoover returned to Washington, and later that month, the first class of 23 officers from across the country began training with the FBI. They took a wide array of classes detailing the latest research and experience on police procedure, forensic science applications, the law, and other important issues. This first class graduated from this 12-week training course on October 19, 1935. Within two years, these classes were accepting foreign law enforcement officers as well" (FBI, 2015). "Courses at that time included scientific aids in crime detection, preparation of reports, criminal investigation techniques, and administration and organization. With the advent of World War II, courses were added in espionage and sabotage" (FBI, 2022a).

Currently, the FBI National Academy's 10-week program is held on the FBI campus in Quantico, Virginia, and is offered four times each year. The students are law enforcement managers nominated by their agency heads because of demonstrated leadership qualities. Approximately 265 officers are selected and college credits may be awarded. The candidates are drawn from state, local, county, tribal, military, federal, and ILEAs. Each session of the National Academy includes up to 35 international students, approximately 10% of each class. Thousands of international police executives from over 160 countries have graduated from the National Academy. Topics in the Academy's curriculum cover: intelligence theory, terrorism and terrorist mindsets, management science, law, behavioral science, law enforcement communication, forensic science, and a fitness challenge (FBI, 2022a). "Officers share ideas, techniques, and experiences with each other and create lifelong partnerships that transcend state and national borders" (FBI, 2022a).

The process of being accepted into a session of the FBI National Academy requires a nomination form to be signed by a commissioner, superintendent, or police chief; a sheriff or head of county policy agency; the chief, superintendent, or executive officer of a state police or highway patrol organization. In the United States, only officers with a minimum rank of lieutenant or the equivalent and who are approved by their respective FBI field office are eligible. Other basic qualifications include being: a regular, full-time officer of a duly constituted law enforcement agency of a municipality, county, or state, having at least five years of substantial and continuous experience; at least 25 years old; in excellent physical condition, capable of strenuous exertion and regular participation in the use of firearms, physical training, and defensive tactics, which will be confirmed by a thorough physical examination (submitted when requested by the FBI) by a medical doctor of the nominee's choosing and at the nominee's expense; having excellent character and a reputation for professional integrity; showing an interest in law enforcement as a public service, a seriousness of purpose, qualities of leadership and enjoying the confidence and respect of fellow officers; having earned 60 college credit hours or equivalent education experience; and agreeing to remain in law enforcement for a minimum of three years after graduating from the FBI National Academy. Prospective students or nominating officials are advised to contact their local FBI field office's training coordinator for assistance and additional information. International students are nominated by their host countries working through the FBI's offices around the globe. These offices—called legal attachés or legats—are located in US embassies (FBI, 2022a). A list of these offices and related information can be found at: https://www.fbi.gov/contact-us/legal-attache-offices. Thus, since 1935 "the FBI's National Academy program has offered training to thousands of law enforcement professionals conducted by experts in law enforcement, legal matters, and scientific applications, and it has graduates spread across the globe" (FBI, 2015).

Graduates of the National Academy have the opportunity to join the nonprofit FBI National Academy Associates, Inc. (FBINAA). According to the association's website, its 16,000 members represent all 50 states, 194 countries, and over 8,200 law enforcement agencies. FBINAA members serve in many senior law enforcement positions throughout the United States and world. There are 44 chapters in the United States and 4 outside the United States (FBINAA, 2022a). The FBINAA organization conducts an annual Youth Leadership Program, an intense eight-day program of classroom study, physical challenges, guest lectures, and leadership experiences. The program is held at the end of the school year in late June for 62 students and focuses on leadership, ethics, and personal development. It is offered through the cooperation of the FBI, and individual participants are selected and sponsored by the various state chapters of the FBINAA, who cover transportation and student sponsorship fees. The highly competitive program is run by a cadre of law enforcement training instructors. Students must have demonstrated high academic standards and good citizenship to be nominated for this program (FBINAA, 2022b).

Various universities in the United States offer tuition discounts for FBINAA members and/or graduation from the FBI National Academy. A number of online master's degree programs provide up to 12 hours of transfer credit.[6] For example, at Tiffin University a maximum of one-third of the required credit hours for a degree can be transfer credits. Transferred credits must not have been used to meet the requirements of any other completed graduate degree (Tiffin, 2022). Other universities also prominently feature the availability of transfer credits for attendance at the National Academy at their websites. Samplings of these are: the University of San Diego, Bethel University, Liberty University, Saint Leo University, and the University of Virginia.

Since June 1972 all FBI National Academy instruction has been conducted at the FBI Academy campus located some 40 miles south of Washington, DC. It is situated on the United States Marine Corps Base at Quantico, Virginia, amid rolling woodlands. The training complex consists of both living and instructional facilities. The following section highlights information about the FBI Academy, where the Bureau trains its own employees.

The FBI Academy

According to Weiser (2020), "by 1907, the Department of Justice most frequently called upon Secret Service 'operatives' to conduct investigations. These men were well-trained, dedicated—and expensive. Moreover, they reported not to the Attorney General, but to the Chief of the Secret Service. This situation frustrated Bonaparte [the US Attorney General], who wanted complete control of investigations under his jurisdiction. Congress provided the impetus for Bonaparte to acquire his own force. On May 27, 1908, it enacted a law preventing the Department of Justice from engaging Secret Service operatives. The following month, Attorney General Bonaparte appointed a force of Special Agents within the Department of Justice. Accordingly, ten former Secret Service employees and a number of Department of Justice investigators became Special Agents of the Department of Justice. On July 26, 1908, Bonaparte ordered them to report to Chief Examiner Stanley W. Finch. This action is celebrated as the beginning of the FBI."

Since the appointment of the first group of special agents, the FBI has continually evolved. By 1924, the Bureau of Investigation had approximately 650 employees, including 441 special agents who worked in field offices in nine cities (Weiser, 2020). Today, the FBI employs approximately 35,000 people, including special agents and support professionals such as intelligence analysts, language specialists, scientists, and information technology specialists. FBI special agents are responsible for conducting sensitive national security investigations and enforcing more than 300 federal statutes. They work on cases involving terrorism, counterintelligence, cybercrime, organized crime, white-collar crime, public corruption, civil rights violations, financial crime, bribery, bank robbery, extortion, kidnapping, air piracy, interstate criminal activity, fugitive and drug-trafficking matters and other violations of federal statutes (FBI, 2022d). A useful online site for exploring FBI career opportunities is: https://www.fbijobs.gov/.

Newly hired FBI special agent recruits must attend the FBI Academy in Quantico, Virginia, having first undergone a rigorous and selective application process. The selection process may take one year to complete or longer.[7] Currently, new agent training lasts approximately 21 weeks for 800 hours of instruction. The curriculum includes "a variety of web-based courses, in four major concentrations: academics, case exercises, firearms training, and operational skills" (FBI, 2022c). In the aftermath of the attacks on America's homeland on September 9, 2001, the FBI transformed itself into an intelligence-driven organization in order "to better discover, understand, and disable a range of national security threats facing America in a global age" (FBI, 2020c, 2022f). The ability to collect, share, analyze, and act on the necessary intelligence information required the recruitment and training of a variety of analysts.

Both special agent and intelligence analyst candidates report to the FBI Academy after passing their respective selection processes. At the Academy, New Agents in Training (NATs) and New Intelligence Analysts in Training (NIATs) have the opportunity to train together in a collaborative environment throughout their time at the Academy. The NIAT curriculum lasts 12 weeks; the NAT curriculum lasts 21 weeks. In the weeks before these trainees arrive at the Academy, they are sent information detailing the requirements, protocols, and rules of the Academy. The NATs and NIATs include people from a variety of diverse backgrounds, such as servicemen and women, teachers, chemists, accountants, lawyers, artists, doctors, engineers, and more. The candidates receive instruction in a variety of areas, such as firearms, defensive tactics, defensive driving, evidence and intelligence collection and analysis, interviewing, negotiation techniques and much more (FBI, 2022e).

The first 12 weeks of training is focused on academic subject areas where NATs and NIATs study together in order to learn the specialized methods the FBI uses in its investigations. A variety of collaborative exercises take place involving threat-based assessments, collecting intelligence, conducting investigations, and planning operations (FBI, 2022e). NATs and NIATs also study a broad range of subjects that grounds them in the fundamentals of law, ethics, behavioral science, interviewing and report writing, interrogation, and forensic science. Students learn how to manage and run counterterrorism, counterintelligence, weapons of mass destruction, cyber, and criminal investigations. As part of their ethics training, students tour the US Holocaust Memorial Museum in Washington, DC, to learn what can happen when law enforcement loses its core values. Students also visit the Martin Luther King, Jr. Memorial in Washington to gain perspective on civil equality (FBI, 2022c). The Holocaust Museum tours, begun in 2000, are part of a program—called "Law Enforcement and Society: Lessons of the Holocaust"—a joint partnership between the Anti-Defamation League and the museum. In 2019, the National September 11 Memorial & Museum in New York City was added to FBI agent and analyst training. Director Christopher Wray wanted the New York Museum to be part of the Basic Field Training Course so participants could gain a greater understanding of an event that had profoundly shaped the FBI (FBI, 2019).

In April 2015, James B. Comey, who served as the director of the FBI during the years 2013–2017, explained in a *Washington Post* article why the FBI has required every new FBI special agent and intelligence analyst to go to the Holocaust Museum since 2000:

> Naturally, I want them to learn about abuse of authority on a breathtaking scale. But I want them to confront something more painful and more dangerous: I want them to see humanity and what we are capable of. . . . Good people helped murder millions. And that's the most frightening lesson of all—that our very humanity made us capable of, even susceptible to, surrendering our individual moral authority to the group, where it can be hijacked by evil. Of being so cowed by those in power. Of convincing ourselves of nearly anything. . . . that's what people do. And that should truly frighten us. That is why I send our agents and our analysts to the Holocaust Museum. I want them to stare at us and realize our capacity for rationalization and moral surrender. I want them to walk out of that great museum treasuring the constraint and oversight of divided government, the restriction of the rule of law, the binding of a free and vibrant press. I want them to understand that all of this is necessary as a check on us because of the way we are. . . . we must know it and we must nurture it now, so that it can save us later. That is the only path to the responsible exercise of power.
>
> *(Comey, 2015)*[8]

At the end of week 12, the NAT candidates attend the graduation of the NIATs. Weeks 13–20 are NAT-only training focusing on the tactical skills required of special agents in the FBI. This training builds upon the educational foundation of the first half of the Academy's curriculum and complements it with a challenging schedule of lessons in firearms, defensive tactics, defensive driving, and more. NAT graduation takes place in week 21 (FBI, 2022e). Since 1934, special agents have been authorized to carry firearms in the performance of their duties. As part of the preparation for potential deadly force encounters, all new agent trainees receive training with a variety of hand-held firearms. Instructors monitor the trainees' progress regarding firearm safety, weapon orientations, weapon handling skills, and practical shooting techniques. To demonstrate proficiency, trainees must successfully qualify with both the pistol and carbine and participate in live-fire familiarization with the shotgun. The present firearms curriculum comprises 28 sessions totaling 110 hours of instruction and includes approximately 5,000 rounds of ammunition (FBI, 2022c). The trainees also receive more than 90 hours of instruction and practical exercises focused on tactics, operations planning, undercover operations, and the development and dissemination of intelligence. At Hogan's Alley, a mock town at the academy that features hired actors playing criminals and terrorists, trainees conduct interviews, plan, and carry out an arrest, perform daytime and nighttime surveillance, and practice street survival techniques taught by their instructors. Real-life exercises include a bank robbery, a kidnapping, an assault on a federal officer, and both compliant and armed and dangerous arrest scenarios. Trainees use paint guns to test their tactical skills (FBI, 2022c).

Throughout their training, the special agent candidates have been supervised by full-time special agents and instructors. Their efforts are supplemented by the availability of a rotating pair of special agents selected from the many FBI field and residential offices. These agents serve as class counselors. At the graduation ceremony a "class spokesperson, chosen by classmates, addresses the recruits and their families on the challenges faced and obstacles overcome during the training. One new agent is selected by his or her peers and staff to receive the Director's Leadership Award, and honors are also handed out for top achievers in academics, firearms, and physical fitness" (FBI, 2022c).

The following section deals with safety in the skies. Passengers sitting in commercial aircraft have had to contend with unruly travelers in their midst, but the overall safety of the planes fall within the province of a relatively unpublicized agency—the Federal Aviation Administration (FAA). In addition, the section reviews aspects of the training of the front-line workers known as transportation security officers (TSOs), who daily operate various screening equipment and technology to identify dangerous objects in baggage, cargo, and/or on passengers in order to prevent those objects or persons from being transported onto aircraft.

The FAA and the TSA Academy

With the invention of the airplane, the world of aviation during the first quarter of 20th century saw the development of many new planes and technologies. "During World War I, the airplane proved its effectiveness as a military tool and, with the advent of early air-mail service, showed great promise for commercial applications" (FAA, 2022b). In 1926, the Aeronautics Branch in the Department of Commerce, the earliest forerunner of the FAA, was established for the purpose of overseeing air transportation, and William P. MacCracken, Jr. became the assistant secretary of commerce for aeronautics. On April 6, 1927, MacCracken as the initial director for this new branch received Pilot License No. 1, the first private pilot license issued by the federal government. However, before accepting License No. 1, MacCracken had offered this honor to Orville Wright, promising to waive the fee and examination. Wright declined because he no longer flew and did not think he needed a federal license to show that he had been the first man to fly. On May 15, 1930, in regulations effective on this date, the Department of Commerce required airlines to obtain a certificate of authority to operate if they engaged in interstate passenger service. A fully illustrated timeline of FAA and aerospace history from 1903 to 2014 is available at: https://www.faa.gov/about/history/timeline.

UNITED STATES OF AMERICA
DEPARTMENT OF COMMERCE
OFFICE OF THE DIRECTOR OF AERONAUTICS

PILOT'S IDENTIFICATION CARD

This Identification Card, issued on the 6th day of April, 1927, accompanies Pilot's License No. 1

Age 39

Weight 200 Color hair Brown

Height 6'1½" Color eyes Blue

FORM R-19 U. S. GOVERNMENT PRINTING OFFICE Pilot's Signature.

FIGURE 3.1 Pilot License No. 1 issued on April 6, 1927. Public Domain.

Source: https://www.faa.gov/about/history/timeline

Almost from its creation, the FAA found itself facing a number of unexpected challenges. In 1961, for example, the first series of aircraft hijackings in the United States occurred. In August of that year, the federal government began employing armed guards on civilian planes. These guards were border patrolmen recruited from the US Immigration and Naturalization Service. In September 1961, President Kennedy signed an amendment to the *Federal Aviation Act of 1958*, which made it a crime to hijack an aircraft, interfere with an active flight crew, or carry a dangerous weapon aboard an air carrier aircraft. To help enforce the act, a special corps of FAA safety inspectors began training for duty aboard airline flights. In March 1962, Attorney General Robert Kennedy swore in FAA's first "peace officers," as special US deputy marshals. These men worked as safety inspectors for the FAA flight standards organization and carried out their role as armed marshals on flights only when specifically requested to do so (FAA, 2022b).

On September 11, 2001, 19 radical Islamic extremists with the group al Qaeda penetrated security at three major airports, seized four US domestic airliners, and turned three of the aircraft into missiles that destroyed the World Trade Center in New York City and damaged the Pentagon in Arlington, Virginia. Passengers on the fourth plane fought the hijackers, causing the plane to crash in a field near Shanksville, Pennsylvania, killing all 44 people on board. When the plane slammed into the ground at 580 miles per hour, it was about 20 minutes flying time from Washington, DC. To prevent any further hijackings, FAA immediately put a ground stop on all traffic for the first time in US aviation history. In the overnight hours of September 11, members of FAA's Flight Standards Service developed an initial lead identifying the names of potential hijackers and provided those names to the FBI. The tragic events of this day radically changed the FAA. On November 19, 2001, the president signed the *Aviation and Transportation Security Act*, which among other provisions, established a new agency responsible for aviation security—the Transportation Security Administration (TSA), within DOT. FAA remained responsible for aviation security until February 13, 2002, when TSA took over those responsibilities. The November 2002 passage of the Homeland Security Act moved TSA into the new Department of Homeland Security on March 1, 2003 (FAA, 2022b).

TSA is responsible for ensuring that all airline passengers and their properties are screened for items that could pose a threat to airplanes and passengers at 440 airports across the United States. Since 2016, Transportation Security Officers (TSO) Basic Training—initial training for newly hired TSOs, including both TSA-employed and private screeners—has consisted of an intensive two-week course at the TSA Academy located at the FLETC. TSA has obligated about $53 million for the program from its inception through March 2018. In 2015 and 2017, the Department of Homeland Security Inspector General raised questions about the effectiveness of checkpoint screening, which prompted concerns about training. A study ensued, conducted by the US Government Accountability Office (GAO), and it recommended that TSA establish specific goals and performance measures for the TSO Basic Training program. This recommendation was subsequently acted upon by the TSA (GAO, 2018).

Prior to the establishment of the TSA Academy's Basic Training program at FLETC in Glynco, Georgia, in 2016, TSO training was conducted at individual airports, often by TSOs for whom instruction was a collateral duty. TSA implemented its Basic Training program to provide efficiencies to the delivery of new-hire training for TSOs and to enhance the professionalism and morale of newly hired screeners. These facilities "have airport checkpoint equipment and x-ray image simulators for students to practice skills, eliminating the challenge of finding available equipment and training times in a busy airport environment. According to program officials, centralized training also provides trainees with an increased focus on the TSA mission and instills a common culture among TSOs. TSA's Office of Training and Development (OTD) updates and modifies the TSO Basic Training curriculum in response to evolving security threats and evaluations of effectiveness, among other factors. For example, OTD holds regular meetings with TSA's Office of Security Operations—the office responsible for managing TSO performance—to discuss issues such as imminent threats. The offices also discuss analyses of TSO effectiveness identified through covert tests, in which role players attempt to pass threat objects—such as knives, guns, or simulated improvised explosive devices—through the screening checkpoints. The two offices identify ways to address issues identified in covert testing, which are then incorporated into TSO Basic Training. OTD also gathers input from TSO Basic Training instructors and from participants to adjust training curriculum" (GAO, 2018).

All TSOs are eventually required to complete the 80-hour intensive training program at the TSA Academy. TSA covers all travel expenses and lodging, as students must reside on-campus or in FLETC-provided housing for the entirety of the program. Improvised explosive devices, or IEDs, are the greatest threat to be prevented by TSOs. At the academy, the trainees learn firsthand what happens if they fail their mission by observing the explosive power of IED devices. They are given specialized instruction in order to identify the various IED components they may detect on the job. According to Bill Morgan, an explosives specialist and TSA Academy instructor, "An IED is limited only by the imagination of the bomber and the materials readily at hand" (qtd. in Gillet, 2016). While the TSA Academy provides an initial overview of the duties required of TSOs, the training continues throughout their TSA career (TSA, 2022a). Upon completion of the two-week academy, TSOs immediately begin new hire on-the-job training at their home airports, a process that can take up to six more months. TSA encourages its officers to pursue higher educational opportunities by reimbursing "up to $5,000 of tuition expenses on eligible coursework within a calendar year depending on available funding" (TSA, 2021). One way to get started on a college education is the TSA Associates Program. The Des Moines Area Community College (DMACC) and the TSA are working together to offer qualified TSA employees three online credit courses in DMACC's Criminal Justice program, all at no cost to TSA employees with at least six months of work experience and who satisfy other requirements. The program is available on a first come, first served basis (DMACC, 2022). The on-the-job training component provide TSOs with a minimum of 60 hours of instruction before they are allowed to make independent judgments with respect to screening persons and property for entry into airport sterile areas or clearing checked baggage (ACE, 2022).

In 2021, the TSA undertook an effort to recruit thousands of new officers for airport checkpoints due to an expected rise in air travel. They were to be added to an existing complement of about 47,000 agency officers who were serving as part of a total TSA workforce of approximately 60,000 employees charged with protecting US transportation systems and the traveling public (TSA, 2022b). The agency hosted virtual recruitment fairs and sought candidates using social media. During the height of the pandemic passenger numbers plunged, and airlines received billions of dollars in aid to keep workers on their payrolls and many TSA officers were kept home. "Those who continued to work risked exposure to a virus that has infected more than 7,700 agency employees. Sixteen TSA employees and a contractor have died of covid-19" (Duncan, 2021). According to John Hubert, an officer's union vice president in Florida, the on-the-job training could prove to be an especially lengthy process because officers don't see serving as a mentor to recruits as a desirable opportunity. "It's one thing to hire them—you still have to train them to do the job" Hubert said (qtd. in Duncan, 2021).

The US Marshals Service National Training Academy is also conducted at the FLETC in Glynco, Georgia. Glynco is located near Brunswick, Georgia, mid-way between Savannah, Georgia, and Jacksonville, Florida. New Deputies are hired as GS-0082 series Deputy US Marshals. Basic Deputy US Marshal Integrated (BDUSMI) training consists of 19 weeks of basic training instructed by the FLETC and US Marshals Service instructors. Students are strongly encouraged to be in excellent physical condition prior to attending their training program as it includes "numerous hours of strenuous physical conditioning and intensive control tactics training" (US Marshals, 2022b). The following section provides an overview and history of FLETC.

FLETC History and Courses

> Prior to 1970, the quality of training received by Federal law enforcement officers and agents varied greatly from agency to agency. Standardized training was an unexplored concept, and inadequate facilities and duplication of effort were prevalent as each agency independently trained its own personnel. Studies conducted in the late 1960's revealed an urgent need for high-quality, cost-effective training by a cadre of professional instructors using modern training facilities and standardized course content. Congress responded by authorizing funds for planning and constructing the Consolidated Federal Law Enforcement Training Center (CFLETC). In 1970, the CFLETC was established as a bureau of the Department of the Treasury (Treasury Order #217) and began training operations in temporary facilities in Washington, D.C.
>
> *(FLETC, 2022a)*

"The permanent location of the training center was originally planned for the Washington, D.C., area. However, a three-year construction delay resulted in Congress requesting that surplus Federal installations be surveyed to determine if one could serve as the permanent site. In May 1975, after an extensive review of existing facilities, the former Glynco Naval Air Station near Brunswick, Georgia, was selected. In the summer of 1975, the newly renamed Federal Law Enforcement Training Center (FLETC) relocated from Washington, D.C., and began training in September of that year at Glynco. Glynco is the headquarters site and main campus for the FLETC, which has grown over the years to include facilities in Artesia, NM, Charleston, SC, and Cheltenham, MD, and Gabarone, Botswana. On March 1, 2003, the FLETC formally transferred from the Treasury Department to the newly created Department of Homeland Security, along with some 20 other agencies. The move reflected the centrality of the FLETC's mission in support of the unified homeland security effort, which was initiated following the terrorist attacks of Sept. 11, 2001" (FLETC, 2022a). A list of more than a hundred of the current agencies, also known as Partner Organizations (POs), who send their employees for training at FLETC campuses, is available online at: https://www.fletc.gov/current-participating-organizations.

In 2016, the US Department of Homeland Security (USDHS) published a review of the DHS government-owned training centers. It sought to: promote standardization where possible in order to "eliminate overlap and duplication with regard to underutilized infrastructure to produce tangible cost savings . . . across the Department" (USDHS, 2016, p. 3). At that time DHS had an inventory with more than 1,400 training courses for its 25 training centers. The report indicated that various steps had already been taken to consolidate the delivery of operational training, but due to the Department's vast training enterprise, management and reporting of training data could be greatly strengthened (USDHS, 2016, p. 3). The review defined " 'operational training' as training that develops, maintains, or improves individual or unit performance and is essential to the Department's ability to accomplish its assigned missions" (USDHS, 2016, p. 5). Significantly, the study noted an essential drawback in its data collection efforts—despite best efforts, a comprehensive curriculum level review was not conducted. Therefore, according to the report, this limitation meant that further study would be needed to determine any appropriateness of relocation/consolidation (USDHS, 2016, p. 8).

The DHS study disclosed that the bulk of the training fell into three categories: law enforcement, disaster response, and service-unique (i.e., Coast Guard). "In fact, FLETC, U.S. Customs and Border Protection (CBP), Federal Emergency Management Agency (FEMA), and the United States Coast Guard (USCG) account for 77.9% of the operational training identified in this study. Despite the study team's expectation to find training programs meeting the criteria for further study and/or possible consolidation/relocation across Components, there were relatively few areas of overlap and/or redundancies found in training programs" (USDHS, 2016, p. 8). The researchers noted that various consolidation steps had taken place in recent years and that for the most part newly hired personnel were being trained at a common basic course at a FLETC facility for their particular track (i.e., Criminal Investigator Training Program or Uniformed Police Training Program). "For the follow-on training, each Component has a separate Academy for training specific to that particular Component. Most of these academies are located on FLETC facilities with some exceptions; U.S. Secret Service, (USSS) which conducts its follow-on training at the James J. Rowley Training Center [in Laurel, MD]; and the Transportation Security Administration (TSA), which conducts its follow-on specialty training for its Federal Air Marshals at the TSA Training Center in Atlantic City, NJ" (USDHS, 2016, p. 9). Currently, the TSA Training Center (TSATC) is responsible for both initial and recurrent training for all Federal Air Marshals, provides leadership training for TSA executive leaders, and trains members of the Federal Flight Deck Officer Program. The TSATC main campus is located on the grounds of the William J. Hughes FAA Technical Center in Atlantic City, New Jersey, with satellite locations on the FLETC campuses in Artesia, New Mexico, and Dallas, Texas.

The TSA's Canine Training Center (CTC) is located on the Joint Base, San Antonio, TX. The CTC is responsible for training TSA's passenger screening canine teams, as well as canine teams for local law enforcement entities. CTC staff selects, purchases, and provides early training to TSA canines prior to pairing them with handlers as they are trained as a team. Located at Joint Base San Antonio-Lackland in San Antonio, Texas, the $12 million Canine Training Center includes 25,000 square feet of space with seven classrooms, office space that accommodates 140 employees, and a 100-seat auditorium. There are 17 indoor venues on the premises that mimic a variety of transportation sites and modes. This includes a cargo facility, an airport gate area, a checkpoint, a baggage claim area, the interior of an aircraft, a vehicle parking lot, a light rail station, a light rail car, an air cargo facility, two mock terminals, and open area search venues for air scenting. The facilities kennels can accommodate approximately 350 dogs. The canine training center also utilizes a variety of training venues in and around the San Antonio area, including San Antonio International Airport, local shopping malls, the ATT Center, and the VIA Bus Terminal. The conventional explosives detection canine handlers undergo an 11-week training course. Passenger screening canine handlers undergo a 16-week training course. After successful completion of the training canine course by demonstrating proficiency in various venues inclusive of all transportation environments, they return to their duty station to acclimate and familiarize the canine to their assigned operational environment (TSA, 2021).

A large majority of the partnering agencies send their new hires to FLETC in order to complete its "Uniformed Police Training Program" (UPTP). The new employees must meet their agency's recruitment standards and the physical performance requirements established by FLETC prior to arriving for their training programs. "The program is designed to provide the new officer [or agent] with the specific knowledge and skills necessary to perform at the entry level in a Federal law enforcement position. . . . FLETC maintains liaison with Partner Organizations (POs) to keep abreast of their changing needs and to provide current information to students concerning federal laws, jurisdiction, policies, procedures, and basic operations. The program of instruction is constantly upgraded and modified to meet the collective training needs of those organizations which participate in the UPTP training platform. Suggestions for improvement and/or modifications are considered by the FLETC and discussed with POs. When a general consensus is reached regarding a change to the program, it is implemented" (FLETC, 2022b).

The major subject areas covered in the basic federal law enforcement course are: behavioral science; counterterrorism; computer safety and evidence; vehicle stops, investigations, and driving skills; enforcement operations; investigative operations; firearms; leadership training; law; and physical techniques. The program's 64-day curriculum includes a wide range of topics, such as: interviewing; recognizing and responding to individuals in mental health crisis; weapons of mass destruction; suicide bomber mitigation; report writing; officer safety and survival; one-hand shooting techniques; crime scene preservation; federal criminal law and procedures; community first aid and safety (CFAS); control tactics; and many more topics (FLETC, 2022b).

In addition to its basic federal law enforcement course, FLETC currently offers 83 different training programs, which may be conducted both on and off the FLETC's various campuses. A current list of these courses is available in their online Training Catalog at: https://www.fletc.gov/training-catalog. For the general public, FEMA's Emergency Management Institute's (EMI) Curriculum Standards and Instructional Technology Branch provide an Independent Study Program (ISP) online and free of charge. The ISP currently offers over 200 training courses at their training website: https://training.fema.gov/is/. Readers may also be interested in a series of free online first aid courses, available online at: https://www.firstaidforfree.com/. According to John Furst, an experienced emergency medical technician and qualified first aid and CPR instructor, "First aid is one of the basic life skills that everyone should equip themselves with. If anything, times like these remind us of the importance of saving lives and being there for other people. It is always good to be prepared for any medical emergency" (Furst, 2020).

In 2015 FLETC hosted a first-ever "Private/Public Partnership Academy" (PPPA). This special two-day training program involved nearly 175 shopping mall executives, mall security directors, and local LEOs and was held at the Glynco campus. The training program included such topics as: terrorism awareness, weapons of mass destruction, improvised explosive devices, and leadership in a crisis situation. Participant feedback indicated that one of the greatest values of the PPPA was learning about others' roles, which leads to improved coordination during emergent situations. Additionally, participants observed that the PPPA underscored the private and public sectors' collective responsibility in ensuring safety and security (FLETC, 2015). Finally, the FLETC campuses host a variety of specialized federal law enforcement agency academies. Eight of these academies are highlighted below.

US Probation and Pretrial Services National Training Academy

The United States Probation and Pretrial Services National Training Academy was established in 2005 at FLETC's Charleston, South Carolina campus. The purpose of the Academy is to provide newly appointed US Probation and Pretrial Services officers with the skills necessary to safely begin their new careers. The Academy also provides instruction to those US probation officers who are serving as their district's firearms instructor or officer safety instructor. In the basic six-week course, the student officers engage in both classroom learning and real-life simulations. Approximately 400 new officers graduate from the academy each year and another 800 graduate from one of the Academy's advanced programs. Use of the state-of-the-art training facility is made possible through a partnership between the Administrative Office of the US Courts and the FLETC (US Courts, 2017).

US Capitol Police Training Academy

The USCP force dates back to 1800 when the Congress moved from Philadelphia to Washington, DC. A lone watchman, John Golding, was hired to protect the Capitol Building. After a number of incidents occurred in 1827 that could have been prevented with sufficient security and surveillance, President John Quincy Adams asked that a regular Capitol Police force be established. On May 2, 1828, Congress passed an Act that expanded the police regulations of the city of Washington to include the Capitol and Capitol Square. The new force consisted of four officers including its captain. It is on this date that the USCP commemorates its founding. By 1935, the Capitol grounds footprint was expanded to 126 acres. As a result, additional officers were employed to augment the 132-man force, which consisted of men ranging from 19 to 75 years old. The USCP expanded its force after the terrorist attacks on September 11, 2001, and again following the historic merger with the Library of Congress Police in 2009 (USCP, 2022a). Today, the USCP comprises more than 2,300 officers and civilian employees and has an annual budget of approximately $460 million (USCP, 2022b).

Following the January 6, 2021, attack on the Capitol grounds, a day unlike any other in American history, various reviews and reports about the event were conducted and improvements recommended to "enhance security around the Capitol Complex, and pivot towards an intelligence-based protective agency" (USCP, 2021). Some of the improvements included: joint training with the National Guard, riot training, shoot/don't shoot scenarios, and less-than-lethal force exercises. Internally, the Department increased the information shared with sworn officers about obtained intelligence and event planning. In addition, the USCP initiated an internal peer support program (USCP, 2021). As of March 2022, more than

775 individuals have been arrested in nearly all 50 states for crimes related to the breach of the US Capitol, including over 245 individuals charged with assaulting or impeding law enforcement. The investigation remains ongoing. It is expected that many individuals will be charged with entering and remaining in a restricted building or grounds as well as disorderly and disruptive conduct in a restricted building or grounds, both misdemeanor crimes. Their actions disrupted a joint session of the US Congress that was in the process of ascertaining and counting the electoral votes related to the presidential election.

Once hired, the new Capitol Police trainees undergo seven months of rigorous, professional training at the FLETC and the US Capitol Police Training Academy. The new police officer trainees receive full pay and are appointed to the rank of private. Generally, the first week of training consists of orientation at the USCP Training Academy in Cheltenham, Maryland. Next, trainees typically will participate in basic 12 weeks of intensive training at FLETC in Georgia. After graduating from FLETC, trainees will return to the US Capitol Police Training Academy in Cheltenham for 13 weeks of specialized training. Graduates from the Academy are appointed to the rank of "Private with Training" and are assigned to an experienced training officer in the field to continue their skills development through on-the-job experience (USCP, 2022c).

US Coast Guard Maritime Law Enforcement Academy

The US Coast Guard is a unique service since it is a multi-missioned organization safeguarding the nation's homeland, but it can also come under the Department of Navy following a declaration ordered by the president. "The common link that the USCG has with many nation-states navies throughout the world is that the USCG is a small maritime service. Most nation-states have small navies that concentrate on coastal patrols and other regional maritime security efforts" (Traina, 2013, p. 58). The USCG is the only branch of the armed forces that has both a law enforcement role and military role (Traina, 2013). Incidentally, the U.S. Space Force became the sixth branch of the military on December 20, 2019, becoming the smallest branch of the armed forces (see https://www.spaceforce.mil/).

The Coast Guard is the only military service within DHS and has unique requirements inherent to its missions and operations. Consequently, it has training facilities scattered throughout the United States. The US Coast Guard Maritime Law Enforcement Academy was established in November 2004 at the FLETC in Charleston, South Carolina, to prepare Coast Guard personnel to perform as "Maritime Law Enforcement Officers." Attendance at its various training courses is for active duty personnel who meet specific prerequisites. However, the Academy has protocols in place for the attendance by qualified visiting public safety personnel from federal, state, local, and international agencies in order to enhance their maritime security skills. A selected list of the Academy's courses include: Maritime Enforcement Specialist "A" School; Basic Boarding Officer Course; Boarding Officer Qualification Support Program; Boarding Officer E-Learning Course; Boarding Officer Practical Course; Law Enforcement Instructor Course; Boarding Officer Certified Ashore (BOCA); Radiation Detection Level II Operators Course; Maritime Counter-Trafficking Course; Integrated Cross-Border Maritime Law Enforcement Operations; and Non-Compliant Vessel Pursuit (USCG, 2022a).

The scope of the Maritime Enforcement Specialist "A" School is to train Coast Guard personnel to provide security and law enforcement support for United States Coast Guard missions. The course is held for 47 training days over 9.3 weeks. Subject areas include:

Leadership, Physical Fitness, Communications, Safety, Rate Training & Administration, Security, Maritime Law Enforcement, Tactical Operations, Port Readiness, Weapons Familiarization & Qualification, Ports Waterways & Coastal Security, Anti-Terrorism, and Force Protection. To ensure compliance with standards indicated in the terminal performance objectives, students are evaluated during role-plays, labs, scenarios, practical, and written exam (USCG, 2022b). The American Council on Education (ACE) has given this course the following credit recommendation: "In the lower-division baccalaureate/associate degree category, 3 semester hours in law enforcement, 2 in law enforcement practicum, and 1 in leadership" (USCG, 2022e).

The Basic Boarding Officer Course (BBOC) is offered to Coast Guard personnel and foreign naval officers. The purpose of the BBOC is to prepare Boarding Officers for the arduous duties associated with enforcing laws and treaties at sea. Graduates of the BBOC possess the skills and knowledge necessary to lead a Coast Guard boarding team in the enforcement of US laws and regulations in a safe and professional manner. This five week course covers such topics as: authority and jurisdiction; criminal law; defensive tactics; boarding procedures; boating safety; hostage situations; and many others (USCG, 2022c). ACE has given this course the following credit recommendation: "In the lower-division baccalaureate/associate degree category, 2 semester hours in law enforcement practicum, 3 in criminal investigation, and 3 in criminal evidence and procedures" (USCG, 2022e).

The Academy offers the Coast Guards only Non-Compliant Vessel Pursuit (NCVP) course. These courses are offered to "Coast Guard personnel at designated Pursuit Units. The purpose of the NCVP courses are to prepare pursuit crews for the dangerous and difficult tasks associated with stopping non-compliant vessels at sea. Graduates of the NCVP courses possess the skills and knowledge necessary to pursue and gain compliance of vessels in a safe and professional manner. During these five day courses, the majority of the training is performed hands on while underway" (USCG, 2022d). The ACE has given this course the following credit recommendation: "In the lower-division baccalaureate/associate degree category, 3 semester hours in maritime law enforcement" (USCG, 2022d).[9]

The Border Patrol Academy

Robert Olson (2012), the former Chief of Party Export Control/Border Security Program, at the US Embassy, Russian Federation, in summarizing the history of the Customs Service (now US Customs and Border Protection within the Department of Homeland Security) noted that "it is a story of a new country that creates a Customs Service as its first federal agency . . . for the sole purpose of raising revenue. It fulfills that role very well, and suddenly other responsibilities are added, things like maintaining lighthouses, marine hospitals, a coast guard, immigration responsibilities and many more" (p. 125). Even prior to the passage by Congress on July 31, 1789, of a law for the organization of a Customs Service, there were customs officers who held office in the colonies and during the Revolutionary War a system for collection of fees existed in all ports not under British control. Following the adoption of the Articles of Confederation the control of shipping was continued by the several states so long as the duties (i.e., those taxes paid to the government, on imported or exported goods) did not conflict with treaties entered into with France and Spain (Schmeckebier, 1924, p. 2). The 1789 statute provided for custom districts and ports of entry, the appointment and specific tasks of customs officers, as well as other details concerning the collection of duties. Three specific types of customs officers were described—collectors of customs, surveyors, and naval officers. The surveyors directed other workers known as inspectors, weighers, measurers, and gaugers to examine the imported goods on ships, in particular, distilled spirits. The initial appointments of these customs officers were made by the President with advice and consent of the Senate (Schmeckebier, 1924, pp. 3–5).

Today, "the Border Patrol is responsible for watching over 8,000 miles of U.S. border and is generally believed to be one of the busiest federal law enforcement organizations" (Army.com, 2022). The US Border Patrol was officially established in 1924 by act of Congress as the "US Immigration Service Border Patrol." In addition to its deep roots connected with the need to collect import duties, a significant historical event took place in 1853 when the Secretary of the Treasury authorized the collectors of customs to hire "Customs Mounted Inspectors" for patrol duty along the nation's land borders (CBP, 2019). In the year 1904, there were mounted watchmen of the US Immigration Service who patrolled the border in an effort to prevent illegal crossings. These early inspectors commonly referred to as "Mounted Guards," operated out of El Paso, Texas. In March 1915, Congress gave additional workers broader arrest powers largely to pursue Chinese immigrants trying to avoid the Chinese exclusion laws along the southwest border. "These patrolmen were Immigrant Inspectors, assigned to inspection stations, and could not watch the border at all times" (CBP, 2020b). In 1920, the passage of the 18th Amendment to the Constitution of the United States and the numerical limits placed on immigration to the United States by the *Immigration Acts of 1921 and 1924* placed new burdens for America's border safety and law enforcement efforts. These stressors led to the passage of the *Labor Appropriation Act of 1924*, officially establishing the US Immigration Service Border Patrol in the Department of Labor to expand patrols between border inspection stations and along the seacoast. This required hiring hundreds of new officers. "Many of the early agents were recruited from organizations such as the Texas Rangers, local sheriffs and deputies, and appointees from the Civil Service Register of Railroad Mail Clerks" (CBP, 2020b).

During the years of the "Prohibition Era" of the 1920s and early 1930s, the majority of the Border Patrol was assigned to the Canadian border (CBP, 2020b). In June 1933, the Bureau of Immigration and the Bureau of Naturalization in the Department of Commerce and Labor were merged and transferred into the newly created Department of Labor as the US Immigration and Naturalization Service (INS). In December 1934, the INS Border Patrol Training School opened at Camp Chigas in El Paso. In addition to such hands-on classes as fingerprinting, marksmanship in rifle and pistol, and horsemanship, the first class of 34 trainees attended lecture courses in immigration law, Spanish, documents, citizenship, leadership and duties, and authorities of patrol inspectors. "Classroom instruction was four hours per day and there was no physical training program. The first session graduated March 17, 1935" (Army.com, 2022).

In 1935, the first US Customs Service School of Instruction opened at the Port of New York. Harry F. Worley developed the training program consisting of more than 40 lesson plans, including a history of customs. His career with Customs covered a period of over 44 years and in 1943 he was elected president of the National Customs Service Association. "In 1936 the Customs Border Patrol was place under the Customs Agency Service and 4 Customs Patrol Districts were established. A training center for the Customs Border Patrol was established in Havre, Montana" (Olson, 2012, p. 118).

On the eve of America's entry in World War II, the Immigration Service was moved from the Department of Labor to the Department of Justice in July 1940, where it remained until March 1, 2003. In 1948, the Customs Patrol Service was abolished (CBP, 2019). Over 1,400 people were employed by the Border Patrol in law enforcement and civilian positions by the end of WWII. During the war, the Patrol strengthened its control over the nation's borders, "manned alien detention camps, guarded diplomats, and assisted the U. S. Coast Guard in searching for Axis saboteurs. Aircraft proved extremely effective and became an integral part of operations" (CBP, 2020b). In 1956 the official name of the INS Border Patrol Training School was changed to the Border Patrol Academy. In June 1970, all officer personnel titles were changed from "Immigration Patrol Inspector" to "Border Patrol Agent." In 1968, the US Customs National Training Center opened at Hofstra University in Uniondale, New York (CBP, 2019), and the Hofstra site fulfilled this purpose until 1977. Hundreds of new agents and inspectors were hired into the Customs Service in 1970. This required quadrupling the number of classes held at the National Training Center during the fiscal year "some 500 inspectors and 150 special agents completed basic and advanced training courses" (US Treasury, 1970, p. 76). During the Vietnam War in 1970, several Vietnamese Customs officers underwent a 2-month training program at the Hofstra campus. In addition, customs personnel from 29 nations received training at Hofstra and at training facilities in Laredo, Texas (US Treasury, 1970, p. 74).

"The training facility for Border Patrol Agents remained at Camp Chigas in El Paso until 1951. From 1951 through 1960, training schools were held in five different locations in the southwest. In July 1961, the Academy was moved to a permanent location in Los Fresnos, Texas" (Army.com, 2022). Los Fresnos is located at the southern tip of Texas, near the Gulf of Mexico. After considerable negotiations between the INS and FLETC in 1977, the Border Patrol Academy at Los Fresnos closed and new recruits began their training at FLETC in Glynco, Georgia (CBP, 2019). Due to continuing training needs, other locations were also used for training purposes and in 2004 the Border Patrol basic training program moved to Artesia, New Mexico, formerly the site of the College of Artesia. "It's made up of dorms, classroom buildings and gyms, plus firing ranges and driving courses that span more than 1,000 acres. Everything the trainees need is on campus, including a grocery store, dry cleaners and even a bar" (Yurkevich, 2018). It is a challenging program as "each Border Patrol Agent trainee must complete a 940 hour (117 training days) paid, resident course of instruction in U.S. law, Border Patrol operations, physical training, firearms instruction, driving, law enforcement and Border Patrol tactical training, and Spanish" (CBP, 2021). "After completing the 19 week program of the Border Patrol Academy, trainees receive additional post-academy and on-the-job training in the field during their 12 month probationary period of employment" (Army.com, 2022).

In addition to the Border Patrol Academy, FLETC's Artesia campus is home to the Bureau of Indian Affairs Law Enforcement Academies as well as a TSA Training Center, which trains private pilots from across the industry to become certified as Federal Flight Deck Officers and a portion of the basic training for Federal Air Marshals. The Uniformed Police Training Program is another basic training program taught at Artesia. This program resides at both the Artesia and Glynco locations. FLETC Artesia provides many other basic and advanced training programs taught both locally and at various hosted locations in the United States and overseas (FLETC, 2022c). (For additional information about the US Indian Police Academy, see US Dept. of Interior, 2022).

In recent years, the Border Patrol has begun hiring civilians to deal with the care of detained asylum seekers, checking holding areas and cells as well as the time-consuming work of collecting information for immigration reports and other documents needed for court appearances. Each coordinator position was to be filled for a period of 13 months, renewable up to four years. The Border Patrol graduated its first class of these civilian "processing coordinators" in January 2021 "with the goal of eventually hiring 1,200. The position requires less training than for LEOs and pays [about 20 percent] less. It is also seen as a recruiting tool for an agency that has struggled to find qualified applicants, particularly women" (Attanasio & Spagats, 2021). U.S. Rep. Nanette Barragan, a member of Congress from Los Angeles, California, told the members of the second graduating class in June 2021 that they were needed to help process the many unaccompanied children who had made illegal crossings from Mexico into the United States. At that time, most single adults were being expelled without an opportunity to seek asylum under the public health order known as Title 42, the pandemic-related authority designed to prevent the spread of the coronavirus. However, unaccompanied children and most families could "seek humanitarian protection, giving them little incentive to elude capture because they will be released in the U.S. with notices to appear in court" (Attanasio & Spagats, 2021).

US Customs and Border Protection —Field Operations Academy

The Border Patrol's parent agency is Customs and Border Protection. The US CBP is one of the Department of Homeland Security's largest components, with a priority mission of keeping terrorists and their weapons out of the United States. Customs and Border Protection is also one of the world's largest law enforcement organizations. The agency also has a responsibility for securing and facilitating trade and travel while enforcing hundreds of US regulations, including immigration and drug laws (CBP, 2022a). On a typical day, CBP employs over 64,000 men and women including law enforcement and trade personnel. This number, in part, includes nearly 26,000 CBP officers, 20,000 Border Patrol agents, and 2,700 agriculture specialists. In addition, there are a combined total of over 1,300 air interdiction agents (pilots), marine interdiction agents, and aviation enforcement agents (CBP, 2022e).

The US Customs and Border Protection is the nation's first comprehensive border security agency with a focus on maintaining the integrity of the nation's boundaries and ports of entry, merging customs officers, Border Patrol agents, and immigration and agricultural inspectors on March 1, 2003 (CBP, 2022b). Before CBP, security, compliance, and facilitation of international travel and trade were conducted by these separate organizations. The consolidation of their roles and responsibilities allowed CBP to develop seamless security procedures while ensuring compliance with the nation's immigration, health, and international trade laws and regulations. However, "the uniformed ranks are only a portion of CBP's specialized corps. They are joined by forensic scientists, international trade specialists, public affairs officers and cadres of other specialists and employees who work together to make CBP's processes more secure, cost effective and efficient" (CBP, 2022c).

The CBP Field Operations Academy (FOA) is responsible for the analysis, design, development, implementation, and evaluation of training that supports the mission of the CBP Field Operations Office. The FOA provides basic and advanced training to address the mission requirements of not only CBP officers but also specialists in such fields as agriculture, import and entry Specialists, and seized property.

> The FOA employs a fully accredited program to prepare new trainees to become CBP Officers. Law enforcement awareness and demeanor are exemplified and reinforced throughout the rigorous 89 day training program. Upon arrival, trainees are immediately indoctrinated into the law enforcement environment. While the training can be intense, the FOA ensures trainees have a fundamental understanding of the duties, obligations, and philosophies that are essential to work within a dynamic and fluid law enforcement environment. Initial instruction teaches trainees basic drill and ceremony procedures, and provides an awareness of the Field Operations Academy guiding principles of Pride, Esprit De Corps, Professionalism, and Integrity, and CBP's core values of Vigilance, Service to Country, and Integrity.
>
> *(CBP, 2022a)*

"During their time at the FOA, trainees learn the technical and legal requirements of the job, and participate in a vigorous physical fitness and conditioning program. Trainees learn the proper methods for handling firearms, learn to safely operate a law enforcement vehicle, and comprehensively employ these skills in more than 200 interactive scenarios that replicate situations routinely encountered in the field. In order to graduate, trainees must successfully pass a total of eight written exams and 25 practical exercises specifically designed to demonstrate skills necessary for success in the field. . . . [For example,] trainees receive expert instruction in Firearms Safety and Maintenance, Basic Marksmanship, CBP Specific Tactical Training, Scenario Based Training, Interactive Cover Drills, Situational Response, Reduced Light scenarios, and the CBP Practical Pistol Course that is recognized as the industry standard for LEOs. CBP Officer Trainees receive a total of 77 hours of weapons handling training including familiarization with the Remington 870 shotgun and the Colt M4/A1 carbine" (CBP, 2022a).

In addition to driver training and physical conditioning activities, trainees undergo "extensive training in arrest techniques, defensive tactics, electronic control weapon (ECW), collapsible straight baton (CSB), oleoresin capsicum spray (OC), ground defense, and edged weapons. To graduate, trainees must successfully meet the following Fitness Graduation Standards: 220 yard run in 45 seconds or less; 24 or more push-ups in one minute; and completion of a 1.5 mile run in 15 minutes or less" (CBP, 2022a)

"The CBP Field Operations Academy developed the curriculum for the CBP Officer basic course by incorporating topics and training from the former U.S. Customs Service, U.S. Immigration and Naturalization Service and the U.S. Department of Agriculture. By melding training topics into a single, seamless course that refines all aspects of the CBP Officer duties, the CBP Officer basic course provides the foundation necessary for new officers to perform their critical anti-terrorism mission alongside their traditional border enforcement missions" (CBP, 2020a). Officers and specialists work at international airports, seaports, land border crossings, as well as assignments worldwide. In addition, US Customs and Border Protection, Air and Marine Operations "conducts its mission in the air and maritime environments at and beyond the border, and within the nation's interior" (CBP, 2022d).

Occasionally, Customs and Border Protection, Air and Marine Operations (AMO) will be engaged in sea rescues. For example, while coastal interceptor boat training was taking place in March 2022, AMO agents rescued four adults from a sinking vessel, approximately three nautical miles south of Marathon, Florida. According to Supervisory Marine Interdiction Agent Robert Sellers, "when someone is in distress, their safety and well-being comes before their citizenship, nationality, or immigration status. The same resources used for border security are immediately directed to those in need" (CBP, 2022d).

Immigration and Customs Enforcement (ICE) Training Academy

US ICE serves as the principal investigative arm of the Department of Homeland Security. Its primary mission is to promote homeland security and public safety through the criminal and civil enforcement of federal laws governing border control, customs, trade, and immigration. The ICE Training Academy came to the FLETC - Charleston site in 2007. In September 2011, a newly renovated ICE Academy, costing $2.5 million, opened on the Glynco, Georgia, FLETC campus. The ICE Academy is a three-story facility containing four computer labs, nine classrooms, two electronics labs, and two breakout rooms. At that time, ICE Director John Morton stated: "With more than 20,000 employees in over 400 offices in the United States and around the world, ICE agents and officers play a crucial role in protecting the security of our homeland. The ICE Academy at FLETC is a vital first step providing a strong educational foundation to prepare our agents and officers to take on all types of law enforcement challenges" USDHSICE (2011). The new facility is dedicated to training and preparing the agency's special agents and officers to enforce the nation's immigration and customs laws (USDHSICE, 2011). One division of the ICE Academy trains personnel for careers as an officer of the ICE Office of Detention and Removal Operations (DRO). Such personnel are required to successfully complete both the five-week DRO Spanish Language Training Program (SLTP) and the DRO Basic Immigration Law Enforcement Training Program (ICE-D). ICE-D is a 13-week FLETC integrated basic training program that consists of both FLETC training and ICE training (USDHSICE, 2008).

The CBP Global Borders College

Since the 1950s, there have been both routine and special initiatives undertaken to stem the illegal flow of aliens and the smuggling of drugs crossing America's borders. At the same time, there has been a phenomenal growth in travel and tourism. The hospitality sector, prior to the start of the pandemic at the end of the second decade of the 21st century, had "become one of the most important sectors in the world economy, accounting for 10 percent of global GDP and more than 320 million jobs worldwide. . . . In 1950, at the dawn of the jet age, just 25 million people took foreign trips. By 2019, that number had reached 1.5 billion, and the travel and tourism sector had grown to almost too-big-to-fail proportions for many economies" (Behsudi, 2020). In so many ways, Americans and citizens the world over are now living in an ever-increasing globalized world due to the interconnectedness of financial systems and marketplaces.

In 2011, a Global Borders College located on the campus of the CBP Advanced Training Center in Harpers Ferry, West Virginia, was opened. Its 60,000 square foot facility houses six classrooms and class break-out rooms, a computer lab, several conference rooms, and over 80 staff offices (CBP, 2019). On the occasion of its opening ceremony, CBP Commissioner Alan D. Bersin stated: "The inauguration of the Global Borders College will further our ability to prepare and educate the future leaders of CBP. The knowledge and expertise that this institute will foster will allow our agency to continue to be at the forefront of international border security." Also, in attendance at the opening ceremony was West Virginia Senator Jay Rockefeller who noted, "It has been my absolute privilege to play a role in helping the new Global Borders College find a great home here in Harpers Ferry. The men and women who will train in this building are on the front lines of protecting us from threats outside our borders. At this state-of-the art college, they will get advanced training and learn new skills and tactics—making them an even smarter and more capable part of our national security team. Intensive training here in West Virginia will keep the entire nation [safer]" (CBP, 2011).

In 2013, Dominic Traina, a certified homeland security instructor who has taught at the FLETC, outlined a curriculum proposal for a joint professional law enforcement program with foreign partners to be offered at the Global Borders College (GBC). He noted that this facility, located only one hour from Washington, DC, has become a world-class training facility for DHS border security officials. International participants would be recommended by the Department of State and vetted for this program. The program would provide a networking opportunity for regional law enforcement officials to discuss mutual concerns. Such regions might include West Africa, the Middle East, or Eastern Europe, depending on the problems of the times. They would have an opportunity to live on campus throughout the training session, participating in such courses as the Rule of Law, Internal Security, Good Governance and Transparency, Universal Values, and Respect for Human Rights. All such programs would follow a seminar format and strive to encourage new and creative thinking. Each cohort would also have the chance to engage in field studies, visiting historical sites, seaport facilities, and some private sector corporations. This aspect of the program would be designed to promote an understanding of US institutions and society. A significant goal of the program would be "to create a network of alumni that is available to peacefully assist in resolving future problems and in the case of law enforcement the sharing of information to enhance investigations and intelligence. . . . it [is] easier to have a friend in place during times of crises than to try to find a friend or develop a friendship when it is too late" (Traina, 2013, p. 74). Traina (2013) also reviewed a variety of past and existing professional exchanges and international training efforts sponsored by US Customs and Border Protection, US Coast Guard, and the ILEAs.[10] Ideally, the proposed program would lead to the formation of an international group of alumni composed of the senior leaders and decision makers in their organizations. "These leaders will have developed personal relationships with their U.S. counterparts" (Traina, 2013, p. 78).

Commission on the Advancement of Federal Law Enforcement (CAFLE)

The Commission on the Advancement of Federal Law Enforcement (CAFLE) was established by the *Anti-Terrorism and Effective Death Penalty Act of 1996* (Pub. L. 104–132). Congress's charge to the Commission was extremely broad and directed the Commission to "review, ascertain, evaluate, report and recommend" action to the Congress on a broad array of issues affecting federal law enforcement priorities for the 21st century. In particular, the Commission was mandated to consider in its study of federal law enforcement entities their respective functions, programs, responsibilities, jurisdictions, training, coordination, and their interaction with each other, as well as with state and local law enforcement bodies.

Five full-day public comment hearings were held at various locations in Washington, DC, from May to September during 1998. The Commission was terminated following the submission of its final report in February 2000 (CAFLE, 1998). Over its two-year tenure, it met more than 20 times and took verbal and sometimes written testimony from some 70 witnesses, including two members of President Clinton's Cabinet and numerous presidential appointees. In addition, the Commission prepared surveys, performed literature reviews, and commissioned and received relevant research papers. In its final report, the Commission concluded that global crime, cybercrime, and terrorism pose emerging security threats to the nation and present the greatest challenges to the federal law enforcement community (see US Senate Hearing, 2001, pp. 50–53).

During the afternoon of February 3, 2000, the US Senate's Subcommittee on Criminal Justice Oversight, Committee on the Judiciary, met to discuss the findings and recommendations of the Commission's final report—a 185-page document entitled "Law Enforcement in a New Century and a Changing World: Improving the Administration of Federal Law Enforcement" (available online at: https://www.ojp.gov/pdffiles1/Digitization/181343NCJRS.pdf). Three Senators were present: Strom Thurmond of South Carolina (chairman of the subcommittee), Senator Jeff Sessions (R-Alabama), and Senator Charles Schumer (D-New York). Testimony was given at the hearing by a panel consisting of the five members of the Commission, which included: William H. Webster, former director, Federal Bureau of Investigation, and the chairman of the Commission; Donald C. Dahlin, professor, Department of Political Science, University of South Dakota; Robert M. Stewart, chief, State Law Enforcement Division, State of South Carolina; Gilbert G. Gallegos, the national president of the Fraternal Order of Police; and Robert E. Sanders, former assistant director of Criminal Investigations, Bureau of Alcohol, Tobacco and Firearms (ATF) (US Senate Hearing, 2001).

The hearing followed the usual pattern of most Congressional hearings—opening remarks from the sub-committee's chair and his introductions of each of the panelists, comments by the present members of the subcommittee, an individual statement by each of the panelists, and lastly questions by the Senators and answers from the panelists. The first panelist to testify was William Webster. His professional career included service as the US Attorney in the Eastern District of Missouri before becoming a Federal judge for the Eastern District of Missouri and then the US Court of Appeals for the Eighth Circuit. Judge Webster resigned from the bench to become the director of the Federal Bureau of Investigation, and later became director of the Central Intelligence Agency. In his initial statement, Judge Webster summarized the five major findings of the Commission's unanimous report. In his final and fifth point, he urged Congress to: "Focus on professionalism, integrity, and accountability. We believe that there are vast differences in professionalism and accountability especially among the Federal agencies, different standards for such things as use of deadly force, for example. There ought to be one Federal standard for the use of deadly force. And so we recommend that the President and Congress should require that Federal law enforcement agencies establish new standards for professionalism, integrity, and public accountability that are standard across the board" (US Senate Hearing, 2001, p. 10).

Following Judge Webster, Robert M. Stewart, the chief of the South Carolina Law Enforcement Division (SLED) made his opening statement. He started his law enforcement career at age 17 as a cadet with the Cheraw Police Department. He joined SLED in 1975, was promoted to deputy director in 1987, and became chief of SLED in 1988. During his career in law enforcement he completed the FBI National Academy. In the area of accreditation, Chief Stewart, in part, explained that "there are two accreditations available in law enforcement today. The one for laboratories is by the American Society of Crime Laboratory Directors, or ASCLD, and the other is from the Commission for Accreditation of Law Enforcement Agencies, CALEA. Now, a number of the Federal agencies are . . . beginning to come about and be involved in the laboratory accreditation. The FBI lab in the last year or so has become ASCLD-accredited. . . . That is just an absolute must in this day and time to assure the public and the people that the labs are being run correctly. . . . About half of the crime labs in the Nation are accredited, and surely all the Federal crime labs should be accredited. . . . As far as agency-wide accreditation, that was begun by a Federal grant from a congressional program. Jim Cotter, with the FBI, was the first director of that commission [speaking about CALEA],[11] and it does a whole lot to standardize policy and procedure and see to it that agencies live up to the mandate they have and are run properly. It also fosters better relationships with local and State law enforcement, and I think it is something that really the Federal agencies ought to look at. . . . I would hope that all Federal agencies would be involved in that program. . . . we found over 140 Federal law enforcement agencies, which is somewhat mind-boggling" (US Senate Hearing, 2001, pp. 13–14).

Senator Thurmond asked Chief Stewart the following question, "the report recommends that Federal agencies be required to regularly undergo accreditation by outside agencies. Based on your experience with accreditation on the State level, do you think accreditation is important for federal law enforcement?" In part, Chief Stewart replied: " 'Yes, sir, I do, and you are talking about a number of issues here. You are talking about the integrity of law enforcement, you are talking about professionalism, you are talking about standardization and uniform policies and procedures that every law enforcement agency, no matter whether it is Federal, State or local—no matter what the level, they should live up to these standards. . . . As I said, [referring to the hundreds of standards established by CALEA] it was created by a Federal grant from Congress. A lot of time and effort has been put into creating this. . . . [CALEA] is made up of law enforcement officials and academics from different levels that meets and comes up with these standards. And then an inspection team comes out and inspects the organization to see to it that all these standards are met. I can't think of anything the federal agencies could do better to encourage public confidence and relationships with State and local law enforcement than the national accreditation program. As I have said, a number of Federal agencies are now in the lab accreditation program with ASCLD, and the Marshals Service and the U.S. Capitol Police are now involved in aspiring to obtain this accreditation from CALEA. I don't see a downside. Some Federal agencies say, well, it doesn't apply to us. . . . Most of the Southeast State criminal investigative agencies—Florida, South Carolina, Georgia, North Carolina, Tennessee—are all nationally accredited. It is one thing, if nothing else, that the Southeast is clearly a leader in and we are proud of that and hope that the Federal agencies will become more involved' " (US Senate Hearing, 2001, p. 27).

Senator Joe Biden submitted the following written question to the Commission: "In your report you call for an external review of Federal law enforcement. Do you have concern that this is just going to add another layer of bureaucracy to a system that you are criticizing for being too bureaucratic?" In a written response to Senator Biden's question, who was not present at the sub-committee's hearing, the Commission submitted the following written response: "No. External review will not create a new bureaucracy review and accreditations are handled by the Commission on Accreditation of Law Enforcement Agencies, Inc. (CALEA), which already exists and was, in fact, created under a grant from the U.S. Department of Justice. Moreover, as the Commission reported (page 103), accreditation is a voluntary process of self-study and peer-review based on some 436 law enforcement standards developed by law enforcement professionals around agency missions and mandates. Since CALEA began in 1979, some 500 law enforcement agencies in the United States have been accredited through the program. The U.S. Marshals Service has already earned accreditation from CALEA and the Capitol Police are currently in the process of obtaining such accreditation" (US Senate Hearing, 2001, p. 42).

More discussion by members of the Legislative branch eventually led to the establishment of an independent accreditation program under the direction of the "Federal Law Enforcement Training Accreditation" (FLETA) Board. The US Office of Management and Budget (OMB) provided funding to establish FLETA's Office of Accreditation as well as the development of standards and an accreditation process for federal law enforcement training.

> The standards for FLETA Accreditation were established by a core group of training professionals from Federal agencies and approved by the FLETA Board of Directors in March of 2005. On September 8, 2005, the Federal Law Enforcement Training Accreditation (FLETA) Board of Directors granted its first accreditation certifications to the US Department of Energy National Training Center's (NTC's) Basic Security Police Officer Training Program (BSPOT) and to the US Department of State, Bureau of Diplomatic Security, Office of Training and Performance Support.
>
> *(FLETA, 2005)*

The following year the FLETA Board awarded accreditation to the Air Force Special Investigations Academy (AF-SIA) and to the FLETC's two-week "Law Enforcement Instructor Training Program." The accreditation of the AF-SIA for OSI special agents marked the first Defense Department law enforcement school to receive federal accreditation (FLETA, 2006).

Federal Law Enforcement Training Accreditation Board

The year 2022 marked the 20th anniversary of the establishment of the independent FLETA Board program. Its establishment represented the culmination of the work of a task force expressly formed to research a model for the accreditation of federal law enforcement academies and training courses. The Commission on Accreditation for Law Enforcement Agencies, Inc. (CALEA) proved to be a good example. In order to implement the accreditation process a board of directors was selected and an "Office of Accreditation" (OA) was created to help with the administration of the first set of FLETA standards and procedures. The FLETA Board comprises 27 senior law enforcement and training professionals from federal and independent agencies or organizations. Beginning in 2002, the FLETA Board was tasked with development of a set of standards for federal law enforcement training as well as the administration of an accreditation process for all federal law enforcement training (FLETA, 2021). Lists of all current and past members of the FLETA Board are posted online at: https://www.fleta.gov/board-of-directors. The work of this board is probably unknown to most Americans, but the FLETA process was created to instill public confidence in federal law enforcement through compliance with its standards. There are five steps to the FLETA accreditation process: application; applicant preparation, FLETA assessment, FLETA accreditation; and reaccreditation. An accredited academy or program must be reaccredited every five years using the current standards and process. In addition, during the five years, agencies are required to submit annual reports (FLETA, 2021, p. 26). "The FLETA standards are the direct result of a committee process involving representatives from numerous federal law enforcement training organizations. The standards do not supersede training organizations' responsibilities to comply with all applicable federal laws, regulations, and other governances. The standards describe 'what' the applicant must accomplish. The academy or training organization determines 'how' to meet the standard. Applicants are expected to work under properly approved administrative controls and guidelines and must follow their own written guidance. The Standards Steering Committee (SSC) reviews the standards regularly and conducts a comprehensive review of the standards and procedures every five years" (FLETA, 2021, p. 5).

Federal Law Enforcement Training in Retrospect

For the most part, the reforms suggested in the last chapter of this book are not easily applicable to federal law enforcement agencies. This is because the reframing ideas focus more on the community level of enforcement and local problems. Thus, the authors have recommended the establishment of a decentralized police training program at the community precinct level in order to help address some of the critical problems generated by incidents in which police officers have used overly aggressive arrest tactics or engaged in outright misconduct at the local level. Such training emphasizes the importance of community involvement and collaboration.

However, the training programs of most of the federal law enforcement agencies have been developed out of concern for national security and, in many cases, have an international scope. On the other hand, a great deal of the frontline work of federal LEOs and agents center on people in transit. Such work is quite labor intensive, involving cultural sensitivity, concern for human welfare, the ability to be understood, and a high level of alertness. These skills cannot neatly be characterized as representing the "traditional styles of policing" known as "reactive" or "proactive."[12] The training of federal officers and agents must utilize a comprehensive approach to address an ever-expanding list of federal crimes as well as being focused on officer protection and responding to crimes after they are encountered or reported. Significantly, the vast majority of federal law enforcement agents do not have a stable list of community resources to draw upon but must rely on whatever is at hand near their units and outposts.

Moreover, federal law enforcement training efforts, by necessity, must center attention on highly technical matters and crimes that cross state borders. This is a matter of special importance to those agents performing criminal investigations, obtaining warrants, conducting surveillance, wiretapping, and clandestine operations. Examples of specific federal crimes abound, including: tax evasion; wire fraud; money laundering; taking bribes in violation of the federal *Anti-Kickback Act*; foreign travel to engage in illicit sexual conduct with minors; identity theft; and firearms trafficking. The *Anti-Kickback Act of 1986*, 41 U.S.C. § 51 et seq., prohibits attempted as well as completed "kickbacks," which include any money, fees, commission, credit, gift, gratuity, thing of value, or compensation of any kind involving the award of any government contract.

Oftentimes several federal agencies are involved in an investigation involving perpetrators of federal crimes. For example, in 2022, one defendant was sentenced to nearly four years in federal prison for illegally trafficking guns to St. Lucia, a sovereign island nation in the West Indies, despite his not having a license to deal in firearms or a license to export. The case was investigated by: the US Department of Commerce, Office of Export Enforcement, New York Field Office; the Bureau of Alcohol, Tobacco, Firearms, and Explosives; and the Federal Bureau of Investigation (US Attorney's Office, 2022a). In addition, federal cases, such as interstate drug distribution conspiracies, can involve several federal, state, and local police agencies. For example, also in 2022, one successfully investigated case of drug trafficking was carried out by an Organized Crime Drug Enforcement Task Force (OCDETF), whose members were assisted by: the Maryland State Police, U.S. Postal Inspection Service (USPIS), Drug Enforcement Administration (DEA), and the Los Angeles Police Department (US Attorney's Office, 2022b). These types of task forces seek to identify, disrupt, and dismantle the highest-level criminal organizations that threaten the United States using a prosecutor-led, intelligence-driven, multi-agency approach. Additional information about the OCDETF Program can be found at https://www.justice.gov/OCDETF.

Another significant example of interagency cooperation among law enforcement agencies was the establishment of the Task Force Klepto Capture by the US Department of Justice in March 2022. Its role involved enforcing the sweeping sanctions, export restrictions, and economic countermeasures that the United States had imposed, along with allies and partners, in response to Russia's unprovoked military invasion of Ukraine. The new task force comprised interagency LEOs from the FBI, Marshals Service, IRS, Postal Inspection, Homeland Security Investigations and Secret Service (Macias & Schwartz, 2022).

The Establishment of a National Volunteer Training Institute

Community involvement in federal law enforcement activities is possible. Everyday citizens may keep abreast of new federal crime statutes and adhere to them. They can also contribute by volunteering to assist as actors in training scenarios; responding to federal jury notices; serving on agency selection and promotion boards; staying informed about national commission studies and agency reports in order to caste informed votes for federal officials; and cooperating in federal investigations.

Several roles for community participation in aspects of federal law enforcement are rather basic examples of ordinary or everyday citizen responsibilities. As such, they require no new initiatives by any federal agency. In contrast, Congress could mandate the establishment of an institute for the express training of volunteer police at one or more of the existing sites where LEOs are currently being trained. In 2020, the Centers for Disease Control and Prevention (CDC) reported that from 1999 to 2019, nearly 500,000 people died from an overdose involving any opioid, including prescription and illicit opioids (CDC, 2020). Significantly, the volunteers could receive specialized "train the trainer" style courses so that these volunteers could return to their communities and pass on the knowledge they receive on various topics, such as learning how opioid abuse affects communities across the nation and the proper use of naloxone, a life-saving medication that can reverse an overdose.[13] If naloxone can be administered in time, it may be possible to save lives due to heroin, fentanyl, and the like overdoses (CDC, 2022).

Civilian training could take place at any of the existing federal training centers, such as at the Marine Corps Base in Quantico, VA and the training campuses established by the

FLETC in: Glynco, Georgia; Charleston, South Carolina; Artesia, New Mexico; and Cheltenham, Maryland. FLETC's facilities are known for their flexibility; namely, the availability of spaces that can be converted and rearranged to mimic a variety of scenarios as public safety threats. Individuals who have demonstrated their leadership of local volunteer police units should be eligible to attend advanced courses at the FBI National Academy.[14]

Presently, eligibility to participate in FLETC training programs extends to over 90 different federal agencies; state, local, tribal law enforcement; ILEAs; and even private sector corporate employees provided they have a federal sponsor and meet other criteria (DHS, 2022a). These eligibility options do not automatically extend to part-time volunteer police unit members and any training programs that might be available for non-partnering federal agency employees is based on a space-available and self-paid basis. Course and instructor fees, in such instances, need to be covered by the agency or student. Moreover, private sector agencies requesting such training must have the endorsement of a federal law enforcement agency such as the FBI, the U.S. Marshals Service, U.S. Secret Service, or the Internal Revenue Service Criminal Investigations Division, etc., stating that the applicant's training would be mutually beneficial to the agency and the applicant (DHS, 2022b). These burdens can be bypassed if legislation was adopted by Congress to establish the recommended institute. The quality of volunteer police education and training is just as important as that which is provided to full-time LEOs. There is no reason, except for the need for adequate training, to discourage volunteer police from effectively advocating for violence reduction, serving in child welfare capacities, and rendering assistance to victims of crime and substance abuse.

Given Russia's unprovoked attack on Ukraine in 2022 and Russia's threats regarding nuclear war should other nations intervene, a new "Cold War" atmosphere may be in the process of developing. In case of emergencies from natural or manmade causes, home front units will be needed to preserve communities. Training opportunities are vitally necessary to ensure that patrols of neighborhoods or industrial complexes are properly carried out. After the attack on America on September 11, 2001, many people asked, "But what can I do?" More than ever before, community involvement is changing as people take more interest in their communities and are willing to assist their neighbors. However, the productive use of citizen volunteers for homeland security needs federal support. It is a terrific waste of resources if the hundreds of courses available through FLETC are restricted only to paid employees. Moreover, such an institute for volunteer training should be invaluable for discerning the full potential of the volunteer police movement in the United States.

Throughout the United States, there are voluntary and community-based: auxiliary and reserve police units; citizen patrols; search and rescue units; CERT units, mounted posses; Law Enforcement Explorer Posts; local, state, and federal Citizen Police Academy Alumni associations; volunteer and unsworn police administrative aide units; etc. A new volunteer training institute at the federal level could help determine through carefully designed studies how such volunteers can best contribute to greater public safety and make recommendations for their future roles. In particular, such an institute can examine how citizen participation in the field of law enforcement affects the practices and development of community policing, human rights, and the rule of law. Oftentimes, in the field of public safety, the stakes are high since a life or lives will depend upon the initial performance of first responders.

The establishment of a volunteer policing training institute will do much to create community leaders who can more effectively engage with the problems of crime and society's responses. Law enforcement should be best considered as "a collaborative and complex undertaking that requires an investment in meaningful engagement" (Hutchins, 2021).

According to the Rev. Markel Hutchins, president and CEO of MovementForward, Inc. and the One Congregation One Precinct (OneCOP) initiative, "Americans must have searching and difficult conversations about policing. Only 28 percent of Black Americans believe the police treat all races equally and only 40 percent have a favorable view of law enforcement. The cost of this discord between residents, particularly Black men, and police are feelings of alienation, oppression, and an unwillingness to report crimes. If we are to create a safe and inclusive nation, all Americans must lean into our shared humanity by creating substantial nonenforcement interactions with law enforcement. We must create platforms for meaningful engagements that reduce our shared biases. This means dialogues and forums, social opportunities, outreach, and conversations" (Hutchins, 2021).

Notes

1 The *Act* specified in its wording that the agreements between a covered federal law enforcement agency and the Metropolitan Police Department shall include the following subjects: (1) sending personnel of the agency on patrol in areas of the District of Columbia which immediately surround the area of the agency's jurisdiction, and granting personnel of the agency the power to arrest in such areas; (2) sharing and donating equipment and supplies with the Metropolitan Police Department; (3) operating on shared radio frequencies with the Metropolitan Police Department; (4) permitting personnel of the agency to carry out processing and papering of suspects they arrest in the District of Columbia; and (5) such other items as the agency and the Metropolitan Police Department may agree to include in the agreement (see: H.R.1538 - District of Columbia Police Coordination Act of 1997;105th Congress 1997–1998).

2 The other federal agencies in 2016 with more than 1,000 full-time federal LEOs were the Bureau of Alcohol, Tobacco, Firearms, and Explosives with 2,675 officers; the US Postal Inspection Service with 1,891 officers; the US Capitol Police with 1,773 officers; the Bureau of Diplomatic Security with 1,215 officers; and National Park Service Rangers with 1,119 officers (Brooks et al., 2019, p. 7).

3 Two online videos provide histories of the US Postal Inspective Service (USPIS). A 9-minute video involves a tour of a USPIS exhibit at the National Postal Museum in Washington, DC. It is available at: https://www.youtube.com/watch?v=A0rXi2o3uVU. A longer 21-minute video on the history of the US Postal Inspection Service is also available. This video presents a 246-year timeline, the USPIS having dated its existence to the date of August 7, 1775. There is one excerpt from this fascinating video about an "historical factoid you probably didn't know. In 1963 postal inspector Harry Holmes interviewed Lee Harvey Oswald about the mail-order rifle used to assassinate President John F. Kennedy. Minutes later Oswald was gunned down by Jack Ruby." The video along with its full transcript are accessible at: https://www.uspis.gov/about/history-of-uspis.

4 According to 18 U.S. Code § 1385 - Use of Army and Air Force as posse comitatus, the Posse Comitatus Act consists of just one sentence: "Whoever, except in cases and under circumstances expressly authorized by the Constitution or Act of Congress, willfully uses any part of the Army or the Air Force as a posse comitatus or otherwise to execute the laws shall be fined under this title or imprisoned not more than two years, or both." Joseph Nunn, who is an expert counsel in the Brennan Center for Justice and the author of the Brennan Center report "Martial Law in the United States" (2020), has provided a brief overview of the meaning and importance of this statute in question and answer format. For example, he notes that not all federal military personnel are covered. "While the Posse Comitatus Act refers only to the Army and Air Force, a different statute extends the same rule to the Navy and Marine Corps. The Coast Guard, though part of the federal armed forces, has express statutory authority to perform law enforcement and is not bound by the Posse Comitatus Act. Members of the National Guard are rarely covered by the Posse Comitatus Act because they usually report to their state or territory's governor. That means they are free to participate in law enforcement if doing so is consistent with state law. However, when Guard personnel are called into federal service, or "federalized, " they become part of the federal armed forces, which means they are bound by the Posse Comitatus Act until they are returned to state control" (Nunn, 2021).

5 In 2000, the NTSB undertook a significant initiative to increase employee technical skills and investigative expertise available to the transportation community by establishing the NTSB Academy.

The George Washington University's Virginia campus was selected as the Academy's home. The NTSB took occupancy of the new facility in August 2003. On October 1, 2006, the name of the NTSB Academy was changed to the NTSB Training Center to better reflect the internal training mission of the facility (NTSB, 2022).

6 It is important to point out that sub-standard D.3 of the "Quality Standards for College/University Criminal Justice/Criminology Master's Degree Programs" adopted by the Academy of Criminal Justice Sciences (ACJS) Executive Board on May 2, 2005, plainly states that: "Only credit from institutions that are accredited by their regional higher education accrediting body is accepted for transfer into a graduate criminal justice program and only on a strictly limited basis. No more than six hours of acceptable transfer credit are awarded at the Master's degree level. There are no waivers of credit. No academic credit for criminal justice courses counting in the degree program is awarded by the criminal justice/criminology program for life experience or for military, police academy, or other professional training, except for internship and service learning courses that originated from accredited academic institutions rather than a training academy, the military, or continuing education credits." A similar standard applies to both associate and baccalaureate degree criminal justice/criminology programs. All current academic standards of the ACJS are available at: https://www.acjs.org/page/ProgramStandards.

7 There are seven basic eligibility requirements for applying to be an FBI special agent: (1) US citizenship; (2) be between 23 and 36 years of age; (3) have a bachelor's degree or higher from a US accredited college or university; (4) have at least two years of full-time professional work experience; (5) have a valid driver's license and six months of driving experience; (6) meet the physical requirements; and (7) must be able to obtain a "Top Secret SCI Clearance" (FBI, 2022d, p. 12). In addition, there are a number of immediate "employment disqualifiers," such as currently having a federally funded student loan in default and/or failure to file income tax returns (FBI, 2022d, p. 9). For the full list of these disqualifiers and other essential information applicants need to know, see the 26-page "Special Agent Selection System" guide available online at: https://www.fbijobs.gov/sites/default/files/how-to-apply.pdf.

8 The US Holocaust Memorial Museum (USHMM) "engages with law enforcement at the federal, state, and local level to learn about the role of police in Nazi Germany and to reflect on their role in a democratic society today. . . . During the Holocaust, the police were central figures not just in maintaining public order but also in combating so-called racial enemies of the Nazi state. They also played a key role in the concentration, deportation, and murder of Jews in Nazi-controlled Europe. . . . [The] Law Enforcement and Society: Lessons of the Holocaust (LEAS)is presented in partnership with the Anti-Defamation League. Established in 1999 at the request of DC Metropolitan Police Department, the program is suitable for recruit, in-service, and command professionals in law enforcement at the federal, state, and local levels. To date, this innovative program has reached more than 150,000 officers from the US and 80 countries worldwide" (USHMM, 2022). The St. Louis Kaplan Feldman Holocaust Museum was one of the first institutions to pilot the program and it is regularly held at the museum to emphasize the importance society places on law enforcement as our nation's first line of defense to insure that the constitutional rights of everyone are protected. For additional details, see: https://stlholocaustmuseum.org/about-us/programs/law-enforcement-society/.

9 For more than a half century, ACE has evaluated educational experiences offered in various settings. Their published online guide contains the ACE recommendations. Search the ACE National Guide for other courses using the keyword "Law Enforcement" at: https://www.acenet.edu/national-guide/Pages/default.aspx. There you will find ten courses which were previously offered through FLETC which have recommended college credits. The Transportation Security Administration (TSA) has ten current courses with credit recommendations.

10 "The Department of State is the lead agency for the ILEAs. However, the DOJ, DHS, and Treasury along with foreign counterparts implement ILEA training programs. These academies were initially established in 1995 by President Clinton to strengthen the global community in order to combat international drug tracking, transnational criminal organizations, and terrorist networks. The U.S. initiated this effort and over the years has developed five ILEA Academies: Europe (Budapest), Africa (Gaborone), Central America and South America (San Salvador), Asia (Bangkok), and a Regional Training Center in North America located in Roswell, New Mexico" (Traina, 2020, p. 53).

11 James (Jim) V. Cotter, came to CALEA in 1980 as the first Executive Director. He "is credited with having the foresight and diplomatic skills to form the coalitions that developed the standards,

bylaws, and procedures that evolved into the current Commission on Accreditation for Law Enforcement Agencies, Inc. Mr. Cotter died in December 2008" (CALEA, 2022).

12 "The three cornerstones of traditional policing are preventive patrol, rapid response, and investigations. Police have three opportunities to impact crime. First, they can prevent it from happening through deterrence, usually by their mere presence in a neighborhood. Second, when they respond to a call of a crime in progress, they can intervene and stop the criminal activity, such as in a case of domestic violence. Lastly, the police can solve the crime after it has occurred through investigations" (SAGE Publications, Inc., 2021, p. 7). Moreover, "traditional policing can separate police departments from the communities they serve. Departments that use more traditional policing also tend to be more reactive and can create a disconnect with the community" (Gibbs, 2022).

13 "Naloxone is a medication approved by the Food and Drug Administration (FDA) designed to rapidly reverse opioid overdose. It is an opioid antagonist—meaning that it binds to opioid receptors and can reverse and block the effects of other opioids, such as heroin, morphine, and oxycodone. Administered when a patient is showing signs of opioid overdose, naloxone is a temporary treatment and its effects do not last long. Therefore, it is critical to obtain medical intervention as soon as possible after administering/receiving naloxone. The medication can be given by intranasal spray (into the nose), intramuscular (into the muscle), subcutaneous (under the skin), or intravenous injection" (SAMHSA, 2022).

14 For example, FBI field offices provide public speakers on a limited basis on a variety of topics pertaining to the Bureau's investigative mission. All requests for speakers must be submitted online a minimum of four weeks prior to the presentation date. Requests are subject to availability. The FBI also offers, on occasion, a Collegiate Academy-Teen Academy, a Citizens Academy, a Leadership Award, a Child ID App, and programs that promote cyber citizenship and drug abuse prevention (FBI, 2022g). The FBI has over 1,000 video items (many quite short) posted at: https://www.fbi.gov/news/videos. There are also dozens of podcasts to listen to. One of special interest is entitled: "The FBI Turns 113: A Brief History." It can be heard at: https://www.fbi.gov/news/podcasts/inside-the-fbi-the-fbi-turns-113-072621. The podcast provides a short story of how a friendship built on a shared passion for civil service helped birth the Federal Bureau of Investigation. A full transcript of each program is posted online.

References

ACE. (2022). *ACE national guide: On-the-job training (OJT) program: Checkpoint.* Retrieved March 8, 2022, from https://www.acenet.edu/National- Guide/Pages/Course.aspx?org=Transportation+Security+Administration&cid=a8062773- 6549-eb11-a813-000d3a33232a

Attanasio, C., & Spagats, E. (2021, September 18). *US border patrol hires civilians to free up agents for field.* Retrieved February 22, 2022, from https://apnews.com/article/business-health-texas-immigration-coronavirus-pandemic-b6915d675bf5adff78aae38d92c4c6ec

Army.com. (2022). *CBP announces new CBP border patrol academy.* Retrieved March 23, 2022, from http://armyreal.com/blog/item/2098

Behsudi, A. (2020). *Tourism-dependent economies are among those harmed the most by the pandemic.* Retrieved March 28, 2022, from https://www.imf.org/external/pubs/ft/fandd/2020/12/impact-of-the-pandemic-on-tourism- behsudi.htm

Brooks, C., Whyde, A., & Mueller, S. (2019, October). *Federal law enforcement officers, 2016 statistical tables.* U.S. Department of Justice, Office of Justice Programs, Bureau of Justice Statistics. https://bjs.ojp.gov/content/pub/pdf/fleo16st.pdf

CAFLE. (1998). *Hearings: A notice by the commission on the advancement of federal law enforcement on 05/08/19981998.* https://www.federalregister.gov/documents/1998/05/08/98-12273/hearings

CALEA. (2022). *James V. Cotter award.* Retrieved March 12, 2022, from https://calea.org/es/node/12389

CBP. (2011). *National Boarders College to be training, educational crossroad for CBP.* Retrieved May 20, 2023, from https://www.cbp.gov/newsroom/national-media-release/new-global-borders-college-be-training-educational-crossroad-cbp

CBP. (2019). *Timeline: April 30, 1789 - February 2019.* Retrieved March 23, 2022, from https://www.cbp.gov/about/history/timeline

CBP. (2020a, October 28). *What is the CBP field operations academy?* Retrieved March 13, 2022, from https://help.cbp.gov/s/article/Article-1023?language=en_US
CBP. (2020b). *Border patrol history*. Last modified: July 21, 2020. Retrieved February 22, 2022, from https://www.cbp.gov/border-security/along-us-borders/history
CBP. (2021, April 27). *CBP border patrol academy*. Retrieved March 23, 2022, from https://help.cbp.gov/s/article/Article-1017?language=en_US
CBP. (2022a). *The field operations academy: What to expect*. Retrieved March 8, 2022, from https://www.cbp.gov/careers/cbpo-basic-training-academy
CBP. (2022b). *About CBP*. Retrieved March 13, 2022, from https://www.cbp.gov/about
CBP. (2022c). *CBP through the years*. Last modified: May 5, 2021. Retrieved March 20, 2022, from https://www.cbp.gov/about/history
CBP. (2022d, March 18). *United States citizens rescued from sinking vessel*. Retrieved March 21, 2022, from https://www.cbp.gov/newsroom/local-media-release/united-states-citizens-rescued- sinking-vessel
CBP. (2022e, January). *Snapshot: A summary of CBP facts and figures*. Retrieved March 28, 2022, from https://www.cbp.gov/sites/default/files/assets/documents/2022-Feb/CBP- Snapshot-20220103.pdf
CDC. (2020). *Drug overdose: Understanding the epidemic*. Retrieved March 6, 2022, from https://www.cdc.gov/drugoverdose/epidemic/index.html
CDC. (2022). *Opioids: Reverse overdose to prevent death*. Retrieved March 6, 2022, from https://www.cdc.gov/opioids/overdoseprevention/reverse-od.html
Comey, J. B. (2015, April 16). Why I require FBI agents to visit the Holocaust Museum. *The Washington Post*. Retrieved March 4, 2022, from https://www.washingtonpost.com/opinions/the-scariest-lesson-of-the- holocaust/2015/04/16/ffa8e23c-e468-11e4-905f-cc896d379a32_story.html
DHS. (2022a). *Learn about law enforcement training opportunities*. Retrieved March 3, 2022, from https://www.dhs.gov/learn-about-law-enforcement-training-opportunities
DHS. (2022b). *FLETC Registration: Private sector registration*. Retrieved March 3, 2022, from https://www.fletc.gov/registration
DMACC. (2022). *TSA homeland security certificate program*. Retrieved March 3, 2022, from https://www.dmacc.edu/tsa/Pages/welcome.aspx
Duncan, I. (2021, April 28). The TSA wanted 6,000 new officers by summer. Most positions are unfilled as airlines expect a passenger surge. *The Washington Post*. Retrieved February 21, 2022, from https://www.washingtonpost.com/transportation/2021/04/28/tsa-hiring/
FAA. (2022a). *National security programs and incident response*. Retrieved February 26, 2022, from https://www.faa.gov/about/office_org/headquarters_offices/ash/ash_programs/investigati ons
FAA. (2022b). *A brief history of the FAA*. Retrieved February 21, 2022, from https://www.faa.gov/about/history/brief_history
FBI. (2015, July 29). *National Academy: Training law enforcement partners for 80 Years*. Retrieved February 27, 2022, from https://www.fbi.gov/news/stories/national-academy-training-law-enforcement-partners-for-80-years
FBI. (2019, March 13). *National September 11 memorial & museum visit added to FBI agent and analyst training*. Retrieved March 4, 2022, from https://www.fbi.gov/news/stories/911-memorial-visit-added-to-agent-and-analyst- training-031319
FBI. (2022a). *National academy*. Retrieved February 23, 2022, from https://www.fbi.gov/services/training-academy/national-academy
FBI. (2022b). *History: Timeline*. Retrieved February 14, 2022, from https://www.fbi.gov/history/timeline
FBI. (2022c). *New agent training*. Retrieved February 28, 2022, from https://www.fbi.gov/ser vices/training-academy/new-agent-training
FBI. (2022d). *FBI jobs: Special agent selection system*. Retrieved February 28, 2022, from https://www.fbijobs.gov/sites/default/files/how-to-apply.pdf
FBI. (2022e). *Working at FBI: The academy*. Retrieved February 28, 2022, from https://www.fbijobs.gov/working-at-FBI/academy
FBI. (2022f). *Intelligence analyst training*. Retrieved February 28, 2022, from https://www.fbi.gov/services/training-academy/intelligence-analyst-training

FBI. (2022g). *Community outreach*. Retrieved March 7, 2022, from https://www.fbi.gov/contact- us/field-offices/albany/community-outreach
FBINAA. (2022a). *About us: Leadership*. Retrieved February 27, 2022, from https://www.fbinaa.org/FBINAA/About_Us/Leadership/FBINAA/NationalBoard.aspx?hkey=9e6d448b-8dd0-434b-95aa-0dbc2b844e8a
FBINAA. (2022b). *Youth leadership program (YLP)*. Retrieved February 28, 2022, from https://www.fbinaa.org/FBINAA/Training/Youth_Leadership_Program.aspx
FLETA. (2005, September 8). *Federal law enforcement training accreditation (FLETA) board of directors grant academy accreditation status*. Retrieved March 13, 2022, from https://www.fleta.gov/press-release/2014/05/29/federal-law-enforcement-training-accreditation-fleta-board-directors-grant
FLETA. (2006, July 4). *FLETA Board announces more accreditations*. Retrieved March 13, 2022, from https://www.fleta.gov/press-release/2014/03/27/fleta-board-announces-more- accreditations
FLETA. (2021). *FLETA procedures and standards (2020 edition)*. Retrieved March 11, 2022, from https://www.fleta.gov/sites/default/files/FLETA%20Procedures%20and%20Standards%2 0Manual%202020%20Edition%20Published%201-1-2021.pdf
FLETC. (2015, June 2). *FLETC hosts first private/public partnership academy*. Retrieved February 27, 2022, from https://www.fletc.gov/press-release/fletc-hosts-first- privatepublic-partnership-academy
FLETC. (2022a). *FLETC history*. Retrieved February 27, 2022, from https://www.fletc.gov/site- page/fletc-history
FLETC. (2022b). *Uniformed police training program*. Retrieved February 27, 2022, from https://www.fletc.gov/uniformed-police-training-program
FLETC. (2022c). *Artesia, New Mexico*. Retrieved March 31, 2022, from https://www.fletc.gov/artesia-new-mexico
Furst, J. (2020, June 25). *Top five advantages of online first aid training*. Retrieved March 7, 2022, from https://www.firstaidforfree.com/top-five-advantages-of-online-first-aid- training/
GAO. (2018, July). *Aviation security: Basic training program for transportation security officers would benefit from performance goals and measures*. Retrieved March 7, 2022, from https://www.gao.gov/products/gao-18-552
Gibbs, N. (2022). *Community policing vs. traditional policing*. Retrieved March 5, 2022, from https://movementforward.org/community-policing-vs-traditional-policing/
Gillet, R. (2016, August 25). *'You're at war': I went inside the new TSA academy, where officers learn to detect bombs, spot weapons, and find out why failure isn't an option*. Retrieved March 7, 2022, from https://www.businessinsider.com/tsa-academy-airport- security-training-2016-8
Hermann, P., Davies, E., Clement, S., & Guskin, E. (2022, February 25). 3 in 10 District residents do not feel safe in their neighborhoods, post poll finds. *The Washington Post*. https://www.washingtonpost.com/dc-md-va/2022/02/25/police-poll-violence-dc/
Holcombe, R. G. (1996). The growth of the federal government in the 1920s. *Cato Journal*, *16*(2), 175–199.
Hutchins, M. (2021, December 29). *A path forward in policing in 2022*. Retrieved March 5, 2022, from https://insidesources.com/a-path-forward-in-policing/
Hyland, S. S., & Davis, E. (2019, October). *Local police departments, 2016: Personnel*. U.S. Department of Justice, Office of Justice Programs, Bureau of Justice Statistics. https://bjs.ojp.gov/content/pub/pdf/lpd16p.pdf
IACP. (2018). *The types of law enforcement agencies*. Retrieved February 20, 2022, from https://www.discoverpolicing.org/explore-the-field/types-of-law-enforcement-agencies/
Lipson, M. (1975). *On guard: The business of private security*. Quadrangle.
Macias, A., & Schwartz, B. (2022, March 2). *Biden administration launches new 'KleptoCapture' task force to go after Russian oligarchs*. Retrieved March 6, 2022, from https://www.cnbc.com/2022/03/02/biden-administration-launches-new-task-force-to-go- after-crimes-of-russian-oligarchs.html
McCraw, T. K. (1984). *Prophets of regulation*. Belknap.
NLEOMF. (2022, January 11). *2021 was deadliest year for law enforcement officers in history*. Retrieved February 27, 2022, from https://nleomf.org/2021-deadliest-year-for-law- enforcement/

NTSB. (2022). *History of the national transportation safety board*. Retrieved February 26, 2022, from https://www.ntsb.gov/about/history/Pages/default.aspx

Nunn, J. (2021, October 14). *The posse comitatus act explained*. Retrieved February 20, 2022, from https://www.brennancenter.org/our-work/research-reports/posse-comitatus-act- explained

Olson, R. E. (2012, April). The history of the development of the US customs administration and its influence on the development of the country. *Customs Scientific Journal CUSTOMS*, 1, 114–128. http://www.wcoomd.org/-/media/wco/public/global/pdf/topics/capacity-building/resources/scientific- journal/scientific-journal_1_2012.pdf

Potter, G. (2013, June 25). *The history of policing in the United States, part 1*. Retrieved February 14, 2022, from https://ekuonline.eku.edu/blog/police-studies/the-history-of-policing-in-the-united-states-part-1/

SAGE Publications, Inc. (2021). *Chapter 1: Community policing and community issues*. Retrieved March 5, 2022, from https://us.sagepub.com/sites/default/files/upm- assets/114427_book_item_114427.pdf

SAMHSA. (2022). *What is naloxone?* Retrieved March 31, 2022, from https://www.samhsa.gov/medication-assisted-treatment/medications-counseling-related- conditions/naloxone

Schafer, J. A., & Jarvis, J. P. (2017). The landscape of police education and training 2037. *The Police Chief*, *84*(10), 56 & 58. https://www.policechiefmagazine.org/wp- content/uploads/PoliceChief_October-2017_F_LR.pdf

Schmeckebier, L. F. (1924). *The customs service: Its history, activities and organization*. The John Hopkins Press. Copyright by the Institute for Government Research. https://www.google.com/books/edition/The_Customs_Service/wUIiAQAAIAAJ

Tiffin. (2022). *Tiffin University: FBI national academy transfer credit*. Retrieved February 28, 2022, from https://go.tiffin.edu/fbi-national-academy-transfer-credit/

Traina III, D. J. (2013, December). *Advancing U.S. foreign policy through homeland security: The logic for international training and professional exchanges* (M.A. Thesis in Security Studies). Naval Postgraduate School. Retrieved March 28, 2022, from https://apps.dtic.mil/sti/pdfs/ADA620493.pdf

TSA. (2021, May 19). *TSA canine training center*. Retrieved March 11, 2022, from https://www.tsa.gov/news/press/factsheets/tsa-canine-training-center

TSA. (2022a). *Training*. Retrieved March 7, 2022, from https://jobs.tsa.gov/transport-security- officer

TSA. (2022b). *Leadership and organization*. Retrieved March 7, 2022, from https://www.tsa.gov/about/tsa-leadership

US Attorney's Office. (2022a, March 1). US Attorney's Office, Eastern District of Pennsylvania: Bucks County man sentenced to nearly four years for trafficking firearms to St. Lucia. *US Department of Justice, Press Release*. Retrieved March 2, 2022, from https://www.justice.gov/usao- edpa/pr/bucks- county-man-sentenced-nearly-four-years- trafficking-firearms-st-lucia

US Attorney's Office. (2022b, March 1). US Attorney's Office, District of Maryland: Hanover man sentenced to 15 years in federal prison for distribution of fentanyl, cocaine, and marijuana shipped through the mail from California to Maryland. *US Department of Justice, Press Release*. Retrieved March 2, 2022, from https://www.justice.gov/usao-md/pr/hanover-man-sentenced-15-years-federal-prison- distribution-fentanyl-cocaine-and-marijuana

US Courts. (2017, March 30). *Probation and pretrial officers train at state-of-the-art facility*. Retrieved March 8, 2022, from https://www.uscourts.gov/news/2017/03/30/probation-and-pretrial-officers-train-state-art-facility

US Dept. of Interior. (2022). *U.S. Indian police academy - Bureau of Indian affairs - Office of justice services*. Retrieved March 8, 2022, from https://www.fletc.gov/site-page/us-indian-police-academy-bureau-indian-affairs-office-justice-services

US Marshals. (2022a). *History: Oldest federal law enforcement agency*. Retrieved February 14, 2022, from https://www.usmarshals.gov/history/oldest.htm

US Marshals. (2022b). *Training academy*. Retrieved March 4, 2022, from https://www.usmarshals.gov/careers/trainingacademy.html

US Senate Hearing. (2001). *Report of the commission on the advancement of federal law enforcement: Hearing before the subcommittee on criminal justice oversight of the committee on the judiciary, US Senate, 106th Congress, 2nd Session, February 3, 2000, Serial No. J-106–63*. US Gov't. Printing Office. https://www.govinfo.gov/content/pkg/CHRG-106shrg72524/pdf/CHRG-106shrg72524.pdf

US Treasury. (1970). *Annual report of the secretary of the treasury on the state of the finances for the fiscal year ended June 30, 1970*. US Gov't. Printing Office.

USCG. (2021a). *The coast guard: America's oldest maritime defenders*. Retrieved February 21, 2022, from https://www.gocoastguard.com/about-the-coast-guard/learn-the-history

USCG. (2022a). *Maritime law enforcement academy*. Retrieved March 8, 2022, from https://www.forcecom.uscg.mil/Our-Organization/FORCECOM-UNITS/MLEA/

USCG. (2022b). *Maritime enforcement specialist "A' school*. Retrieved March 8, 2022, from https://www.forcecom.uscg.mil/Our-Organization/FORCECOM-UNITS/MLEA/ME/

USCG. (2022c). *Basic boarding officer course*. Retrieved March 8, 2022, from https://www.forcecom.uscg.mil/Our-Organization/FORCECOM-UNITS/MLEA/Course-Offerings/Boarding-Officer-Course/

USCG. (2022d). *Non-compliant vessel pursuit*. Retrieved March 8, 2022, from https://www.forcecom.uscg.mil/Our-Organization/FORCECOM-UNITS/MLEA/Non- Compliant-Vessel-Pursuit-Course/

USCG. (2022e). *American council on education: MLE Academy courses with current A.C.E. military programs evaluations*. Retrieved March 8, 2022, from https://www.forcecom.uscg.mil/Our-Organization/FORCECOM- UNITS/MLEA/Accreditation/American-Council-on-Education/

USCP. (2021). *After the attack: The future of the U.S. capitol police*. Retrieved March 9, 2022, from https://www.uscp.gov/media-center/press-releases/after-attack-future-us-capitol- police

USCP. (2022a). *Our history*. Retrieved March 9, 2022, from https://www.uscp.gov/the-department/our-history

USCP. (2022b). *USCP fast facts*. Retrieved March 9, 2022, from https://www.uscp.gov/media-center/uscp-fast-facts

USCP. (2022c). *Police officer academy training*. Retrieved March 9, 2022, from https://www.uscp.gov/police-officer-academy-training

USDHS. (2016, September). *Government owned training centers: Pre-decisional*. Retrieved March 11, 2022, from https://www.dhs.gov/sites/default/files/publications/FLETC%20Presidential%20Transitio n%20Records.pdf

USDHSICE. (2008). *Immigration and customs enforcement academy, DRO division, revised April 2008, basic immigration law enforcement training program*. Retrieved March 21, 2022, from https://www.ice.gov/doclib/about/offices/ero/pdf/ice_d_handbook.pdf

USDHSICE. (2011). *FLETC opens $2.5M state-of-the-art ICE academy classroom complex*. Retrieved March 21, 2022, from https://content.govdelivery.com/accounts/USDHSICE/bulletins/11f337

USHMM. (2022) *Outreach programs: Law enforcement*. Retrieved March 4, 2022, from https://www.ushmm.org/outreach-programs/law-enforcement

USPIS. (2022). *History of the U.S. Postal inspection service*. Retrieved February 20, 2022, from https://www.uspis.gov/about/history-of-uspis

USPS. (2018). *Who do I call for USPS law enforcement?* Retrieved February 20, 2022, from https://faq.usps.com/s/article/Who-Do-I-Call-for-USPS-Law-Enforcement

Weiser, K. (2020). *Legends of America: History of the FBI*. Retrieved March 1, 2022, from https://www.legendsofamerica.com/20th-fbi/

Wright Jr., R. K. (1992). *Military police*. Defense Dept., U.S. Army, Center of Military History. Retrieved February 13, 2022, from https://history.army.mil/html/books/060/60-9-1/index.html

Yurkevich, V. (2018, August 11). *Training to be a Border Patrol agent in the age of Trump*. Retrieved March 23, 2022, from https://edition.cnn.com/2018/08/11/us/border-patrol-academy-agents-trnd/index.html

4

PRE-SERVICE, PRE-EMPLOYMENT, AND COLLEGE-BASED ACADEMIES

In 1829, one of the 12 basic principles of the new police force created by Sir Robert Peel in London concerned the importance of "securing and training of proper persons" (Germann et al., 1977, p. 62).[1] "In recent years, as cellphones and other cameras have become ubiquitous, Americans from all backgrounds have become aware of complaints of excessive force by police, particularly against people of color. And some departments have paid out millions of dollars in settlements to people because of such complaints" (Martin et al., 2017). The availability of new communication and data storage technology may have, in fact, spawned a new era in the history of policing—an "Era of Information" (see Hooper, 2014). Although former St. Louis Police Chief Daniel Isom has noted that "chiefs don't really have the mechanisms to hold officers accountable for repeat violations of abuse. And . . . it's also very difficult to get rid of officers who are exhibiting behaviors that we don't want officers to have" (qtd. in Martin et al., 2017), a lot of the new technology, such as citizen held cellphone cameras and police body cameras have begun to play an important role in obtaining police accountability. There are occasions where one or more officers, for whatever reason, lose their sense of control as happened in the murder of George Floyd and the beating of Rodney King. At such times, as taught in many academies, there is a responsibility and a duty for other officers to immediately intervene.

Today, almost 200 years after the introduction of Peel's police, many police officers are still having "problems with poor image, low status, and limited training, while at the same time they [were being] asked to perform the most skilled, important, and dangerous police work" (Wrobleski & Hess, 1979, p. 489). "Few persons would deny that police officers have a very difficult and demanding job, not to mention the danger involved. They go out, every day, into a world where they face suspects and crimes. They place themselves in harm's way in the name of protecting the lives and property of the people in their respective jurisdictions. It is an extremely stressful job, and exposes them to many situations where they could lose their lives or justly or mistakenly take someone else's life" (Greenberg, 2021, p. 204). In the United States, about 18,000 police departments and more than 660 state and local law enforcement academies provide basic training to police officer recruits (BJS, 2013). The police officer's job has become more difficult over the years and the multiplicity

DOI: 10.4324/9781003307396-6

of training facilities and agencies appears to have increased the complexity of the police role. According to Chuck Wexler, executive director of the PERF, "It's always hard to get consistency. But that is a responsibility. . . . And that's just another failure" (qtd. in Martin et al., 2017).

On the other hand, according to Austin Police Chief Joseph Chacon, it is also important to continually remind police officers that "when they're out there and they're doing their job, they need to concentrate on that and not on any false narrative there might be about how policing is just absolutely broken. Can we do things better? Certainly. But there's many things that I think that we do very well" (qtd. in Pelley, 2021). Moreover, there is some evidence that the concentration in police training based on a "stress model" is giving way to a format that is less stressful. An example of a new approach to recruiting instruction is taking place in the state of Washington under the direction of former King County Sheriff Sue Rahr, who now heads the state's Criminal Justice Training Commission. Rahr served 33 years with the King County Sheriff's Office, the last seven as the elected sheriff. She "has pioneered an academy-training approach centered on a vision of police as guardians, not warriors. Rahr calls her training method 'LEED,' for 'Listen and Explain with Equity and Dignity.' Instead of an emphasis on yelling and standing at attention, her recruits are trained to engage others in courteous conversation, and are evaluated during role-play exercises on their ability to listen, show empathy, explain their actions, de-escalate tense situations, and leave everyone they encounter 'with their dignity intact' " (Brooks, 2020; see also Rahr & Rice, 2015, pp. 3, 7–11).

According to Rosa Brooks, a law professor at Georgetown University and a former US Defense Department official as well as a four-year veteran of the volunteer police reserve corps in Washington, DC, "the nation is now debating how to 'fix' American policing, and much of the criticism of current police practices relates to the paramilitary aspects of policing. It's an important critique, but one that often focuses narrowly on police uniforms, weapons, and equipment, rather than on underlying issues of organizational culture and structure. If we want to change policing, we need to also turn the spotlight onto police academies, where new recruits are first inculcated into the folkways of their profession" (Brooks, 2020).

This chapter explores the characteristics of pre-service, pre-employment, and college-based police training programs in the United States. Pre-service police academies are those police training institutions that provide basic training to students who have already been hired by their agencies and are therefore on that agency's payroll, and the cost of the training is paid by the employing agency. In the state of Kansas all regional police academy recruits must be sponsored by a police agency (Wilburn, 2021). By state law in Kansas, the police academy is a "closed enrollment" academy for providing basic law enforcement training. Police academy recruits that attend the academy must first be employed by their agencies, and they are then sent to a regional academy to receive their basic training (Wilburn, 2021; see also JCCC, 2021). Pre-employment academies provide basic police training for individuals who have not yet been hired by any police agency, and the cost of the police training is borne by the individual. In some instances, as a cost-savings measure, pre-service academies will reserve some spaces for pre-employment students. Such a combined program is frequently found in college-based police training programs. According to a 2013 study by the Bureau of Justice Statistics (BJS), nearly half (46%) of training academies that provided basic training in the United States were based at an educational institution (BJS, 2013).

The college-based academy is typically located on or near the campus of the co-sponsoring college and oftentimes includes a college credit optional benefit. Such an academy is the Johnson County Regional Police Academy located in Overland Park, Kansas, on the west side of the campus of Johnson County Community College (JCCC) (JCCC, 2021). In some states, the completion of a basic police academy has been included in the curriculum for an associate's degree at the host campus; one such program option is offered at North Central State College (NCSC) in Ohio (NCSC, 2021). The provision of college credits for police academy attendance may depend upon an agreement between the host campus and the academy training program. This has occurred because of the growth of criminal justice-related college degree programs and the competition among colleges for students. For example, students who successfully complete a Florida state-certified police academy are eligible to receive 15 college credits from Broward College (Broward College, 2021). Moreover, students who have successfully completed training at the Philadelphia Police Academy can earn up to 57 credits in Peirce College's Criminal Justice degree program (Peirce College, 2021). However, the award of such academic credits for professional training experiences has met with a division of opinion among educators (see Hummer & Byrne, 2021; Schafer & Castellano, 2005). The mixed assortment of training programs has arisen in the United States because the nation's police system is highly decentralized, existing at the local, state, and federal levels. Unlike many countries in the world, in the United States, there is a wide range of facilities and curriculums for the training and education of LEOs.

History of Police Training

Policing in Colonial America was a divided affair involving appointed or elected sheriffs and constables as well as members of the night watch. The constables "often brought in suspects and witnesses to court—frequently for such conduct as working on the Sabbath, cursing in public and failing to pen animals properly" (Sorrell, 2019). The "night watch" first involved volunteers who sought to deter prostitution or gambling but watch participation later became compulsory except that wealthier colonists could pay for a substitute. As early as 1631, watchmen patrolled the streets of Boston at night to protect the public from criminals, wild animals, and fire. In 1658, paid watchmen were hired to replace drafted citizens in what is now the city of New York (Schmalleger, 2001, p. 171). The southern parts of Colonial America relied on slave patrols to supplement these arrangements. Due to inefficiency, the quality of the persons selected for the watch, and the growth of cities, the night watch and a day watch gave way to a more consolidated approach, in part, based on the London police model. The city of Boston is most often cited as having created the first official American police force in 1838 (Sorrell, 2019; City of Boston, 2021). Boston's first police force consisted of six men under the supervision of a City Marshal. The Boston Watch of 120 men continued to operate separately. In 1854, the city replaced its watch organizations with the Boston Police Department. The department was composed of 250 officers. Each appointed officer received a payment of $2 per shift, walked his own beat, and was forbidden to hold outside employment (City of Boston, 2021).

Generally, as summarized by Gary Potter, Emeritus Professor of Criminal Justice and Police Studies, Eastern Kentucky University, the early "American police departments shared two primary characteristics: they were notoriously corrupt and flagrantly brutal. . . . Police systematically took payoffs to allow illegal drinking, gambling, and prostitution. Police organized professional criminals, like thieves and pickpockets, trading immunity for bribes or information. They actively participated in vote-buying and ballot-box-stuffing. Loyal political operatives became police officers. They had no discernible qualifications for policing and little if any training in policing" (Potter, 2013a). "By the end of 19th century municipal police departments were firmly entrenched in the day-to-day political affairs of big-city political machines—the primary modality through which crime was organized in urban areas" (Potter, 2013b). In time, reform-minded police commissioners and chiefs sought to lessen the hold of politicians, and particularly ward leaders on police officers. "Among the reforms instituted within police organizations were the establishment of selection standards, training for new recruits, placing police under civil service, and awarding promotion as a result of testing procedures" (Potter, 2013c). By the 1990s, new trends in law enforcement had come to prominence including community policing; a new emphasis on science and technology, particularly related to citizen surveillance; and the spread of paramilitary units, such as SWAT. However, the more recent trends are likely "to replay the failures of history as the policies of the future" according to Potter (Potter, 2013d).

In 1908 the first police academy was opened in Berkeley, California, when August Vollmer realized that many officers lacked the skills necessary to solve crimes (Oliver, 2013, p. 8). But it took another 50 years for there to be statewide standards for the training of newly appointed police officers. New York became the first state in the nation to accomplish this by creating the Municipal Police Training Council (MPTC) in 1959. For the greater part of the 20th century, the emphasis on police training has not been on academic work but rather on physical training and experience. After the 1960s, the usefulness of a college education began to emerge as one of the most valuable assets a police officer can have, especially if there was an interest in promotion and advancement (Armstrong & Polk, 2002). In 1943, August Vollmer had predicted that

> Regardless of the opinion of the many police executives today, college level police training is on its way and nothing that they or any other group might do can stop it . . . college trained police officials will be the rule rather than the exception.
>
> *(qtd. in Oliver, 2013)*

Warren (1999) indicates that it is important for law enforcement agencies to partner with organizations such as colleges and professional organizations in order to ensure a quality training program. He points out that there is also an increased need for training that is focused on police ethics, cultural diversity, and methods of stress adaptation. After the widespread media coverage involving the physical abuse of Rodney King and other high-profile incidents of police violence, some training academies have added a selection of topics dealing with cooperative interaction with the public. "But that movement was blunted after the terrorist attacks on the World Trade Center and the Pentagon in 2001" (Kindy, 2015). In its place, there arose an enhanced interest in domestic security, also known as "homeland security" (Oliver, 2006).

During the ensuing years, the issue of police training has arisen after each incident of the police use of excessive force (Kindy, 2015). In April 2015, Sue Rahr, a former sheriff and the current executive director of the Washington State Criminal Justice Training Commission, co-authored with Stephen K. Rice a 14-page paper entitled "From Warriors to Guardians:

Recommitting American Police Culture to Democratic Ideals." It was published by Harvard University's Kennedy School of Government with funding support from the National Institute of Justice, US Department of Justice. The report warned that too many academies are training police officers to go to war with the very people they have been sworn to protect (Rahr & Rice, 2015, p. 1). Both the President's Task Force on 21st Century Policing and the PERF have endorsed this sentiment (see Kindy, 2015). But according to Alexis Artwohl, a former police psychologist and consultant to the International Law Enforcement Educators and Trainers Association, "in a cop's world it's kill or be killed" (qtd. in Kindy, 2015). Rahr and Rice (2015), appear to recognize this cliché, when they state: "Don't misunderstand—we are not advocating a reduction in tactical training or equipment. Officer safety is critical, and we must maintain vigorous instruction on physical control tactics and weapons. Those skills will always be necessary for dealing with individuals who refuse to comply and present an immediate threat. But we need to significantly increase the level of training and importance placed on communication skills and human behavioral science if we truly care about the safety of our officers" (p. 5). Samuel Walker, a national expert on police training, believes that "the two approaches have long been present in American policing," and the final resolution over which style of training (i.e., creating a culture of warriors or a culture of guardians) should dominate remains uncertain (Kindy, 2015).

In the United Kingdom, due to economic conditions, there has been a shifting of some police training responsibilities from the police service to colleges and universities as well as recommendations to do a lot more in this regard (Neyroud, 2011). It is a way of shifting the cost of training onto individuals rather than the government. However, "this trend is in full swing in many U.S. states, where individuals pay their own way to attend the basic police academy and then go in search of police employment" (Cordner & Shain, 2011, p. 282). At some college campuses, this training takes place in a separate facility or in a section of a building somewhat removed from the academic department. College credits may be offered for the completion of the academy, but it is usually for elective credits that may be applied for a current or future degree.[2]

Basic police academies exist throughout the United States, mostly at the regional and state levels of government for newly qualified members of municipal, county, and state law enforcement agencies. These academies are the typical entry point for police who have been recruited through their state's civil service system. They are too numerous to describe here, but details about several police training systems are discussed below, including the states of Maine, New York, and New Jersey. These states also have a variety of different types of pre-employment police training programs. While all jurisdictions now provide their own or have access to regional basic training academies, the development of each state's police training system has followed its own unique path. Various key aspects of the history of police training in each of these states are presented. In particular, police training in Maine illustrates the linear development of one state's training program. Another type of police training program involves combining college education and tuition assistance, salaried civilian police work, police academy attendance, and police officer certification. New York City adopted this type of "cadet program" in 1985, and its first students were enrolled by 1986. The first cohort of 133 cadets was hired in June of 1986 and a second cohort of 140 Cadets was hired a year later (Pate & Hamilton, 1991, p. 23). The program is still functioning.

Maine

After New York State provided a model for statewide standards, other states adopted similar mandates. In some cases, the availability of federal funds accelerated the process. Thus, the development of police training programs with a governing body on the state level is of fairly recent origin. The origin of organized law enforcement training in Maine dates back to the late 1960s. Title 25, Chapter 342, §2801 of the laws of the State of Maine states:

> The purpose of the Maine Criminal Justice Academy is to provide a central training facility for criminal justice personnel. The academy shall promote the highest levels of professional law enforcement performance and facilitate coordination and cooperation between various criminal justice agencies.

A brief look at Maine's early history as well as the history of the origin of the Maine Criminal Justice Academy illustrates the long road traveled and milestones reached to arrive at the present-day status of police training in Maine. In 1622, Sir Fernando Gorges (1565–1647) along with Captain John Mason were granted ownership of land, to be called the Province of Maine, by the Great Council of New England.[2] In 1629, Mason and Gorges divided their property. Mason took the land west of the Piscataqua River and named it New Hampshire. Later, Sir Fernando Gorges was granted exclusive rights to Maine in 1639 by King Charles. However, after his death in 1647, the British parliament declared his grant invalid, contributing to a period of confusion regarding landownership in the province, and the growing Massachusetts Bay Colony eventually claimed jurisdiction over Maine and purchased proprietary rights from Gorges' heirs in 1677. From these early times, the origins of the name Maine or Mayne have been obscure (Celebrating Maine's Bicentennial, 2021). The present government of the State of Maine was organized in 1820 upon the general political principles of the Commonwealth of Massachusetts. On March 3, 1820, the Congress of the United States passed an act that completed the separation and declared Maine to be an independent state. In 1827, after seven years of heated debate, the State legislature agreed that Augusta would be its capital city. Through the years, there have been periods of reorganization and expansion to meet the increased demands upon the state's governing agencies (Maine Human Resources, 2013, p. 3).

By the end of the 1960s, the availability of federal funding helped Maine to establish its state level governing body to systemize police training. The funding source was the Federal Law Enforcement Assistance Agency. The funds enabled the Maine Municipal Association to initiate a two-week law enforcement training program offered in the Portland, Augusta, and Bangor regions. A Board of Directors, consisting of law enforcement officials, was charged with overseeing the program and encouraging law enforcement agencies to support the training. In 1994, two citizen positions to the Board were added, bringing the Board membership to 17 members (Maine.gov, 2021a).

The early 1970s saw passage of Maine's Mandatory Training Act to ensure that no person could serve as a LEO without meeting minimal training standards. The new law required the Board of Trustees of the Maine Criminal Justice Academy to establish standards for training for municipal and county LEOs. In 1972 the former Thomas College in Waterville was purchased to provide permanent facilities for the Maine Criminal Justice Academy (MCJA) (Maine.gov, 2021a). The mandate called for officers to attend a basic course within the first year of employment. Since that time, the scope of activities at the Academy has steadily increased. In 1976 the program was expanded from ten to 12 weeks. In 1990 a survey was conducted that identified over 800 police tasks, equipment, and physical activities. It was distributed to personnel from different local police and sheriff departments. Line personnel reviewed each item and indicated how frequently, if at all, they performed each task. Supervisors rated each task in terms of its importance and when it should be learned. The responses were analyzed to ascertain the essential skills and knowledge that should be known prior to certification as a full-time police officer. Maine's "Law Enforcement Officer's Certification Examination" was instituted based on the various critical tasks identified in this study (Maine.gov, 2021c).

New legislation passed in 1990 required that all LEOs at all levels of government (state, county and municipal) with the power of arrest and the authority to carry a firearm, be regulated by the Academy's Board of Trustees. This has greatly increased the responsibilities and tasks of the Academy. The Academy is responsible for the development and implementation of comprehensive training programs both at the Academy and through outreach programs across the state (Maine.gov, 2021a). In the same year, the state purchased the Oak-Grove Coburn School complex, which is located north of Augusta on Route 201 in the town of Vassalboro. The site consists of over 105 acres with a main facility complex suitable for a new training site. In 1998, the Legislature appropriated over $11 million to renovate the former Oak-Grove Coburn School and build a specialized training facility. In 2000, the Legislature appropriated an additional $2 million to complete Phase II of the project. The move from Waterville to Vassalboro occurred on December 22, 2000. Construction was completed in the spring of 2001. The mission of the new facility is to support Academy training and educational functions in an effective, economical, and safe manner. The new facility has: an indoor running track; a fully equipped weight/exercise room; a lecture hall to seat 75 students; 8 additional classrooms seating up to 70 students; extensive meeting space; housing for up to 130 students; and on-site dining facilities (Maine.gov, 2021b).

In 1995, the Board of Trustees established minimum physical fitness and academic standards for all officers entering the Municipal/County Basic Police School. A report from the Board to the legislature was submitted recommending the implementation of joint training of Municipal/County and all state LEOs. In 2001, a new joint training curriculum was approved by the Board of Trustees for all LEOs. This new curriculum, which expanded the Municipal/County Basic Police School from 12 to 18 weeks, is known as the Basic Law Enforcement Training Program and was implemented in June of 2001 (Maine.gov, 2021a). The revised course is continually reviewed and updated to include the latest skills and knowledge needed by LEOs. Each of the employing police agencies pays the tuition costs for their newly hired police recruits attending the basic school. Only on a very rare occasion will a cadet be self-sponsored in this program (Desjardins, 2021).

A wide range of curriculum changes took place during the1980s including: a revised Municipal/County Basic Police School curriculum; a new course for operating emergency vehicles; training for part-time and reserve police officers as mandated by the Legislature; and the development of a standardized LEOs Manual. Other new curriculums and certification programs developed and initiated during this decade included: basic training for public safety dispatchers; Advanced Arson Investigation; Domestic Violence; Radar Operator; Specialized Instructor Certification (e.g., firearms, DARE—Drug Abuse Resistance Education); Intermediate and Advanced Officer Certification; Intoxilyzer Operator Certification; and a municipal ordinance prosecutor's course. In 2001, the Municipal/County Basic Police School, Maine State Police Academy and the State Law Enforcement Basic School were combined into one 18-week Basic Law Enforcement Training Program (Maine.gov, 2021a). This Basic (18-week) Law Enforcement Training Program is held twice a year at the Maine Criminal Justice Academy in Vassalboro (Maine.gov, 2021b).

Today, the mission of the Maine Criminal Justice Academy centers on the training and certification to Maine's law enforcement and corrections officers. The Academy provides basic law enforcement and corrections training to all newly hired officers, specialized in-service training programs at the Academy in Vassalboro and support to the regional training councils. With respect to becoming a certified LEO in Maine, the Academy offers two types of programs—an 18-week residential "Basic Law Enforcement Training Program" and a "Law Enforcement Pre-Service Course" (LEPS). Only full-time LEOs who are employed in a law enforcement capacity or a person making an application to and being accepted as a tuition student can attend the Basic Law Enforcement Training Program (BLETP). The LEPS course provides the least amount of education needed in the state of Maine to carry a firearm on duty and to have powers of arrest as either a part-time or full-time LEO. The present Basic Program consists of 720 hours of training. In addition, various in-service courses are offered throughout the year for LEOs. In 2021, the Academy added a mandatory two-hour continuing education course dedicated to de-escalation techniques with carefully planned scenarios. In scenario-based training, actors are brought in and officers must assess a staged call and how it can be defused and solved through de-escalation tactics. According to Rick Desjardins, the Academy's director, communication training is intertwined in all academy training. De-escalation Desjardins said, "is at the core of what we do when we're interacting with people, is to try to resolve problems, with the least restrictive means possible" (qtd. in O'Brien, 2021).

Completion of the residential 18-week Basic Law Enforcement Training Program does not guarantee employment as a LEO. It enables graduates to state to prospective law enforcement employers that they have fulfilled the mandatory training requirements of a full time municipal, county or state LEO. Upon employment, graduates are eligible to take the Maine Law Enforcement Officer's Certification Examination. The age and educational qualifications for this Academy course includes being a high school graduate, or having obtained scores as follows on the General Education development Test: not lower than 35 on any one of the 5 parts, and an average not lower than 45 for all five parts. Applicants must be at least 21 years of age unless the applicant has an associate's degree or 60 credit hours of post-secondary education in which case the applicant must be at least 20 years of age (Maine.gov, 2021e; see also Maine State Statute Title 25: 2804-G). The application process for the Basic Law Enforcement Training Program is mandated by the director of the Maine Criminal Justice Academy with the approval of the Board of Trustees. Interested persons apply through a two-stage process. The first stage involves the following four steps: (1) submission of the academy's official application form and personal history statement with a non-refundable $150 application fee; (2) taking a reading and writing examination; (3) successfully passing a physical fitness examination at the 40th percentile level for their age and gender; and (4) being interviewed and recommended to the academy's director in order of their finish. After receiving a conditional offer of acceptance, candidates move to the second stage in the process involving a polygraph examination and three additional screening evaluations: medical fitness; background investigation; and a psychological evaluation. Applicants are responsible for any fees associated with each of these four evaluations. Those individuals meeting the entrance requirements are placed on a roster and accepted into the program on a space available basis. Preference is given to individuals who have been hired as LEOs by a governmental entity (Maine.gov, 2021d).

In 1989, the 114th Maine Legislature passed laws mandating the Board of Trustees of the Maine Criminal Justice Academy to establish standards for pre-service training for certification as a part-time LEO. The Law Enforcement Pre-Service is the required training program for all part-time officers. The purpose of this mandate was to ensure that no person could "serve as a law enforcement officer with the power to make arrests or the authority to carry a firearm until certified as satisfying pre-service training requirements." This resulted in the first Law Enforcement Officer Pre-Service Training Program. For this training course, applicants 19 years of age are eligible to qualify for the program as a courtesy to colleges and universities that offer course credits for this program (Maine.gov, 2021e). The program has been especially designed to accommodate students attending such academic programs and includes completion of an initial set of specific online training modules. Students must be 21 years old, or 20 years old with at least 60 credits from an accredited college, or age 19, currently enrolled in an accredited post-secondary education program, with at least 40 credit hours (Maine.gov, 2021f).

In 2009 the Board of Trustees of the Maine Criminal Justice Academy proposed changes to the Law Enforcement Pre-Service Training Program, updating the existing program to change its format, number of hours required, and adding a supervisory component. The revised curriculum is presented in three phases. In the first phase, students must meet the age and education requirements to apply as well as a 40-hour on-line training program. Students must also complete the MCJA application and pay a $350 fee. At the completion of the Phase I training students need to contact MCJA and take a final exam in Vassalboro. From the Phase I completion date, the student has two years to start Phase II. There is no time limit to complete the Phase I of the training. During Phase II, students must complete an 80-hour interactive, scenario-based classroom program. Prior to the start of Phase II, students must complete another application, requiring an additional fee of $350. All students must also satisfy additional requirements involving reading and writing, medical fitness, background investigation, and physical fitness. Significantly, the classroom-based program is held at several different locations throughout Maine. Phase III involves being hired by a law enforcement agency as a LEO and having a provisional certificate issued upon receipt of an official "MCJA Notice of Employment and a MCJA Firearms Proficiency Form signed by a Certified MCJA Firearms Instructor. The employing agency must provide 80-hours of documented supervision before certification as a Law Enforcement Officer is granted by the Criminal Justice Academy. . . . The part-time law enforcement officer will have one year to complete the 80 hours of supervision. An officer may receive an extension by the MCJA Board in extenuating circumstances" (Maine.gov, 2021f). Course administrators try to maintain an even mix of self-sponsored and agency sponsored cadets (Desjardins, 2021).

A separate and distinct program related to police education is available from the University of Maine at its Augusta Regional Community Policing Institute. The institute was established in 1998. In 2019, under the leadership of Noel C. March, the institute became the Maine Community Policing Institute (MCPI). Noel March is a former police chief and served as the 39th United States Marshal for the District of Maine. The institute provides "education, training, and technical assistance to members of the public and the police who protect them with the goal of creating proactive problem solving to enhance community wellbeing and quality of life through public safety partnerships" Three new certificate programs, Community Policing, Community Corrections, and the Advanced Certificate in Criminal Justice Management, help support the MCPI. "Community policing promotes organizational strategies that create problem-solving partnerships targeting the reduction of crime, fear of crime, and social disorder" (MCPI, 2021). The Certificate in Community Policing is open to all students. Maine Criminal Justice Academy graduates of the Basic Law Enforcement Police Training Program (BLETP) are eligible for 15 transfer credits toward completion of this certificate (MCPI, 2021).

New York State

New York, by virtue of Chapter 446 of the Laws of 1959, became the first state in the nation to establish statewide basic training for newly appointed police officers. This was accomplished through the creation of the Municipal Police Training Council (MPTC). The MPTC was empowered to devise rules and regulations with respect to the content and presentation of required training, including the minimum requirements for conducting a "Basic Course for Police Officers." In this way, the MPTC had responsibility of making recommendations regarding police training schools, instructor qualifications and categories of in-service training. All persons seeking permanent appointment as a municipal police officer (including sheriff's deputies) after July 1, 1960, had to complete the basic course. Basic police training had to be completed within one year from the date of original appointment. In 1965, Chapter 326 gave the MPTC the authority to promulgate regulations establishing, height, weight, and physical fitness requirements for police officer candidates. These standards, which were amended in 1996 to comply with the *Americans with Disabilities Act*, are set forth in the New York State Official Compilation of Codes, Rules, and Regulations (NYCRR). In 1967, Chapter 671 increased the responsibilities of the MPTC by requiring establishment of a course of training for police officers appointed to supervisory positions. Initially, the Basic Course for Police Officers consisted of 80 hours of instruction. By 1971, 285 hours was the requirement. The hours were increased incrementally throughout the 1980s, advancing to 445 hours by 1991. In 2008, the minimum hours of instruction was raised to 639 (DCJS, 2021a).

> The Division of Local Police was created in the Office for Local Government by Chapter 168 of the Laws of 1967. The new Division consisted of staff of the Municipal Police Training Council and the Division for Police Administrative Services. The Division was later renamed the Bureau for Municipal Police (BMP), and more recently, the Office of Public Safety (OPS), and was placed within the Division of Criminal Justice Services by virtue of Chapter 399 of the Laws of 1972. Like its predecessors, OPS today provides assistance to municipal law enforcement agencies. With respect to police training, the statutory design requires the MPTC to be the standard setting and monitoring group, while actual instruction is executed locally. OPS is responsible for the review and approval of basic, supervisory, and in-service training curricula and instructors submitted by municipal law enforcement agencies and training academies. This mechanism ensures that the training meets statutory requirements with respect to curriculum content, instructor qualifications/certification and hours.
>
> *(DCJS, 2021a)*

In New York State, the Division of Criminal Justice Services (DCJS), oversees basic police training as well as a wide range of other courses for criminal justice and private security personnel. All persons seeking permanent appointment as a municipal police officer in the state must complete an approved "Basic Course for Police Officers" as a condition of appointment. In recent years, the DCJS has approved the creation of a number of "Pre-Employment Police Basic Training Courses" primarily located on college campuses throughout the state. The course provides an alternative to the conventional manner of conducting the basic training course and it is completed in two distinct parts (DCJS, 2021b). Significantly, this type of pre-employment training represents an alternative to the conventional basic police training model in New York State. Law enforcement administrators of police departments or sheriff's offices decide what method of basic training best suites their individual needs (DCJS, 2021c). "Pre-Employment Police Basic Training is not a new concept. Thirty-seven other states in the United States conduct it with great success. It relieves law enforcement agencies of the burden and expense of providing Phase I training, but all aspects of regular academy training are essentially the same, except that the student is not a sworn police officer and enters the program as a civilian" (Cazenovia College, 2021).

The first component (Phase I), pre-employment training, includes most of the instructional material in the Basic Course for Police Officers. It may be completed by civilian students as well as appointed police officers. This is a distinct departure from past practices within the state. After appointment, a police officer who has successfully completed the Pre-Employment Police Basic Training Course must complete the second component, which includes at a minimum law enforcement skills and supervised field training. The second component may only be completed by sworn police officers (DCJS, 2021b).

This form of pre-employment police training involves collaboration between a municipality and an accredited college, junior college, or two-year college having an active criminal justice, public safety program, or other similar or equivalent program registered and approved by the New York Department of Education. It provides interested persons with the opportunity to begin preparation for a career as a police officer prior to being hired by a law enforcement agency. Most importantly, as a further benefit, the program may provide law enforcement agencies and municipalities with a diverse pool of trained police officer candidates. Prospective students are required to directly contact one of the 14 approved schools of their choice for enrollment information. Descriptive materials regarding three of these school programs are described below. The list of approved schools may fluctuate from year to year (see DCJS, 2021c).

Anyone who meets the entrance requirements established by state regulations and any further requirements established by the school conducting the program can attend. The minimum entrance requirements for students are US citizenship, or lawful residency, no felony convictions, and either a high school diploma or a General Education Diploma (GED). There is no minimum or maximum age requirement for students. Although, a background investigation is not required, citizenship and possession of a high school diploma (or GED) must be verified by the school. Any determination to conduct student background investigations is solely at the discretion of the school. Students must be provided with a clear written warning notice describing the conditions of this training program, and how those conditions will affect them immediately and, in the future, including the fact that successful completion of the course is not a guarantee of employment as a police officer. It is recommended that students are medically evaluated to determine that they are physically able to safely participate in fitness training and testing (DCJS, 2021c). The warnings emphasize that before being appointed as a police officer, a person must meet various New York State Civil Service Law requirements and appointing agency hiring standards will apply, including minimum and maximum age and residency requirements. Additionally, police officer candidates must take and successfully complete a written examination, a physical fitness examination and a medical examination that may include drug screening. Further, before being appointed as a police officer, a person may be required to submit to a psychological examination and a background investigation. A person with a criminal conviction or with a felony conviction may be disqualified from employment (DCJS, 2021c). Thus, successful completion of the course is not a guarantee of employment as a police officer. Training and the pre-employment training are just one step in the process.

After a student completes the pre-employment trainings course and is appointed as a police officer, further training is still required. This post-appointment component of the basic training requirement will include at minimum, additional law enforcement skills and supervised field training. Law enforcement agencies and academies may add topics and increase the length of post-appointment training to meet their individual needs. Students are informed that the completion of their New York State-approved course may or may not be acceptable in other states. Any such decision to accept basic training to satisfy basic police training requirements in other states is made pursuant to the rules established by such state where a person is seeking appointment as a police officer as well as the law enforcement agency considering that candidate (DCJS, 2021c).

SUNY Potsdam

The State University of New York's (SUNY's) 64 campuses are within commuting distance of virtually all New Yorkers and comprise the nation's largest comprehensive system of public higher education. SUNY is a mix of 29 state-operated campuses and five statutory colleges—including research universities, liberal arts colleges, specialized and technical colleges, health science centers, land-grant colleges—and 30 community colleges. When founded in 1948, the University consolidated 29 state operated but unaffiliated institutions whose varied histories of service date as far back as 1816. SUNY has a total enrollment of nearly 445,000 full-time and part-time students, serving 37% of New York State's higher education student population. SUNY also employs 88,000 faculty and staff and counts more than three million living alumni, residing in New York State and throughout the world (SUNY, 2021a).

SUNY Potsdam is the oldest of the system's 64 campuses. It traces its origins to a one-room schoolhouse when the residents of Potsdam, New York, founded the St. Lawrence Academy in 1816, one of America's first 50 colleges. At its founding, the institution had 42 students and one teacher. Over the next two centuries, the college became a public university, eventually joining the new State University of New York system upon its founding in 1948. Two highlights of the college's development include the time when St. Lawrence Academy officially became Potsdam Normal School and New York State's purchase of the campus lands and buildings in 1867. In 1922, both the general elementary teachers' curriculum and the Normal course were lengthened to three years. In 1938, a law was adopted that elevated all Normal Schools in New York to the status of a college, requiring four years of study, entitling student to a degree. In 1942, another act of the Legislature, converted all

Normal Schools into State Teachers Colleges. In 1948, with the founding of the State University of New York, Potsdam State Teachers College officially becomes the State University of New York College at Potsdam. However, it is not until 1964 that the College first began to offer degrees in the liberal arts (SUNY, 2021b).

The SUNY Potsdam Law Enforcement Training Institute (LETI) has been offered every semester since spring 2017. The first cohort of men and women consisted of 20 students (SUNY Potsdam, 2021b). The program is an approved pre-employment basic police training program involving 485 total contact hours. Students receive 12 upper division credits towards their bachelor's degree upon completion of the course. The Institute's program includes topics in defensive tactics, emergency medical services, emergency vehicle operation; applying field sobriety tests to intoxicated individuals in a controlled setting, processing crime scenes, military drill and ceremony, and other law enforcement training topics. Prospective attendees must have: a minimum of a 2.5 cumulative grade point average (GPA); Junior or Senior status or higher (students may apply in their sophomore year and enroll in the academy in their Junior or Senior year); and pass an interview with the program's director (SUNY Potsdam, 2021b). Students enrolled in the Institute train for ten hours a day, five days a week, as part of a demanding semester-long program. While running their field sobriety tests, students are able to see first-hand how intoxicated subjects' eyes jerk involuntarily while tracking a pen, or how they reacted poorly to standing on one leg and counting out loud. Potsdam's senior Crystal Washington, a double major in criminal justice and sociology, has stated that "the institute expands upon what she has already learned in the classroom. 'This is what I want to do for a career. I want to be a police officer, so it's definitely preparing me for a job and what to expect' " (SUNY Potsdam, 2017).

SUNY Erie

In 2021 SUNY Erie celebrated its 75th anniversary. Over the past seven plus decades, the college has grown from a small two-year technical institute to a three-campus college (City, North, South) serving over 10,000 students (SUNY Erie, 2021a). SUNY Erie is the second largest college in Western New York. The college offers over 90 different degree and certificate options, including eight different programs in public service, safety, and law: Corrections Officer (Certificate); Crime Scene Technology (Certificate); Criminal Justice (Associate in Science); Criminal Justice/Law Enforcement (Associate in Applied Science); Homeland Security (Certificate); Paralegal (Associate in Applied Science); Police Basic Training (Certificate); and Police Science (Associate in Applied Science) (SUNY Erie, 2021b). SUNY Erie is one New York's 30 locally sponsored two-year community colleges offering programs that are directly and immediately job related as well as degree programs that serve as educational experience or a transfer opportunity to a baccalaureate degree at a four-year campus.

In 1946, the Legislature of the State of New York, recognizing the need for technical-vocational education at the junior college level, established the New York State Institute of Applied Arts and Sciences at Buffalo as one of the five, tuition-free, two-year technical institutes for high school graduates. Two years later, in 1948, when the New York State Legislature founded the State University of New York, the Institute at Buffalo became one of the units of the University. In 1953, while maintaining ties with the State University of New York, Erie County assumed sponsorship of the college, changing its name to the Erie County Technical Institute (ECTI). In 1969, the name of the college was once again changed, this time to Erie Community College. In 2017, the college changed its name to SUNY Erie. (SUNY Erie, 2021a).

SUNY Erie's MPTC approved pre-employment Police Basic Training Certificate Program also illustrates how students have the opportunity to complete many aspects of basic police training before being appointed as a police officer in New York. Based on the approach already used in 36 states, SUNY Erie's is another example of one the 14 programs in New York with an approved police academy. Upon successful completion of the program, students are eligible for hiring. If hired by a police agency, students will then need to attend an abbreviated ("Phase II") Police Equivalency Course (six-week course). The academy is held Monday through Friday, from 7 am to 4 pm, for a 20-week session. The Phase I training at SUNY Erie begins each August and January. In this way, it is a concentrated program designed to be completed in one extended semester. In 2021, the basic tuition was about $6,000 and there was an additional cost for books, supplies, uniforms, and equipment (SUNY Erie, 2021c).

According to the 2021–2022, SUNY Erie online catalog, students may receive credit for following courses when enrolled in the college's Police Science AAS Degree major and completing the Phase I Law Enforcement Academy: PB 201 Police Physical Fitness (4 cr.); PB 202 Basic Law for Police (4 cr.); PB 203 Emergency Medical Services/First Responder (3 cr.); PB 204 Police/Community Relations (4 cr.); PB 205 Police Administration of Justice (4 cr.); PB 206 Police Arrest Techniques (4 cr.); PB 207 Police Investigative Procedures (4 cr.); PB 208 Police Patrol Functions (4 cr.); PB 209 Police Traffic Procedures (4cr.); and PB 210 Emergency Vehicle Operations (3 cr.) (SUNY Erie, 2021d).

New Jersey

The Police Training Commission (PTC) staff, under the authority of the state's *Police Training Act*, are responsible for the development and certification of basic training courses for county and local police, sheriffs' officers, state and county investigators, state and county corrections officers, juvenile detention officers, and a number of other law enforcement positions. Several instructor development courses are also under the purview of the PTC. Generally, PTC's certification responsibilities include the certification of training course curricula, instructors, trainees, and academies authorized to conduct anyone of 35 different PTC-certified training courses (PTC, 2021).[3]

In New Jersey, a "Police Officer" means any employee of a law enforcement agency, a correctional agency, or a juvenile justice agency who, by statute, comes under the jurisdiction of the Commission or any member of a fire department or force who is assigned to an arson investigation unit pursuant to public law 1981, Chapter 409. Each year, the Ocean County Police Academy trains more than 300 recruits in various law enforcement disciplines such as Basic Police Officer, Special Police Officer, County Correction Officer and Humane LEO. In addition to basic recruit training, the academy is also host to in-service and specialized law enforcement training programs for newly certified and veteran officers (OCPA, 2021a).

In New Jersey, there are two classifications for "special officers" determined by the general duties to be performed by the officers. "Class One Special Police Officers are authorized to perform routine traffic details, spectator control and other similar duties. If authorized by township ordinance, Class One Officers are empowered to issues summons for disorderly persons and petty disorderly person's offenses, violations of municipal ordinances and violations of Title 39. Class One Officers are not authorized to carry a firearm and [cannot] be assigned to any duty that may require the carrying of a firearm. Class Two Special Police Officers are authorized to exercise full police powers and duties similar to those of a permanent, regularly appointed full-time police officer. Class Two Officers may only carry a firearm while engaged in the actual performance of the officer's official duties and when specifically authorized by the Chief of Police. While not every law enforcement agency utilizes Special Police Officers, many do, especially shore towns during the peak summer months" (OCPA, 2021b). Several community colleges in New Jersey offer special police officer qualification training including Camden County College,[4] Essex County College, and Rowan College of South Jersey, which is affiliated with the Gloucester County Police Academy in Sewell, NJ. At the Essex County Police Academy (ECPA) in Cedar Grove, the Special Officer Class II course consists of over 460 hours of training mandated by the Police Training Commission. This course covers similar material as the basic class. Upon graduation, students will be PTC certified as a Class Two Special LEO (ECPA, 2021).

The Ocean County Police Academy (OCPA) is a law enforcement training academy located in central New Jersey. It is one of 15 law enforcement training academies certified by the New Jersey Police Training Commission. In the late 1950s the police chiefs serving towns throughout Ocean County recognized the need for standardized training for new police officers. Based on this need, an agreement for joint responsibility between the police chiefs and the Ocean County Board of Chosen Freeholders was drawn up. The County Board assumed financial responsibility and the chiefs assumed the responsibility of organizing and staffing the new police academy. By 1960, the Ocean County Police Academy (OCPA) became a reality. The site of the academy is in Ocean County Park at a former carriage house on the estate of oil magnate and philanthropist John D. Rockefeller. The original carriage house was constructed in 1902. It overlooks a nine-hole golf course. It was first used as housing for the estate's gardeners, caretakers, and other employees. The facility later went on to serve as the locker room for the New York Giants baseball team (now the San Francisco Giants) during their spring training from 1943 to 1945. After a six weeks course ending in October of 1961, the first group of 14 officers graduated. The 50th class of the OCPA included 24 officers who attended a 15-week course ending in May of 1988. The 15 recruits in the academy's 100th class graduated in August of 2015, following a 22-week course (OCPA, 2021c). Clearly, this training academy has greatly progressed from a part-time six-week police recruit course to its present organization.

There are three primary ways for becoming a police officer in New Jersey. The first route is the New Jersey Civil Service Commission, which governs the hiring practices of the state government, involving 20 of the 21 counties in the state, and more than 200 towns. In order to be considered for employment in an entry-level law enforcement position, candidates must pass a written exam, the Law Enforcement Examination (LEE). Those who pass the examination remain on an eligibility list for two years. The eligible candidates that result from the LEE are used to fill positions for law enforcement titles in all of the state's Civil Services jurisdictions.

Civil Service requirements include: graduation from high school or vocational high school or possession of an approved high school equivalent certificate; not less than 18 or more than 35 years of age at the announced closing date for filing applications for the position (in determining maximum age eligibility of veterans, the time spent in active military service may be deducted from the attained age); US citizenship; appointees may be required to pass a thorough medical and psychiatric examination to be administered by the appointing authority; and possess a driver's license valid in New Jersey. Additional information can be found at the New Jersey Civil Service Commission website www.state.nj.us/csc/ and specifically in the "Frequently Asked Questions" section (OCPA, 2021b).[5]

The second route for becoming a police officer is making a direct application to a non-civil service town or borough, which are commonly known in New Jersey as the "Chief's Departments." In Ocean County, in particular, there were 14 such agencies at the time of the research for this book. These agencies "can essentially establish their own requirements as their governing body deems appropriate. Some require college and/or military experience, or a combination of both. Most will require a written examination, physical fitness assessment, and an oral interview. Generally speaking, most will require the same age, citizenship, medical and license requirements as the New Jersey Civil Service Commission and the general qualifications defined in N.J.S.A. 40A:14–122" (OCPA, 2021b). General qualifications include such requirements as having the ability to read, write and speak the English language well and intelligently; being of good moral character; not convicted of any criminal offense, and being a resident of the State of New Jersey. Additional information can be found on most of the non-civil service departments' websites (OCPA, 2021b).

The third pathway is known as the "Alternate Route Program." The Alternate Route Program was designed to give individuals interested in becoming police officers, the opportunity to attend a certified police training academy at their own expense, prior to being hired by a police, sheriff's, or campus police department. The Alternate Route candidate trains alongside the regular police recruit and is treated as their equal during training. Although successful completion of the program does not guarantee a candidate a position in law enforcement, the graduates from a certified police academy and are able to pursue employment as a certified police officer for a three-year period from the date of graduation. In accordance with the provisions of *N.J.S.A. 52:17B-69.1,* an Alternate Route candidate is a person who does not hold a probationary or temporary appointment as a police officer, but who is seeking such an appointment. An Alternate Route candidate may enroll in the Basic Course for Police Officers provided upon meeting the general qualifications for a police officer set forth in *N.J.S.A. 40A:14–122*, and such other qualifications as the Commission may deem appropriate; and applies to and is accepted by a Commission approved school for admission to a police-training course (OCPA, 2021b). In addition, Alternate Route applicants must meet the standards required under *N.J.S.A. 52:17B-69.1* (OCPA, 2021b).

It should be noted that the *New Jersey Police Training Act* requires that all persons must receive a probationary or temporary appointment prior to attending the Police Academy. The only exception is those individuals enrolled in the Alternate Route Program (OCPA, 2021b). A critical qualification needed for this third pathway to becoming a police officer in New Jersey is the need for having earned college course credits. The NJ Police Training Commission has established an education standard for Alternate Route police academy applicants, requiring a minimum of 60 college credits earned from a regionally accredited or Middle States accredited college or university, in order to be considered for admission to the Alternate Route Program. In recognition of the contributions and sacrifices made by military veterans, any individual who has served in the military and who is otherwise qualified, but has not earned 60 college credits, may substitute two years of full-time, active duty military service to satisfy the educational requirement. Applicants must supply a copy of their DD214 as proof of military service (OCPA, 2021b).[5]

Applicants for police or related careers discussed in this chapter or any other jurisdiction should carefully review the current state information about the specific selection processes and academy entrance rules for their state's agencies and their academies.

Merger of Training with College Degrees

Most of the police academies previously discussed in this chapter have close affiliations with colleges. In the United States, there are now hundreds of training facilities based on or in some manner affiliated with colleges (BJS, 2013). "The value of post-secondary education for police officers and others working in the justice system has been written about extensively. Going back to the 1967 President's Commission on Law Enforcement and the Administration of Justice's assessment of justice issues during a period of civil unrest, the idea that the quality of policing could be best improved by establishing higher educational requirements is stated clearly. The Police Foundation followed with recommendations for criminal justice programming (mostly targeted to future law enforcement personnel) in U.S. colleges and universities" (Hummer & Byrne, 2021). At that time, the President's Commission (1967) stated "The struggle to maintain a proper balance between effective law enforcement and fairness to individuals pervades the entire criminal justice system. It is particularly crucial and apparent in police work because . . . every police action can impinge directly, and perhaps hurtfully, on a citizen's freedom of action" (p. 93). Such a statement about American justice is applicable just as much today as it was in yesteryear.

During the decades that followed, many college programs in the United States began to offer college credits for police academy attendance and found ways to incorporate these into their degree programs in the field of criminal justice. Thereafter, a variety of such institutions with the support of state laws and regulations began to co-sponsor police academies on their campuses thereby enabling graduates to become eligible for police employment upon graduation. In New York, a program such as at SUNY Potsdam was cited.

New Jersey's "Alternate Route Program" is distinctive because it requires completion of 60 college credits (or appropriate military service) as a prerequisite for admission into its police training academy. Today, many states have adopted regulations authorizing pre-employment police training on college campuses. In turn, the schools have integrated police academy participation into their degree programs and a number of these colleges offer flexible schedules for the completion of their programs. Some additional examples of campus-based programs include: Stark State College in North Canton, OH; Yuba College in Marysville, CA; Santa Rosa Junior College; Alvernia University in Reading, PA; East Texas Baptist University in Marshall, TX; and Niagara University in Lewiston, NY. Several of these are reviewed below.

The Yuba College Administration of Justice program offers academy, degree, and certificate programs designed for entry into law enforcement, corrections, and related fields. Additionally, advanced courses for law enforcement personnel who are already employed are available for professional development and continuing education goals. Courses are offered days, evenings, and weekends to accommodate a wide variety of needs. Yuba College considers itself to be one of the finest providers of law enforcement and corrections training in Northern California (Yuba College, 2021). Yuba College's Law Enforcement

Academy has prepared an 85-page "Rules and Regulations" manual setting forth its policies and procedures for students (see Yuba College, 2018).

Santa Rosa Junior College's (SRJC) police academy program, like the program offered by Yuba College provides two pathways for students to become a California peace officer: modular and intensive. The Academy is certified by the California Commission on Peace Officer Standards and Training (POST). Successful completion of either course serves to make graduates eligible for employment as a police officer or deputy sheriff anywhere in California.

Santa Rosa's Modular Police Academy (MPA) provides students a path to become a California Peace Officer by attending classes on weeknights and Saturdays. The Modular Police Academy format at Santa Rosa Junior College is actually three courses (AJ 222A, AJ 222B, and AJ 222C), which are offered in sequence in one calendar year. The classes meet on Tuesday, Wednesday, and Thursday evenings from 6:30–10:30 pm and Saturdays from 8:00 am to 5:00 pm, totaling 20 hours of training per week. All training takes place at SRJC's Public Safety Training Center in Windsor. This training center has modern facilities including classrooms, gym, indoor firing range, and driver training track. Its full-scale "Scenario Village" provides realistic settings for practice and the assessment of student skills. Each class is mentored by working police officers serving as part-time Recruit Training Officers. Completion of each modular course earns the student a specific level of certification by the California Commission on POST. When all three courses are successfully completed, the student earns the POST Level I Certification (the equivalent of the 20-week Regular Basic Academy) and makes students eligible to work as full-time California Police Officers or Deputy Sheriffs. The MPA format is sometimes referred to as an "extended" or "reserve" academy due to the modular structure (SRJC, 2021a). The basic module is labeled Module III, the intermediate course is labeled Module II, and the final course is Module I. Module III is 195 hours of basic police training where students earn 4.5 college units (PC 832 Arrest & Firearms) and POST Level III Certification. Entry-level topics include ethics, law, evidence, search and seizure, first aid, defensive tactics, and firearms. Module II is 289 hours of training where students earn six college units and POST Level II Certification (or Reserve Level II). Topics include criminal law, arrest, report writing, crimes in progress, community relations, defensive tactics, chemical agents, and firearms. Students must have passed Module III as a prerequisite before taking Module II. Module I is the final and most extensive module where students earn 11 college units. Topics include controlled substances, alcohol and traffic laws, emergency vehicle operations, high-risk vehicle stops, accident and crime scene investigation, domestic violence, communications, lifetime fitness, firearms, and defense tactics. Students must have passed Modules III and II as prerequisites before taking Module I (SRJC, 2021a).

Santa Rosa Junior College's intensive 20-week academy meets from 7 am to 4 pm Monday through Friday in addition to some evenings and weekends. The Academy provides instruction in each of the previously listed modules. As with the modular program option, the intensive course is held at the Public Safety Training Center in Windsor (SRJC, 2021b).

In Pennsylvania, Alvernia University in Reading offers an optional Police Academy certification program for criminal justice majors. When Alvernia's criminal justice four-year degree program was introduced, the discipline of criminal justice as an academic field was emerging on a rather wholesale level throughout the academic world. The process was accelerated in the late 1960s and 1970s due to concerns about rising crime rates, social change, urban unrest, and the availability of significant federal funding for educating both pre-service and in-service peace officers.

Alvernia's criminal justice program was founded in 1974 by the late Sister Mary Pacelli. At the time of the program's initiation, it was part of an assortment of career-related programs seeking to keep pace with the needs of society as well as to ensure the viability of Alvernia College. "At the time, Sister Pacelli was the only woman in the nation to head a college's criminal justice program. In the first year, a large group of male students, mostly police officers who came to be known as 'Pacelli's boys,' joined the forward-thinking program, virtually making the Pennsylvania college co-ed overnight. In 2009, with support of a grant, the criminal justice program received new classroom and lab space, complete with a state-of-the-art interrogation room and lie detector equipment that gives students exposure to situations that they would face in the real world" (CJ Program History, 2018).

By 1999, Alvernia College had established a very creative and advanced approach to providing this type of criminal justice career education. Namely, students could receive not only a baccalaureate degree in four years of study, but also the certification necessary to be appointed a police officer in most jurisdictions throughout the Commonwealth of Pennsylvania. Students with career goals to enter into a police career were now able to pursue the Criminal Justice Program's Law Enforcement Track option and attend the on-campus Reading Police Academy to obtain Municipal Police Officer Certification (ACT 120) in Pennsylvania as part of their four-year degree without extended time or expense. Students apply for the Academy during their junior year. If accepted, such students attend the Academy during the fall semester of their senior year. Upon successfully completing the Academy, they are awarded 15 Alvernia University college credits.

The academy is located on the Alvernia University's campus. The basic training course as prescribed by *Pennsylvania Act 120*, is designed to provide students with the initial skills necessary to begin their police careers. The *Act 120* course is required training for all Pennsylvania municipal police officers. Two types of students attend the academy. The first are newly hired police officers enrolled to satisfy the requirements of *Act 120*. The second are pre-employment students who have not yet been hired by a police department. The pre-employment students are taking the course in the hopes of enhancing their chances of police employment. To be accepted into the academy, applicants must pass physical fitness tests, a criminal background check, and a psychological exam. The course consists of 820 hours and is completed in a 20-week program. The college students start the academy in July and are in training at the Academy until December (Reading Police Academy, 2013).

East Texas Baptist University (ETBU) is located in Marshall, Texas, a city of 25,000, 150 miles east of Dallas. The university is affiliated with the Baptist General Convention of Texas. It is a private, Christian university of liberal arts and sciences. ETBU was founded as the College of Marshall in 1912. It became East Texas Baptist College in 1944. ETBU is accredited by the Southern Association of Colleges and Schools Commission on Colleges to award baccalaureate and master's degrees. Enrollment is approximately 1200 students and more than 85% of full-time faculty members have earned doctorates or terminal degrees (ETBU, 2013a).

At East Texas Baptist University students can complete a four-year university degree and be eligible to test for a Basic Texas Peace Officer's license without the need for additional police academy training. The ETBU program was approved by the Texas Commission on Law Enforcement (TCOLE) in December 2013 to serve as an academic alternative peace officer basic training provider. In the past, students who graduated with either a Bachelor of Science or Bachelor of Arts degree in Criminal Justice from ETBU had to continue their training by attending a certified law enforcement academy elsewhere for licensure. The Criminal Justice program at ETBU had to demonstrate the ability and the commitment to meet all of the standards for law enforcement training and education within the State of Texas. The program was designed to exceed state requirements in several areas, including classroom contact hours, internship requirements, physical fitness, and skills training. Prior to acceptance into the program, students must pass the same background, medical and psychological exams required for any officer entering a department or training program (ETBU, 2013). Students who successfully complete this program are also eligible for part-time paid or unpaid reserve officer appointments.

For several decades, the New York City (NYC) Police Department has had a cadet program for city residents who are college students age 18 or over with at least 45 college credits and a 2.0 GPA. The program provides tuition assistance (up to $20,000), an hourly wage, flexible work hours during the school year, and the cadet-students have the opportunity for full-time summer employment. Cadets who take advantage of this program will not have to re-pay the amount after completing two years of service as a New York City Police Officer. Students must earn a minimum of 12 credits each semester with at least a 2.0 GPA and be enrolled in a four-year degree program at an accredited college within NYC, Nassau, or Westchester counties (NYC.gov, 2021). The NYCPD began recruiting the first group of cadets in the fall of 1985. Forty-four colleges and universities in New York City were determined to be eligible for the program and were contacted by representatives of the police department and informed of the program. In actuality, applications were received from students at 87 schools, several of which were outside of New York City. The most common college majors of the first Cadet Corps Program were criminal justice/police science, business, and social science (Pate & Hamilton, 1991, pp. 27, 29, and 43).

Hummer and Byrne (2021) have stated that "criminal justice education is at an inflection point. A set of factors including changing demographics, technological innovation, a global pandemic, and a pervasive view of systemic bias in the justice system, are compelling the field to re-assess how to best educate both pre- and in-service students." There is surely no place for "cookie-cutter" like curriculums to contend with such a diverse set of ever-changing circumstances; consequently, Hummer and Byrne (2021) conclude that moving forward such "an education will include components of a liberal arts education, practical learning, and work and life experiences that produce justice system actors who look at deviant behavior –and justice-involved individuals– through a broader lens than simple punitiveness or deterrence." While the merging of police training with the curriculums of degree programs at colleges and universities is a trend, caution is recommended since "higher education can be quite an intransigent institution in its own right, so one should not approach it naively when looking for better models for police education and training" (Cordner & Shain, 2011, p. 283).

The interconnectedness of world affairs and travel has offered mankind numerous opportunities to share commerce, governance principles, and technology. For the most part, the Western nations of the world have also participated in a variety of crime control projects of mutual benefit. Cross-cultural initiatives are commonplace among these nations, including many student exchange programs. Educational exchanges have also been routinely conducted with Asian countries and these have often included police representatives. The following chapter explores police education and training in five nations.

Notes

1 Peel's Metropolitan Police force consisted of "some three thousand men, headed by two civilian justices (later called 'commissioners'), and organized like an army, with each superintendent overseeing four inspectors, sixteen sergeants, and a hundred and sixty-five constables, who wore coats and pants of blue with black top hats, each assigned a numbered badge and a baton. Londoners came to call these men 'bobbies,' for Bobby Peel" (Lepore, 2020).
2 The Great Council of New England was "an outgrowth of the Plymouth Company founded in 1606, the . . . Council of New England was a company, created and led by Sir Ferdinando Gorges. It was granted a royal charter in 1620 to found colonies in New England from the 40th parallel to the 48th. The Pilgrims of the Plymouth Colony were given a contract or patent for their land from the Council. The Council was dissolved in 1635" (Council of New England, 2021).
3 In addition, "PTC staff develop operational guidelines to implement applicable training standards, monitor the operation of all PTC certified academies, review all trainee injuries, investigate possible violations of the *Police Training Act* or PTC Rules occurring during authorized training courses, and handle appeals involving challenges to PTC decisions regarding, for example, trainee dismissals from PTC-certified courses, training waivers, and drug screening practices of PTC-certified academies" (PTC, 2021).
4 An 11-minute video talk about the entrance and other requirements for attending the Camden County College Police Academy Alternative Route program can be viewed at: https://www.camdencc.edu/police-academy/police-academy-alternate-route/.
5 A complete listing of the New Jersey Civil Service jurisdictions can be found at www.state.nj.us/csc/about/divisions/slo/jurisdictions.html.

References

Armstrong, D., & Polk, O. E. (2002, September/October). College for cops: The fast track for success. *Journal of the Institute of Justice and International Studies*, *17*(5), 24–26.
BJS. (2013). State and local law enforcement training academies, 2013. *Bureau of Justice Statistics Bulletin*, July 2021. Retrieved November 29, 2021, from https://bjs.ojp.gov/sites/g/files/xyckuh236/files/media/document/slleta13_sum_3.pdf
Brooks, R. (2020, June 10). *Stop training police like they're joining the military*. Retrieved November 28, 2021, from https://www.theatlantic.com/ideas/archive/2020/06/police-academies-paramilitary/612859/
Broward College. (2021). *Note to police academy recruits and graduates*. Retrieved November 28, 2021, from https://www.broward.edu/academics/public-safety/_docs/experlearn-polacad.pdf
Cazenovia College. (2021). *About the program*. Retrieved November 21, 2021, from https://www.cazenovia.edu/academics/adult-and-continuing-education/police- academy/about-program
Celebrating Maine's Bicentennial. (2021). *Celebrating Maine's Bicentennial: A brief history of Maine*. Retrieved November 14, 2021, from https://maineanencyclopedia.com/brief- history-of-maine/
City of Boston. (2021). *Brief history of the Boston police*. Retrieved November 29, 2021, from https://www.boston.gov/departments/police/brief-history-boston-police
CJ Program History. (2018). *Criminal justice program history*. Retrieved May 1, 2018, from http://www.alvernia.edu/academics/professional-programs/criminal-justice/history.html
Cordner, G., & Shain, C. (2011, August). Editorial: The changing landscape of police education and training. *Police Practice & Research*, *12*(4), 281–285.
Council for New England. (2021). *Council for New England*. Retrieved November 15, 2021, from https://penobscotmarinemuseum.org/pbho-1/glossary/council-new-england
DCJS. (2021a). *History of the basic course for police officers*. Retrieved November 15, 2021, from https://www.criminaljustice.ny.gov/ops/training/bcpo/index.htm
DCJS. (2021b). *Pre-employment police basic course*. Retrieved November 3, 2021, from https://www.criminaljustice.ny.gov/ops/training/bcpo/bcpo04.htm
DCJS. (2021c). *Pre-employment police basic course FAQ*. Retrieved November 3, 2021, from https://www.criminaljustice.ny.gov/ops/training/bcpo/bcpo05.htm

Desjardins. (2021, December 2). Personal communication from Richard R. Desjardins, Director, Maine Criminal Justice Academy.

ECPA. (2021). *Basic course for special law enforcement officer class II*. Retrieved November 25, 2021, form https://essexcountypoliceacademy.org/event/basic-course-for-special-law-enforcement-officer-class-ii/

ETBU. (2013). *ETBU gets approval for peace officer training*. Retrieved December 22, 2013, from http://www.marshallnewsmessenger.com/news/etbu-gets-approval-for-peace-officer-training/article_9f2ba857-d034-5122-8d05-78a3f191a1f6.html

ETBU. (2013a). *History*. Retrieved December 22, 2013, from http://www.etbu.edu/about/glance/

Germann, A. C., Day, F. D., & Gallati, R. R. J. (1977). *Introduction to law enforcement and criminal justice, 26th Printing*. Charles C. Thomas Publisher.

Greenberg, M. A. (2021). *Everyone a sheriff: The democratization of crime prevention in America*. Lexington Books.

Hooper, M. K. (2014). Acknowledging existence of a fourth era of policing: The information era. *Journal of Forensic Research and Crime Studies*, *1*, 1–4. Retrieved November 29, 2021, from http://www.jscholaronline.org/articles/JFRC/Acknowledging-Existence-of-a-Fourth-Era-of-Policing-The-Information-Era.pdf

Hummer, D., & Byrne, J. (2021). Rethinking criminal justice education: Applying experience credits towards CJ degree completion—Generates dollars, but does it make sense? *Journal of Criminal Justice Education*, *32*(4), 415–455.

JCCC. (2021). *Johnson county regional police academy*. Retrieved November 29, 2021, from https://www.jccc.edu/academics/credit/police-academy/

Kindy, K. (2015, December 15). *Creating guardians, calming warriors*. Retrieved November 27, 2021, from https://www.washingtonpost.com/sf/investigative/2015/12/10/new-style-of-police-training-aims-to-produce-guardians-not-warriors/

Lepore, J. (2020, July13). *The invention of the police*. Retrieved November 30, 2021, from https://www.newyorker.com/magazine/2020/07/20/the-invention-of-the-police

Maine.gov. (2021a). *History*. Retrieved November 13, 2021, from https://www.maine.gov/dps/mcja/about/history.htm

Maine.gov. (2021b). *About the facility*. Retrieved November 14, 2021, from https://www.maine.gov/dps/mcja/about/about.htm

Maine.gov. (2021c). *Basic law enforcement*. Retrieved November 13, 2021, from https://www.maine.gov/dps/mcja/training/basiclaw/index.htm

Maine.gov. (2021d). *Pre-employment training*. Retrieved November 13, 2021, from https://www.maine.gov/dps/mcja/training/basiclaw/preemployment.htm

Maine.gov. (2021e). *Entrance standards*. Retrieved November 15, 2021, from https://www.maine.gov/dps/mcja/training/basiclaw/standards.htm

Maine.gov. (2021f). *Law enforcement pre-service*. Retrieved November 13, 2021, from https://www.maine.gov/dps/mcja/training/preservice/index.htm

Maine Human Resources. (2013). Maine human resources and administrative and financial services, "state of Maine employee handbook 2013." *Human Resources Documents*. Paper 2. Retrieved November 14, 2021, from http://digitalmaine.com/hr_docs/2

Martin, M., Wexler, C., & Isom, D. (2017, May 30). *How police training has evolved*. Retrieved November 28, 2021, from https://www.npr.org/2020/05/30/866204394/how-police- training-has-evolved

MCPI. (2021). *Maine community policing institute*. Retrieved November 14, 2021, from https://www.uma.edu/academics/programs/justice-studies/mcpi/

NCSC. (2021). *Criminal justice-law enforcement (police academy), AAS*. Retrieved November 29, 2021, from https://ncstatecollege.edu/associate-degrees/criminal-justice-law- enforcement/

Neyroud, P. (2011). *Review of police leadership and training*. Home Office. Retrieved December 23, 2013, from https://www.gov.uk/government/publications/police-leadership- and-training-report-review

NYC.gov. (2021). *Cadet Corps requirements & benefits*. Retrieved December 5, 2021, from https://www1.nyc.gov/site/nypd/careers/cadets/police-cadets-program.page

O'Brien, K. (2021, May 20). Amid heightened concern over police use of force, law enforcement trains to talk. *The Times Record*. Retrieved December 2, 2021, from https://www.pressherald.com/2021/05/20/more-police-training-on-de-escalating-potentially-violent-interactions-needed-in-maine-and-the-nation/

OCPA. (2021a). *Ocean county police academy*. Retrieved November 9, 2021, from http://www.oceancountypoliceacademy.org/

OCPA. (2021b). *How to become a police officer in New Jersey*. Retrieved November 9, 2021, from http://www.oceancountypoliceacademy.org/how-to-become-a-police-officer-in- new-jersey/

OCPA. (2021c). *Academy history*. Retrieved November 9, 2021, from http://www.oceancountypoliceacademy.org/academy-history/

Oliver, W. M. (2013). *The history of the academy of criminal justice sciences (ACJS): Celebrating 50 years, 1963–2013*. Retrieved November 29, 2021, from https://cdn.ymaws.com/www.acjs.org/resource/resmgr/Historian/ACJS50thAnniversaryH istoryBo.pdf

Oliver, W. M. (2006, March). The fourth era of policing: Homeland security. *International Review of Law, Computers & Technology*, *20*(1–2), 49–62.

Pate, A., & Hamilton, E. E. (1991, November 13). *The New York city police cadet corps: Final evaluation report*. Police Foundation. https://www.ojp.gov/pdffiles1/Digitization/133389NCJRS.pdf

Peirce College. (2021). *Law enforcement training*. Retrieved November 29, 2021, from https://www.peirce.edu/pla/law-enforcement-training

Pelley, S. (2021, November 21). *Reimagining police departments with safety and justice in mind*. Retrieved November 29, 2021, from https://www.cbsnews.com/news/police-reform-austin-texas-60-minutes-2021-11-21/

Potter, G. (2013a, July 2). *The history of policing in the United States, part 2*. Retrieved November 28, 2021, from https://ekuonline.eku.edu/blog/police-studies/the-history-of-policing-in-the-united-states-part-2/

Potter, G. (2013b, July 2). *The history of policing in the United States, part 4*. Retrieved November 28, 2021, from https://ekuonline.eku.edu/blog/police-studies/the-history-of- policing-in-the-united-states-part-4/

Potter, G. (2013c, July 2). *The history of policing in the United States, part 5*. Retrieved November 28, 2021, from https://ekuonline.eku.edu/blog/police-studies/the-history-of-policing-in-the-united-states-part-5/

Potter, G. (2013d, July 2). *The history of policing in the United States, part 6*. Retrieved November 28, 2021, from https://ekuonline.eku.edu/blog/police-studies/the-history-of-policing-in-the-united-states-part-6/

President's Commission. (1967). *The challenge of crime in a free society: A report by the president's commission on law enforcement and administration of justice*. U.S. Government Printing Office. https://www.ojp.gov/sites/g/files/xyckuh241/files/archives/ncjrs/42.pdf

PTC. (2021). *Police training commission*. Retrieved November 25, 2021, form https://www.njoag.gov/about/divisions-and-offices/division-of-criminal-justice- home/police-training-commission/

Rahr, S., & Rice, S. K. (2015, April). From warriors to guardians: Recommitting American police culture to democratic ideals. In *New perspectives in policing bulletin* (pp. 1–14). U.S. Department of Justice, National Institute of Justice. Retrieved November 27, 2021, from https://www.ojp.gov/pdffiles1/nij/248654.pdf

Reading Police Academy. (2013). Retrieved December 23, 2013, from http://www.readingpa.gov/content/reading-police-academy

Schafer, J., & Castellano, T. C. (2005). Academe versus academy: Faculty views on awarding academic credit for police training. *Journal of Criminal Justice Education*, *16*(2), 300–317.

Schmalleger, F. (2001). *Criminal justice today: An introductory text for the twenty-first century* (6th ed., Annotated Instructor's edition). Prentice Hall.

Sorrell, R. (2019, April 18). *History of constable system as old as the United States*. Retrieved November 29, 2021, from https://heraldcourier.com/news/history-of-constable-system-as-old-as-the-united-states/article_b902b704–3474–5cec-ab7d-02f7df29e176.html

SRJC. (2021a). *What is modular police academy and how does it work?* Retrieved December 1, 2021, from https://pstc.santarosa.edu/police-academy-modular

SRJC. (2021b). *Police academy –intensive.* Retrieved December 1, 2021, from https://pstc.santarosa.edu/police-academy-intensive

SUNY. (2021a). *History of SUNY.* Retrieved November 22, 2021, from https://www.suny.edu/about/history/

SUNY. (2021b). *Historical resources.* Retrieved November 22, 2021, from https://www.potsdam.edu/about/college-history/historical-resources

SUNY Erie. (2021a). *History and traditions.* Retrieved November 22, 2021, from https://www.ecc.edu/about/history-and-tradition.html

SUNY Erie. (2021b). *Find your program.* Retrieved November 22, 2021, from https://www.ecc.edu/academics/find-your-program.html

SUNY Erie. (2021c). *Police basic training.* Retrieved November 3, 2021, from https://www.ecc.edu/academics/police-basic-training.html

SUNY Erie. (2021d). *Law enforcement academy.* Retrieved November 3, 2021, from https://catalog.ecc.edu/preview_program.php?catoid=25&poid=2741&returnto=1324

SUNY Potsdam. (2021a). *Past cohorts.* Retrieved November 22, 2021, from https://www.potsdam.edu/academics/appliedlearning/law-enforcement-training- institute/past-cohorts

SUNY Potsdam. (2021b). *SUNY Potsdam law enforcement training institute.* Retrieved November 20, 2021, from https://www.potsdam.edu/academics/appliedlearning/law-enforcement-training- institute

SUNY Potsdam. (2017). *SUNY Potsdam's new Law Enforcement Training Institute offers real- world training for students.* Retrieved November 22, 2021, from https://www.potsdam.edu/academics/appliedlearning/law-enforcement-training- institute/suny-potsdams-new-law-enforcement

Warren, G. A. (1999). *Police academy training for 21st century law enforcement.* Delaware Law Enforcement Institute.

Wilburn, S. (2021, November 29). Personal communication from Sonta Wilburn, director of the Johnson County Regional Police Academy.

Wrobleski, H., & Hess, K. (1979). *Introduction to law enforcement and criminal justice.* West Publications.

Yuba College. (2021). *Administration of justice: About our program.* Retrieved December 1, 2021, from https://yc.yccd.edu/publicsafety/home-page/administration-of-justice/

Yuba College. (2018, April). *Yuba college public safety program: Rules and regulations manual.* Retrieved December 1, 2021, from https://yc.yccd.edu/publicsafety/wp- content/uploads/sites/14/2020/04/Rules-Regulations-Revised-April-2018-Most- Current.pdf

5

POLICE EDUCATION ON THE INTERNATIONAL LEVEL

Culture's Influence on Policing

Culture influences every aspect of a society. Social institutions mirror cultural values and norms. Rules that permeate a society reflect a society's culture, highlighting what a society values (Nickerson, 2022). Theories are utilized to establish frameworks for better understanding how culture impacts offending behavior in a nation and theoretical criminology has become a popular academic pursuit.[1] Culture and history intertwine to impact how societal groups are represented (or not represented) within a nation's criminal justice system (Strauss-Hughes et al., 2019). The criminal justice system itself, and thus policing activities, of any nation is largely evolves through culture, providing a society with rules and structures for justice. In the United States, for example, federal agencies, state organizations, and local jurisdictions have vastly different police activities and cultures. Much of the available research looking at cross-national policing activities examines other countries' policing activities with United States as a comparison. The United States has a decentralized policing (and training) model with various (federal, state, local) levels of law enforcement. This structure is not in place universally across the globe, largely due to differences in political and governmental organization. For example, Sweden has a single police force, centralized with federal government oversight. France has multiple forces with different jurisdictions, with some focusing on cities, others focusing on rural areas, and a municipal police force. The United States has over 18,000 total police agencies, which is more than many other first-world nations. Canada has a decentralized model comparable to the organizational levels of the United States but has fewer than 200 agencies. Despite its numerous forces, spending on policing in the United States falls somewhere in the middle range for countries within the Organization for Economic Cooperation and Development (OSCE) (Cheatham & Maizland, 2022).

As national culture is a driving force behind policing on an international level, it is impossible to broadly conceptualize "policing" generally or police training globally. Perceptions of police, histories of policing, and evolution of police training differ dramatically based on the culture and political climate of a nation—and even in different within a single nation.

DOI: 10.4324/9781003307396-7

In the United States, policing can differ based on factors such as geographic location, level of policing, type of police department, and resources available. Further, policing is a highly politicized activity. Political climate (which can drastically change over time and space) influences every aspect of police activity, including training. According to Brewer and colleagues (1996), the cultural components of beliefs, resources, politics, policies, and values of an area influence the connection between politics of a given nation and policing. This connection lies on a spectrum from weak to strong, based on other cultural and geographic factors. External inputs such as the media, public opinions, and historical events further influence the nature of policing in a specific location (Lo, 2016).

The way police view themselves, their profession, and their internal police culture also vary by place and the larger culture of that location. Factors like the widely-accepted police philosophy of a nation, the level of trust by the police of the national populace, and use of media are quite different when explored by position or department, and are drastically between different between countries (Bayerl et al., 2014). While some efforts have been made to categorize police officer "types," much less has been done to generalize police culture more generally across nations. Looking across European countries' police agencies, Bayerl and colleagues (2014) found varying policing perspectives, still with some overlap among nations, highlighting the social and political influence on the profession of policing in an international context.

International Police Structures

Information about international policing and police training is not always readily available to the public. Still, it is important to explore the differences among nations in the areas of law enforcement and beyond (Sullivan & Haberfeld, 2005). In this pursuit, Saferworld (2022) has compiled a document that summarizes issues of decentralization (i.e., local, state, federal in the United States) of police structure for various policing systems around the world: the United Kingdom, Canada, Brazil, India, South Africa, and Japan. The summaries of the policing structures of these nations offer a glimpse into the variation in policing activities across the globe, and how they vary by location and culture. The UK has separate but uniform agencies covering specific geographic locations, with a federalist-like law enforcement structure (though the larger government is structured differently than a federalist society) that gives various responsibilities to police officials in different parts of the system. Canada has a federalist-type system with a decentralized national policing organization and is home to ten province-based agencies with many more departments at the municipal level. Still, Canada has trended toward a more centralized system as the Royal Canadian Mounted Police (a federal agency) does a fair amount of law enforcement at lower levels. In Brazil, a federally structured system, three federal agencies handle law enforcement in communities, on highways, and railways. Each state police agency operates independently. India is home to a federally structured system with a variety of national-level, state-level, and local-level police departments. South Africa has a centralized police system where all levels of policing are handled under one commissioner. Japan's policing is divided among six decentralized, regional police agencies though the National Police Agency promotes standards and offers leadership across the country (Saferworld, 2022).[2] While examples of police training across the world can be found in a wide variety of articles and books, the content often lacks exploration of the essential details of training. And many sources use the United States as the standard for comparison to explore controversial topics such as how many police officers kill civilians; in the United States a relatively high number of civilians are killed each year and the discussion often centers around cultural factors (such as high firearm ownership) alongside of training practices (i.e., Cheatham & Maizland, 2022; Horton, 2021) that lead to those fatal outcomes in the United States. Length of training is another source of comparison of law enforcement practices across nations, and how this training time influences policing outcomes. Estimates for length of training for US police officers vary based on sample, but overall training takes approximately 21 weeks. In European nations, on the other hand, training can take over three years (OSCE, 2018).[3] Scandinavian countries require higher levels of education for new police officers, as compared to the United States where typically only a high school diploma is needed (Cheatham & Maizland, 2022).

The profession of policing parallels socio-political factors, and police training is also largely dictated by cultural elements reflecting the socio-political climate of a nation. This chapter gives broad overviews of five different nations (the UK, the Netherlands, Finland, Kenya, and India) and their police academies, or police training activities, with the acknowledgement of the role that culture plays in policing and, thus, police training. Only a small sample of the global community is discussed here, largely due to the protected nature of what happens in police academies and the limited academic and popular research specifically detailing the topics of training and education. The discussions that follow are not meant to be exhaustive even for the countries explored; the goal is to discuss the spectrum of police academies across the globe rather than analyze, in detail, any one nation. This exploration allows for a snapshot of the variation in police training that exists across the world. It provides substance for a general comparison of different countries' (with varying cultures, governments, and norms) approaches to preparing police officers for duty. Looking at a small sample of nations' police academies provides insight into the spectrum of police training that occurs throughout the world.

Police Training in the UK

The United Kingdom is home to 52 police forces (called constables), which are organized administratively with 43 agencies in England and Wales, eight in Scotland, and one in Northern Ireland. The UK law enforcement structure also includes the Serious Organized Crime Agency (which operates largely independently) and the British Transport Police (who provide law enforcement on the railways) (Organization for Security and Co-Operation in Europe, 2022). The UK's model for police typically requires that training begin after recruits are hired into a police agency (Belur et al., 2020). Potential recruits have the option to train to work with special police forces (British Transport Police, Civil Nuclear Constabulary, Ministry of Defense Police, and National Police Air Service). Most individuals entering police service in the UK have a college degree, are working toward a degree, or are part of an apprenticeship program (Higgenbothem, 2022). These three paths have been advanced by professional agencies seeking to better professionalize law enforcement across the UK (Belur et al., 2020).

England and Wales have experienced massive shifts in their philosophies of policing and police training in recent years, with the goal of increased professionalism (Belur et al., 2020). The new millennium has brought an increase in the popularity of "neighborhood policing" (evolving from a community policing model) in the UK, alongside calls for evidence-based practices and promoting the importance of ethical practices in the field (Ramshaw & Soppitt, 2018). A series of investigations and reports on how best to handle police training has resulted in modified entry requirements with a larger focus on higher education for police, now allowing for the three separate entry points (as mentioned above). Findings and recommendations have suggested that police training and education should connect more closely with universities. Proponents suggest that modeling future police training should be similar to nurse and teacher training programs that partner directly and deliberately with institutions of higher education (White, 2012). As policing has changed from primarily crime-fighting to a more all-encompassing social service role, training is being redesigned to better help new officers reconstruct and align with the identity of the larger police profession to build better community-police relationships. Studies of this transition have highlighted potential challenges to bridging the academic and practitioner communities in the fields of policing. Nonetheless, forward momentum to increase formal education (beyond tactical training, etc.) of police officers in the UK continues (Ramshaw & Soppitt, 2018).

The UK's education system, including higher education, differs considerably from that of the United States. In addition to terminology being different ("college" and "university" do not mean exactly the same thing in the UK as they do in the United States), the cost of attending a university is much lower and can be completed in less time than the traditional bachelor's degree in the UK as compared to the United States (Kopaczewski, 2018).[4] "Higher education" of police officer is not an equivalent term in the United States and the UK. For example, the College of Policing (2022) in the UK is not what US citizens would typically think of in terms of a "college"—it is not a four-year institution open to any qualified applicant to continue their formal education. Instead, the College of Policing is an independent agency that acts as a professional organization for those working in various areas of law enforcement across the UK. The organization is also active in research on crime and crime prevention, offers guidance for those in the field of policing, and assists individuals working or interested in working in the field.

In the UK, the College of Policing was founded in 2012 during global calls for increased professionalism in policing. The goals of this College are to "develop the knowledge, standards of conduct, leadership and professionalism required by police officers in England and Wales" (House of Commons, 2016). The College of Policing sets standards, promotes ethical policing, and recruits qualified instructors to train and educate future law enforcement personnel (House of Commons, 2016). It has put forth a Police Education Qualifications Framework (PEQF) to help advocate for higher levels of education in policing. The PEQF promotes the idea that increased education levels and professional training will support the public by providing citizens with enhanced safety and service. Currently, the UK's field training section for police recruits is somewhat shorter than what is more common in the United States, yet both nations recognize the importance of field training in combining theory and practice for a new officer's understanding of the job, and success on their own. As the College of Policing and the PEQF note, it is difficult to find scholarly research on evidence-based practices for police training, which can make determining how to improve programming more difficult. As such, the PEQF states that to improve training, agencies must begin properly measuring the successes of training currently in place. Evaluation tools are crucial to assist in better examining outcomes for the three entry points into policing to assist in improving training and enhancing the work of police officers once they are on the job (College of Policing, 2022).[5]

The UK, through the PEQF, has developed additional opportunities for recruitment and training of police: Police Constable Degree Apprenticeship (PCDA), Degree Holder Entry Program (DHEP), and Pre-Join Degree (PJD).[6] With the continued focus on professionalism and education, the UK's College of Policing, the Association of Police and Crime Commissioners (APCC), and the National Police Chief's Council (NPCC) have developed a "Policing Vision 2025," which further advances policing as a professional field. Recognizing the importance of higher education to expand into graduate-level education is a key component of this vision. The PEQF also states that more standardized education and training will be important in adequately preparing police forces to operate professionally while allowing officers to have high levels of autonomy and exercise appropriate, professional judgment. Through these efforts, the additional opportunities and pathways to recruitment are integral in the development of a more professional, higher-educated force. The PCDA is an apprenticeship program that takes approximately three years to complete. Individuals who have some level of training and/or have been in the armed forces are eligible for this program. Apprentice students work through a specific, tailored set of modules during a set period of time to obtain full credentials. The DHEP is a two-year program that allows those who have a university degree in another field to enter into the policing profession. Again, students work through a structured set of modules until completion. The PJD program is a more traditional academic program that allows students to complete a university degree in Professional Policing and then enter directly into police work. All of these programs collaborate with institutions of higher education to assist in providing appropriate training and education to students in their respective pathway to a law enforcement career (Shohel et al., 2020).

Scotland provides another opportunity to explore police training within the UK, as well. Probationary training for new police officers in Scotland lasts approximately two years. These trainees, called probationers, begin with an 11-week educational course where they learn and are tested on issues related to safety, legislation, and physical education. From there, probationer's complete information technology (IT) training before moving into the operational phase where they work alongside of tutor constables and complete additional education via distance learning. Assessments are required around weeks 44, 60, and 92. Not successfully completing these assessments can result in dismissal from the policing pipeline (Police Scotland, 2022). Many Scottish police officers are unarmed. While some of their officers do end up involved in physical altercations, the deadly violence seen in the United States is extremely rare in Scotland. Certain groups within Scotland perceive the police negatively and they deal with difficult situations of poverty and crime, as do many policing units across nations. However, the subculture of policing and expectation of police officers in Scotland stand out from that of the United States. Constables live and work in the same general geographic area and "embrace their role as 'guardians of the community,' not warriors from a policing subculture" in Scotland (Baker, 2015).[7]

Police Training in the Netherlands

Policing in the Netherlands falls under the Ministry of Justice, getting its foundation from the Constitution's Police Act of 1993. The nation's law enforcement agencies consist of 25 regional forces as well as the National Police Services Agency. The Police Academy is the central agency providing training (basic and ongoing), education, and research for law enforcement in nine police training centers across the Netherlands (OSCE, 2018). Basic training includes both on the job and classroom portions (Politieacademie, 2023). New recruits can enter The Police Academy in one of six levels (voluntary police officer, assistant police officer, police officer, full police officer, bachelor in police studies, or master's in police studies), depending on their educational level and experience at the time of entry. To move up the ranks, police officers must complete additional training and education through The Police Academy and have a minimum number of years (depending on goal rank) working as police officers (OSCE, 2018).

With one national police force, training of the Dutch Police is completely centralized (Government of the Netherlands, 2022) and training is standardized and streamlined, though it takes place in various locations. The Netherlands police forces have received accolades for their use of digital technology in training (Ahern, 2022), something that is not widely reported on in other police training programs across the world. Even decades ago, the Dutch Police forces recognized the importance of higher levels of education in training officers (Junger-Tas, 1977). Since its inception in 1992, The Police Academy of the Netherlands has undergone various shifts and status changes in response to changing times and philosophies of police training. Beginning in 2006, the Academy became a University of Applied Sciences, which allows the institution to grant bachelor's and master's degrees that are accredited by the national government. Upwards of 2000 students have completed initial training and the policing bachelor's degree and over 25,000 have attended more advanced training programs (Heinen & Peeters, 2018). The Netherlands Institute for the Study of Crime and Law Enforcement (NSCR) does ongoing research into policing and police education in the nation to continue to enhance the profession and education of LEOs across the nation (NSCR, 2023).

While much of what is publicized about the police agencies and activities in the Netherlands is positive, the Dutch Police still face scrutiny due to minority mistreatment. Instances of racial profiling and unequal treatment have prompted public outcry in the nation, particularly after Amnesty International reported such actions and when former police officers corroborated them (Nieuwenhuis, 2015). As a response, efforts have been under way to improve diversity within the ranks of the Dutch Police and tackle structural issues that lead to racism in law enforcement activities, largely through training activities (DutchNews, 2022). A recent documentary was released about racism within the ranks of the police in the Netherlands.[8] Citizens have begun to question whether their loved ones should even consider a career in policing (Quell, 2022), bringing to the surface the familiar question of how recruiting and training can be improved for less negative outcomes as well as a more professional police force.

Police Training in Finland

Finland offers an approach to police training that other nations often seek to model, including the United States. Finland's law enforcement structure includes national, provincial, and local agencies. The three national units are the National Bureau of Investigation, National Traffic Police, and Security Police, with each handling crime respective to their specialty on a national level. Provincial police commands coordinate law enforcement activities at the state level and help coordinate, when necessary, between local and national agencies. The local police are made up of 90 departments, with a total of 280 service points. These local offices oversee public order and daily crime response and control within their geographic locations (OSCE, 2023).

Each year, Finland sees approximately 400 new students interested in joining the police on some level. With a formalized education and training protocol, these future officers begin basic training and work toward a Diploma in Police Studies, which takes approximately two and a half years to complete. To move up in rank, police officers can take the Police Sergeant's Exam and work toward the Senior Police Officer's Degree while completing police work, taking about two to three years to finish. After that, interested parties can complete a police-related master's degree and then have the option to continue toward doctoral studies (OSCE, 2023). Since 2008, Finland has had a single institute for beginning police education—The Police University College (Polamk). Training includes both higher-education and practical training. About 200 staff members serve Police University College; about 40% of them are employed as police officers (POLIISI, 2023b). Master's degrees are offered at both the University of Tampere and the University of Turku. The expectation of professionalism dictates all police education and training in the nation (OSCE, 2023); this professional focus in police training is gaining traction across the globe.

The Finnish police explicitly recognize the importance of international collaboration in law enforcement activities. The Police University College participates in exchange programs to allow future officers to study in varying environments and broaden their education. Students who take the option to study elsewhere must have completed one full year of studies at the Police University College and then spend a full three months at a partner institution (POLIISI, 2023a).[9]

Police Training in Kenya

Kenya has experienced significant political change in recent decades, including within the realm of policing. Kenya's current Constitution became law in 2010. At this time, a National Police Service as well as a National Police Service Commission were established. (The Constitution also has stipulations and regulations for human rights along with an Independent Policing Oversight Authority.) A new structure for policing was prompted by the Ransley Report (also known as the Police Reform Taskforce Report) in efforts to better professionalize the field of policing and increase public trust of police in Kenya after much violence. With the new constitution, police activities have been organized into four distinct but connected areas. The National Police Service (NPS) oversees public safety. The National Police Service Commission oversees the recruiting and training activities for the NPS. The Independent Policing Oversight Authority handles complaints and investigations of police activities and personnel. Multiple County Policing Authorities are responsible for community policing and ensuring that police are accountable to citizens (Release Political Prisoners Trust, 2012). Each of the three acts creating the NPS, the NPS Commission, and the Independent Policing Oversight Authority details the functions of each service. For example, the NPS Act, an approximately 69-page document, details rights and duties of officers and other positions within the NPS (National Council for Law Reporting with the Authority of the Attorney General, 2012).[10]

The Kenya Police Service (operating under the NPS) states as its vision: "To be a world class police service, with a people-friendly, responsive and professional workforce" (Kenya Police Service, 2022b). To ensure the proper training of police personnel, the 2010

Constitution set forth a mandate to the Kenya Police Training College-Kiganjo, one of five institutions that can offer diplomas in police training (Rachel, 2015), to "train staff to the highest possible standards of competence and integrity and to respect human right and dignity as provided for under Article 244 (d) of the Constitution of Kenya, 2010" (Kenya Police Service, 2022a). The College trains new police officers as well as those going for promotion and providing a range of training and education services for new and veteran police officers in Kenya (Kenya Police Service, 2022a). Their active Facebook page (Kenya Police College, 2022) chronicles training programs and recruitment activities to promote the work and progress in the relatively new system.

Individuals interested in becoming part of Kenya's police forces must be citizens of the nation and hold valid official identification. They must meet a minimum score on the Kenya Certificate of Secondary Education (KCSE), an exam taken by individuals at the end of four years of secondary education, including minimum scores in English or Kiswahili languages. Applicants must demonstrate physical and medical fitness and should not have a criminal record, including pending charges. Police candidates must be between the ages of 18 and 28 if they hold a KCSE Certificate, but can be up to age 30 if they already have a degree. Women may not be recruited or attend training if they are pregnant (KNEC, 2022).

Once training begins, recruits can expect a demanding training schedule, with a combination of academic, physical, and tactical training. Showcasing their relatively new training curriculum, the Kenya Police Service now boasts a greater police presence across the nation, fighting against terrorism and other criminal enterprises. Training includes a significant amount of time spent outdoors doing physical tasks (Kenya Police Service, 2018). The entire training process takes about 15 months, at which time successful candidates complete the requirements to become a police officer (Kenyadmission, 2022).

Formal policing is not the only source of law enforcement in Kenya. Kenya's overall culture is quite diverse, and the nation is highly stratified socially and with varying geographic characteristics. Historically, rural areas often have had little formal police presence. At times, violence between various groups within Kenya has spurred police action, which brings additional violence (Sobania, 2003). Due to the landscape and habitability, many arid and semi-arid (mostly rural) parts of the nation are largely protected and secured by the Kenya Police Reserve (KPR). This force is often considered unprofessional and recent movements and research have encouraged more training and increased professionalism of the KPR, in addition to the more formal and traditional police services in the nation. Historically, a lack of funding and little oversight have led to problems with public trust and professionalism. Some citizens living in areas with more of a KPR presence have resorted to using other, private sources for protection. Scholars and activists have called for the state to take a larger role in providing formal training to the KPR to increase security, particularly in rural areas of the country (Mkutu & Wandera, 2013). Limited information is available on reserve policing in Kenya, even though they do a significant amount of work in rural, arid areas. Without in-depth analyses of training and outcomes, research simply suggests that the professionalization of reserve forces should include more intensive, formal training on proactive, community policing and working with populations who have low literacy skills and are isolated in rural areas. Additionally, recruiting citizens from these areas will be necessary to help in the training process (Asembo & Lumadi, 2013)

With governmental upheaval in Kenya, the profession of policing has evolved and continues to adapt to political and social conditions of the nation. The Constitution adopted in

2010 mandates professional police forces to operate as government agencies. Training has increased and philosophies mirror those of other nations in contemporary society, recognizing the need for more community involvement to build trust and confidence among enforcers of the law. Even within the reserve police forces, calls continue for increased training and professionalism including the need for more financial resources to better support police activities in all areas of Kenya (Lemarleni et al., 2017).

Police Training in India

The government structure in India, per its constitution, delegates most policing and "law and order" activities to the states (Ministry of Home Affairs, 2017). With relatively recent cultural changes in India and the shift to independence and democracy, the goal of policing has been to mirror this political progress. However, there is some question as to whether the administrative processes of law enforcement have lived up to that ideal (Sharma, 2013). The Police Act of 1861 with subsequent amendments details the rules for and responsibilities of police in the nation of India. A Code of Conduct for the Police in India (1985) was issued by the Ministry of Home Affairs in 1985 to ensure police officers avoid misconduct and maintain responsibility of their duties. India has a structured, formal system for police training that includes multiple levels and layers, based on function and locality. As of 2013, the Bureau of Police Research and Development (BPRD, 2022) had hundreds of training options for police in different departments across the nation. Historically, police training in India has not placed any significant emphasis on social sciences or the humanities (Scott et al., 2009), suggesting that higher education is considered disadvantageous to work in the field. Training instead has focused on national, state, and local policies as well as procedures (not unlike traditional US academies). Also mirroring some criticisms of training of police officers in the United States, Indian police officers sometimes have difficulties gaining public trust because of a lack of academic subjects in police training (Patterson, 2011). Calls for improvements have resulted in slow changes. For example, for police across the nation, the Bureau of Police Research and Development (2006) notes that training should be required continually, not just a one-time, entry-level experience. The government has sought to have exceptional trainers who can adapt curricula and training to the current needs of the many police forces in India as a response. Also, like police systems in the United States, there are aspects of the police world that are very resistant to change. Of note, in India (as well as in Kenya and the United States) the military rank policies were directly inherited from the British (Lane, 1977).

The Indian Police Service (IPS) is a national body of elite officers charged with border policing, counterterrorism, crime prevention, investigations, high-profile security, management of disasters, and other high-level responsibilities. As opposed to more traditional and local crime-fighting law enforcement officials, members of the IPS are considered civil servants. A federal agency, the IPS trains officers for higher-level command positions. Recruits are already employed in civil service or who have ample experience to enter into civil service. Much like most US forces, the IPS has certain requirements for recruits including Indian citizenship, minimum age of 21 (with variance in maximum age dependent on position), university graduation, and physical standards. If the initial screening standards (which are higher than for other portions of policing in India) are met, a series of exams is required and, if passed, recruits enter into a year or more of formal training (BYJU's Exam Prep, 2022).

The National Police Academy in India, the Sadar Vallabhbhai Patel National Police Academy, has two phases of basic training followed by three phases of more intense leadership and management training. Beginning in the basic courses, future IPS officers explore a variety of academic subjects with a focus on national acts, codes, and procedure. They are required to write 15 papers on these subjects over the course of their classroom training. The "outside" courses of the basic phase include a variety of physically challenging tests, drill, and map reading. The later phases include more specific leadership and managerial training in preparation for future promotion (Sadar Vallabhbhai Patel National Police Academy, 2016). Training for police officers in India may differ by locale, level, and charge, but the nation recognizes the need for ongoing training at different levels for their specialized forces. Similar to other nations including the United States, deficiencies in training and education of LEOs are cited as problems for police-community relations, putting (ongoing) training at the forefront of the discussion on how to improve policing for the country.

International Law Enforcement Training

The ways in which various police agencies interact, across jurisdictions and boarders, is an integral part to any law enforcement training. Training police officers across international borders is a popular activity. Formalized International Police Academies (ILEAs) are a relatively new development in this history, increasing the ability of different nations to fight crime in innovative and ever-evolving ways (Akgul & Marenin, 2007).[11] Academic research examining policing in countries beyond the United States is growing. And across the globe, nations are looking for ways for police "training" to morph into police *education,* often through institutions of higher education, to carry law enforcement personnel through a more professional career path and improve public safety (Patterson, 2011). But often overlooked in these (limited) theoretical and philosophical discussions is even the mention of the police academies (or police training within the linguistically appropriate terminology) in different nations. Nonetheless, when exploring different types of police academies, international police training must be mentioned.

Crime does not always occur exclusively within a single nation—crime can cross borders, continents, and oceans. A discussion on international police training would be incomplete without recognizing the agencies that operate between different nations. Through the State Department in the United States, the Bureau of International Narcotics and Law Enforcement Affairs helps to oversee six academies in partnership with other nations to help address international crime. In 1995, then-President Bill Clinton called for the establishment of a network of police agencies across the globe to work together for international safety. The ILEA program has academies in Accra, Ghana (to serve West Africa); Budapest, Hungary (to serve Central Europe, Eastern Europe, and Centra Asia); Bangkok, Thailand (to serve Southeast Asia and China); Gaborone, Botswana (to serve nations south of Sahel and portions of West Africa); San Salvador (to serve Latin America and the Caribbean); and Roswell, New Mexico (to serve officials from all nations who participate in the ILEA) (US Department of State, 2022). The United States has the most dominant role in ILEA's governing structure. "A Policy Board governs the ILEA Program. The State Department chairs the Board, which includes senior representatives from the Departments of Treasury, Homeland Security, and Justice. The ILEA Interagency Steering Group, which comprises of representatives from these same departments and other federal law enforcement, provides functional program oversight. Each overseas academy is staffed by one U.S. Director, and one or two U.S. Deputies, in addition to locally employed staff and host government personnel seconded to the academy" (US Department of State, 2022).

ILEAs offer education and leadership training in a variety of areas, taught by instructors with expertise in areas such as cybercrime, human trafficking, money laundering, and a multitude of topics of regional interest (US Department of State, 2023). Led by US efforts, the interests of the United States are well-protected through the training.

> The regional ILEAs offer three different fields of programs. The CORE program, specialized training courses, and regional seminars. The CORE program typically includes 50 participants and is focused on improving the investigative and management skills of selected police officials. The specialized courses, comprised of about 30 participants, are normally one or two weeks long and often run simultaneously with the CORE course. These courses provide in-depth instruction on areas of concern or of urgent need. Topics of the Regional Seminars include transnational crimes, counter-terrorism and financial crimes.
>
> *(US Customs and Border Patrol, 2014)*

Graduates of ILEA courses have access to a Global Portal allowing practitioners to work together to identify and combat criminal concerns across an international landscape (US Department of State, 2023).

INTERPOL Virtual Global Academy

INTERPOL is also integral in assisting nations across the globe with law enforcement training efforts. To note, INTERPOL, contrary to popular belief, is not a police force. Instead, it "is a global organization established to do two things: to foster better cooperation between police agencies and to improve information sharing," according to John Cohen who is a contributor for ABC News but previously held the position of acting undersecretary of the Department of Homeland Security (Margolin, 2018). INTERPOL is integral in assisting police forces around the world with education and training. In 2019, the organization launched a virtual academy that connects institutions of law enforcement education, which has gained interest and has helped educate LEOs across the globe during the Covid-19 pandemic. This academy provides a variety of courses to help professionals learn about and collaborate crime in areas such as the Darknet, counter-terrorism, and organized crime. After requesting and being granted credentials, law enforcement officials can access the secure platform to utilize information and take courses (INTERPOL, 2020a). Materials available to users consist of a library, educational webinars, and I-Le@rn, which offers self-paced courses. Additionally, small-group instructor-led courses are available in real time. The INTERPOL Virtual Academy also allows access to the Intellectual Property Crime Investigators College[12] and the INTERPOL Global Knowledge Hub, which is "a secure online environment for real-time knowledge exchange and law enforcement networking. It has specialized work spaces which are accessible only on invitation by the work space community managers" (INTERPOL, 2023). INTERPOL also continues to educate law enforcement officials on a global scale through events like the INTERPOL Police Training Seminar, the 23rd of which took place in September 2022 in Riyadh, Saudi Arabia. The theme of this seminar was Law Enforcement Training in a Post-Pandemic World. Those involved used the opportunity to look for the future to continue to collaborate and better address crime on a global level (Saudi Press Agency, 2022).

Discussion

Since crime knows no borders, the existence of a network of international police academies may enhance a global arrangement for dealing with transnational criminal threats some day in the future. Due to the alleged commission of war crimes and other atrocities in Ukraine in the wake of Russia's unprovoked invasion in 2022, there is also an ongoing need to hold accountable those who have committed such crime to maintain a stable world order. Hence, there is an obvious need for trained investigators and prosecutors to augment and ultimately deter such crimes.[13] In the meantime, an organization such as the ILEA Program initiated by the United States in partnership with several host nations and 17 federal US law enforcement agencies serves as a prototype for such a development in international cooperation. A trend in this direction has already been shown with the establishment in 2019 of the INTERPOL Global Academy—"a network of trusted law enforcement national or regional education institutions providing a global approach to law enforcement training" (INTERPOL, 2020b). It also has a Virtual Academy with courses covering INTERPOL policing capabilities, transnational crimes, and professional policing skills.

In addition to exploring police training and education from a multi-national context, there is also much to be gained by looking at the ways that police are currently trained across the globe in individual nations. The cultural differences of each nation are going to dictate specifics and offer variation among policing activities, training, and education. Additionally, similarities begin to emerge by examining general information about different police academies in different parts of the world. While the nations discussed in this chapter are only a tiny portion of the diverse law enforcement agencies across nations and continents, we can still glean some global trends even among culturally different nations. For example, movements toward combining police training with higher education, more training, and raising standards for police recruits and trainees are not unique to the United States; and neither are scandals or concerns with community-police relations. A global push towards ongoing education to professionalize policing is currently in full swing.

The protective nature of what happens during police training is a barrier to an exhaustive summary of what happens within a police academy in any nation. These barriers can be magnified when looking beyond one's own nation and culture. Although it can be difficult to glean nuances of policing to fully comprehend the magnitude of severity in public news stories, it is a sound research practice to seek out information about policing and police training among the nations of the world. In so doing, the issues of increasing professionalism and bridging higher education with police training appear in discussions across nations. The international differences are largely connected to the cultural and sociopolitical climates of different nations. The history of a nation, and its police force(s), is key to understanding its police training, not only in the present time but also in context of prior years. For example, recognizing that Kenya underwent a large government and political shift with the implementation of a new constitution in 2010 is important in understanding shifts in policing philosophies and training. Such a system is relatively new and, therefore, will not have significant research and information available on long-term outcomes or progress. When comparing nations, one must not lose sight that these are broad generalizations and, just as within the United States, there is also significant variation within these nations. From rural to urban areas, among citizens living in wealth to poverty, there will be differences in policing goals, activities, and outcomes. Still, taking a larger view of policing outside of the confines of one's own nation allows for a deeper understanding and exploration about how police officers are trained to perform their duties in communities across the globe. It also allows for the opportunity for nations to learn from one another and enhance safety and police-community relations across the world.

Yet, America's domestic crime control issues persist, especially as it concerns police brutality. Many persons want to see more body cameras, community oversight of police, stringent use of force policies and more consequences for police officers who do harm while on the job. In addition, there are also advocates for cities to spend less on policing efforts and more on health care, education, and job training. According to Erika Maye, a senior leader for the nonprofit civil rights organization Color of Change, "Police violence is not an issue of representation. To really protect Black lives, we feel we really need to upend the current policing system" (qtd. in "Diversity in Law Enforcement," February 11, 2021). The subject of the racism in American history and diversity in policing is considered in the following chapter.

Notes

1 Many articles and books are available exploring theories of crime and responses to crime. See Burke (2018) for a broad look at criminological theory.
2 See National Police Academy (2023).
3 In addition to country-specific training and police forces, the European Union Agency for Law Enforcement Training (CEPOL), established in 2005, provides law enforcement training for the EU to help with collaboration and knowledge-sharing across EU nations. See European Union (2023). Additionally, Fehérváry (1997) offers a historical discussion on the Central European Police Academy (MEPA).
4 See Kopaczewski (2018) for more information on differences in higher education in the United States and the UK.
5 See College of Policing 2022 and House of Commons 2016 for more detailed information on continued efforts for enhancing and improving police training in the UK.
6 For additional information on the history of police training and new, specialized training routes in the UK, see Shohel et al. (2020).
7 Large police departments in the United States have looked to Scotland for guidance on improving training and police subculture to decrease violence. However, Scottish police officers have noted that the Scottish approach might not be appropriate or might not work in American cities. See Baker, 2015, for a more in-depth discussion.
8 The documentary in the Dutch language can be found at: https://nos.nl/artikel/2429926-politiechef-racisme-en-discriminatie-structureel-probleem-binnen-de-politie.
9 Students have multiple options for where to study internationally. Information and details on the Erasums and Nordcop programs can be found at on the Police University College website (POLIISI, 2023a).
10 See National Council for Law Reporting with the Authority of the Attorney General (2012) for specifics.
11 See Akgul and Marenin (2007) for a more in-depth discussion on the history of collaboration among international police agencies in training and beyond.
12 Information available at https://college.iipcic.org/#/public-dashboard.
13 More than ever before, the nations of the world must stand together to confront war crimes and other acts of inhumanity. In late September 2022, as the Russian armed forces continued to attack the Ukrainian nation, US Attorney General Merrick B. Garland and Ukrainian Prosecutor General Andriy Kostin discussed efforts to hold accountable individuals responsible for war crimes committed by Russia in Ukraine. They outlined areas for enhanced collaboration and signed a

memorandum of understanding (MOU) to facilitate appropriate cooperation, coordination, and deconfliction between each country's respective investigations and prosecutions. At that time, the United States had already initiated investigations of potential war crimes over which the United States possesses jurisdiction, such as the killing and wounding of US journalists covering the unprovoked Russian aggression in Ukraine (US Dept. of Justice, 2022). In addition, Ukraine had already begun to prosecute war crimes committed by members of the Russian Armed Forces. An unusual move while a war is still going on. According to NPR's correspondent Greg Myre, "one reason it wants to start prosecutions now is to show Russian soldiers currently fighting in Ukraine that being put on trial is a real possibility if they commit war crimes" (Myre, 2022).

References

Ahern, L. (2022). How the Dutch academy streamlines and secures education. *Itslearning*. Retrieved October 28, 2022, from https://itslearning.com/global/news/dutch-police-academy-lms-security/

Akgul, A., & Marenin, O. (2007). Global developments in transnational police training: TADOC (Turkish International Academy against Drugs and Organized Crime). In H. Durmaz, et al. (Eds.), *Understanding and responding to terrorism*. Retrieved January 5, 2023, from https://www.researchgate.net/profile/Arif-Akgul/publication/320978623_Global_Developments_in_Transnational_Police_Training/links/5bc8e47da6fdcc03c79099f8/Global-Developments-in-Transnational-Police-Training.pdf

Asembo, K. O., & Lumadi, M. W. (2013). Professionalizing peripheral police officers in Kenya: Implications for curriculum development. *Mediterranean Journal of Social Sciences*, *4*(13), 781–789. doi:10.5901/mjss.2013.v4n13p781

Baker, A. (2015, December 11). US police leaders, visiting Scotland, get lessons on avoiding deadly force. *The New York Times*. Retrieved December 15, 2022, from https://www.nytimes.com/2015/12/12/nyregion/us-police-leaders-visiting-scotland-get-lessons-on-avoiding-deadly-force.html

Bayerl, P., Horton, K. E., Jacobs, G., Rogiest, S., Reguli, Z., Gruschinske, M., Costanzo, P., Stojanovski, T., Vonas, G., Gasco, M., & Elliott, K. (2014). Perspectives on the police profession: An international investigation. *Policing: An International Journal of Police Strategies & Management, 37*(4), 728–745.

Belur, J., Agnew-Pauley, W., McGinley, B., & Tompson, L. (2020). A systematic review of police training programmes. *Policing: A Journal of Policy and Practice*, *14*(1), 76–90. https://doi.org/10.1093/police/paz022

BJYU's Exam Prep. *Details about IPS training*. Retrieved October 14, 2022, from https://byjus.com/free-ias-prep/details-about-ips-training/

Brewer, J. R., Guelke, A., Hume, I., Moxon-Browne, E., & Wilford, R. (1996). *The police, public order, and the state*. Macmillan.

Bureau on Police Research and Development. (2006). *Training policy*. Retrieved October 14, 2022, from https://bprd.nic.in/content/205_1_TrainingPolicy.aspx

Bureau on Police Research and Development. (2022). *Updated list of police training institutions in India*. Retrieved October 14, 2022, from https://bprd.nic.in/WriteReadData/CMS/File1217.pdf

Burke, R. H. (2018). *An introduction to criminological theory*. Taylor & Francis. https://doi.org/10.4324/9781315204871

Cheatham, A., & Maizland, L. (2022). How police compare in different democracies. *Council on Foreign Relations*. Retrieved October 28, 2022, from https://www.cfr.org/backgrounder/how-police-compare-different-democracies

Code of Conduct for the Police in India. (1985). Retrieved October 14, 2022, from https://police.py.gov.in/MHA%20-%20Model%20Code%20of%20Conduct%20-%20Indian%20Police.pdf

College of Policing. (2022). Retrieved October 24, 2022, from https://www.college.police.uk/

Diversity in Law Enforcement. (2021, February11). *Diversity in law enforcement may improve policing, study shows*. Associated Press. Retrieved February 15, 2023, from https://www.nbcnews.com/news/nbcblk/diversity-law-enforcement-may-improve- policing-study-shows-n1257515

DutchNews. (2022, May 23). *Police need to tackle 'structural problem' of racism and discrimination.* Retrieved January 9, 2023, from ttps://www.dutchnews.nl/news/2022/05/police-need-to-tackle-structural-problem-of- racism-and-discrimination/

European Union. (2023). *European union agency for law enforcement training (CEPOL).* Retrieved January 6, 2023, from https://european-union.europa.eu/institutions-law-budget/institutions-and-bodies/institutions-and-bodies-profiles/cepol_en

Fehérváry, J. (1997). Central European police academy (MEPA). *European Journal of Crime, Criminal Law and Criminal Justice, 5*(4), 411–420. doi:10.1163/157181797x00239

Government of the Netherlands. (2022). *Police.* Retrieved October 28, 2022, from https://www.government.nl/topics/police

Heinen, J., & Peeters, H. (2018). Higher police education in the Netherlands. In C. Rogers & B. Frevel (Eds.), *Higher education and police.* Palgrave Macmillan. https://doi.org/10.1007/978-3-319-58386-0_11

Higgenbothem, D. (Ed.). (2022). *Prospects: Joining the police.* Retrieved September 10, 2022, from https://www.prospects.ac.uk/jobs-and-work-experience/job-sectors/law-enforcement-nd-security/joining-the-police

Horton, J. (2021, May). How US police training compares with the rest of the world. *BBC.* Retrieved October 28, 2022, from https://www.bbc.com/news/world-us-canada-56834733

House of Commons. (2016, July 9). *College of policing: Three years on.* Retrieved January 7, 2023, from https://publications.parliament.uk/pa/cm201617/cmselect/cmhaff/23/23.pdf

INTERPOL. (2020a, April 29). *INTERPOL launches virtual academy to support police learning during COVID-19.* Retrieved January 5, 2023, from https://www.interpol.int/en/News-and-Events/News/2020/INTERPOL-launches-Virtual-Academy-to-support-police-learning-during-COVID-19

INTERPOL. (2020b, September 2). *INTERPOL global academy welcomes three new members.* Retrieved October 30, 2022, from https://www.interpol.int/en/News-and- Events/News/2020/INTERPOL-Global-Academy-welcomes-three-new-members

INTERPOL. (2023). *INTERPOL virtual learning academy.* Retrieved January 5, 2023, from https://www.interpol.int/en/How-we-work/Capacity-building/INTERPOL-Virtual-Academy

Junger-Tas, J. (1977). *Basic police training and police performance: Some preliminary findings of an evaluation study on police training.* Research and Documentation Centre of the Ministry of Justice. Retrieved October 28, 2022, from https://www.ojp.gov/pdffiles1/Digitization/48524NCJRS.pdf

Kenya National Examinations Council (KNEC). (2022). *Kenya certificate of secondary education.* Retrieved October 27, 2022, from https://www.knec.ac.ke/services/school-exams/k-c-s-e/

Kenya Police College. (2022). *Facebook page.* Retrieved October 25, 2022, from https://www.facebook.com/KenyaPoliceCollege/

Kenya Police Service. (2018). *Career in policing: Police training in Kenya (New Curriculum).* [Video]. YouTube. Retrieved October 17, 2022, from https://www.youtube.com/watch?v=nARNOIQGiLM

Kenya Police Service. (2022a). *Kenya police training college Kiganjo.* Retrieved October 25, 2022, from https://www.kenyapolice.go.ke/2015-09-07-17-41-13/kenya-police-college.html

Kenya Police Service. (2022b). *Vision and mission.* Retrieved October 25, 2022, from https://www.kenyapolice.go.ke/pages/links.html

Kenyadmission. (2022). *How long does police training take?* Retrieved October 27, 2022, from https://kenyadmission.com/how-long-does-kenya-police-training-take/

Kopaczewski, C. (2018, June). 6 ways college is different in the US and the UK. *Business Insider.* Retrieved October 24, 2022, from https://www.businessinsider.com/how-college-is-different-in-the-us-and-the-uk-2018–6

Lane, R. (1977). *Policing the city: Boston, 1822–1885.* Harvard University Press.

Lemarleni, J. E., Ochieng, I., Gakobo, T., & Mwuara, P. (2017). Effects of resource allocation on strategy implementation at Kenya police service in Nairobi county. *International Academic Journal of Human Resource and Business Administration,* 2(4), 1–26.

Lo, S. S. (2016). *The politics of policing in greater China*. Palgrave Macmillan.

Margolin, J. (2018, October 6). Beyond the myth of Interpol, the world's police organization. *ABC News*. Retrieved January 19, 2023, from https://abcnews.go.com/International/myth-interpol-worlds-police-organization/story?id=58325721

Ministry of Home Affairs. (2017). *Law and order*. Retrieved October 14, 2022, from https://www.mha.gov.in/commoncontent/law-and-order

Mkutu, K., & Wandera, G. (2013). Policing the periphery: Opportunities and challenges for Kenya's reserve police. *Small Arms Survey*. Retrieved October 27, 2022, from https://ciaotest.cc.columbia.edu/wps/sas/0027675/f_0027675_22533.pdf

Myre, G. (2022, May 14). *Ukraine begins prosecuting Russians for war crimes*. Retrieved October 30, 2022, from https://www.npr.org/2022/05/14/1098941080/ukraine-begins-prosecuting-russians-for-war-crimes

National Council for Law Reporting with the Authority of the Attorney General. (2012). *National police service act, chapter 84*. Republic of Kenya. Retrieved October 25, 2022, from https://www.ilo.org/dyn/natlex/docs/ELECTRONIC/97347/115467/F-467123398/KEN97347.pdf

National Police Academy. (2023). *Police of Japan*. Retrieved January 9, 2023, from https://www.npa.go.jp/english/Police_of_Japan/2020/poj2020_full.pdf

Nickerson, C. (2022, June). Social institutions in sociology: Definitions and examples. *Simply Sociology*. Retrieved September 4, 2002, from https://simplysociology.com/social-institution.html

Nieuwenhuis, M. (2015, July 23). The Netherlands' disgrace: Racism and police brutality. *openDemocracy*. Retrieved January 9, 2023, from https://www.opendemocracy.net/en/can- urope-make-it/netherlands-disgrace-racism-and-police-brutality/

NSCR. (2023). *Police program*. Retrieved January 8, 2023, from https://nscr.nl/en/research-area/police-program/

Organization for Security and Co-Operation in Europe. (2022). *Country profile: United Kingdom*. Retrieved September 10, 2022, from https://polis.osce.org/country-profiles/united-kingdom

OSCE. (2018). *Police education and training in the OSCE region*. Retrieved October 28, 2022, from https://www.osce.org/files/f/documents/f/7/423401.pdf

OSCE. (2023). *Finland*. Retrieved January 9, 2023, from https://polis.osce.org/country- profiles/finland

Patterson, C. (2011). Adding value? A review of the international literature on the role of higher education in police training and education. *Police Practice and Research*, *12*(4), 286–297.

Police Act of India. (1961). Retrieved October 14, 2022, from https://www.mha.gov.in/sites/default/files/police_act_1861.pdf

Police Scotland. (2022). *Training*. Retrieved December 15, 2022, from https://www.scotland.police.uk/spa-media/tblf33gs/police-officer-training.pdf

POLIISI. (2023a). *International exchange programs*. Retrieved January 6, 2023, from https://polamk.fi/en/international-exchange-programs

POLIISI. (2023b). *The police university college in brief*. Retrieved January 6, 2023, from https://polamk.fi/en/the-police-university-college-in-brief

Politieacademie. (2023). *Police training*. Retrieved January 9, 2023, from https://www.politieacademie.nl/en/Pages/policetraining.aspx

Quell, M. (2022, May). Racism in the ranks: Dutch police film spurs conversation. *Associated Press*. Retrieved October 28, 2022, from https://apnews.com/article/death-of-george-floyd-entertainment-politics-race-and-ethnicity-racial-injustice-8d37956fce12df831a151eede7b9f70c

Rachel, B. (2015, April). Kenya police recruiting and training process. *Strategic Intelligence*. Retrieved October 26, 2022, from https://intelligencebriefs.com/kenya-police-recruitment-process-and-training/

Ramshaw, P., & Soppitt, S. (2018). Educating the recruited and recruiting the educated: Can the new police education qualifications framework in England and Wales succeed where others have faltered. *International Journal of Police Science & Management*, *20*(4), 243–250. https://doi.org/10.1177/1461355718814850

Release Political Prisoners Trust. (2012). *Your guide to: The national police service act, the national police service commission act, and the independent policing oversight authority act.* Retrieved October 25, 2022, from https://humanrightsinitiative.org/publications/police/CHRI%20and%20RPP%20Guide%20to%20the%20new%20Kenya%20Police%20Laws_Final.pdf
Sadar Vallabhbhai Patel National Police Academy. (2016). Retrieved October 14, 2016, from https://www.svpnpa.gov.in/
Saferworld. (2022). *Police decentralization.* Retrieved September 7, 2022, from https://www.saferworld.org.uk/downloads/police-decentralisation-saferworld.pdf
Saudi Press Agency. (2022, September 25). *23rd INTERPOL police training symposium kicks off tomorrow in Riyadh.* Retrieved January 5, 2023, from https://www.spa.gov.sa/viewfullstory.php?lang=en&newsid=2387019
Scott, J., Evans, D., & Verma, A. (2009). Does higher education affect perceptions among police personnel: A response from India. *Journal of Contemporary Criminal Justice, 25*(2), 214–236.
Sharma, A. (2013). Police culture in Indian democratic system. *The Indian Journal of Political Science, 74*(2), 295–302.
Shohel, M. M. C., Uddin, G., Parker, McLoed, J., & Silverstone, D. (2020). Police education in the United Kingdom: Challenges and future directions. In M. Nugmanova, H. Mikkola, A. Rozanov, & V. Komleva (Eds.), *Education, human rights and peace in sustainable development.* Retrieved January 7, 2023, from https://www.intechopen.com/chapters/72435. doi:10.5772/intechopen.02705
Sobania, N. (2003). *Culture and customs of Kenya.* Greenwood Press.
Strauss-Hughes, A., Heffernan, R., & Ward, T. (2019). A cultural-ecological perspective on agency and offending behavior. *Psychiatry, Psychology, and Law, 26*(6), 938–958. https://dx.doi.org/10.1080/13218719.2019.1644250
Sullivan, L., & Haberfeld, M. (2005). *Encyclopedia of law enforcement* (Vol. 3). Sage Publications. Retrieved January 20, 2023, from https://iuristebi.files.wordpress.com/2011/07/law-enforcement-volume-3.pdf
US Customs and Border Patrol. (2014, January). *International law enforcement academy (ILEA) program overview.* Retrieved January 3, 2023, from https://www.cbp.gov/border-security/international-initiatives/international-training-assistance/law-enforce
US Dept. of Justice. (2022, September). *U.S. Attorney General and Ukrainian Prosecutor General met to strengthen joint efforts to hold accountable perpetrators of war crimes and other atrocities committed in Ukraine.* Press Release Number: 22–994. Retrieved October 30, 2022, from https://www.justice.gov/opa/pr/us-attorney-general-and-ukrainian-prosecutor-general-met-strengthen-joint-efforts-hold
US Department of State. (2023). *International law enforcement academies (ILEAs).* Retrieved January 3, 2022, from https://www.state.gov/international-law-enforcement-academy-ilea/
White, D. (2012). Educating, legitimizing, or accessorizing? Alternative conceptions of profession training in higher education: A comparative study of teacher, nurse, and police educators. *Police Practice and Research: An International Journal, 13*(4).

PART III

Police Academy Issues

6

ADVANCING DIVERSITY IN LAW ENFORCEMENT

The subject of diversity permeates many, if not most, of the social and political realities of America today. Diversity may be a drain on an organization or a dynamic contributor to its mission, vision, and strategy. Diversity represents both a choice and a challenge (Thomas, 2005). According to Rashawn Ray, a senior fellow at The Brookings Institution and professor of sociology at the University of Maryland, College Park, "America remains a deeply racist country and until we recognize and deal with that fact . . . [we] will not alter the status quo in a meaningful way. To make real progress and create systemic change, we need comprehensive police reform at the federal, state, and local level. Anything short of that will not ease the pain and suffering that takes place regularly in the United States" (Ray, 2021). While overt discrimination may be less pervasive than it was in past decades, various types of subtle forms of discrimination remain (Malhotra et al., 2022). For example, the New York State Police "remains overwhelmingly white—an imbalance some troopers say is rooted in a legacy of racism" (Mustian & Fassett, 2021). According to Major Albert Guerra of the Miami Police Department, "People from different cultures and backgrounds have different demeanors and ways of carrying themselves. Diversity in the force ensures that we are prepared for these cultural differences and help us avoid unfortunate misunderstandings" (qtd. in Flavin, 2018). However, mere diversity in the ranks is insufficient without also a course of instruction to transmit the proper attitudes for new police officers. Over a half century ago, the President's Commission on Law Enforcement and the Administration of Justice (1967) emphasized that the education of police will play a major role in future attempts to combat crime rates (p. 124). The ensuing years have certainly confirmed that prediction. Before men and women can be better trained and educated to perform the difficult tasks associated with police work, they must: first be attracted to the law enforcement profession; obtain the necessary preliminary qualifications (such as minimum education, age, and residency requirements); pass various background, written, physical, and psychological exams; be hired; and successfully complete basic and probationary periods of training. Agency selection standards and the processes involved vary as there are more than 18,000 law enforcement agencies in the United States.

DOI: 10.4324/9781003307396-9

One of the most difficult yet critical responsibilities of law enforcement leaders and administrators is the management of their personnel (Heintze et al., 2019, p. 94). "Police hiring standards vary by state and agency. States typically have minimum standards for their local police agencies, often established by a Commission on POST or similar state agency. Usually, all police agencies within the state are required to meet the minimum standards; and some departments may require higher standards than the state minimums" (CRC, 2022, p. 3). However, statewide minimum and individual agency hiring or other standards must be backed-up by a strong set of cultural values so that all officers are capable of safeguarding the public's trust to perform their jobs effectively. Since "ethical conduct greatly impacts public trust, law enforcement agencies must closely examine their policies, reward systems, and training to ensure that their agency fosters a culture of firm ethical values" (Fitch, 2011). Cultural sensitivity and culturally appropriate practices specific to a given location should be central to police training, as different locations serve various cultural groups and policing in general should embrace people from a multitude of cultures and backgrounds within their ranks.

At the federal level, the *Census of Federal Law Enforcement Officers* (CFLEO) conducted by the Bureau of Justice Statistics, identified 94 federal law enforcement agencies. Nonetheless, these federal agencies employ nearly 137,000 officers (including over 17,000 correctional officers and nearly 4,000 officers serving in the Offices of Inspectors General) "compared to 701,000 full-time sworn officers in general-purpose state and local law-enforcement agencies nationwide" (Brooks, 2019, p. 1, 2020, pp. 1 and 4).[1] In 2002, the Federal Law Enforcement Training Accreditation (FLETA) Board was established to accredit training academies and programs. The FLETA Board is the accrediting body for all federal law enforcement training and support programs. It provides an opportunity for the members of the federal law enforcement community to voluntarily demonstrate that they are meeting an established set of professional standards (FLETA, 2022). State and local law enforcement agencies are eligible to apply for accreditation through a national program administered by the Commission on Accreditation for Law Enforcement Agencies (CALEA) as well as by individual state entities (see Vracar, 2022).

Efforts to advance diversity within the law enforcement profession have been particularly challenging. In fact, this is one of the issues that led Congress, in 1972, to provide the Federal government with greater authority to enforce the employment discrimination provisions of Title VII of the landmark *Civil Rights Act of 1964* against state and local public employers, including law enforcement agencies. Samuel Walker (1985) has explained that "virtually every national report on the police over the past twenty years has recommended increased employment of minorities and women" (p. 55). Since the late 1960s, many law enforcement agencies as well as organizations that work with law enforcement have tried to recruit and retain workforces that have reflected the diversity within their jurisdictions. According to the U.S. Equal Employment Opportunity Commission (EEOC), "despite their efforts, law enforcement agencies of all sizes have not always been successful in recruiting and attracting individuals that reflect the communities they serve." The EEOC is an independent Federal agency originally created by Congress in 1964 to enforce Title VII of the *Civil Rights Act of 1964*. Additional details about the EEOC will be addressed in this chapter.

While police departments are more diverse than ever before, "recruiting, retaining, and promoting women, people of color, and members of LGBTQ groups remain a challenge nationwide (Heintze et al., 2019, p. 98). The hiring of police officers during a healthy economy can be problematic because private industry can offer better salaries. But in recent years, other matters have led some police agencies to struggle in achieving their hiring goals. The reasons cited include (1) strained relations and a lack of trust in law enforcement by eligible candidates; (2) high-profile police incidents involving the use of force undermining respect for police authority; (3) unease among potential candidates concerned about the paramilitary operational practices of law enforcement agencies; (4) an intense competition for skilled candidates in some areas; (5) burdensome bureaucratic and personnel regulations; and (6) lack of awareness about police work as a career. Consequently, each law enforcement agency must devote considerable planning time to recruit and retain adequate numbers of qualified personnel. The "methods and processes used to recruit and hire employees must be valid and fair and comply with federal, state, and local laws and guidelines" (Heintze et al., 2019. p. 95).

A fundamental theme of the President's Task Force on 21st Century Policing (2015) was the need to augment "trust and legitimacy" in police-community relations. One way to help accomplish this purpose is to have personnel who reflect the communities they serve. The Task Force called upon law enforcement agencies to "strive to create a workforce that encompasses a broad range of diversity including race, gender, language, life experience, and cultural background to improve understanding and effectiveness in dealing with all communities" (p. 2). It also addressed the need to develop "systematic and comprehensive diversification" policies for establishing a "greater trust and legitimacy with all segments of the population" (pp. 16–17).

One of the specific ways to build trust and legitimacy for the implementation of the Task Force recommendations is to employ qualified police candidates who reflect the community's diversity as well as to "examine hiring practices to better involve the community in recruiting and screening of recruits. For example, the Sarasota (Florida) Police Department involves the community in recruiting, selecting, and hiring officers as a way to encourage a more diverse workforce. The city works with residents to identify culturally responsive and qualified multilingual candidates for consideration. The community gives input into the hiring priorities considered in selection" (Implementation Guide, 2015, p. 10).

This chapter considers the problems associated with the recruitment and selection of qualified minority and women candidates in police agencies. The involvement of the community in the recruitment, selection, and hiring of officers is recognized as a major step toward overcoming the existing obstacles impeding recruitment efforts. Community members need to be invited to partner with law enforcement agencies through participation in meetings, surveys, and other initiatives. A few of these other initiatives may involve reporting to the public on recruiting activities and their outcomes by using the mainstream media, social media, and the agency's website. Perhaps, even more effective is for community stakeholders to serve as ambassadors to help in the recruiting process (Heintze et al., 2019, p. 102). At the same time, it would be most beneficial for police officers to possess "the knowledge and skills to be culturally responsive and to treat each person with dignity and respect" (Implementation Guide, 2015, p. 16). Additional matters relevant to the selection of police personnel as well as expanded activities to engage community members in the hiring process are discussed throughout the chapter. However, the road to federal and more local initiatives for the sake of a more diverse workforce and a more peaceful society has been paved with racism.

The Long March for Racial Equality

The lack of trust existing between minority groups, especially Black and White citizens, has been attributed to the development of a system of "structural racism" in the US stemming from the nation's history of: slavery and slave patrols; the South's Black Codes; lynching; the practice of convict leasing of freed people to plantation owners and to southern industrialists; the fire hoses and police violence used against Black freedom marchers; "redlining" practices associated with housing; federal policies directly aiding in militarizing local police; President Nixon's wars on drugs and crime; as well as the discriminatory effects of mandatory minimum sentences and the adoption of three strikes laws. Today, there are not only significant racial tensions between police and minorities, but a major political divide among state and federal lawmakers.

Due to the protests and disturbances associated with the civil rights movement led by a number of heroic figures including the Rev. Dr. Martin Luther King, Jr., President Kennedy sent a civil rights bill to Congress. In support of Kennedy's initiative, President Lyndon B. Johnson signed into law the *Civil Rights Act of 1964*. One section of the *Act*, referred to as Title VII, prohibits employment discrimination based on race, sex, color, religion, and national origin. The *Act* applies to private employers, labor unions and employment agencies. The *Act* also created the Equal Employment Opportunity Commission (EEOC) to enforce Title VII and eliminate unlawful employment discrimination, but the new agency had no authority to file lawsuits directly against employers. On July 2, 1965, EEOC began operations—one year after Title VII became a federal law. EEOC had an initial budget of $2.25 million and approximately 100 employees. Congress passed the *Age Discrimination in Employment Act of 1967* (ADEA) protecting individuals who are between 40 and 65 years of age from discrimination in employment. At that time EEOC was not authorized to file lawsuits directly against employers, but the agency did begin to submit *amicus* or "friend of the court" briefs in cases brought by individual employees. Finally, in 1972 Congress provides EEOC with the authority to file lawsuits against private companies. It also applied Title VII to the entire federal government and to all state and local government agencies with at least 15 employees (EEOC, 2022a).

The EEO Commission is composed of five Commissioners and a General Counsel appointed by the President and confirmed by the Senate. Commissioners are appointed for five-year staggered terms; the General Counsel's term is four years. The US President designates a Chairman and Vice Chairman. The Chairman is the Chief Executive Officer of the Commission. The Commission has authority to establish equal employment policies and to approve litigation. The General Counsel is responsible for conducting litigation. (For more specific information on the history of the EEOC, see the timeline of important EEOC events at: https://www.eeoc.gov/youth/timeline-important-eeoc-events and/or request additional information at: info@eeoc.gov.)

Currently, with headquarters offices in Washington, DC, 53 field offices serving every part of the nation, approximately 2,200 personnel, and a budget that exceeded $350 million in FY2020, "the U.S. Equal Employment Opportunity Commission (EEOC) is responsible for enforcing federal laws that make it illegal to discriminate against a job applicant or an employee because of the person's race, color, religion, sex (including pregnancy, transgender status, and sexual orientation), national origin, age (40 or older), disability, or genetic information. Most employers with at least 15 employees are covered by EEOC laws (20 employees in age discrimination cases). Most labor unions and employment agencies are also covered. The laws apply to all types of work situations, including hiring, firing, promotions, harassment, training, wages, and benefits. The EEOC has the authority to investigate charges of discrimination against employers who are covered by the law" (EEOC, 2022b). Administrative Law Judges conduct the hearings on EEO complaints and adjudicate the appeals from administrative decisions made by federal agencies on EEO complaints (EEOC, 2022b). If discrimination has been found to have taken place, the agency will try to settle the charge. If it isn't successful, it can file a lawsuit to protect the rights of individuals and the interests of the public. "When deciding to file a lawsuit, the EEOC considers several factors such as the strength of the evidence, the issues in the case, and the wider impact the lawsuit could have on the EEOC's efforts to combat workplace discrimination" (EEOC, 2022b). In addition, to enforcing EEOC laws and providing oversight and coordination of all Federal EEO regulations, practices, and policies, the agency tries to prevent discrimination before it occurs through outreach, education, and technical assistance programs (EEOC, 2022b).[2] "On any given day, the EEOC averages about 4,000 charges in intake, over 1,000 charges in conciliation, and 7,500 to 8,000 charges in mediation, in addition to the tens of thousands in investigation" (EEOC, 2019).

In the 1960s, the creation of a federal agency to address the barriers to fair employment was long overdue as the seeds of discrimination on the North American continent were planted centuries earlier. Beginning in 1619, the European settlers who relied on planting crops for their survival "increasingly purchased and enslaved Africans who had been kidnapped and brought to America by Dutch and English slavers; unlike indentured servants, these laborers had no contracts and their bondage was passed on to their children" (Blakemore, 2019). The institution of slavery became codified between 1690 and 1740 in South Carolina. Thus, more than 250 years before the creation of the U.S. Equal Employment Opportunity Commission (EEOC), the repression of African Americans included almost all aspects of life including freedom of movement, religious worship, and work habits. The laws were enforced by sheriffs, constables, night watch, and slave patrols (Henderson, 1976, pp. 34–35). Militia members helped to fill the ranks of the night watch and slave patrols. Militia membership provided a sense of affiliation and identification with one's settlement, town, and county. According to Reichel (2022), "as early as 1704 and continuing through the antebellum period, Southern slave states used local patrols with specific responsibility for regulating the activity of slaves. Those slave patrols were comprised of citizens who did patrol duty as their civic obligation, for pay, rewards, or for exemption from other duties" (p. 26). The slave patrols served specific regions and they were the main enforcers of the laws pertaining to runaway slaves, stolen property, and weapons. However, their main concern was to forestall insurrections. "Enslaved people didn't just engage in passive resistance against slaveholders—they planned and participated in armed revolts. Between the 17th and 19th centuries, enslaved Africans and African Americans in British North America and the United States staged hundreds of revolts" (Blakemore, 2019). For a well-researched review of the topic of slave patrols, the book by Sally Hadden (2001) entitled *Slave Patrols: Law and Violence in Virginia and the Carolinas* is recommended.

Slavery divided the nation until the conclusion of the Civil War. But for many generations it was replaced by "Jim Crow laws" that fostered segregation and second-class citizenship for Black Americans that continued until new national civil rights laws were enforced. "Jim Crow was the name of the racial caste system which operated primarily, but not exclusively in southern and border states, between 1877 and the mid-1960s. Jim Crow was more than a series of rigid anti-black laws. It was a way of life. Under Jim Crow, African Americans were relegated to the status of second class citizens. Jim Crow represented the legitimization of anti-black racism" (Pilgrim, 2012).

"During the era of Reconstruction, Black Americans' political rights were affirmed by three constitutional amendments and numerous laws passed by Congress. Racial discrimination was attacked on a particularly broad front by the *Civil Rights Act of 1875*. This legislation made it a crime for an individual to deny 'the full and equal enjoyment of any of the accommodations, advantages, facilities, and privileges of inns, public conveyances on land or water, theaters and other places of public amusement; subject only to the conditions and limitations established by law, and applicable alike to citizens of every race and color'" (National Archives, 2022).

"In 1883, the Supreme Court struck down the 1875 act, ruling that the 14th Amendment did not give Congress authority to prevent discrimination by private individuals. Victims of racial discrimination were told to seek relief not from the federal government, but from the states. At the same time, state governments were passing legislation that codified inequality between the races. Laws requiring the establishment of separate schools for children of each race were most common; however, segregation was soon extended to most public and semi-public facilities through 'Jim Crow' laws" (National Archives, 2022).

In 1896, the US Supreme Court affirmed a segregation law in Louisiana in the case of *Plessy v. Ferguson*, which required either separate railroad passenger coaches or partitioned coaches to provide segregated accommodations for each race. The *Plessy* case "gave Jim Crow states a legal way to ignore their constitutional obligations to their black citizens" (Pilgrim, 2012). The *Plessy* decision set the precedent that "separate" facilities for Blacks and Whites were constitutional as long as they were "equal." The "separate but equal" doctrine was quickly extended to cover many areas of public life, such as restaurants, theaters, restrooms, and public schools. The doctrine was a fiction, as facilities for Black citizens were always inferior to those for Whites. Not until 1954, in the equally important Supreme Court decision of *Brown v. Board of Education of Topeka*, would the "separate but equal" doctrine be struck down. Nonetheless, *de facto* segregation remains in many urban school systems.

In 1909, reform-minded Black and White citizens established the National Association for the Advancement of Colored People (NAACP). This association and other organizations led the efforts against discrimination and segregation in the United States. The NAACP pursued voting rights and worked to dismantle various forms of segregation through the courts. Painstakingly, one case at a time, one law at a time, they confronted the racial inequities in the legal system. In addition, Black artists, actors, and writers led the battle against intellectual and artistic bias. Even during the deprivations of the Great Depression, their artistic achievements became known as the "Harlem Renaissance." Paintings, drawings, classical music, jazz, blues, poetry, novels, plays, and dance abounded during this era and won world acclaim. On the other hand, more than a century after the end of World War I, "African Americans, whether in the military, the halls of Congress or in local communities, continue to stand on the front lines in the fight to make democracy a reality in the United States" (Williams, 2018).

An early date found for the hiring of Black police personnel was 1861 in Washington, DC. In 1867, African American police officers were appointed to the police department in

Selma, Alabama; they would be followed in 1868 by officers in Jackson, Florida, and in 1870 by officers in Houston and Galveston, Texas. In 1870, New Orleans, Louisiana had 177 African American officers, and three of five police board members were African American (US Dept. of Justice, 2017). In 1872, Chicago, Illinois employed that city's first Black officer. Other cities with Black officers prior to 1890 include: Philadelphia, Pennsylvania in 1874; Columbia and Charleston, South Carolina in 1873; and Meridian, Jackson, and Clinton, Mississippi in 1871 (Kuykendall & Bums, 1980, p. 4).

> In Los Angeles, California, prior to 1959 blacks were restricted in geographical assignments and at one point, all non-whites were assigned to an industrial district in one division of the city. . . . In Charlotte, North Carolina, prior to civil service, black officers received a lower salary than did White officers. In Birmingham, Alabama, until the mid-1950's police examinations were not given to black applicants. In 1962, in some southern communities, black officers were not allowed access to police headquarters and, at times, were not permitted to attend training programs.
>
> *(Kuykendall & Bums, 1980, p. 8)*

Moreover, it wasn't until 1948, three years after the end of WWII, that Black people were hired by the cities of Memphis, Tennessee and Atlanta, Georgia (Kuykendall & Bums, 1980, p. 8).

In the field of federal law enforcement, in 1875 Bass Reeves became, perhaps, the first African American Deputy U.S. Marshal (US Dept. of Justice, 2017). He escaped from slavery during the Civil War where he had served as his master's body servant during battle. He was able to make his way to Indian Territory and after learning the languages of the region's tribes was hired by Judge Isaac Parker, the famous "Hanging Judge," who presided between 1875 and 1896 over the US District Court for the Western District of Arkansas in Fort Smith. At one time, it was the largest criminal court in the country. He was employed as a deputy for 32 years, retiring in 1907. "Newspaper accounts from the time celebrate the frontier lawman's skill" (Trent, 2019).

In late 1919, an African American Army captain in World War I named James Wormley Jones, age 37, became a special agent in the Bureau of Investigation, the forerunner of the FBI. "As an agent, Jones was employed exclusively in an undercover capacity, working directly under the head of the General Intelligence Division (GID), future director J. Edgar Hoover" (FBI, 2011). However, it appears that only a few other black agents were hired until 1962 when Aubrey Lewis and James Barrow "became the first African-American agents accepted to the FBI Academy, ushering in a new era for minority agents in the Bureau" (FBI, 2011).

"The National Organization of Black Law Enforcement Executives (NOBLE) was founded in September 1976 during a three-day symposium to address crime in low-income urban areas. The symposium was co-sponsored by the Police Foundation and the Law Enforcement Assistance Administration (LEAA). The Joint Center for Political Studies (JCPS) coordinated this unprecedented event in which 60 top-ranking Black law enforcement executives representing 24 states and 50 major cities gathered in the Washington, DC, area to participate. They exchanged views about the critically high rate of crime in the Black urban communities and the socio-economic conditions that lead to crime and violence. They raised questions about relevant issues such as fairness in the administration of justice, police community relations, the hiring and promotion of Black police officers, and the unique problems of the Black police executive. Recognizing Black law enforcement executives could have a significantly more effective impact upon the criminal justice system through a unified voice, the symposium participants departed from the planned agenda to create NOBLE. They unanimously elected Hubert Williams, then Director of the Newark, New Jersey Police Department, and the first Black police chief of a major city, temporary chairman of NOBLE. During that meeting, the initial purpose and the objectives of the organization were developed and a working committee to devise the organizational structure was formed" (NOBLE, 2022).

While various civil rights organizations and artists pursued efforts to fostering the ideals of American democracy and racial equality, a number of minority individuals saw opportunities for personal advancement in public service careers due to the availability of the new civil service merit systems and/or personal initiatives. For example, Samuel Jesse Battle (1883–1966) may have been the first or at least one of the earliest Black police officers in New York City. After attending segregated schools in North Carolina, Battle moved north, first to Connecticut, then to New York City where he worked as a train porter (Secret, 2015). He worked as a "Red Cap" at Grand Central Terminal for seven years and at the same time began studying for the New York City Police Department (NYPD) civil service exam. He was sworn in on March 6, 1911, rising to the rank of lieutenant. Later, he served as a commissioner of parole from 1941 to 1951. His initiation into a police career was facilitated through the support of his brother-in-law, Moses P. Cobb, who started working for the Brooklyn Police force in the early 1890s before Brooklyn officially was absorbed into New York City with the adoption of the Greater New York Charter in 1898. Battle's successful career in law enforcement surely inspired other minorities to enter the field of police work. In 1960, Battle provided various details about his career for Columbia University's oral history project (see Battle, 1960).

Over two decades before Battle joined the NYPD, Robert William Stewart (1850–1931) became the first Black police officer in Los Angeles. He was born in Garrard County, Kentucky and is believed to have been the eldest of 11 children who were born into slavery. He was a member of the local Colored Republican Club (CRC), "a political force at the time, helping to sweep Republican politicians into office. When it came time for those politicians to make political appointments, the CRC wanted their due. At this time, police positions were subject to annual approval and re-approval by the city's police commission. Appointments at the time were even released in lists separated by Democratic and Republican appointments" (Mendez & Cagle, 2020). In 1889, Stewart was one of two Black persons on the published Republican police officer appointees' list. The two had become the first Black police officers in the city of Los Angeles. However, just a year later, Joseph H. Green, his fellow appointee was laid off and he died in 1903. On the other hand, "Stewart was given a post directing traffic at the intersection of Spring and First streets, then one of the city's busiest intersections. Stewart's career was lauded in the press. Newspaper articles described both his arrests and court appearances and the fascination the public had with seeing a 'colored giant in blue.' He was wildly popular as a subject and well-respected in the community. At one point in his career, Stewart posed for a photograph with his arms folded in front of his bare chest along with other members of a 'strong man' team (Mendez & Cagle, 2020). In 1892, Stewart resigned from the LAPD to run as a Republican for one of two positions as a county constable, as the region's first major-party Black candidate for elected office, he finished third in the race. However, he was quickly reappointed as a police officer early in 1893. However, Stewart's police career suddenly ended on May 10, 1900. "That day, as he prepared to patrol his beat, Stewart was arrested by LAPD detectives and charged with the rape of Grace Cunningham, a white 15-year-old girl. . . . Stewart was quoted as saying that he did meet and speak with a girl while walking his beat, but that he did not walk her home, and that he likely wouldn't even be able to recognize her . . . the city's Police Commission voted, 3–2, to fire Stewart without allowing him to defend himself—only after voting to provide themselves with the power to fire an officer" (Mendez & Cagle, 2020). Stewart's first trial ended with a hung jury and three months later he was found not guilty by a second trial's jury. Stewart worked as a janitor and a laborer for the remainder of his life. Currently, historians are seeking to ensure that Stewart and Green's stories will be properly acknowledged (Mendez & Cagle, 2020).

An early pioneer in the history of African American woman in the field of law enforcement was Georgia Ann Hill Robinson (1879–1961). She was born in Opelousas, Louisiana, never knowing her parents. She was initially cared for by her older sister and later grew up in a Roman Catholic convent. When she was 18, Robinson moved to Kansas to work as a governess. There, she met and married Morgan Robinson. The couple moved first to Leadville, Colorado, and then to Los Angeles with their daughter Marian. In Los Angeles, Robinson's desire to serve led her to get involved with various community organizations, and it was through her work with these groups that she was approached and convinced by an LAPD recruiter to join the force. On July 25, 1916, at the age of 37, she first became a volunteer for the LAPD. Three years later, on June 10, 1919, Robinson became the city's first Black policewoman when she was hired as a jail matron. Later, she investigated juvenile and homicide cases. In her position as an investigator, Robinson discovered the need for a women's shelter in Los Angeles and helped to establish the Sojourner Truth Home for destitute women and girls. Unfortunately, at the age of 49, she tried to break up an altercation between two drunken women in her jail and lost her sight. Nevertheless, Robinson continued to serve her community. She worked with community leaders to end local discriminatory practices, including Dr. Claude Hudson, the longtime president of the Los Angeles branch of the National Association for the Advancement of Colored People (NAACP) (Bryan, 2016).

The long police career of Samuel Battle was exceptional since most police officers of African American heritage, including Battle at times, had to cope with discriminatory behavior by their agencies and many of their White colleagues. For example, in Philadelphia, Pennsylvania, the first Black officers were assigned in or near Black areas and were limited in opportunities for promotion (Kuykendall & Bums, 1980). In the late 1960s, Black Americans were just beginning to enjoy broader employment opportunities, including in urban police and fire departments. On the other hand, African American police officers were often faced with a dual challenge. Firstly, they had to aggressively seek out fair treatment and advancement opportunities; and secondly, they had to walk a very thin line because many people in their own communities viewed them as members of a "menacing, racist force" (Blythe, 2021). According to Stark and Little (2018), "despite a successful push in 2016 to attract more Black applicants to the police force, the Chicago Police Department has hired relatively few African-Americans." Charles Wilson, chairman of the National Association of Black Law Enforcement Officers, said prescreening exams have been used to discriminate against Black recruits. "They bang us out on the agility exam," he said. "We do not typically go into the exam being 'fit and ready.' We go out into the yard and shoot hoops, but we

FIGURE 6.1 Lt. Samuel Battle, with his four-year-old granddaughter, at City Hall in New York City on September 4, 1941. He was sworn in at that time as NYPD's first Black parole commissioner by the city's mayor during graduation exercises of the police department.

Source: AP Photo.

don't get into the idea of doing a daily run. Our counterparts are heavily into that. So, they are more prepared for the agility examination" (qtd. in Stark & Little, 2018). In addition, Chicago Alderman Anthony Beale said the hiring process systematically excludes minorities. The biggest issue is the background check, which "really wipes out minorities. . . . If you have bad credit you can't be a police officer" (qtd. in Stark & Little, 2018). Black applicants need more of a support system throughout the application process, according to

Tracey Ladner, former director of the Chicago Police Department's human resources division. "You have to have that support group off the job as well as a support group you have from being on the job" (qtd. in Stark & Little, 2018).

Trends in Hiring

Absent an infusion of federal funds, there have been only modest changes in the numbers of in-service LEOs. Policing is a secure job, according to Peter Moskos, a professor at the John Jay College of Criminal Justice. "They are financially locked in. If you quit, you don't get your pension. Cops are human, too. They have a mortgage to pay. You can't quit" (qtd. in Li & Mahajan, 2021). Recent reports have indicated only a small declining trend in the number and quality of applicants for law enforcement careers. From 2019 to 2020, the number of people working at local police departments and sheriffs' offices decreased by less than 1%, according to monthly data from the Bureau of Labor Statistics.[3] On the other hand, there is a nationwide correctional officer shortage in prisons. In order to attract more correctional officers, "states are raising salaries, offering hiring bonuses, reducing the minimum age to 18 and ratcheting up recruiting efforts with advertisements on billboards and social media" (TCR Staff, 2022). "The shortages have had a severe impact on daily prison life, forcing officers to work mandatory overtime and undercutting their fundamental duty to oversee and escort people who are incarcerated, heightening tensions inside the prison walls" (PEW Stateline, 2022).

The utility of increasing police force numbers has been the subject of much research (see Tella & Schargrodsky, 2004; Donahue & Ludwig, 2007; Lin, 2009; Mello, 2018). For example, Steven Mello (2018) found that additional police leads to reductions in robbery, larceny, and auto theft, with suggestive evidence that police reduce murders as well. "Crime reductions associated with additional police were more pronounced in areas most affected by the Great Recession [2007–2009]. The results highlight that fiscal support to local governments for crime prevention may offer large returns, especially during bad macroeconomic times" (Mello, 2018).[4]

The slight decline in police numbers has been attributed to a "confluence of factors—diminished public respect for the profession, a more complex and dangerous job, greater public scrutiny often with bystander or body-worn camera video, and a post-pandemic desire for different ways of working that include remote work and flexible schedules, neither of which is typically available in the law enforcement field" (Wiseman, 2021). In some cities, the increased calls for police accountability and reform since the death of George Floyd in May 2020 have contributed to a drop-off in police officer retention as police morale has suffered and retirements and resignations have increased. In some cases, city officials voted to reduce the size of their police force. For example, the Burlington (VT) City Council passed a resolution in 2020 to decrease the size of the police department from 105 to 74 officers by attrition. After the Council voted to decrease the officer count, the number of officers kept falling in the department. In August 2022, there were 61 officers, but only 53 were available for deployment, including 21 available to be on patrol. City officials are now attempting to rebuild the agency and have raised officer salaries and are offering a substantial sign-on bonus in the amount of $15,000. "Burlington Police hope to increase the number of officers up to 85 in three years. However, they will need to double the number of recruits annually and improve retention rates to 55% to achieve that" (Huntley, 2022).

According to a widely reported PERF survey of nearly 200 departments, there has been a "45% increase in the retirement rate and a nearly 20% increase in resignations in 2020–21 compared to the previous year. . . . Exit interviews in the PERF survey and other data show that a key factor in the police resignations and retirements is the national conversation and protests that center on changing what the police do, how they're funded, and how to better hold officers accountable for abuse of force and racial bias" (Westervelt, 2021). Conversely, Li and Mahajan (2021) point out that while the 2020 numbers appear dramatic when compared to year 2019, "looking across the past decade, police employment in 2020 was roughly the same as in 2018."

The Chicago Police Department seemed to be on verge of hiring many new Black officers in 2016 due to a rise in the number of applications received as a result of a widespread advertising campaign. Yet, in 2017 the "police department hired whites and Latinos at rates more than double that of African-Americans, who made up just 17 percent of the . . . 1,126 new hires" (Stark & Little, 2018). "Historically, the Chicago Police Department has had a hard time recruiting black officers, who are 23 percent of the force in a city that is about one-third African-American" (Stark & Little, 2018). However, this problem appears to lie not in attracting applicants, but retaining those Black applicants during the multistep process leading-up to academy graduation. Like most police agencies, the process includes initial entry testing, followed by extensive background checks and physical, psychological and drug exams, but many of the applicants fall out along the way. According to Shari Runner, the chief executive officer for the Chicago Urban League, whose organization has been active in police reform, "You can't just recruit. You can't just say we've got thousands of applications from African-Americans or people of color without really understanding what the culture is that allows people to succeed in that [process] and then move forward" (qtd. in Stark & Little, 2018).

In order to recruit more Black officers with a goal of improving the department's relations in African American communities, in November of 2016 Chicago hired a leading public relations firm to oversee the recruitment. Recruitment among Black citizens significantly increased, but the selection process was time-consuming, and many Black applicants lacked a support group. According to Tracey Ladner, former director of the Chicago Police Department's human resources division, "You have to have that support group off the job as well as a support group you have from being on the job. . . . You have to assure their mother that you know the chances of them getting shot are relatively low" (qtd. in Stark & Little, 2018). Other critics of the department's hiring process claim that it is discriminatory. Charles Wilson, chairman of the National Association of Black Law Enforcement Officers, explained: "They bang us out on the agility exam. . . . We do not typically go into the exam being 'fit and ready.' We go out into the yard and shoot hoops, but we don't get into the idea of doing a daily run. Our counterparts are heavily into that. So, they are more prepared for the agility examination" (qtd. in Stark & Little, 2018).

Undoubtedly, the problems associated with the recruitment of Black police officers in Chicago have also arisen in other comparable cities. The process is slow and many candidates who may already have family members on the force or the backing of legacy officer associations will likely be provided coaching so that they will have better chances of performing well on the screening exams. Therefore, it is one thing to fill out an interest card and be given a date for an entry exam and quite another to do well enough to advance to the next step in the process.

Best Practices

Over the past half century, there have been wide ranging efforts to help cultivate police recruits. One program that was developed in the mid-1970s for the city of Miami involved training young people to serve as police paraprofessionals. The program initially offered 55 men and women aged 18 to 20 opportunities to work as "public service aides" (PSAs). They were paid $3 an hour during a 30-hour work week to perform non-law enforcement duties and to undertake part-time coursework at a local college in a law enforcement associate degree program. Of the first 40 PSAs to enter the program, seven became police officers upon reaching age 21 (Young People, 1976, p. 11).

After the 9/11 attacks on America, the International Association of Police Chiefs (IACP) received US Department of Justice support to develop a model to assist local and state law enforcement agencies improve their recruiting efforts in general and with minority groups in particular. It was deemed desirable for the purposes of building-up the public trust to seek out minority applicants who mirrored local populations. A three-step model was created and piloted in cooperation with the Hartford (CT) Police Department. The three steps included (1) building block activities; (2) stakeholder action planning; and (3) strategy implementation, monitoring and evaluation (Needle & Rollins, 2003).

Step 1 of the Hartford model involved diagnosing the problem in collaboration with the community and conducting such building block activities as: a market survey of potential candidates; recruitment targeting of minorities and women; studying the efforts of other agencies; ascertaining the availability and practices of the local human resources system; and gathering information about the best practices of other agencies regarding recruitment, selection, and retention. Step 2 involved moving to a stakeholder action planning mode for the purposes of: determining specific diversification and agency's goals. During this step civic groups, police, and other concerned community partners target and survey future applicants to determine interest and design initiatives for recruiting purposes. Step 3 involved implementation of these action initiatives by such means as: management reforms; training; action plan implementation; the generation of evaluation data; monitoring implementation actions; mid-course corrections; new conceptualizations; action plan revisions; and evaluation of outcomes (process and impact measures) (Needle & Rollins, 2003, pp. ii–iv).

Jane Wiseman (2021), drawing upon the insights gathered from recent research, recommended that the hiring of a diverse force to improve trust and confidence could be enhanced by (1) widening outreach strategies to attract more candidates; (2) making the process more efficient; (3) supporting recruits so that fewer abandon the process; (4) employing targeted recruitment strategies to attract candidates of color; (5) employing targeted recruitment strategies to attract female candidates; and (6) developing the most beneficial recruiting messages (p. 3). She noted that "many of the recommendations put forth here can be done with little cost, or at no cost at all. Any combination of approaches may yield improvements now, which can compound over time to create significant impact in the future" (Wiseman, 2021, p. 10).

Oliver (2017) has indicated that creating a diverse workforce should be an intentional priority since they should help "to offset potential implicit conceptions of bias." An important first step involves the development of selection criteria aimed at recruiting officers who will be effective in their assignments, possess leadership skills, and have the capacity to exercise authority in a prudent manner. He recommended seeking candidates who "have integrity, dedication to service, human relations skills, compatibility with a team, and a drive to excel. . . . These qualifications are vital because even the newest officers have considerable authority in the community and the potential to become leaders in their agencies" (Oliver, 2017). In order to reach such candidates permanent recruitment units are needed to streamline "the application process as much as possible (to prevent losing applicants during the extended process); and varying assessment measures to include job-simulation and interpersonal skills testing" (Oliver, 2017).

The strategies for the recruiting, hiring, retaining, and promoting a diverse law enforcement should include the need to reflect the diversity found in the communities where they serve. The Commission on Accreditation for Law Enforcement Agencies (2022) has adopted a mandatory standard to encourage the recruitment and selection of culturally diverse police departments proportionate to the community. Standard 31.2.1 states, in part "The agency has a recruitment plan for full-time sworn personnel outlining the steps to achieve the goals of an ethnic, racial, and gender workforce composition in approximate proportion to the available workforce in the agency's service community."

One area of concern that has been routinely problematic is the entry interview. Heintze and his associates (2019) indicate that "an interview, no matter how standardized, is an interaction. As a result, it is inherently subjective and involves human judgment as a critical component of the decision-making process. In any interaction, there are verbal and non-verbal cues—as well as subtle interactions between the parties—that affect and can influence responses. Even in the most standardized interview process, a decision will come down to several people interpreting data to form an opinion about the risks and benefits associated with hiring a particular individual" (p. 96). In addition, "many of the traditional selection practices used to screen applicants—including physical ability and cognitive tests as well as background checks—have been shown to have an unwarranted disproportionate impact on underrepresented populations" (Heintze et al., 2019, pp. 96–97).

Minority Recruitment Strategies

At a PERF meeting held in 2018 of 250 law enforcement executives, there was near unanimity of belief that police agencies were having problems recruiting for diversity. Tempe (Arizona) Police Chief Sylvia Moir remarked that making departments more welcoming to minorities and women, in part by providing them with mentors and physical training, has enabled her department to maintain its recruitment numbers.[5] Other top police commanders also shared their ideas about "how to recruit, and retain, quality police officers, including lowering the requirement of a college degree, relaxing rules on prior drug use and easing tattoo policies" (Jackman, 2018).

Two law enforcement agencies that have adopted new selections procedures that effectively select qualified individuals and have a less adverse impact on racial minorities and women are the Madison (WI) and St. Paul (MN) Police Departments. The Madison Police Department "has made significant progress in increasing the number of women it hires to be officers. The agency's physical agility test used to require a bench press component, which deterred some candidates from applying and led others to fail - in part because they were not familiar with the specific weight lifting equipment or exercise. Recognizing these challenges, the agency began to give candidates the option to do push-ups, instead of the bench press, to test their upper body strength. Department leadership believes this change resulted in more women competing and passing the physical agility test. Overtime, the bench press was completely removed from the exam" (EEOC, 2016). In St. Paul, the police department "determined - after analyzing the breakdown of pass rates for African American, Latino, and Asian-American applicants - that its testing process was having a disproportionately harmful impact on candidates of color without a commensurate job-related benefit. The department found that candidates of color performed worse on the situational and written tests but significantly better than white candidates during the in-person interview. The department re-evaluated its hiring criteria to ensure that its testing criteria accurately aligned with the qualities that were most important on the job. It changed its written tests to focus more on the candidate's personal history and community engagement and removed the entire situational component. The department reported that it was able to hire more diverse, but equally qualified applicants using this new approach" (EEOC, 2016).

At a summit meeting held in December 2018 regarding the progress of women in policing, conference attendees expressed frustration at the state of existing marketing materials about policing and the reality of the job. One attendee stated, "Marketing materials should show what policing is really about, not all shooting and rappelling from helicopters. We always show all the sexy stuff, but not conflict resolution, problem solving, helping people access resources. These are the talents and skills we need to reflect in our marketing materials" (Starheim, 2019, p. 16). With respect to the recruitment and retention of female officers, it has been recommended that law enforcement leaders must address issues of concern to female candidates, such as sexual harassment from male officers and maternity leave. Credibility on these and other issues is more likely to occur if women officers are used in efforts to recruit female officer candidates. Women officers are best able to explain what it is like to work and have a career in a traditionally male-dominated occupation. In addition, in order to find greater numbers of female candidates, departments should focus on areas where they are likely to find women who are interested in nontraditional careers. This can include distributing literature and sponsoring activities at gyms and women's sporting events, as well as female health clinics and grocery stores. Recruiters participating in college job fairs should not limit their efforts to criminal justice graduates, but also focus on those who have majored in physical education, journalism, and sociology (Orrick, 2009). A recruitment video from New Zealand, one of several, is an example of an effective recruitment tool. This highly entertaining video features several male and female officers who run through obstacles, doing backflips and rolls in the air, while explaining and interacting with the community. It emphasizes the value of communication and relationship building, and uses humor to promote a different image of police and police work. This three-minute recruiting video may be viewed online at: https://www.youtube.com/watch?v=f9psILoYmCc#action=share.

Shortly after the onset of the 21st century, Needle and Rollins (2003) surveyed law enforcement agencies from coast to coast that had planned and conducted successful minority recruitment programs. At that time, Needle and Rollins (2003) noted that in many parts of the nation the search for qualified "educated, intelligent, and technologically capable applicants [was] . . . fierce" (p. 42).

Women Police in History

Women LEOs have been participating in police work for well over 100 years. According to Rick Barrett, a former Drug Enforcement Administration agent and amateur historian, Marie Owens was not only the first policewoman in Chicago but also the first known female officer in the United States. In 1888, her husband "died of typhoid fever, one of several illnesses then plaguing the city. Left to raise five children, Owens landed a job in 1889 with the city health department, working as one of five female factory inspectors who enforced child-labor and compulsory education laws. At the time, public outrage was growing over sweatshop conditions in factories across the city. But the inspectors' powers were limited; they couldn't enter buildings without a warrant. As pressure mounted on public officials to step up enforcement of child labor laws, Owens was transferred to the Police Department in 1891. She was given powers of arrest, the title of detective sergeant and a police star" (Mastony, 2010). In 1906, during a newspaper interview about her career, "Owens described how she had discovered children—'frail little things' as young as 7 years old—working in factories all over the city. Some assembly lines were staffed by scores of kids, many looking suspiciously younger than 14, the age at which children were legally allowed to work. 'In my sixteen years of experience I have come across more suffering than ever is seen by any man detective.' Her work affected thousands of children. She established schools within department stores so young workers could get an education, and she persuaded other employers to shorten their workdays. In 1923, she retired after 32 years with the department. Four years later, she died at age 74 (Mastony, 2010).

On April 1, 1908, Lola Baldwin, 48, was sworn in as a "female detective to perform police service" for the city of Portland, Oregon (Horne, 2006). Los Angeles appointed its first woman officer in 1910—Alice Stebbin Wells. A community petition helped her achieve this appointment. Mina C. Van Winkle (1875–1933) was a crusading social worker, suffragist, and police lieutenant who led the Women's Bureau of the Metropolitan Police Department in Washington, DC. Her public statements about gender and morality brought her national attention. On one occasion, she proclaimed that the role of women police should be greatly enlarged since in nearly "all the cities where women are employed and given a free hand they have proved themselves most efficient and useful" (Winkle, 1921). Before serving in her police position, Winkle headed the Speaker's Bureau of the newly created US Food Administration. "The Speaker's Bureau consisted of teachers, scientists, and other volunteers who traveled the country encouraging food conservation during war time" (Biondi, 2022). During her career she became a national leader in the protection of girls and other women involved in the criminal justice process.

Prior to the entry of Owens, Baldwin, Wells, and Van Winkle into police service, as early as 1845 in New York City, women in law enforcement were limited to assignments involving the oversight of the women's quarters in various lockups—jails, prisons, holding cells in police stations and taking them to and from court. By 1916, policewomen existed in 25 cities in 20 states (Peak, 1997, p. 94). By 1921, it was estimated that there were 300 cities in the United States where women police served. In nearly all police departments their assignments concerned preventive or protective work related to female offenders of all ages. Such women officers were placed at posts in or near movie theatres, dance halls, railroad depots and similar places. They also engaged in limited types of investigations involving runaways, petty gambling in stores frequented by children, the sale of liquor to minors, child desertion, truancy, shoplifting, prostitution, and narcotics addiction (Winkle, 1921; Graper, 1921, pp. 225–226).

By 1960, there were 5,617 female police officers and detectives in the United States. Of these, all but 400 served in urban areas. However, their role was primarily in juvenile divisions, "where they performed investigative and social service-oriented activities for women,

FIGURE 6.2 Women taking the qualifying exam for the New York City Police Department in 1947. A New York World-Telegram & Sun photo by Dick De Marsico. Library of Congress Prints and Photographs Division Washington, D.C. Reproduction Number: LC-USZ62–136823 (b &w film copy neg.). In 1942, the NYPD added the requirement of a college degree for female officers—which did not exist for men. Immediately following WWII, there was a shift for many women to return to the traditional gender roles they held before. However, many women fought to maintain the sense of freedom they held during wartime. This image shows women who are breaking away from the gender norms of the past.

teenage females, preteen youngsters (both male and female), and infants. In addition, some larger forces, including those of New York, Detroit, and Los Angeles, routinely [assigned] female officers to other operational commands, where they [participated] in narcotics and gambling law enforcement and routine patrolling (The President's Commission, 1967, p. 125). Over the next two decades, the roles of women officers began to diversify due to new federal equal employment opportunity laws and the lawsuits pursued by women in police service. New studies found that having women on street patrol duty could be beneficial (e.g., see Weldy, 1976; Morash & Greene, 1986; McDowell, 1992). McDowell (1992) indicated that as the police job description has been expanding beyond crime fighting into community service, the growing presence of women should help improve community relations and foster a more flexible and less violent approach to keeping the peace. By the beginning of the 21st century, women police officers were serving in all types and sizes of police agencies, in all ranks, in all kinds of work assignments, and in all parts of the country (Horne, 2006). By 2007, women occupied about 11.8% of all sworn positions and 18.3% of the positions in the nation's largest cities. In addition, they held 13.7% of first-line police supervisory positions and 23.2% of the criminal investigative positions, but only 5% of the chief executive positions (Orrick, 2009).

While much of society has come to accept the fact of women police officers, many of them "often feel excluded from the informal networks of policing, providing an added source of stress" (Peak, 1997, p. 99) and there remains underrepresentation of women in many police agencies. In the first decades of the 21st century, female police applicants and officers continued to file discrimination lawsuits against law enforcement agencies, seeking change through the courts (Horne, 2006).

There is no escaping the fact that the employment of women in police work presents special problems for the women involved, their families, and the employing agencies. Yet, according to Cara Rabe-Hemp (2018), despite the struggles that women face to survive in the "all-boys club" of policing, women not only survive, most thrive in this almost exclusively male occupation. However, the entry of women into the field of policing is complex and officer's experiences are wide-ranging. Stories of resistance and harassment by colleagues, the glass ceiling in promotion, and gender specific obstacles related to pregnancy and childcare are common.

On December 3–4, 2018, the National Institute of Justice (NIJ), a sub-division of the US Department of Justice, hosted a prepandemic summit meeting of nearly 100 sworn and civilian LEOs, researchers, representatives from professional organizations and foundations, and federal agencies to discuss the state of research on women in American policing. Their mandate was to identify priority questions and to form a compendium of the issues for future research. A report, based on conversations at the conference set forth many of the issues and related research on women in policing across the areas of culture, performance, recruitment and retention, and promotion. It also outlined a wide grouping of research questions in each of these areas. With regard to the theme of recruitment and retention, the report noted that there existed no standardized, empirically supported programs to increase the representation of women in policing (Starheim, 2019, p. 13). Nonetheless, the impact of popular national television shows portraying the effectiveness and acceptance of women as full partners with men in police work has surely enhanced interest in women entering police careers. Such programs as *Cagney and Lacey*, *NCIS*, and *Law and Order: SVU* come readily to mind.

On the other hand, there was consensus among attendees at the summit conference held in late 2018 that the difficulty of balancing professional and personal responsibilities was a major factor driving women to leave policing or simply to choose a different career. According to one attendee, "The biggest obstacle for women in police work is the ability to balance work and family life [and] a lot of women simply opt out of policing for this reason" (Starheim, 2019, p. 19). In addition, the "attendees agreed that departments must prioritize policy changes that would help officers balance their professional and personal lives better . . . if departments did not frame the conversation in that way, they would risk wasting significant resources in their talent pool" (Starheim, 2019, p. 19)

Milestones for Women in Policing

According to Rebe-Hemp (2018), the potential for enduring change in the field of policing is growing as women continue to make strides in achieving high ranks, breaking down assignments barriers, and ensuring just opportunities for future generations of female police officers. However, as noted above the progress has only been gradual. For example, the *2001 Status of Women in Policing Survey* by National Center for Women and Policing (NCWP) found that "despite evidence that women and men are equally capable of police work, widespread bias in police hiring, selection practices, and recruitment policies keeps the numbers of women in law enforcement artificially low. Entry exams overemphasize physical prowess and block many qualified women from serving even though research shows that such tests are not job-related and they do not predict successful job performance. Many women are discouraged from applying to law enforcement agencies because of the aggressive and authoritarian image of policing; an image based on the outdated paramilitary model of law enforcement. On the job, women often face discrimination, harassment, and intimidation, and are maliciously thwarted, especially as they move up the ranks. Research has shown that women police officers use a style of policing that relies less on physical force and more on communication skills. As a result, women are often better at defusing potentially violent confrontations, and are less likely to become involved in use of excessive force situations. Women are substantially less likely to be named in a citizen complaint, sustained allegation, or civil lawsuit for excessive use of force. Women officers respond more effectively to domestic violence incidents. The disparity between the numbers of men and women involved in policing adversely impacts the culture, operations, and efficacy of law enforcement agencies" (NCWP, 2002). Most of these thoughts have been echoed by law enforcement leaders in subsequent decades. According to Michael Koval, who served as the police chief in Madison, Wisconsin from 2014 to 2019, "Enforcement of the law is about 20 percent of what we do. The other 80 percent is a lot of relational stuff, a lot of mediation, diagnostics, referral—a lot of collaboration that has nothing to do with law enforcement" (qtd. in Ripley, 2017). On occasion, in Madison, women have made up nearly 30% of the police force—one of the highest ratios in the United States.

Moyca Newell and Katherine Mayo led the publicity campaign to establish the New York State Police in the early 1900s, but it was not until 1974 when four women were selected and completed the basic training school to become state troopers. In 2011, Maureen Tuffey, a member of this groundbreaking group, retired after 38 years of service from the New York State Police. At the time she was sworn-in, she didn't think that any more women were going to be hired and that she felt like a spectacle, because most people weren't accustomed to seeing troopers with long hair. "They'd stare at you for a little while until they figured it out" (qtd. in Mason, 2011).

In 1975, the first female woman trooper joined the ranks of her graduating class of 80 men and was sworn in as a member of the New Jersey State Police (NJSP). Gail Just, the lone female graduate said that the training program was "rigorous," but that she had neither asked nor was offered any mitigation of the requirements, except for some slight alterations based on "consideration for the physiological differences" between men and women. "I ran the five-mile course here, although I was required only to do three miles" (qtd. in Johnston, 1975, p. 71). Jane Hostetler Bulaga was able to attend all but the final week of the training program, but was dismissed at the end of 17 weeks of the program for her "failure" to meet minimum standards for shooting and running. She had instituted the original civil rights lawsuit that brought about the end of the long-standing barrier to admission of women into the NJSP. She described her 17 weeks of training as "hell." "I brought a lawsuit against them and they don't want me" (qtd. in Johnston, 1975, p. 71).

According to Brandon Kooi, professor of criminal justice at Aurora University, Penny Harrington (1942–2021) was the first major-city female police chief in US history. She sued the Portland Police Bureau 42 times, half in federal court, in an effort to allow women to be promoted the same way male officers were, and she suffered a great deal as a consequence of her courageous trailblazing efforts (Kooi, 2021). She became Portland's chief of police in 1985 and the following decade co-founded of the National Center for Women and Policing. "When Harrington started as an officer with the Portland Police Bureau in 1964, there were only 12 women in the department. She faced widespread challenges over the course of her career, ranging from blatant harassment and sexism to many iterations of body armor that did not fit or protect women's bodies" (Starheim, 2019, p. 3). In 1999, her autobiography was published (see Harrington, 1999). In an interview, Harrington explained three reasons for why she wrote her book: "First, I want to set the record straight about why I was forced out of the Portland Police Bureau. Second, it is my special way to mentor—to extend my reach to women in law enforcement who may learn from my experiences. Third, I want to reach out to all women, regardless of their career choices—to let them know we can succeed despite the obstacles" (qtd. in Brittany Publications, Ltd., 1999).

Other Experiences of Women Police

"Women are dramatically underrepresented in American law enforcement, yet there is limited research exploring why this underrepresentation persists. Women make up more than half of the U.S. population but fewer than 13% of law enforcement officers" (Starheim, 2019, p. 3). Nonetheless, with well over 100,000 female police officers currently serving throughout the United States and its territories, it is not easy to generalize about the nature of their experiences. The authors feel it worth indicating at least a few of the contemporary personal experiences of officers from two local police agencies: Burke County Sheriff's Office and the Morganton Public Safety Department. The following reflections by women police officers were reported in the *Morganton News Herald*, serving Burke County, North Carolina.

Becky Weatherman of the Burke County Sheriff's Office was promoted to the rank of Detective Lieutenant in 2005. She "always wanted to work in law enforcement. She was aware that males dominated the field, but that didn't make her hesitate. She began her career in the 1980s as a dispatch officer in the communications division and as a female jailer. Through the years, she took on many duties: road officer, bailiff, school resource officer and detective. During her early years she encountered some tough times 'since it was like females didn't belong, males tried to make you not succeed'" (qtd. in Chang, 2010). Morganton Officer Sherry Hunt is a road patrol officer. "It's a difficult job. When you put this uniform on, you better be prepared because you don't know what's going to happen next" (qtd. in Chang, 2010). During her basic academy program, she had to run just as much as the other students and do just as many pushups. There were no free passes for anyone. Sheriff's Deputy Melanie Robinson was hired in 2009. She "strongly believes that female and male officers have their own strengths and weaknesses, and a strong organization should make efforts to include both. Robinson was 16 when she decided to enter the field. She took a criminal justice course at Western Piedmont Community College and was 'pretty much hooked from day one. She delayed pursuing a career in law enforcement because her friends and family initially were apprehensive, but 'it was in my blood. . . . I've got some good partners. . . . It's like a family at the sheriff's office'" (qtd. in Chang, 2010). "Weatherman and Robinson said they always work hard, but sometimes feel pressure to put in more effort to prove they can pull their load. Robinson said, 'I always try to put in extra effort, but sometimes I have to go the extra mile to prove myself to the boys.' Weatherman said, 'I constantly felt like I had to prove myself every day (in the early days). I don't feel that way at all now' " (qtd. in Chang, 2010). Weatherman and Hunt also spoke about balancing a growing family and their careers. "Hunt said it's hard to tell her 12-year-old daughter that she can't participate in certain activities. The look of disappointment in her daughter's eyes hurts her too. . . . Weatherman said her oldest daughter as a child hated it when she was working. Robinson encourages future female officers not to give up. 'If it's your dream, follow it. Don't let anyone talk you out of it. The rewards are just priceless'. . . . Weatherman said confidence in your own abilities and good communication skills are necessary to perform the job. Also, building a level of trust with fellow officers is the only way to put their minds at ease. 'I just hope that you've got the strength mentally and physically. It's tough. . . . It takes a toll on your whole body' " (qtd. in Chang, 2010).[6]

Other Underrepresented Groups in Policing

While diversity practices often focus on the race and biological sex, it is important to note that other minority groups in the United States are underrepresented in the ranks of police officers. For example, people with disabilities, minority ethnic/cultural/linguistic groups, and members of the LGBTQ+ community are not typically widely represented in policing jobs. As these groups are vast and cover many different individuals in society, it is not possible to cover each minority group and why they are not typically found among the ranks of law enforcement. Nonetheless, people from all of these groups (with some intersectionality) represent citizens in the communities police officers serve. While it may not be possible to hire individuals from these groups as sworn officers (physical demands, for example, may prohibit some individuals from being able to perform daily duties of a police officer), it is possible to hire such individuals within police agencies themselves; this can offer diversity within departments and expand inclusion of traditionally underrepresented groups within the workspace. It is also possible to more comprehensively educate police officers on the diverse groups of people within the communities they serve.[7]

Conclusion: Community Engagement

In order to achieve desired levels of diversity in the police workforce it is urged that police leaders and government officials engage with their community's resources—be they schools, religious institutions, or civic organizations. According to former Chicago Police Superintendent Eddie Johnson, "If we're going to get there, we have to ensure that we have a viable pool of people to constantly pull from" (qtd. in Stark & Little, 2018). Police agencies can broaden their applicant pool by reaching out to prospective candidates at high schools, university classrooms, and job fairs. They can specifically enhance diversity by targeting their efforts at youth and young adults from underrepresented groups. Agencies may consider transitional workers—such as cadets who do not yet qualify to go into the police academy or promising students who have not yet completed educational or age requirements—to serve in a "civilian" position until they reach qualification for a sworn personnel position. Examples of such programs include the Explorer and Cadet programs, as well as programs like the LAPD's partnership with a magnet high school to offer a special police officer preparation program. In this five-year program "graduates earn both a high school diploma and an associate's degree. These graduates can then enter the department's reserve program; at age 21, they are eligible to enter the police academy" (Heintze et al., 2019, p. 102). Recommendations for the inclusion of Explorers, a cadet program, and internship programs to augment the recruitment of minority youth has been a consistent theme in the relevant literature (e.g., see Oliver, 2017; Digh, 1999). In particular, more than 50 years ago it was recommended that interns "could assist police officers and police agents, or could serve as community service officers. The police department, with Federal, State or local financial assistance, could defray the college expenses of the intern as well as pay him a salary and these expenses would have to be repaid only if he did not enter the police department and serve a specific length of time upon his graduation from college. . . . If cadet programs are utilized in this way, their attractiveness will be enhanced and they could serve as a valuable method of recruiting qualified persons into the police service" (*Task Force Report: The Police*, 1967, p. 137).

In order to improve the ranks of minorities in local and state police agencies it will be necessary to include all those community and government stakeholders "who have an interest in enhancing minority recruitment and selection and groups/individuals that can influence the desired outcome, positively or negatively. Core stakeholders for this issue normally include police executives; police human resources specialists; city/county human resources executives and specialists; the jurisdiction's chief administrative officer (city/county executive, mayor's office); the jurisdiction's legislative body; neighborhood associations; minority interest groups; and special interest groups" (Needle & Rollins, 2003, p. 6). Ideally, the local chief of police should lead this mobilization effort and thereafter diligent and sustained effort must be accorded to implementation, monitoring, and evaluation (see Needle & Rollins, 2003, pp. 6, 8, and 14).

However, it is not enough for police leadership to take charge of diversity initiatives. Critiques of police operations will continue as long as incidents of police brutality persist. Police chiefs and other agency supervisory personnel must inculcate a clear set of moral standards throughout their departments. In the contemporary world of American law enforcement, the establishment of ethnic representation in proportion to a community's population is but one facet of agency management. Police leaders must also create a culture of ethics within their agency by establishing "standards for employees' behavior at all levels and illustrate that ethics play a crucial role in an officer's success in the agency. If managers neglect ethics or, even worse, behave poorly themselves, this demonstrates to officers that neither the agency nor its leaders care about proper conduct. Strong moral behavior at all levels sends officers a clear, consistent message that the agency will not tolerate inappropriate behavior" (Fitch, 2011).

Thus, diversity in law enforcement includes more than just racial, national origin, religious and ethnic values, sexual orientation, gender identity, and so on among the ranks, but also the need to create a culture of ethics and inclusion. Inclusion helps to spur involvement and empowerment, where the inherent worth and dignity of all people are recognized. At the same time, pre-service and in-service curriculums need to reflect the police philosophy emphasized under "community policing." According to the Office of Community Oriented Policing Services (COPS Office, 2014), a component of the US Department of Justice, "Community policing is a philosophy that promotes organizational strategies that support the systematic use of partnerships and problem-solving techniques to proactively address the immediate conditions that give rise to public safety issues such as crime, social disorder, and fear of crime" (p. 1).[8] The police strategies emphasized under community policing include greater police communication, interaction, and cooperation with the community in forging community-based priorities and practices in crime prevention and crime control. Police education must focus on: the ethics and practices of inclusion; training in the principles and tactics of community policing at all levels—academy, field, and in-service; the application of learning rather than memorization; the use of a problem-solving model at training sessions; and the use of scenarios as the basis for learning (COPS Office, 2014; Chappell, 2008). In these ways, law enforcement agencies may not only strengthen their reputations as trustworthy guardians and reflective of the communities they serve but also enrich the police profession by being representative of the diversity of the human experience.

A critical role for guardian style policing is to refrain from any use of force that might be unreasonable under the circumstances of the situation. The following chapter explores how police academies address the problem of violence prevention. It also considers the need for developing higher-level thinking skills and how to deal with systemic inadequacies within the field of policing.

Notes

1 About 15% of federal LEOs were female in FY 2020, up from 14% in FY 2016. In FY 2020, about 61% of federal LEOs were White, 10% were Black, 21% were Hispanic, 3% were Asian, 1% were American Indian or Alaska Native, and less than 1% were Native Hawaiian or Other Pacific Islander. A little more than 2% of officers identified as being two or more races (Brooks, 2020, p. 8).

2 EEOC field office information is available at www.eeoc.gov or in most telephone directories in the U.S. Government or Federal Government section. Additional information about EEOC, including information about charge filing, is available at www.eeoc.gov. For a concise two-page flyer revised in November 2009 regarding the protections provided by federal law from discrimination see: https://www.dol.gov/sites/dolgov/files/ofccp/regs/compliance/posters/pdf/eeopost.pdf.

3 "The decrease [in police employment] is much slower than the overall employment, or industries such as restaurants, education and healthcare. Even as many industries started to bounce back, local police hiring hasn't picked up because it takes months, or even years, to train to become a police officer. . . . The Bureau of Labor Statistics' The Quarterly Census of Employment and Wages program collects employment and wages data from private companies as well as local, state and federal governments. In some cases, local governments do not break down their number of employees by industry (police, education, sanitation, etc.), which means police employment data from some local governments is missing in the dataset" (Li & Mahajan, 2021).

4 "The Great Recession began in December 2007 and ended in June 2009, which makes it the longest recession since World War II. Beyond its duration, the Great Recession was notably severe in several respects. Real gross domestic product (GDP) fell 4.3 percent from its peak in 2007Q4 to its trough in 2009Q2, the largest decline in the postwar era (based on data as of October 2013). The unemployment rate, which was 5 percent in December 2007, rose to 9.5 percent in June 2009, and peaked at 10 percent in October 2009" (Rich, 2013).

5 On September 15, 2020, an abrupt announcement was made that Tempe Police Chief Sylvia Moir, the first female chief of police in Tempe's history, was resigning effective October 25. The announcement was made without any explanation. "She had been in charge of the department since March of 2016. Like many cities, Tempe has faced calls from protesters to defund the police in the wake of the Black Lives Matter movement. The Tempe police department has been criticized for use of force incidents and the officers' use of deadly force—so it's unclear if the cumulative effect of all of that had an impact on Moir's tenure at the department. But Tempe Mayor Corey Woods shared a statement praising Moir's years of service and her contributions to the community" (Jenkins & Goldstein, 2020). In September 2022, Moir became the Undersheriff of the Marin County (California) Sheriff's Office. In this role she is second in command, Undersheriff Sylvia Moir, was sworn in to her new role this week. Immediately prior to this appointment, Moir served as interim chief

for the Napa Police Department. She worked for the Sacramento Police Department for nearly two decades, from 1990 to 2008, serving in every division of the department and was the incident commander on hundreds of planned and spontaneous events. From 2010 until 2016 she was chief in El Cerrito and was a member of the California Commission on Peace Officers Standards and Training, which sets standards for selection and training for law enforcement candidates (Gecan, 2022). Moir holds a Bachelor of Science (1993) in Criminal Justice from California State University, Sacramento, a Master of Arts (1996) in Organizational Management from University of Phoenix, and a Master of Arts in Security Studies (2016) from the Naval Postgraduate School- Center for Homeland Security and Defense in Monterey, California. Her 65-page Naval Postgraduate School Master's Thesis is titled: *Fluid Leadership: Inviting Diverse Inputs to Address Complex Problems*. In one section of her thesis, Moir asks: "Are leaders born, or are they made?" She responds that "Research shows that, while genetics plays a role, life context and experience play the most significant role in leadership emergence. This suggests that leaders are both born and made" (p. 12). Her unclassified thesis can be found online at: https://www.hsdl.org/?view&did=792234. For additional information about Moir, see: https://www.policinginstitute.org/executive-fellows/sylvia-moir/.

6 Police work is also a dangerous vocation. Natalie Corona was a City of Davis (California) police officer who was shot and killed January 10, 2019 while responding to a routine traffic call. The daughter of a 26-year veteran police officer, she was 22 years young and only a couple of weeks into her duty as a police officer in Davis. The gunman was identified as a 48-year-old man with a conviction record who was banned from owning firearms and took his own life following an hours-long standoff with officers. Corona was ambushed as the man was on a bike and shot her without warning (see: Fry & Willon, 2019; Fernandez, 2019). In honor of Corona's ideals of excellence and service, there exists an Officer Natalie Corona Odd Fellows Memorial Scholarship program, providing financial assistance to high school students in Davis, CA, and Arbuckle, CA, who are pursuing a career in law enforcement, criminal justice, or as a first responder. For additional details about the life of Officer Corona, scholarship details, and recipients, see: https://www.davislodge.org/officer-natalie-corona-odd-fellows-memorial-scholarship/. To view a two-minute video of women officers reflecting on being a woman in law enforcement taped at the location of the memorial service for Officer Corona in January 2019, see: https://www.youtube.com/watch?v=tPX0ZnqMPJM.

7 Chapter 7 expands the discussion on the importance of cultural education for police officers and how this can assist in the reduction of violence and greater trust of the community toward law enforcement.

8 Community policing comprises three key components: Community Partnerships; Transformation; Problem Solving. Community partnerships are collaborative partnerships between the law enforcement agency and the individuals and organizations they serve to develop solutions to problems and increase trust in police. Organizational transformation is the alignment of organizational management, structure, personnel, and information systems to support community partnerships and proactive problem solving. Problem solving is the process of engaging in the proactive and systematic examination of identified problems to develop and evaluate effective responses (COPS Office, 2014, p. 1).

References

Battle, S. J. (1960). *The first Black policeman remembers*. Retrieved February 8, 2021, from http://c250.columbia.edu/c250_celebrates/harlem_history/battle.html

Biondi, T. (2022). Biographical sketch of Mina Van Winkle. In *Part III: Mainstream suffragists—national American woman suffrage association*. Retrieved Octobers 3, 2022, from https://documents.alexanderstreet.com/d/1010113657

Blakemore, E. (2019, March 8). *How two centuries of slave revolts shaped American history*. Retrieved October 16, 2022, from https://www.nationalgeographic.com/history/article/two-centuries-slave-rebellions- shaped-American-history

Blythe, R. (2021). *The Afro-American Patrolmen's League*. Retrieved February 7, 2021, from https://www.chicagohistory.org/aapl/

Brittany Publications, Ltd. (1999). *An interview with Penny Harrington about Triumph of Spirit.* Retrieved October 24, 2022, from https://brittanypublications.com/uploads/1/2/1/1/121180366/interview_with_penny_harri ngton.pdf

Brooks, C. (2019, October). *Federal law enforcement officers, 2016—Statistical tables.* U.S. Department of Justice, Bureau of Justice Statistics. https://bjs.ojp.gov/content/pub/pdf/fleo16st.pdf

Brooks, C. (2020, September). *Federal law enforcement officers, 2020—Statistical tables.* U.S. Department of Justice, Bureau of Justice Statistics. https://bjs.ojp.gov/sites/g/files/xyckuh236/files/media/document/fleo20st.pdf

Bryan, E. (2016, March 19). *Georgia Ann Hill Robinson (1879–1961).* Retrieved February 9, 2021, from https://www.blackpast.org/african-american-history/robinson-georgia-ann- hill-1879-1961/

Chang, J. (2010, August 11). 'It's tough' being a female officer. *Morganton News Herald.*

Chappell, A. T. (2008). Police academy training: Comparing across curricula. *Policing: An International Journal of Police Strategies and Management, 31*(1), 36–56.

Commission on Accreditation for Law Enforcement Agencies. (2022). *Standards for law enforcement agencies: The standard manual of the law enforcement agency accreditation program* (6th ed.). Commission on Accreditation for Law Enforcement Agencies, Inc. (CALEA).

COPS Office. (2014). *Community policing defined.* US Department of Justice, Office of Community Oriented Policing Services. Retrieved November 12, 2022, from https://cops.usdoj.gov/RIC/Publications/cops-p157-pub.pdf

CRC. (2022). *Community relations services (CRC) toolkit for policing: Policing 101.* U.S. Department of Justice, Community Relations Services. Retrieved October 6, 2022, from https://www.justice.gov/file/1376626/download

Digh, P. (1999, October). Getting people in the pool: Diversity recruitment that works. *HR Magazine, 44*(10), 94–98.

Donahue, J., & Ludwig, J. (2007, March). More COPS. *Brookings Institution Policy Brief,* pp. 1–7.

EEOC. (2016, October). *Advancing diversity in law enforcement.* Retrieved October 12, 2022, from https://www.eeoc.gov/advancing-diversity-law-enforcement

EEOC. (2019, March). *Fiscal Year 2020 Congressional budget justification U.S. equal employment opportunity commission.* Retrieved October 16, 2022, from https://www.eeoc.gov/fiscal-year-2020-congressional-budget-justification-us-equal- employment-opportunity-commission

EEOC. (2022a). *Timeline of important EEOC events.* Retrieved October 16, 2022, from https://www.eeoc.gov/youth/timeline-important-eeoc-events

EEOC. (2022b). *About EEOC: Overview.* Retrieved October 16, 2022, from https://www.eeoc.gov/overview

FBI. (2011, February 15). *A byte out of history: Early African-American agents.* Retrieved October 25, 2022, from https://www.fbi.gov/news/stories/early-african-american-agents

Fernandez, L. (2019, January 12). *The story behind this image of slain Davis police officer Natalie Corona.* Retrieved October 7, 2022, from https://www.fox4news.com/news/the- story-behind-this-image-of-slain-davis-police-officer-natalie-corona

Fitch, B. D. (2011, October 1). Focus on ethics: Rethinking ethics in law enforcement. *FBI Law Enforcement Bulletin.* Retrieved October 25, 2022, from https://leb.fbi.gov/articles/focus/focus-on-ethics-rethinking-ethics-in-law-enforcement

Flavin, B. (2018, December 10). *Police officers explain why diversity in law enforcement matters.* Retrieved November 8, 2022, from https://www.rasmussen.edu/degrees/justice-studies/blog/diver sity-in-law-enforcement/

FLETA. (2022, August 23). *President Joe Biden congratulates the FLETA board on its 20th anniversary.* Retrieved October 6, 2022, from https://www.fleta.gov/press- release/president-joe-biden-congratulates-fleta-board-its-20th-anniversary

Fry, H., & Willon, P. (2019, January 11). Davis police officer Natalie Corona, 22, was gunned down, but first she lived her dream. *Los Angeles Times.* Retrieved October 7, 2022, from https://www.latimes.com/local/la-me-ln-davis-police-shooting-profile- 20190111-story.html

Gecan, A. N. (2022, September 9). Former bay area police chief sworn in as Marin undersheriff. *Marine Independent Journal*. Retrieved September 30, 2022, from https://www.marinij.com/2022/09/07/former-bay-area-police-chief-sworn-in-as-marin- undersheriff/

Graper, E. D. (1921). *American police administration: Handbook on police organization and methods of administration in American cities*. MacMillan.

Hadden, S. (2001). *Slave patrols: Law and violence in Virginia and the Carolinas*. Harvard University Press.

Harrington, P. (1999). *Triumph of spirit: An autobiography*. Brittany Publications Ltd.

Heintze, H., Zoll, A., Davis, A., Ambrose, A., Heintze, A., et al. (2019). *Law enforcement best practices: Lessons learned from the field*. U.S. Department of Justice, Office of Community Oriented Policing Services. Retrieved September 28, 2022, from https://cops.usdoj.gov/ric/Publications/cops-w0875-pub.pdf

Henderson, W. C. (1976). The slave court system in Spartanburg county. In *The proceedings of the South Carolina Historical Association* (pp. 24–38).

Horne, P. (2006, September). Policewomen: Their first century and the new era. *The Police Chief*, *73*(9), 56–61.

Huntley, K. (2022, August 7). *Burlington's new plan to get more police in its ranks*. Retrieved September 27, 2022, from https://www.wcax.com/2022/08/08/burlington-has- new-plan-get-more-police-its-ranks/

Implementation Guide. (2015). *The president's task force on 21st century policing: Implementation guide: Moving from recommendations to action*. U.S. Department of Justice, Office of Community Oriented Policing Services. https://cops.usdoj.gov/RIC/Publications/cops-p341-pub.pdf

Jackman, T. (2018, December 4). Who wants to be a police officer? Job applications plummet at most U.S. departments. *The Washington Post*. Retrieved September 30, 2022, from https://www.washingtonpost.com/crime-law/2018/12/04/who-wants-be-police-officer-job-applica tions-plummet-most-us-departments/

Jenkins, J., & Goldstein, S. (2020, September 16). *Tempe police chief Sylvia Moir announces resignation*. Retrieved September 30, 2022, from https://theshow.kjzz.org/content/1618491/tempe-police-chief-sylvia-moir-announces- resignation

Johnston, R. J. H. (1975, January 31). State police swear in first woman trooper. *The New York Times*, p. 71.

Kooi, B. (2021). *Seven highly effective police leaders: 1895-modern times*. Routledge.

Kuykendall, J. L., & Bums, D. E. (1980). The Black police officer: An historical perspective. *Journal of Contemporary Criminal Justice*, *1*(4), 4–12.

Li, W., & Mahajan, I. (2021, September 1). *Police say demoralized officers are quitting in droves. Labor data says no*. Retrieved September 27, 2022, from https://www.themarshallproject.org/2021/09/01/police-say-demoralized-officers-are- quitting-in-droves-labor-data-says-no

Lin, M.-J. (2009, June). More police, less crime: Evidence from US state data. *International Review of Law and Economics*, *29*(2), 73–80.

Malhotra, A., Kysel, I., Sinha, M. G. A., Sankofa, J., & Frankel, A. (2022, August 8). *Racial discrimination in the United States: Human rights watch/ACLU joint submission regarding the United States' record under the international convention on the elimination of all forms of racial discrimination*. Retrieved November 12, 2022, from https://www.hrw.org/report/2022/08/08/racial-discrimination-united-states/human- rights-watch/aclu-joint-submission

Mason, J. (2011, December 17). Last of first female troopers steps aside. *The Daily Gazette*. Retrieved October 4, 2022, from https://dailygazette.com/2011/12/17/1217_tuffey/

Mastony, C. (2010, September 1). Was Chicago home to the country's 1st female cop? *Chicago Tribune*. Retrieved October 24, 2022, from https://www.chicagotribune.com/news/ct-xpm-2010-09-01-ct-met-first-police- woman-20100901-story.html

McDowell, J. (1992, February 17). Are women better cops? *Time*, *139*(7), 70–72.

Mello, S. (2018, February 25). *More COPS, less crime*. Retrieved September 27, 2022, from https://www.princeton.edu/~smello/papers/cops.pdf

Mendez, D., & Cagle, K. (2020, September 27). *The lost history of Robert Stewart, LAPD's first Black cop*. Retrieved February 9, 2021, from https://spectrumnews1.com/ca/la-west/human-interest/2020/09/25/the-lost-history-of-robert-stewart-lapd-s-first-black-cop

Morash, M., & Greene, J. R. (1986, April). Evaluating women on patrol: A critique of contemporary wisdom. *Evaluation Review*, *10*(2), 230–255.

Mustian, J., & Fassett, C. (2021, June 4). *NY State Police struggles to diversify amid national reckoning. Check our database*. Retrieved November 12, 2022, from https://www.democratandchronicle.com/story/news/2021/06/04/database-ny-state-police- diversity/7534745002/

National Archives. (2022). *Milestone documents: Plessy v. Ferguson (1896)*. Retrieved October 17, 2022, from https://www.archives.gov/milestone-documents/plessy-v-ferguson

NCWP. (2002, April). *Equality denied: The status of women in policing, 2001*. National Center for Women & Policing.

Needle, J. A., & Rollins, M. L. (2003, December). *Mobilizing the community for minority recruitment and selection: A strategy to leverage community assets to enhance recruitment and placement of minorities*. U.S. Department of Justice, Office of Community Oriented Policing Services. Retrieved September 26, 2022, from https://www.theiacp.org/sites/default/files/2018-08/FinalCLP Report_0.pdf

NOBLE. (2022). *History*. Retrieved October 25, 2022, from https://noblenational.org/history/

Oliver, P. (2017, March 8). Creating a multicultural law enforcement agency: An intentional priority, *Police Chief Online*. Retrieved September 26, 2022, from https://www.policechiefmagazine.org/creating-a-multicultural-law-enforcement-agency/

Orrick, D. (2009, December). Recruiting female candidates. *Law and Order*, *57*(12), 30–32, 34, 36.

Peak, K. J. (1997). *Policing America: Methods, issues, challenges* (2nd ed.). Prentice Hall.

PEW Stateline. (2022, September 26). *Prison staff shortages take toll on guards, incarcerated people*. Retrieved September 27, 2022, from https://www.pewtrusts.org/en/research-and- analysis/blogs/stateline/2022/09/26/prison-staff-shortages-take-toll-on-guards- incarcerated-people

Pilgrim, D. (2012). *What was Jim Crow?* Retrieved January 21, 2014, from http://www.ferris.edu/jimcrow/what.htm

The President's Commission (1967). *The president's commission on law enforcement and administration of justice, task force report: The police*. U.S. Government Printing Office. Policehttps://www.ojp.gov/pdffiles1/Digitization/147374NCJRS.pdf

President's Task Force. (2015, May). *President's task force on 21st century policing, final report of the president's task force on 21st century policing*. U.S. Department of Justice, Office of Community Oriented Policing Services. http://www.cops.usdoj.gov/pdf/taskforce/taskForce_Finalreport.pdf

Rabe-Hemp, C. (2018). *Thriving in an all-boys club: Female police and their fight for equality*. Rowman & Littlefield.

Ray, R. (2021, May 25). *One year after George Floyd's murder, what is the status of police reform in the United States?* Retrieved November 11, 2022, from https://www.brookings.edu/blog/how-we-rise/2021/05/25/one-year-after-george-floyds- murder-what-is-the-status-of-police-reform-in-the-united-states/

Reichel, P. L. (2022). Reading 1: Southern slave patrols as a transitional police type. In *Section 1 the history of the police* (pp. 16–29). Sage Publications. Retrieved October 12, 2022, from https://www.sagepub.com/sites/default/files/upm-binaries/50819_ch_1.pdf

Rich, R. (2013, November 22). *The great recession: December 2007–June 2009*. Retrieved September 27, 2022, from https://www.federalreservehistory.org/essays/great-recession-of- 200709

Ripley, A. (2017, November 14). *Federal law enforcement has a woman problem*. Retrieved October 4, 2022, from https://www.politico.com/story/2017/11/14/women- federal-law-enforcement-male-dominated-244649

Secret, M. (2015, June 26). *The story of New York's first Black police officer, told with the help of Langston Hughes (published in The New York Times)*. Retrieved February 8, 2021, from https://www.mosisecret.com/features

Starheim, R. P. (2019, July). *Women in policing: Breaking barriers and blazing a path*. U.S. Department of Justice, Office of Justice Programs, National Institute of Justice. https://www.ojp.gov/pdffiles1/nij/252963.pdf
Stark, K., & Little, D. (2018, February 2). *More African-Americans apply to become cops, but few make it to finish line*. Retrieved February 7, 2021, from https://www.chicagoreporter.com/more-african-americans-apply-to-become-cops-but- few-make-it-to-finish-line/
Task Force Report: The Police. (1967). *Task force on the police: The president's commission on law enforcement and administration of justice*. US Government Printing Office.
TCR Staff. (2022, September 27). Staff shortages, inmate anger plague U.S. prisons. *The Crime Report*. Retrieved September 27, 2022, from https://thecrimereport.org/2022/09/27/staff-shortages-inmate-anger-plague-u-s-prisons/
Tella, R. D., & Schargrodsky, E. (2004, March). Do police reduce crime? Estimates using the allocation of police forces after a terrorist attack. *American Economic Review*, *94*(1), 115–133.
Thomas, R. R. (2005). *Building on the promise of diversity: How we can move to the next level in our workplaces, our communities, and our society*. AMACOM Books.
Trent, S. (2019, December 14). The fiercest federal lawman you never knew—and he was African American. *Washington Post*. Retrieved October 25, 2022, from https://www.washingtonpost.com/history/2019/12/14/fiercest-federal-lawman-you-never- knew-he-was-African-American/
US Dept. of Justice. (2017, February). A history of African Americans in law enforcement. *Community Policing Dispatch* (the e-newsletter of the COPS Office), *10*(2). Retrieved October 25, 2022, from Rhttps://cops.usdoj.gov/html/dispatch/02-2017/african_americans_in_law_enforcement.html
Van Winkle, M. C. (1921, August). Municipal policewomen: Their duties and opportunities. *American City*, *25*(8), 93–96.
Vracar, A. (2022, May 10). *Accreditation 101: The benefits of state and national police accreditation*. Retrieved October 6, 2022, from https://www.benchmarkanalytics.com/blog/accreditation-101-the-benefits-of-state-and- national-police-accreditation/
Walker, S. (1985). Racial minority and female employment in policing: The implications of glacial change. *Crime & Delinquency*, *31*(4), 555–572.
Weldy, W. O. (1976, January). Women in policing: A positive step toward increased police enthusiasm. *The Police Chief*, *43*(1), 46–47.
Westervelt, E. (2021, June 24). *Cops say low morale and department scrutiny are driving them away from the job*. Retrieved September 27, 2022, from https://www.npr.org/2021/06/24/1009578809/cops-say-low-morale-and-department- scrutiny-are-driving-them-away-from-the-job
Williams, C. (2018, November 12). African-American veterans hoped their service in World War I would secure their rights at home. It didn't. *Time*. Retrieved October 21, 2022, from https://time.com/5450336/african-american-veterans-wwi/
Wiseman, J. (2021, August). *Recruiting for diversity in law enforcement: Selected recent research*. Retrieved September 26, 2022, from https://scholar.harvard.edu/files/janewiseman/files/police_recruiting_research_summary_ august_2021.pdf
Young People. (1976, April). Young people trained as police paraprofessionals. *The Police Chief*, *43*(4), 11.

7

POLICE EDUCATION AND THE REDUCTION OF POLICE VIOLENCE

Media coverage of police violence and other controversies surrounding "the thin blue line" (see Hernandez, 2020) often overshadows the positive work many police officers are doing on a daily basis. Nevertheless, public opinion surveys suggest that the majority of Americans think that at least some reform is needed in policing. Moreover, different groups in society (e.g., based on race, age, and political affiliation) have differing opinions about the functioning of America's law enforcement establishment (Council on Criminal Justice, 2020). An increase in highly publicized excessive use of force cases in 2020 directly led to an executive order by President Trump concerned with tracking and preventing police misconduct (Breuninger, 2020). The impact of excessive use of force by police officers first touches the lives of individuals and then extends to entire communities as localities will often make large settlements in compensation to the survivors and victims of police misconduct (Elinson & Frosch, 2015). Police leaders have looked to other nations, Scotland in particular, to explore training techniques and cultural aspects of policing that could decrease the excessive use of force in American cities (Baker, 2015b). Of course, it is understood that the culture of each nation is unique and not all tactics used in Scotland or elsewhere may be appropriate in the United States (Baker, 2015a).[1]

The reasons why so many notorious cases of excessive police use of force have occurred continue to be debated. Echoing findings by the National Academies of Science (2018), Trinkner et al. (2019) note, "We know too little about what leads to abuses of police power, and psychological science has yet to engage the issue as seriously as it can" (p. 433). Therefore, research and discussions must continue to examine excessive use of force and violence among police officers in the United States, while also recognizing these cases are not necessarily the norm of the daily activities involved in police work. Exploring what happens both during and after training is an important step toward qualitative change, and recognition of the "why" can help inform the "how" in addressing these problems. The analysis of success stories for departments and training is also imperative to improve police training and outcomes across the nation. The reasons for excessive use of force can include: implicit bias; racial profiling; lack of education; and systemic inadequacies within the field of policing as well as the other components of the administration of justice. These underlying (often

DOI: 10.4324/9781003307396-10

personal) characteristics may also serve as barriers to teaching human relations and violence prevention methods to police officers, suggesting the potential need for additional screening techniques for recruits.

As the idea of police reform gains momentum, some police departments have seen improvements while others are working at making progress when it comes to community-police relations. In Las Vegas, which has been considered a model for police reform, the Department of Justice stepped in to investigate and concluded with 75 recommendations for improvement. Of those recommendations, approximately one-third involved updates to training. Improvements within the Las Vegas Police Department included courses taught by social psychologists, reality-based field training, and in-house efforts to promote accountability for all LEOs (Hernandez, 2015). These types of progressive changes offer a model by which other police departments could begin to reform their culture, training programs, and practices, particularly when seeking ways to prevent violent police encounters. A recent report by the PERF raises issues regarding the saving of money and time with respect to police training in the United States. Improving police training to decrease negative outcomes, such as the excessive use of force, must require a rethinking of the curriculum used, updating technology, and ensuring appropriate leadership and professionalism of those in charge of training new recruits (PERF, 2022).[2] The idea that time and money spent in the early stages of training may serve to benefit communities by decreasing violent encounters in the long-run should not be ignored.

Police training tends to rest on a behaviorist approach, which limits the academic exploration of human relations and reinforces traditional police culture. Police academies are the entry-level step in preparing future LEOs to act on formal police procedures as well as their informal interactions with community members. Prior research (see Doreian & Conti, 2017) has demonstrated the stressful and paramilitary environments of the academy, including the physical and mental breaking down and rebuilding of recruits. The thinking behind such patterns of training is that it encourages a culture of solidarity and mutual respect that is deemed necessary for police officers to adequately do their jobs. But, such socialization can lead to unfavorable consequences. For example, the training process may actually shift the trainees' personalities due to their acceptance of a police culture that leads away from an empathetic view of citizens. When police are in the field completing their academy program, the development of negative perceptions of the general public can result (Doreian & Conti, 2017). In working to create this shared adversity and loyalty to the profession, "The Blue Wall of Silence" (see Kleinig, 2001) can result in police officers participating in questionable behavior to protect their own, even at the expense of the citizens they are sworn to protect. Kleinig (2001) recommends training specifically about loyalty—"its contours, importance, and limitations;" noting that open and honest discussions about the limits of loyalty may help to alleviate negative outcomes as a result of the "blue wall of silence" (p. 10). At such times, there certainly exists a critical need for close guidance, supervision, and support in order to help counteract such biased thinking.

Historically, skills like critical thinking have not traditionally been considered a part of training and academic subjects beyond the law were not thought to be necessary in police academies. Instead, physical abilities were held in high regard along with the need to learn tactics required to perform tasks like coercing confessions (Goldfarb, 2020). However, by the end of the turbulent 1960s there was a critical shift toward a community focus within policing. Consequently, given new federal incentives, police academies switched to topics with a greater focus on community relations rather than only dealing with matters concerning how to respond to specific crimes.

This chapter explores ways academies generally aim to address violence prevention in the current models of training and offers suggestions to include more human relations education for future police officers.[3] Emphasis is placed on the best practices concerning how police academies can train new officers to relate better to the communities they serve and how unnecessary violence can be prevented, while still addressing the goal of public safety. A reasonable place to start is the inclusion of a variety of academic subjects involving the human condition such as psychology, ethics, history, and sociology as part of the academy process—all of which expose students to formal research methodology with a focus on protecting human subjects in the process of collecting data. Hannah Arendt (1906–1975), one of the leading social theorists in the United States, noted the paradox that as human powers increase through technological and humanistic inquiry, we are less equipped to control the consequences of our actions. Arendt (1998) considered humankind from the perspective of the actions of which it is capable. Today our nation's police need to adopt this perspective in order to begin to appreciate the importance of their conduct.

If more police academies choose to partner with their local academic institutions of higher education, police training could be enhanced and the educational backgrounds of all trainees would be elevated. Hannah Arendt's (1998) work challenges people to truly think about what they do. Governmental authorities, such as police administrators need to rethink the weaknesses and strengths of their agencies for the sake of a safer and saner society.

Current Police Academy Training Characteristics

On average, police academies in the United States require somewhere between 623 (Linetsky, 2018) and 833 training hours (Buehler, 2021), often requiring far less training hours than it takes to become licensed in other fields, such as cosmetology (see Linetsky, 2018). During this time, the subject of human relations is often given little attention. Curriculum variation in academies abound because there is no national standard for the training of police in the United States. Moreover, financial considerations limit the times allotted for the tactical and practical aspects of training (PERF, 2022). Consequently, the tactical and physical areas of training typically take priority. Rahr and Rice (2015) call for an overall shift in the culture of policing from "warriors" to "guardians," with suggestions for transforming police training to include more behavioral and social science education, for example. Given the many local and public colleges in the United States, these supplemental courses can be readily added to police training programs.

By the first decade of the 21st century, even with community policing gaining popularity and academies evolving to work on new "types" of socialization among recruits, some researchers (Chappell & Lanza-Kaduce, 2010) found that the authoritarian and paramilitary culture was still prominent in police academies. The focus in academies was on tactical training while neglecting to emphasize subjects like non-violent conflict management (Gutierrez, 2022). Chappell and Lanza-Kaduce (2010) have offered the following suggestions for shifting this trajectory: moving away from the paramilitary structure; finding ways to better integrate formal curriculum with more information types of instruction; and re-envisioning culture to move away from the "us versus them" narrative of policing.

Kirk Burkhalter (2020), a retired NYPD detective and professor at New York Law School, suggests at least two years of formal education be required for all police officers, with an emphasis on subjects such as conflict resolution and sociology, along with field assignments that include the guidance not only of other police officers, but also of academics and other civilians. Furthermore, Christie Gardiner, a professor of criminal justice at the University of California, Fullerton, surveyed 958 law enforcement agencies (116 that employ 250 or more officers and 842 that employ fewer than 250 officers) in all 50 states, concluding "that college-educated officers often excel in critical areas of policing, particularly in report-writing, although other results varied widely by state [and] also found that college-educated officers are more willing to embrace department-wide changes, particularly new policing methods and technology" (Dowd, 2020). Still, most police departments in the United States do not require formal higher education before, during, or after academy training. Gardiner's, 2017, study found that only 1% of US police departments (below the federal level) require a college degree. On the other hand, in recent decades more police officers have earned college credits than ever before; an average of 30.2% of police officers have a four-year college education, compared to just 8.9% in 1974 (Gardiner, 2017, pp. 4 and 12).

Negative press and strained community-police relationships are becoming more common, but every day the nation's police officers stand guard. However, with increasing frequency, the basic or post-academy training provided to them has been found to be too perfunctory or otherwise insufficient. The discussion on how to transform, and further educate, America's police officers seems to be never ending. No sooner does one crisis news story abate when another arises to take its place. In January 2023, the circumstances concerning the death of Tyre Nichols filled media outlets. Within 20 days of Nichols' death—and following that internal investigation—five officers were fired and charged in connection to Nichols' death. The day after video recordings were made available of the officers' actual conduct at the scene of this tragedy, the Memphis Police Department abolished the entire 40-member special tactical unit to which these officers belonged. The released police body-cam and security surveillance footage had shown multiple officers kicking, punching and striking Nichols with a baton as he screamed for help and pleaded for them to stop (Chen, 2023). The nation was rightfully outraged, and this tragedy continued discussions about police violence and debates on how to end these deadly encounters. The administration of the Memphis Police Department was praised (by some) for holding officers accountable, and have said the response should be "a new example of how to maintain trust in the community after fatal police encounters" (Sanchez, 2023).

Philosophy Shifts: Community Policing and the Need for Education

The concepts and practices associated with education versus training can be explicitly differentiated. Searches on topics related to police academy processes suggest that the word "training" is the primary description of the activities recruits undertake to prepare them for their careers in policing. While the terms education and training are commonly used interchangeably, there are some notable differences. Training involves activities to transfer skills into various scenarios (nicely fitting with behaviorism) while the learning process (i.e., education) revolves around the development of individuals by means of an ongoing process of growing knowledge (Jay, 2022). Education requires developing a mindset for individuals to expand their capacity to apply knowledge, including theoretical application, in future unknown scenarios (Mckenzie, 1995).

Traditional police training follows a behaviorist approach, which continues to be a common training philosophy in many contemporary academies. "Behaviorist theories equate humans to machines in that, as with machines, if you introduce input (stimulus) into a human being and control how that input is processed (operant conditioning), you will get a predetermined output (response)" (Birzer, 2003, p. 31). Behaviorism, largely developed by B. F. Skinner (1904–1990) (see Delpato & Midgley, 1992), does not allow or account for the interpretation or creation of meaning, but rather focuses more narrowly on an output (Lewis, 2016). Paramilitary structures with punishment-based behavioral systems within training academies are designed to help weed out those who are not the best performers. Supposedly, such systems create an optimal environment for behavioral approaches that will prepare recruits for police work. On the other hand, such approaches may contribute to the possible use of violence and abusive levels of force in future encounters. Not only are behavioral approaches inflexible, but they do not recognize learning differences among recruits or the cultural differences of the communities they serve. If a shift toward "community policing" is still considered to be a desirable movement with respect to police reform throughout the country, moving away from traditional military-style training models is crucial. Public satisfaction with police agencies has improved, at least in some communities, since the introduction of community policing programs (Crowl, 2017). These types of programs are serving as a catalyst for widespread change and improvement in community-police relationships (Birzer, 2003). Hence, the nature of such community-focused programs should be considered as part of police academy curriculums and for training within the larger law enforcement community.

The two core components of community policing are partnerships with community and problem-solving, concepts that are not easily imparted via traditional training methods and which require deeper levels of education and critical thinking skills in order to evolve with the fluid needs of communities. The shift toward community policing gained popularity and momentum in the last decades of the 20th century. This policing approach, or philosophy, considers a spectrum of services to a community, depending on the needs of differing communities; these needs can change over space and time. Police officers and community members have largely become separate, divided entities; community policing practices attempt to help build bonds between police departments and citizens. Deviating somewhat from a primary focus of crime fighting by police officers within an isolated department or system, community policing has, at its core, the goal of embedding police officers within the fabric of the communities they serve (Community Policing Consortium, 1994). Yet, basic police training has not fully mirrored such a shift. In Gardiner's (2017) sample study, while over 99% of agencies claim to practice this policing philosophy to some level, only about 36% of police agencies provide additional training after attendance at a basic training academy explicitly on community policing. Less than 20% of agencies teach problem-solving, yet about 85% of agencies note that officers must engage in this activity (see Gardiner, 2017, pp. 5, 35–42). Of note, problem-solving is widely expected of students at the collegiate level of education. Such discrepancies suggest the need for non-traditional, updated, and innovative approaches to preparing police officers for their careers. Training must be enhanced to mirror the current, stated philosophies and touted practices of the field—it must shift to the inclusion of education, versus strictly training.

The inclusion of academic subject matter in police training programs has been recognized for more than 100 years, beginning with the efforts of August Vollmer (1876–1955). Moreover, several Presidential Commissions have made similar recommendations. Perceptively, David Geary and his associates (1975) have stated the following rationale: "Sensitive professionals involved in all facets of criminal justice cannot ignore the growing number of alienated, drifting, disordered, and overly suspicious people. The fact that so many unhappy and unfortunate people exist makes it extremely important to improve the police officer's education and training in psychology, social work, and counseling skills" (p. 35).

Birzer (2003) suggests an adult learning model utilizing the theory of andragogy (which allows for self-direction of the student with the assistance of a facilitator) as a more appropriate model for training and educating future police officers than what is currently common practice. Police academy officials have begun to recognize the importance of strengthening higher-level thinking and decision-making abilities among police officers. Consequently, they have implemented various instructional units to enhance the future use of community policing practices. For example, in Idaho, the state agency known as Idaho Peace Officer Selection and Training (or POST), whose mission is "to develop skilled law enforcement professionals" (Idaho POST, 2022), has developed a "Problem Based Learning Exercise" program to help develop and expand such skills (see Werth, 2011). This program was built on the foundation of problem-based learning because of its well-established track record of assisting students' development of skills in solving problems, making decisions, self-direction, and collaboration (Werth, 201; see also, Cleveland & Saville, 2022). This approach offers students opportunities to solve difficult problems in a 10-week structured program, exploring on-the-job-type scenarios. The process engages students in active learning (versus traditional lecture-style courses) and challenges them to use what are sometimes referred to as "soft" skills, such as communication. Student surveys suggest the program is successful in assisting future police officers once they enter the field (Werth, 2011). The shift away from behaviorist training philosophies has the potential to impart skills and knowledge that may better assist future police officers in using approaches and responses that do not result in violence or excessive use of force.

August Vollmer, who is considered the "father of modern policing" in the United States, was an early advocate for police higher education. According to the notable historian Willard Oliver, Vollmer "became Berkeley's first police chief in the early 1900s and began advancing policing in its use of technology, training and, most importantly, education. He influenced so many people within and outside of the Berkeley Police Department that his ideas began gaining traction first in California, then across the United States, and eventually around the world. When people spoke of good policing in the first half of the 20th century, they spoke about August Vollmer. His was a household name by the 1920s, and by the 1940s he was featured in popular magazines such as *Collier's*, *True Detective* and *Reader's Digest*" (qtd. in Kell, 2017). Due largely to Vollmer's work, by 1916, the University of California at Berkeley began to offer law enforcement-related courses (Travis, 1995). For police officers, education and training occurred with great overlap or at least without differentiating between the two. Thus, police science education programs in colleges and universities are not new (though many earlier programs provided "education" that we might now consider training) and many pioneers of such programs did lobby for more traditional types of training as a large part of the curriculum (Cordner, 2016; Vollmer, 1936).

FIGURE 7.1 President Hoover meets with his newly created Wickersham Commission. In the front row, seated, left to right: Roscoe Pound; Ada L. Comstock; William D. Mitchell, Attorney General; President Hoover; George W. Wickersham, chairman of the Commission; and William S. Kenyon. In the back row, left to right: Kenneth R. MacIntosh; Monte M. Lehman; Paul J. McCormick; William J. Grubb; Frank J. Loesh; Newton D. Baker; and Henry W. Anderson. May 28, 1929. White House, Washington, DC in background. Library of Congress Prints and Photographs Division Washington, D.C. 20540. August Vollmer wrote portions of the Commission's final report which was released on January 7, 1931.

Source: https://tile.loc.gov/storage-services/service/pnp/hec/35300/35394v.jpg

The National Commission on Law Observance and Enforcement was appointed by President Herbert Hoover on May 20, 1929. It was initially established to investigate the problem of prohibition enforcement, but its work expanded to include many aspects of the administration of justice. A 286-page final "Report on the Enforcement of the Prohibition Laws of the United States (January 7, 1931), one of 14 reports or volumes, is available online at: https://www.ojp.gov/pdffiles1/Digitization/44540NCJRS.pdf. Two separate reports placed emphasis on the importance of police reform and the need to educate LEOs—report on *Lawlessness in Law Enforcement* (No. 11) and report on *The Police*

(No. 14). The Commission was chaired by George W. Wickersham, who had served as US attorney general under President William Howard Taft. The final report of the Commission is popularly known as the Wickersham Report. The other ten members included some of the most prominent individuals in American law and public life. Most notable was Roscoe Pound, dean of Harvard Law School and widely regarded as the leading expert on American criminal justice. Also serving on the commission were Newton D. Baker, a leading urban reformer during the Progressive Era and secretary of war under President Woodrow Wilson, and Frank J. Loesch, a prominent Chicago attorney and leader of the Chicago Crime Commission, who had led the fight to prosecute Al Capone. The Commission conducted the first national study of the administration of justice in the United States and was a precursor to the President's Commission on Law Enforcement and Administration of Justice (1967), popularly known as the President's Crime Commission. If considered together, the two national commissions helped to influence improvements in the hiring of police officers by the end of the 20th century.

August Vollmer served as a "police consultant" to the Commission and a summary of his report simply entitled *The Police* (Volume 14) was published in 1932 (see Vollmer, 1932; Wilson, 1953, p. 100). However, Samuel Walker, one of America's leading scholars on criminal justice history, considers the 1931 *Report on Lawlessness in Law Enforcement* (Volume 11) prepared by Zechariah Chafee Jr., Walter H. Pollak, and Carl S. Stern for the Wickersham Commission as "one of the most important events in the history of American policing. It was the first systematic investigation of police misconduct and became a catalyst for reforms involving new forms of accountability for the police" (Walker & Boehm, 1997, p. v). In an unwavering tone, the Report on *Lawlessness in Law Enforcement* concluded that the third degree—"the use of physical brutality, or other forms of cruelty, to obtain involuntary confessions or admissions is widespread" (qtd. in Walker & Boehm, 1997, p. ix). "Specific tactics included protracted questioning, threats and methods of intimidation, physical brutality, illegal detention, and refusal to allow access of counsel to suspects. The report declared unequivocally that 'the third degree is a secret and illegal practice'" (Walker & Boehm, 1997, p. ix). Volume 14, *The Police*, was prepared by August Vollmer. In this last report to the Wickersham Commission, Vollmer reiterated his well-known views regarding "the need for strong leadership, the importance of eliminating political influence, [and] the necessity of upgrading recruitment and training standards" (Walker, 1977, p. 132).

The "training" of future police officers often focuses on technical skills and physical development, within a paramilitary structure (Blumberg et al., 2019; Doreian & Conti, 2017). While these may be important and necessary skills for future officers to learn, they are not the only aspects. Once on the job, police officers will experience a multitude of situations, and there is no possible way that any amount of training could fully prepare them to handle those cases where they often have to play the role of mediator, social worker, or confidant. Education, on the other hand, allows academy "trainees" to step into different roles, expanding their minds to learn about aspects of the communities they will serve from a theoretical lens—learning about subjects not always included in training, such as victimization, as police officers are often the first responders when someone has been victimized. Such explorations provide future police officers with a blueprint for better understanding the human beings in the communities they will serve, as well as themselves. Moreover, looking at commonly occurring community scenarios should help trainees improve their abilities to better understand individual behavior, which has the potential to decrease violent encounters. Nationwide, a variety of academies have adopted scholars' suggestions that adult learning models be integrated into police academies to better prepare officers for their future assignments, integrating more traditional college-level academic approaches with traditional police academy training (Schlosser, 2013).

Reducing Violence With Higher Education: Ideas and Inconclusive Results

Gary Cordner, a leading scholar and practitioner in policing, is a senior research advisor for the US Department of Justice, National Institute of Justice. He formerly taught at Kutztown University in Pennsylvania and also at Eastern Kentucky University (EKU) where he founded and directed both the Regional Community Policing Institute and the International Justice and Safety Institute and served as Dean of the College of Justice and Safety (ASU Center, 2022). Cordner (2021) has addressed the need for and benefits of higher education for the preparation of police officers in such areas as: stop/search/arrest; investigation; use of force; use of discretion; and procedural justice for current/veteran police officers. He suggests that police education and training (terms used together throughout his work) focus instruction and practice on the subjects of: procedures; learning new forensic techniques; refreshers on investigations; exploring ways the street officer impacts cases; appropriate use of force; practicing decision-making skills; refreshers on policy; and the reinforcement of the importance of treating people with respect. In other words, training does not and should not end at academy graduation. Education is an ongoing process that should be required of all police officers throughout their careers.

Reform initiatives in programs of police training should be considered an ever-evolving process in order to achieve the twin goals of reducing crime while improving community-police relationships. The planning should include the impacts of the types of initial training received at police academies throughout the United States. While the processes of continuing education and assessments for improvement are imperative, basic training programs need to be well managed in order to start officers off on the right foot and prepare them for successful careers. Ultimately, it will require a great amount of agreement and support for the police to be able to fulfill one of the recommendations of the President's Commission on Law Enforcement and the Administration of Justice, established in 1967, "that all police personnel with general enforcement powers have baccalaureate degrees" (President's Crime Commission, 1967, p. ix).

Cordner (2016) explains that although criminal justice has become a popular major in higher education, that setting alone does not satisfactorily meet the needs of police. There should be a bridge between police academies and academic institutions to more adequately prepare future and current police officers for the realities of the job; meshing together education, training, and experience about the specific and unique communities in which future officers will serve. Such a combined approach has the potential to decrease violent encounters, improve police–citizen relations, and increase job satisfaction for officers throughout their careers. It might also help retain officers, reversing a recent trend seen in the profession. Furthermore, in light of the fact that since 2015 police officers have fatally shot more than 900 people per year in the United States, high-level de-escalation techniques that include both practical training and theoretical education need to become a paramount and constant feature of all training programs for police.[4]

Police academies have historically placed little focus and time on what are considered to be academic topics (Gardiner, 2021). Viewpoints by some still include the belief that police officers get all the training they need in the academy, which can adapt to the needs of time and geographic location. In general, police academy training in the United States typically covers the following areas: strategy; weapons; working with communities; mental preparation; and physical readiness (Police 1, 2021b). The topic of police strategy will include information about law, policy, and procedure. The inclusion of "working with communities" will likely take in some aspects of psychology (Police 1, 2021b). The time constraints in the administration of academy programs limit the breadth and depth of the discussions oftentimes required for teaching about academic topics. Yet, efforts to converse and bring about community policing are taking place in many training programs. On the other hand, the available data indicates much room for improvement. Less than half of police departments across the nation provide additional training on community policing (36.2%) and implicit bias (37.1%). Less than a quarter of departments offer additional training on how to handle issues like civil disobedience (non-violent protests) or problem-solving (problem-oriented policing). Even fewer (less than 15%) provide training on evidenced-based policing (Gardiner, 2017, p. 35). It is worth noting that all of these subjects are commonly taught in college curricula for criminal justice students, and they are all key components of community policing. Thus, time constraints at academies still limit how much and to what extent academic programs can be explored, which again begs the question of whether or not some college requirement is appropriate for future police officers.

The minimum education requirements to become a police officer have remained largely unchanged over the past several decades, though higher levels of education are increasingly necessary for promotion. Most local police departments across the nation–over 80% (Gardiner, 2017) only require a high school diploma to become a sworn officer, while some state and most federal agencies do require some level of higher education (National University, 2022), along with steeper age requirements to enter an academy at state and federal levels. Still, it is approximated that over half of the police agencies in the United States offer some type of incentive (like tuition reimbursement or pay increases) for police officers to pursue college-level education (Gardiner, 2017), suggesting a latent recognition of the utility of college for police officers. Estimates suggest that over half of the individual police officers in the United States have at least a two-year degree, with over one-quarter having a four-year degree and just over 5% having a graduate-level education (Gardiner, 2017, p. 4). Massachusetts, New Jersey, Minnesota, and California have the highest percentages of officers with at least a 4-year degree; Massachusetts and New Jersey have the highest percentage of officers with master's degrees (Gardiner, 2017, p. 4). Still, barriers to education and a culture that does not exactly celebrate academic accomplishments leave the nation, overall, with police officers without 4-year college degrees.

Community colleges have been hailed by some as an ideal institution to assist in bridging higher education with more traditional police training (Etter, 1998) with advocates suggesting a minimum of an associate's degree for incoming police officers in all agencies across the country. The debate on whether or not police officers should be required to have a two- or four-year degree is ongoing, with some jurisdictions pushing for some level of college education while others are not requiring (or are dropping requirements for) any sort of college experience prior to entering a career in law enforcement (Police 1, 2022). For example, some jurisdictions in California have proposed legislation to require police officers to have a minimum number of college credits to assist in better preparing police to work with and understand the communities to which they have been assigned (Zeigler, 2020). Other areas (i.e., Chicago and New York) are considering lowering such requirements citing difficulties in recruitment (Police 1, 2022).

Beyond the academic benefits, higher salaries and greater ease in obtaining promotion are often cited as rationales for police officers to have a college education. Other benefits including being able to better relate to community members support the notion that having a college education before becoming a police officer is important. In addition, the shift in focus toward community policing models throughout the United States further promotes this idea (Police 1, 2021a).

Bouffard and Armstrong (2020) believe that higher education for police officers will result in fewer citizen complaints and police will less likely resort to using violence. Other researchers support their views. For example, Rydberg and Terrill (2010) found that LEOs having a college education may significantly reduce the use of force during police encounters. The development of community policing and problem-oriented policing requires problem solving and creative thinking—skills that most colleges include throughout their curriculums. In addition, internships and service-learning opportunities in college provide future police officers a chance to develop civic engagement skills. It also gives them the chance to get to know the communities they will police. "Among students who participated in a criminal justice service-learning course working with young people in the community, 80% reported a change from stereotypical assumptions that all of them would be criminals to a better understanding of them as individuals with goals and potential—some not so different from the students' own dreams. Almost 90% said they had come to understand the community, which they believed would serve them in their criminal justice careers" (Bouffard & Armstrong, 2020).

A higher education background will help police officers acquire the skills to identify best practices in policing. Further, each academic area will expose future law enforcement officials to research methodology in a variety of fields. They will learn how the scientific method can be utilized in a wide range of settings—assisting police in everything from evidence collection to detective work. Such knowledge is typically gained in college courses rather than in basic training courses. Police work in the future may involve "a new professionalism . . . that relies more on rigorous evaluation of policies, both strategic and managerial, rather than personal experience" (Bayley, 2016, p. 163). At least for senior leadership, a college education that includes a study of the scientific method will be critical for these essential purposes to be achieved.

Highlights From Recent Research

Studies on how a formal college education impacts individuals in police academies and their careers are limited and have produced mixed or inconclusive results; no standardized measure of success in policing careers is identified in the literature. Most of these studies are limited in scope and size, often exploring one or only a few specific police academies or departments. While this research is useful, it cannot and should not be generalized across the United States or beyond, as geographic and cultural factors vary. Still, these limited studies may help broaden the discussion and, hopefully, lay the groundwork for future, large-scale research on these topics. For example, White (2008) suggests that having a certain number of college credits obtained before attending a police academy does not directly translate into successful police performance. However, this study did show that the reading level during one's time at the academy was the largest predictor of successful career performance. Another study (Chappell, 2008) found that with the shift to more community policing-focused academies, education (and other skills that parallel the community policing philosophy) is rewarded in training performance. However, this study was limited to academy performance and not success on the job. Other studies suggest that the attitudes of police chiefs may influence how a college degree is viewed within a department (see Marciniak & Elattrache, 2020). While some skills gained in college are clearly advantageous to the field of policing, for the most part prior research studies showed that a college education had little to no impact on current measures of job performance (Marciniak & Elattrache, 2020). Perhaps current measures of performance in policing roles have not evolved with changing community policing practice or since studies are limited in scope and size, the evaluation of education has not been adequately measured. The authors still urge that there are a number of essential academic subjects that academies, alone or in collaboration with colleges or universities, should adopt to decrease violent encounters.

Essential Academy Subjects

The idea of adding a more academic component to police academies (or requiring a college degree) is not a novel idea (see Cordner, 2016; Vollmer, 1936). Moreover, taking a student-centered approach to training and education may be beneficial, particularly with the shift toward community policing (Birzer, 2003). The development of critical thinking skills along with repeated opportunities to practice those skills, with structured research methodologies, is more likely through an "educational" as opposed to a strictly "training" model. Critical thinking is an important skill needed for policing (Bouffard & Armstrong, 2020), particularly community policing when engaged in problem-solving (Community Policing Consortium, 1994). Completion of an accredited college education has been shown to adequately teach and enhance critical thinking skills (Huber & Kuncel, 2016). Academic subjects in the humanities and such fields as psychology, social work, sociology, anthropology, and law can assist in the development of critical thinking skills and, potentially, better community-police relationships with decreased incidents of excessive use of force. Some have even suggested and explored the possibility of adding training on social interaction to assist in the reduction of use of force in American police departments (Wolfe et al., 2020).

Humanities

Education in the humanities (including the subjects of languages, history, and philosophy) can help broaden perspectives and assist students in becoming more-informed citizens, regardless of their professional path after college. Growing intellectually through an exploration of these subjects can assist individuals in any field (Frank, 2016). Importantly, education in the humanities can introduce people to the concept of culture and its deeper meanings (Leerssen, 2021), which helps students learn about cultures beyond their own. Better understanding larger issues of justice and equality can also be explored by studying humanities (National Endowment for the Humanities, 2013). Arguably, all of these benefits are useful to people who will be interacting with community members as law enforcement officials. Police officers will routinely encounter people who do not share their same language or culture.

The melting pot of the United States includes countless minority groups, but the cultural and linguistic minority of the Deaf (capital D used to denote cultural identity) community provides insight into the importance of the humanities in an education for police officers. Culturally Deaf individuals share beliefs, values, and language (American Sign Language, or ASL) that differ from that of traditional American society (The Outreach Center for Deafness and Blindness, 2023). Communities throughout the nation are home to large groups of Deaf community members. Gallaudet University[5], the world's only liberal arts institution for the d/Deaf and hard-of-hearing, is located in Washington, DC. DC hosts a large Deaf population and, as a response, the Metropolitan Police Department (MPD) created the Deaf and Hard of Hearing unit (DC.gov, 2023). Though federal law requires that all police departments (as well as courts and corrections agencies) provide appropriate accommodations including communication aids (like interpreters) in practice d/Deaf and hard of hearing individuals involved in the justice system often go without what is needed to appropriately communicate with officials or advocate for themselves. Some of these encounters can end in violence, or even lawsuits against police agencies (Wyllie, 2016). MPD is actively working against the negative outcomes that can result by appropriately educating officers about this cultural and linguistic minority that they serve, and may be the only police department in the nation to take such a strong initiative for this community. MPD has been open to helping educate Gallaudet students (as well as faculty and staff) about the services offered by the larger department and the Deaf and Hard of Hearing Unit. Such collaborations can be used as an example or model for ways that communities can come together to better serve citizens through law enforcement activities, lowering potentials for violent encounters by police officers understanding the basic cultural and linguistic aspects of a group they serve. While this is done at the departmental level, it highlights the importance of a humanities-heavy education for police officers who will be interacting with residents of their communities who will not always share their language or culture. The inclusion of a humanities education more broadly during the training phase, and more narrowly based on unique department needs, have the potential to decrease violence and increase trust of police among community members. It can help more professionally and adequately build the human relationships needed to be successful in increasing public safety within a community policing framework.

Psychology and Human Relationships

Police officers are often asked to do much more than the basic job description; for example, having to talk at length with people in the toughest moments of their lives. In their call to action, Blumberg and colleagues (2019) suggest a unique approach to a psychological education for future police officers. They note that helping to develop "cognitive, emotional, social, and moral" skills can better equip officers to handle their stressful jobs and develop better relationships with the members of the communities they will serve. The physical and mental health of police officers should be of the utmost importance throughout their careers, fully supported by department officials. Considering the high levels of stress (personal and familial) experienced by police officers (see Elkins, 2021; Griffin & Sun, 2018), police departments are increasingly making mental health education part of their ongoing training/education process and there are calls to begin this process even earlier at academies. According to Gardiner (2017), nearly half of police departments across the country provide training to all of their officers on handling mental health crises, with about a quarter of agencies providing such training to a small percentage of police in their departments. Having a better handle on one's own mental health could possibly lead to more positive, less violent encounters.

In addition to considering their own mental health, it is imperative for police officers to have an understanding of the psychology of others. The connection between mental health problems and criminal justice system involvement is well-documented (Livingston, 2016). It has been shown that there exists a greater likelihood for individuals with untreated mental illness to be killed by police officers (Treatment Advocacy Centers, 2022). Police officers routinely come into contact with individuals not only dealing with mental health issues, but sometimes in an active mental health crisis. It is estimated that about 80% of police calls are service-related (Patterson, 2008). A number of police departments are developing programs to have social workers present for certain police calls or having people fulfill the requirements/training to be a police officer and social worker (Stone, 2021). These types of initiatives are referred to as "Embedded Police Social Worker" programs and are based on the need for providing mental health services for people in need of counseling rather than a police confrontation. They offer persons experiencing moments of crisis opportunities to receive professional help in tough situations. Unfortunately, social workers are often not trained with the practical skills needed to handle criminal justice-related calls, suggesting even more of a need for ongoing discussion, emerging partnerships, and appropriate education for police officers on mental health issues (Weniger, 2021). Providing education on basic social work practices to new police officers could be a way to address some of needs of both the police and the public.

Sociology explores human relationships and social institutions. Subfields of sociology include criminology and organizational sociology. Anthropology explores the evolution of human beings and their cultures. Exploring such subjects allow students, or potentially police recruits, to develop a more objective lens of the world around them and better understand the subjective "realities" and cultural influences of the community members they will be serving. Some research suggests that police officers are unfamiliar with some of the critical social problems they will be facing in the field. For example, only about 10% of agencies in the United States have officers dedicated and trained to work with the homeless population (Gardiner, 2017). Nonetheless, police officers routinely come into contact with this population and research has long established a link between homelessness, crime, and incarceration (Urban Institute, 2020), Racial issues also continue to be divisive between police officers and community members. Moon et al. (2018) cite a need to teach intercultural competency to police officers to assist in better outcomes. These examples highlight the ways in which college-level courses in sociology, anthropology, and related fields might assist in educating police officers to help perform their daily duties after academy life, improving relations with communities, and decreasing unnecessary violent encounters.

Legal Studies

As common sense as it may sound, it is vital for police academies to ensure that future police officers have an adequate grasp of the law itself. Police officers are responsible for upholding the law, but the legal code is not always at the top of the training agenda. Linetsky (2018) explores various examples of how a lack of understanding of the law can lead to improper arrests and declining relationships between police officers and the community members they serve. While substantive law is a staple in police academies for obvious reasons, constitutional law often falls by the wayside during police training, leading to the potential for improper enforcement of things like traffic laws and criminal misconduct. The highly-publicized uses of excessive force by police officers highlight this discrepancy (Linetsky, 2018). Among police departments in the United States, 35% provide training to patrol officers (beyond the academy) on procedural justice (Gardiner, 2017). Undoubtedly, there is room for improvement and an expanded understanding of the law future police officers are expected to uphold in their jobs after academy life. It is essential to include more in-depth legal education (as it pertains to LEOs' daily interactions) at the most basic levels of the academy program. Hopefully, such an emphasis will open the door for a better understanding and (peaceful) implementation of policy and procedure.

Conclusion

It is important to present higher-level thinking skills as part of the basic police academy educational program. This chapter has offered some potential ways to fulfill this need. The adoption of a philosophy that revolves around or at least includes education in academic subjects (with less or at least not exclusive reliance on the training or vocational models) opens the door for the development of critical thinking skills that can assist future police officers on a daily basis. The addition of human relations and critical thinking applications at academy programs and less emphasis on behaviorist approaches can help decrease violence and improve police–citizen interactions.

In order to encourage progress regarding police education, academies need to continue to address tactics and procedures, but also expand the time devoted to human relations and provide a more enriched curriculum that includes the humanities and other academic areas. "The typical case comes to the attention of authorities not on account of police initiative but through the initiative of a private citizen acting in the role of a complainant" (Black, 1978, p. 171). Thus, the vast influx of cases about crime and disorder are generated by the citizenry and that public expects police to be on-call every minute of the day. Such a constant flow of incidents requires all LEOs to have a firm grasp of the law and to perform many social work functions. While the expectation exists that police officers should perform a wide spectrum of crime-related and social tasks, it is unrealistic to expect that police academies can be responsible for imparting an infinite amount of knowledge and wisdom to future police officers. The challenge is coming up with the right combination of training and education along with an appropriate methodology to give police officers the highest degree of competence in order to handle the situations they will likely encounter. Education in subjects such as the humanities and social sciences can allow the learning process to take hold, encouraging higher-level thinking (beyond practical and tactical responses) to assist police officers in making ethically and legally sound decisions when faced with precarious situations. While ethics can be a difficult concept/subject to teach, it is not without precedent that it can be taught with a focus on policing (see Kleinig, 1990).[6]

More than half a century ago, Loughrey and Freise (1969) explored ways to bring formal, academic education to criminal justice professionals. They placed a certain amount of emphasis on the need for the study of history and government, indicating that "an understanding of our government, its history, its operation, and the relationships that exist among the various branches, will enable the student better to identify his role and the need for it in the area he elects to follow in his professional career" (Loughrey & Freise, Jr., 1969, pp. 266, 270). Furthermore, since the police must come in contact with all members of society they require an intimate understanding about how people behave in groups or as individuals. In essence, a police officer is like a "practicing social scientist, working in what has been described as the greatest living laboratory—the streets of a city. Therefore, to add depth to his experience and understanding to his relationships with the public, we must teach him the social sciences: Psychology, sociology, and anthropology" (Loughrey & Freise, Jr., 1969, pp. 266, 269).

The benefits of obtaining an academic education prior to employment as a full-time peace officer cannot be overemphasized. At the very least, it may help a future student pass competitive civil service examinations and as a trainee to know how to absorb and implement future training. Beyond that, it can assist individuals in better understanding the community members they will serve and work more collaboratively with representatives of other social institutions with whom they often interact (e.g., members of the medical community and of other government agencies).

Police academies need to continue with training for practical and tactical skills, especially de-escalation techniques, but also allow for more opportunities and outlets to address learning about human relations subjects. Longer training times need not be viewed as negative. On the contrary, benefits such as more opportunities for maturity and time to learn as professionals can prepare new police officers for future success and assist in further professionalizing the field. Partnerships with universities and police-sponsored academics may enhance the learning process, encouraging successful careers among police officers and hopefully, help decrease violent interactions with individuals.

Within the current system, practically speaking, it may not be possible (or maybe even necessary) to require a four-year degree across all police departments in the United States. However, including relevant academic work as academy requirements is a good starting point. Expanding training to include more educational processes, requiring some level of higher education and/or partnering with colleges are potential models for moving forward. Evaluation should be part of this process, ensuring that the tools and methods used to evaluate educational programs mirror the goals of community policing philosophies and practices. The design and use of longitudinal studies can best serve as an accurate measure of on-the-job performance. This process requires selecting researchers from outside of the system itself to perform professional assessments to also measure community satisfaction with police programs and new initiatives.

In the last quarter of the 20th century, James Q. Wilson (1931–2012) was quite skeptical of the value of both police higher education and the way human relations training was then being conducted at police academies. He called attention to the injustice that Blacks (and other minorities) faced due to becoming the victims of police shootings in disproportionate numbers (Wilson, 1985, p. 102). Wilson (1985) wrote that "it is natural that black organizations have made the issue a central theme of their criticism of police practice" (p. 102). He learned from discussions with police "that training room discussions of minority groups and police-community relations have little impact, and that such impression as they do produce quickly evaporates when the officer goes on the street and first encounters hostile or suspicious behavior" (Wilson, 1985, p. 106). Accordingly, Wilson (1985) held that the essential remedies to these enigmas lie first in the officer selection process, next in the creation of more relevant academy and post-academy programs, and lastly in a supportive organizational climate.

Police recruitment efforts must be designed so that police candidates will be selected who are honest and have the best capacity to handle the difficult challenges of the street. They must be able to accept responsibility for the consequences of their own actions and able to understand and apply legal concepts in both complex and ambiguous situations. Moreover, police training programs must include lessons "that simulate as far as possible real world conditions" (Wilson, 1985, p. 112). Furthermore, new officer training should "be made continuous rather than . . . sharply segmented into often inconsistent 'academy' and 'street' phases" (Wilson, 1985, pp. 112–113). "Finally, the properly recruited and suitably trained officer must be placed into an organizational setting" that rewards not only good arrests and instances of valor but also working constructively on community concerns and projects (Wilson, 1985, p. 113).

James Q. Wilson was especially interested in a community's capacity to engage in self-regulation. His emphasis on community efforts at self-regulation and how a properly trained and organized police force may contribute to more stable communities, reducing the tensions between the police and the public, are taken up in the proposals set forth in this book's final chapter. The current state of police training is the central topic of the next chapter, but new approaches to police training and education are needed to address the public's justified demands for police reforms in our time.

Notes

1 See Chapter 5 for a discussion of cultural and international police training.
2 See PERF, 2022, for an in-depth discussion on guiding principles to improve and transform police training in the United States.
3 It is useful in an examination of human relations (showing concern for how people treat one another) to understand that it is quite a different subject than police-community relations or public relations. The latter concerns efforts by police departments to try to correct a poor image, especially when public dissatisfaction regarding a specific incident has taken place. Such efforts seek to foster a more favorable view of the department. On the other hand, police-community relation became significant out of the turmoil of police misconduct during the 1960s and has centered upon trying to understand the needs of communities by opening-up lines of communication between the police and the public they serve. This is done with the expectation that solutions to problems may evolve and that both the police and the community will need to share in their resolutions. On the other hand, sound human relations requires police to recognize the human frailties we all have in common and when they encounter others to act in the most professional manner possible given all the circumstances. In this way, the police may come to deal with people on an individual basis, free of stereotypes and preconceptions (Hale, 1973, pp. 15–16).
4 *The Washington Post* has tracked fatal police shootings in the United States since 2015, there latest findings can be found online at: https://www.washingtonpost.com/graphics/investigations/police-shootings-database/.
5 Learn more about Gallaudet's history and mission at https://gallaudet.edu/.
6 See Kleinig (2013) for specific examples of teaching ethics through scenario-based projects.

References

Arendt, A. (1998). *The human condition* (2nd ed.). The University of Chicago Press.
ASU Center. (2022). *ASU center for problem-oriented policing biographies: Gary Cordner*. Retrieved July 3, 2022, from https://popcenter.asu.edu/content/biographies-gary-cordner
Baker, A. (2015a, December 11). On patrol, Scottish officers rely on an important tool: Banter. *The New York Times*. Retrieved December 15, 2022, from https://www.nytimes.com/2015/12/12/nyregion/on-patrol-scottish-officers-rely-on-an-important-tool-banter.html

Baker, A. (2015b, December 11). US police leaders, visiting Scotland, get lessons on avoiding deadly force. *The New York Times*. Retrieved December 15, 2022, from https://www.nytimes.com/2015/12/12/nyregion/us-police-leaders-visiting-scotland-get-lessons-on-avoiding-deadly-force.html

Bayley, D. H. (2016). The complexities of 21st century policing. *Policing: A Journal of Policy and Practice*, *10*(3), 163–170. https://doi.org/10.1093/police/paw019

Birzer, M. L. (2003). The theory of andragogy applied to police training. *Policing: An International Journal of Police Strategies and Management*, *26*(1), 29–42.

Black, D. J. (1978). The mobilization of law. In P. K. Manning & J. V. Maanen (Eds.), *Policing: A view from the street* (pp. 167–187). Goodyear Publ. Co., Inc.

Blumberg, D. M., Schlossler, M. D., Papazoglou, K., Creighton, S., & Kay, C. (2019). New directions in police academy training: A call to action. *International Journal of Environmental Research and Public Health*, *16*(24), 4941. https://doi.org/10.3390/ijerph16244941

Bouffard, L., & Armstrong, G. (2020, June). 5 reasons police officers should have college degrees. *The Conversation*. https://theconversation.com/5-reasons-police- fficers-should-have-college-degrees-140523

Brueninger, K. (2020, June). Trump signs executive order urging police reform, says cops need more funding. *CNBC*. https://www.cnbc.com/2020/06/16/trump-%09signs-%09executive-order-urging-police-reform-says-cops-need-more-funding.html

Buehler, E. D. (2021). State and local law enforcement training academies, 2019–Statistical tables. *Bureau of Justice Statistics*. NCJ 255915. Retrieved August 11, 2022, from https://bjs.ojp.gov/sites/g/files/xyckuh236/files/media/document/slleta18st.pdf

Burkhalter, K. (2020, June). Retired officer: Give police a real education before putting them on the streets. *USA Today*. https://www.usatoday.com/story/opinion/policing/2020/06/11/ex-cop-academy-training-falls-short-police-need-extensive-education/5342917002/

Chappell, A. T. (2008). Police academy training: Comparing across curricula. *Policing: An International Journal*, *31*(1), 36–56. https://doi.org/10.1108/13639510810852567

Chappell, A. T., & Lanza-Kaduce, L. (2010). Police academy socialization: Understanding the lessons learned in a paramilitary-bureaucratic organization. *Journal of Contemporary Ethnography*, *39*(2), 187–214. https://doi.org/10.1177/0891241609342230

Chen, S. (2023, January 28). Memphis Police disband Scorpion unit after Tyre Nichols footage release. *Axios*. Retrieved January 30, 2023, from https://www.axios.com/2023/01/28/tyre-nichols-memphis-police-scorpion-disband

Cleveland, G., & Saville, G. (2022). *Police PBL: Blueprint for the 21st century*. Retrieved July 2, 2022, from https://www.theiacp.org/projects/21st-century-policing-blueprint

Community Policing Consortium. (1994, August). *Understanding community policing: A framework for action*. Bureau of Justice Assistance, U.S. Department of Justice. NCJ 148457. https://www.ojp.gov/pdffiles/commp.pdf

Cordner, G. (2016). The unfortunate demise of police education. *Journal of Criminal Justice Education*, *279*(4), 485–496. https://doi.org/10.1080/10511253.2016.1190134

Cordner, G. (2021, January). How police education and training can contribute to violence reduction. *Police 1*. https://www.police1.com/police-training/articles/how-police-education-and-training-can-contribute-to-violence-reduction-oU4x5bz48otQTK4y/

Council on Criminal Justice. (2020). *Public perceptions of the police*. https://counciloncj.org/public-perceptions-of-the-police/

Crowl, J. N. (2017). The effect of community policing on fear and crime reduction, police legitimacy and job satisfaction: An empirical review of the evidence. *Police Practice and Research: An International Journal*, *18*(5), 449–462. https://doi.org/10.1080/15614263.2017.1303771

DC.gov. (2023). *Metropolitan police department: Deaf and hard of hearing unit liaison*. https://mpdc.dc.gov/page/deaf-and-hard-hearing-liaison-unit

Delpato, D. J., & Midgley, B. D. (1992). Some fundamentals of B.F. Skinner's behaviorism. *American Psychologist*, *47*(11), 1507–1520.

Doreian, P., & Conti, N. (2017). Creating the thin blue line: Social network evolution within a police academy. *Social Networks*, *50*, 83–97.

Dowd, T. (2020, December 10). *Being a cop could soon require a 4-year college degree in California*. https://www.vice.com/en/article/akd7wp/california-bill-require-police-officers-4-year-college-degree

Elinson, P., & Frosch, D. (2015, July). Cost of police-misconduct cases soars big in US cities. *The Wall Street Journal*. https://www.wsj.com/articles/cost-of-police-%09misconduct-cases-soars-in-big-u-s-cities-1437013834

Elkins, F. E. (2021, May). Optimizing mental and physical health in the phoenix police department. *Dispatch*, *14*(5). https://cops.usdoj.gov/html/dispatch/05-2021/optimizing_mental_and_phyiscal_health.html

Etter, G. W. (1998). The role of community colleges in the training and education of law enforcement and corrections personnel: A curriculum for the 21st Century. *Community College Journal of Research and Practice*, *22*, 491–506.

Frank, A. (2016). What is the value of an education in the humanities? *NPR*. https://www.npr.org/sections/13.7/2016/02/02/465239105/what-is-the-value-of-an-education- n-the-humanities

Gardiner, C. (2017, September). Policing around the nation: Education, philosophy, and practice. California State University Fullerton Center for Public Policy and Police Foundation. Retrieved July 2, 2022, from https://www.policinginstitute.org/wp-content/uploads/2017/10/PF-Report-Policing-Around-the-Nation_10-2017_Final.pdf

Gardiner, C. (2021). College cops around the nation: A 30-year and 40-year update on the state of higher education in US policing. *Policing: A Journal of Policy and Practice*, *15*(2), 798–816. https://doi.org/10.1093/police/paz029

Geary, D. P., et al. (1975). *Community relations and the administration of justice*. John Wiley & Sons, Inc.

Goldfarb, B. (2020). *18 tiny deaths: The untold story of the woman who invented modern forensics*. Sourcebooks Inc.

Griffin, J. D., & Sun, I. Y. (2018). Do work-family conflict and resiliency mediate police stress and burnout: A study of state police officers. *American Journal of Criminal Justice*, *43*, 354–370.

Gutierrez, D. (2022). *Why police training must be reformed*. Retrieved July 5, 2022, from https://iop.harvard.edu/get-involved/harvard-political-review/why-police-training-must-be- eformed

Hale, C. D. (1973). *Police community relations*. Delmar Publishers.

Hernandez, D. (2015, December). How one of the deadliest police forces in America stopped shooting people. *Quartz*. https://qz.com/565011/how-one-of-the-largest-police-forces-in-america-stopped-shooting-people

Hernandez, D. (2020, July 6). The thin blue line: The history behind the controversial police emblem. *The San Diego Union Tribune*. https://www.sandiegouniontribune.com/news/public-safety/story/2020-07-06/the-thin-blue-line-the-complex-history-and-thoughts-behind-the-police-emblem

Huber, C. R., & Kuncel, N. R. (2016). Does college teach critical thinking skills? A meta-analysis. *Review of Educational Research*, *86*(2), 431–468. https://doi.org/10.3102/0034654315605917

Idaho POST. (2022). *Mission, vision, and values*. Retrieved July 3, 2022, from https://post.idaho.gov/mission-vision-values/

Jay, S. (2022). *Learning vs. training: What's the difference and why do you need to know?* https://www.aihr.com/blog/learning-vs-training/

Kell, G. (2017, April 19). August Vollmer biography explores famous police chief's UC Berkeley ties. *Berkeley News*. Retrieved February 1, 2023, from https://news.berkeley.edu/2017/04/19/august-vollmer-biography-explores-famous-police- chiefs-uc-berkeley-ties/

Kleinig, J. (1990). Teaching and learning police ethics: Competing and complimentary approaches. *Journal of Criminal Justice*, *18*, 1–18.

Kleinig, J. (2001). The blue wall of silence. *International Journal of Applied Philosophy*, *15*(1), 1–23.

Kleinig, J. (2013). Reflections on teaching police ethics with scenarios. In P. A. J. Waddington, J. Kleinig, & M. Wright (Eds.), *Professional police practice: Scenarios and dilemmas*. Oxford University Press.

Leerssen, J. (2021). Culture, humanities, evolution: The complexity of meaning-making over time. *Philosophical Transactions of the Royal Society B: Biological Sciences*, *376*. http://doi.org/10.1098/rstb.2020.0043

Lewis, M. (2016). *The undoing project: A friendship that changed our minds*. W. W. Norton and Company.

Linetsky, Y. R. (2018). What the police don't know might hurt us: An argument for enhanced legal training of police officers. *New Mexico Law Review*, *48*(1), 1–95.

Livingston, J. D. (2016). Contact between police and people with mental disorders: A review of rates. *Psychiatry Online*. https://ps.psychiatryonline.org/doi/10.1176/appi.ps.201500312

Loughrey, L. C., & Freise, H. C. (1969, June). Curriculum development for a police science program. *The Journal of Criminal Law, Criminology, and Police Science, 60*(2), 265–271. https://scholarlycommons.law.northwestern.edu/cgi/viewcontent.cgi?article=5597&conte xt=jclc

Marciniak, L., & Elattrache, A. D. (2020). Police chiefs' opinions on the utility of college education for police officers. *Journal of Criminal Justice Education*, *31*(3), 436–453.

Mckenzie, P. (1995). Education and training: Still distinguishable? *The Vocational Aspect of Education*, *47*(1), 35–49. https://doi.org/10.1080/0305787950470103

Moon, S. H., Morgan, T., & Sandage, S. J. (2018). The need for intercultural competence assessment and training among police officers. *Journal of Forensic Psychology Research and Practice*, *18*(5), 337–351. https://doi.org/10.1080/24732850.2018.1510274

National Academies of Sciences, Engineering, and Medicine. (2018). *Protective policing: Effects on crime and communities*. National Academies Press.

National Endowment for the Humanities. (2013). *The humanities belong to everyone*. https://www.neh.gov/divisions/fedstate/resource/the-humanities-belong-everyone

National University. (2022). *Law enforcement education: Career boosting options*. Retrieved July 5, 2022, from https://www.nu.edu/resources/law-enforcement-education/

Outreach Center for Deafness and Blindness. (2023). *Understanding the deaf culture and the deaf world*. https://deafandblindoutreach.org/understanding-the-deaf-culture-and-the-deaf-world

Patterson, G. T. (2008, July). *Police social work: A unique area of practice arising from law enforcement functions*. National Association of Social Workers. https://www.naswnyc.org/page/77/Police-Social-Work.htm

PERF. (2022, November). *Transforming police recruit training: 40 guiding principles*. Police Executive Research Forum. Retrieved December 14, 2022, from https://www.policeforum.org/assets/TransformingRecruitTraining.pdf

Police 1. (2021a, October). *Why college educated police officers make more money*. https://www.police1.com/how-to-become-a-police-officer/articles/why-college-educated-police-officers-make-more-money-vNlkNJ6MzOgfBFcY/

Police 1. (2021b, November). *What to expect from police academy training*. https://www.police1.com/how-to-become-a-police-officer/articles/what-to-expect-from-police-academy-training-TphD8qpkqgg68nYc/

Police 1. (2022, May). *State your case: Should prospective cops be required to have college degrees?* https://www.police1.com/police-jobs-and-careers/articles/state-your-case-should-prospective-cops-be-required-to-have-college-degrees-t9MXaJOawkPBvUma/

President's Crime Commission. (1967). *The challenge of crime in a free society: A report by the president's commission on law enforcement and administration of justice*. US Government Printing Office. https://www.ojp.gov/pdffiles1/Digitization/42NCJRS.pdf

Rahr, S., & Rice, S. K. (2015). *From warriors to guardians: Recommitting police culture to American ideals*. NCJ 248654. https://www.ojp.gov/pdffiles1/nij/248654.pdf

Rydberg, J., & Terrill, W. (2010). The effect of higher education on police behavior. *Police Quarterly*, *13*(1), 92–120. https://doi.org/10.1177/1098611109357325

Sanchez, R. (2023, January 30). 'A new era of accountability.' What Memphis got right after the death of Tyre Nichols. *CNN*. Retrieved February 6, 2023, from https://www.cnn.com/2023/01/30/us/memphis-police-tyre-nichols-case/index.html

Schlossler, M. D. (2013). Training adults to become police officers at The University of Illinois Police Training Institute. *Law Enforcement Executive Forum*, *13*, 61–62.

Stone, M. (2021, August). Embedded police social workers. *Dispatch*, *14*(8). https://cops.usdoj.gov/html/dispatch/08-2021/police_social_workers.html#:~:text=PSWs%20work%20to%20identify%20appropriate,and%20are%20being%20used%20effectively

Travis, J. (1995, February 10). *Education in law enforcement: Beyond the college degree.* Retrieved July 3, 2022, from https://nij.ojp.gov/speech/education-law-enforcement-beyond-college-degree

Treatment Advocacy Center. (2022). *People with untreated mental illness 16 times more likely to be killed by law enforcement.* Retrieved July 5, 2022, from https://www.treatmentadvocacycenter.org/key-issues/criminalization-of-mental-illness/2976-people-with-untreated-mental-illness-16-times-more-likely-to-be-killed-by-law-enforcement

Trinkner, R., Kerrison, E. M., & Goff, P. A. (2019). The force of fear: Police stereotype threat, self-legitimacy, and support for excessive force. *Law and Human Behavior*, *43*(5), 421–435. https://doi.apa.org/fulltext/2019-36698-001.html

Urban Institute. (2020, September). *Five charts that explain the homelessness-jail cycle and how to break it.* https://www.urban.org/features/five-charts-explain- omelessness-jail-cycle-and-how-break-it

Vollmer, A. (1936). *The police in modern society.* University of California Press.

Vollmer, A. (1932, Winter). Abstract of the Wickersham police report. *Journal of Criminal Law and Criminology*, *22*, 716–723. https://scholarlycommons.law.northwestern.edu/cgi/viewcontent.cgi?article=2255&conte xt=jclc

Walker, S. (1977). *A critical history of police reform: The emergence of professionalism.* Lexington Books.

Walker, S., & Boehm, R. (1997). *Guide to the microfilm edition of records of the Wickersham commission on law observance and enforcement.* University Publications of America. http://www.lexisnexis.com/documents/academic/upa_cis/1965_wickershamcommpt1.pdf

Weniger, D. (2021, November 26). As law enforcement embeds social workers, police see positives, but training needed. *Police 1.* https://www.police1.com/mental- ealth-outreach/articles/as-law-enforcement-embeds-social-workers-police-see-positives-but-training-needed-0A22fZGKRh1hvCMK/

Werth, E. P. (2011). Scenario training in police academies: Developing students' higher-level thinking skills. *Police Practice and Research*, *12*(4), 325–340.

White, M. D. (2008). Identifying good cops early: Predicting recruit performance in the academy. *Police Quarterly*, *11*(1), 27–49.

Wilson, J. Q. (1985). *Thinking about crime; Revised edition.* Vintage Books.

Wilson, O. W. (1953). August Vollmer. *Journal of Criminal Law and Criminology*, *44*(1), 91–103. https://scholarlycommons.law.northwestern.edu/cgi/viewcontent.cgi?article=4112&conte xt=jclc

Wolfe, S., Rojek, J., McLean, K., & Alpert, J. (2020). Social interaction training to reduce police use of force. *The ANNALS of the American Academy of Political and Social Science*, *87*(1). Retrieved December 15, 2022, from https://journals.sagepub.com/doi/full/10.1177/0002716219887366

Wyllie, D. (2016, November 8). Police contacts with deaf subjects: Tips and resources to keep everyone safe. *Police1.* https://www.police1.com/police-trainers/articles/police-contacts-with-deaf-subjects-tips-and-resources-to-keep-everyone-safe-pcyuNWFjLA9xaq18/

Zeigler, S. (2020, November). California police groups back requiring college classes for recruits. *Police 1.* https://www.police1.com/police-training/articles/calif-police-groups-back-requiring-college-classes-for-recruits-MyzpoHEnZTS5d5T4/

8

POLICE TRAINING VERSUS EXPERIENCE IN THE COMMUNITY

New ideas are needed in the field of police training. It is an historical fact that police training and police education in the United States has followed a rather familiar pattern—with a "local police academy, operating continuously or intermittently, and offering principally a program of recruit training" (MacNamara, 1949, p. 657). However, due to budgetary constraints, ever more frequently in recent years recruit training courses have also involved cooperative arrangements for academy training to be conducted regionally for a multiple number of law enforcement agencies. The new recruits follow-up and supplement this training with field training at their home agencies along with various mandatory refresher courses of short duration. Police training is a necessary requirement in an age marked by such converging crises as: the COVID-19 pandemic; economic problems; climate change; immigration control; racial disparities; cybercrime; new cultural mores; a growing mental health crisis; gun violence; and the havoc caused by mass shooting incidents. The events involving school shootings have reached a breaking point in school districts throughout the US. The police response to the Robb Elementary School massacre in Uvalde, Texas, where an 18-year-old shooter killed 19 children and two teachers and injured an additional 17 people, has been described as an "abject failure." "We failed," said Col. Steve McCraw, director of the Texas Department of Public Safety, a leader for the after-incident investigation (qtd. in Bruggeman et al., 2023). The tragedy unfolded on May 24, 2022, as the gunman rampaged through two fourth-grade classrooms. It was the most shocking attack to have occurred since the loss of 20 first-graders and six school employees at Sandy Hook Elementary on December 13, 2012. Today, most schools and police agencies recognize they must do better to protect children because of the systemic failures at Uvalde. The National Association of School and Campus Police Chiefs (NASCPC) is a not-for-profit based in Stuart, Florida. The organization advances school and campus safety by providing training, advocacy, and collaboration. The association's web pages track school safety incidents across the US at https://www.nascpc.org/statesafetynews. According to Frank J. Kitzerow, the NASCPC President,

> the greater the investment in proactive strategies, the less opportunity for a targeted act of violence to occur. . . . It is important to note that success in this regard requires a strong collaboration between mental health professionals and law enforcement, which

DOI: 10.4324/9781003307396-11

> does not always equate to an arrest. Being able to mitigate a potential attacker's underlying grievance can have a long-term positive impact on maintaining the safety of our students. In short, we are never going to arrest our way out of this problem.
>
> *(Kitzerow, 2022)*

According to John Kleinig, the Emeritus Professor of Philosophy at John Jay College of Criminal Justice and Strategic Research Professor at Charles Sturt University and Professorial Fellow and Program Manager in Criminal Justice Ethics at the Centre for Applied Philosophy and Public Ethics in Canberra, Australia,

> police, like members of every other public agency, fall short of the professional ideals that inform their occupation. . . . Given police powers, performance failures can be socially devastating. In addition, such failures are not randomly distributed. There are social and cultural forces—political and religious ideologies, economic factors, historical traditions and incidents, and even influential individuals—that unfairly skew them.
>
> *(Kleinig, 2016)*

By the mid-1960s, well over half of American cities with a population of more than half a million people were providing their police recruits with at least eight weeks of basic training.[1] This standard owed much to the initiatives undertaken by the Federal Bureau of Investigation "which dramatized the need, set standards, devised techniques and provided personnel for police training" (President's Commission, 1967, p. 112) and for three decades had been providing a training academy for nonfederal senior law enforcement personnel. Candidates had to be nominated by their agency's head and possess at least five years of experience (Nowicki, 1994).[2] However, the advanced FBI training could only accommodate a few hundred officers each year and the vast number of new police recruits had to rely on their basic training received in their communities. While such local training was considered a major advance by the President's Commission on Law Enforcement and the Administration of Justice in 1967, the content offered by the local training academies was found to be "unsophisticated and incomplete" (President's Commission, 1967, p. 112). There was scant coverage of such subjects as: the legal limitations on street policing; the proper use of discretion; the nature of the community; and the role of the police. In addition, the President's Commission noted that the topic of police-minority group relations was given insufficient attention and that civilian instructors were rarely used to teach topics related to criminal law, sociology, and the history of the civil rights movement. Only a small percentage of departments combined classroom work with formal field training that would acquaint recruits with everyday street problems. Moreover, new educational techniques were seldom used in police academies and small rural departments often provided "recruits with no training at all" (President's Commission, 1967, p. 112). Consequently, the President's Crime Commission recommended that: (1) All training programs should provide instruction on subjects that prepare recruits to exercise discretion properly, and to understand the community, the role of the police, and what the criminal justice system can and cannot do; (2) Professional educators and civilian experts should be used to teach specialized courses-law and psychology, for example; (3) Recognized teaching techniques such as problem-solving seminars should be incorporated into training programs; and (4) Formal police training programs for recruits in all departments, large and small, should consist of an absolute minimum of 400 hours of classroom work spread over a four- to six-month period so that it can be combined with carefully selected and supervised field training (President's Commission, 1967, p. 112).

In addition, to the foregoing recommendations, the multi-volume President's Crime Commission report detailed many criminal justice reforms. By the 1970s, field training programs were recognized as an essential supplement to attendance at a basic police training program. An important impetus to having new recruits shadow and serve under veteran officers out on patrol were the practices instituted by the San Jose Police Department beginning in 1972. It took two years for the San Jose Police Department to develop a checklist of 31 traits on which recruits could be rated. In 1974 the California State Legislature adopted Penal Code section 832.3 governing the standards of field training programs. The San Jose model was established as that standard (Moore & Womack, 1975). Subsequently, similar programs "became fixtures in departments across the country" (Weichselbaum, 2020). A favorable survey involving the San Jose Police Department as well as the police departments of Newport News (Virginia), Flagstaff (Arizona) and Largo (Florida) indicated that field training programs "are relatively in-expensive ways to improve selection and training of new officers . . . [and] result in a reduction of civil liability complaints and ultimately increase the agency's effectiveness in the community" (McCampbell, 1987, p. iv). On the basis of these findings, the report recommended "that law enforcement chief executives institute field training programs as a natural extension of their recruit selection and training process" (McCampbell, 1987, p. iv). Several decades later, however, the President's Task Force on 21st Century Policing was highly critical of the San Jose Model and recommended a number of changes for inclusion when revisions are made to new training programs (Delany& Elkins, 2015). In particular, the President's Task Force (2015) urged that "law enforcement agency policies for training on use of force should emphasize de-escalation and alternatives to arrest or summons in situations where appropriate" (p. 20). In addition, the Task Force recommended that "law enforcement agencies should engage youth and communities in joint training with law enforcement, citizen academies, ride-alongs, problem solving teams, community action teams, and quality of life teams" (p. 93).

In the United States, since the 1970s, the availability of increased federal and state funding for police training programs resulted in substantial improvements in the overall training of police personnel, but still not as much as that provided in other nations with comparable wealth. Moreover, by the end of the first decade of the 21st century, despite greater emphasis on community interests and local involvement in public safety initiatives, "the most salient lessons learned in police training were those that reinforced the paramilitary structure and culture" (Chappell & Lanza-Kaduce, 2010, p. 187). Rosa Brooks,[3] Georgetown Law School's Associate Dean for Centers and Institutes and the Scott K. Ginsburg Professor of Law and Policy, has noted that "the nation is now debating how to 'fix' American policing, and much of the criticism of current police practices relates to the paramilitary aspects of policing. . . . If we want to change policing, we need to . . . turn the spotlight onto police academies, where new recruits are first inculcated into the folkways of their profession" (Brooks, 2020). In this regard, Brooks also emphasizes the importance of making changes in the culture and structure of police agencies. "For decades, cities have tried to change the cultures of their police departments, bringing in progressive chiefs and mandating programs to teach officers to become more compassionate and less violent. For the most part, it hasn't worked. . . . Field training officers are a big reason problems persist, according to current and former police leaders, academics and even the U.S. Justice Department" (Weichselbaum,

2020). The current state of police training is the central topic of this chapter. The issue of police training often receives a great deal of media attention where there has been an abject failure in police response at a major crime scene or the occurrence of a mistake resulting in death or serious injury of suspects or bystanders. The problem of assigning officers to mentor new recruits who may not be suitable is given initial attention in this chapter.

Mistakes and Poor Standards in Field Training Programs

According to a Marshall Project review of ten big-city departments, police agency field "trainers get little formal instruction in how to mold young officers' behavior. Becoming a field trainer is seen as a mark of prestige and seniority, rather than a serious and challenging job" (Weichselbaum, 2020). "The low standards create poisonous field training programs that fuel a toxic street-cop culture, marked by too much aggression and too little accountability. Since 2011, the Justice Department has ordered at least five major cities to revamp how they run field training" (Weichselbaum, 2020). Furthermore, there are no national standards for how long a young officer should work under the direction of a veteran (Weichselbaum, 2020).

One infamous case of poor training occurred when veteran Brooklyn Center, Minnesota police officer Kim Potter killed 20-year-old Daunte Wright when she mistakenly used her firearm instead of her Taser during a traffic stop. Potter, who had worked as a police officer for 26 years, had served on the force's negotiation team. She was acting as a field training officer, training a new officer (Anthony Luckey), when she shot Wright (Adams, 2021). Potter was convicted of both first- and second-degree manslaughter in a trial in December 2021. Judge Regina Chu found there to be mitigating factors in the case and sentenced Potter to two years in state custody with the stipulation that the final eight months would be served on supervised release. Chu listed the following factors that she said called for a lighter sentence: that Potter intended to draw her Taser instead of her gun; that the scene was chaotic, tense and rapidly evolving, requiring quick decision-making by Potter; and that Potter's decisions were not driven by personal animosity toward Wright. "Officer Potter made a mistake that ended tragically," Chu said. "She never intended to hurt anyone. Her conduct cries out for a sentence significantly below the guidelines" (qtd. in Sullivan & Wamsley, 2022). Wright was stopped by Potter and the officer she was training after they noticed "expired tabs on his license plate and an air freshener hanging from the rearview mirror [an infraction in Minnesota]. After a polite initial conversation, the officers discovered a warrant for Wright's arrest stemming from a gun charge. They decided to arrest him. Video footage from body cameras and the squad car dashcam show that Wright was initially cooperative, but as he was being handcuffed, he pulled away and ducked back inside his car" (Sullivan & Wamsley, 2022). At her trial, "during questioning by her defense attorney, Potter described her long background in policing and public safety. As a junior high school student, she volunteered as a school patrol officer, she said, and joined a youth police department program in high school. During college, she interned at a local police department" (Sullivan, 2021).

Ironically, the shooting death of Wright took place as the murder trial of former police officer Derek Chauvin was unfolding in nearby Minneapolis. Chauvin was tried and convicted of the murder of George Floyd. Chauvin received a sentence of 22 1/2 years in prison for applying excessive and fatal force during Floyd's arrest on May 25, 2020. Other officers present were charged with related crimes. The sentence fell short of prosecutors' request of a 30-year sentence. According to Minnesota Attorney General Keith Ellison, Chauvin's sentence was one of the longest a former police officer had ever received for an unlawful use of deadly force, calling it a "moment of real accountability" (qtd. in Chappell, 2021). "Chauvin was seen on video pressing his knee onto Floyd's neck for nine minutes and 29 seconds as Floyd lay face down on the asphalt outside a convenience store with his hands cuffed behind his back. The police had been called to the store after Floyd allegedly used a counterfeit $20 bill to pay for cigarettes" (Chappell, 2021).

A notorious example of a major incident of police failure to act took place shortly before noon on May 24, 2022. Multiple officers were present or nearby when an 18-year-old gunman fired at students and teachers in adjoining classrooms at Robb Elementary School in Uvalde, Texas. The gunman's actions caused the deaths of 19 students and two teachers. Initial reports indicated that as many as "19 law enforcement officers stood outside the classroom in the school for roughly 50 minutes as they waited for room keys and tactical equipment [while] children inside the classroom repeatedly called 911 and pleaded for help" (Tucker, 2022). According to Maria Haberfeld, a professor of police science at John Jay College of Criminal Justice, "The way the Uvalde officers responded aligned with the fact that they likely did not have proper training" (qtd. in Tucker, 2022). The Texas active shooter guidelines then in effect stated that "Officer's first priority is to move in and confront the attacker. This may include bypassing the injured and not responding to cries for help from children." According to Thor Eells, executive director of the National Tactical Officers Association (NTAO), "the delayed police response in Uvalde runs contrary to well-established, commonly taught active shooter protocol established after the Columbine school shooting of 1999" (Tucker, 2022). Steven McCraw, the director of the Texas Department of Public Safety who leads both the Texas State Police and Texas Rangers, called the mass shooting event "an abject failure" that ran counter to decades of training (Goodman, 2022). At present, there are still "no national guidelines to standardize law enforcement's training and response to active shooter situations" (Tucker, 2022).

Generally, the nearly 18,000 police agencies in the United States are not bound by any national standards on training, procedures, and basic training. Academy content and duration varies across the country. However, when the US Supreme Court rules on the basic rights of citizens, the Court has in effect promulgated specific national legal standards to guide the conduct of law enforcement officials. On average, US officers spend about 21 weeks at their basic training academies before they are qualified to go on patrol, a period that is much less than in such other countries as Finland, Germany, Australia, the United Kingdom, and Canada. Furthermore, "many other countries require officers to have a university degree - or equivalent - before joining the police, but in the US most forces just require the equivalent of a high-school diploma" (Horton, 2021). A number of police educators have indicated their support for a national curriculum for policing, or a national certification and minimum qualifications, especially for police chiefs. John DeCarlo, a former police chief who directs the master's program in criminal justice at the University of New Haven, supports this view. DeCarlo believes that federal and state governments should incentivize officers to get higher levels of education and that non-police specialists should be more involved in teaching future officers. He has said: "Where cops learn to be cops in the United States is sometimes from TV and that's where we don't want them learning to be cops. We want them to be educated. We don't want them to be mirroring the Dirty Harrys of the world. . . . I want gender scholars and race scholars and criminal justice scholars to be teaching future cops, not TV" (qtd. in Preston, 2020). New national guidelines should be considered for upgrading the content of training, the time allotted for each topic, and the qualifications of instructors.

On the other hand, the police actions at the time of Uvalde school massacre cannot readily be simply explained as an example of the lack of standard training practices. Confusion about command responsibility and common sense seemed lacking. A year prior to the Uvalde shootings, Randy Shrewsberry, a veteran officer and the founder of the Institute for Criminal Justice Training Reform, was asked about what he thinks needs to change with policing in the United States. He stated:

> We are asking our officers to run towards danger for which the rest of us are running away from. And I never want to minimize the responsibility that police officers are taking on in doing that. But it can't be the sole thing. We have to give them the tools for de-escalation, for dealing with mental health. We have to rely on policy changes so that we can reduce the interactions. This is critical.
>
> *(qtd. in Elliott, 2021)*

Moreover, it is possible that some people cannot be trained. This was the sentiment of Jason Sole, a former president of the Minneapolis NAACP, who has noted that training is not a "catch all" (Adams, 2021). Although he was stating his belief in the context of the lasting impact of implicit bias training for police officers, the same sentiment may apply in other cases. It may be that the day-in and day-out experience of people also plays an important part in the way people may react in a crisis situation.

Limitations and Opportunities in Police Training

There are many issues associated with police training in the United States. According to Dennis Slocumb, a 32-year veteran of the Los Angeles County Sheriff's Department who has held such positions as detective lieutenant and Vice President Emeritus of the International Union of Police Associations (IUPA) and is now serving as the principal IUPA federal legislative liaison regarding law enforcement issues, "Police officers, police chiefs, and everyone agree that we do not get enough training in a myriad of fields" (qtd. in Khazan, 2021). "Police in the United States receive less initial training than their counterparts in other rich countries—about five months in a classroom and another three or so months in the field, on average" (Khazan, 2021). In recent years the work of field-training officers (FTOs) has become the focus of significant news media attention due to the convictions of Derek Chauvin and Kim Potter, who shouted "Taser! Taser! Taser!" just before fatally shooting Daunte Wright with her service firearm. Both former officers were acting as field-training officers for their respective police departments when their actions took place. In light of these circumstances, some persons may be justly concerned about whether any new officer who has been paired with a field-training officer is at risk of being taught the wrong techniques from veteran officers who have themselves learned incorrect techniques.

According to David Harris, the Sally Ann Semenko Endowed Chair and Professor of Law at the University of Pittsburg who studies, writes and teaches about police behavior, law enforcement and race, search and seizure law, "Once a person is out [of the police academy], and picks up habits and gets acculturated, it becomes harder to change directions. . . . How do you shift their worldview and their way of doing the job that they've been in already?" (qtd. in Khazan, 2021). Harris' (2020) most recent book, *A City Divided: Race, Fear and the Law in Police Confrontations*, begins with a notorious police use of force incident in Pittsburgh. He uses the case to help explain why police confrontations with Black Americans go wrong far too often, and what can be done to stop this.

The Marshall Project is a nonpartisan, nonprofit news organization whose investigative reports have been awarded Pulitzer Prizes. Its stated mission is "to create and sustain a sense of national urgency about the US criminal justice system" (Marshall Project, 2022). The organization's name is a tribute to Thurgood Marshall who was an Associate Justice of the US Supreme Court and a leader in the civil rights movement. One Marshall Project study focused on ten big-city police departments and found that most allow officers who have faced allegations of aggressive behavior to become trainers. Additional research disclosed that officers whose trainers had a history of citizen complaints were more likely to draw complaints themselves in their first two years on the job (Weichselbaum, 2020).

An exception to the trend for police to go along with their field trainers' bad advice is illustrated by the brief career of Deputy Sheriff Andrew Rodriguez in Los Angeles County. After completing basic training, Rodriguez was assigned to detention/custody duty and after a period of time he sought and obtained a transfer to patrol duty to the City of Industry station in Los Angeles County on December 1, 2013. He then encountered field training officers who tried to bully him in order to have him comply with practices he found unacceptable and illegal. While on medical leave, in late February 2018, Rodriguez commenced a lawsuit against the County of Los Angeles and the County's Sheriff's Department alleging a hostile work environment, unlawful retaliation, and interference with his civil rights by threats, intimidation, or coercion (see *Rodriquez v. County of Los Angeles et al.*). In October 2019, a jury awarded him $8.1 million for workplace harassment (Weichselbaum, 2020). In February 2020, Los Angeles County Superior Court Judge Susan Bryant-Deason denied motions by lawyers for the county for a new trial or for the judge to declare that there was no factual basis for the jury's verdict since there was insufficient evidence presented at trial to support Rodriguez's claims of a hostile work environment and retaliation. Both motions rested on the county's claims that the jury was not properly instructed before rendering its October 4th verdict in favor of 37-year-old Andrew Rodriguez (City News Service, 2020).

Due to the negative publicity surrounding the Floyd incident and others, many police departments now require personnel to intervene when they spot misconduct or are now seeking to implement such policies, although substantial numbers of officers still lack the appropriate training to follow through. "Intervening can be tricky in a community in which one might face retaliation for speaking up" (Mark, 2022) as the Rodriguez case illustrates. On the other hand, there have been occasions when body-cam footage reveals that an officer has successfully restrained a colleague over actions toward a suspect.[4]

The Marshall Project has noted that field training program at the Grand Prairie Police Department, in a suburb west of Dallas, has taken important steps toward building up their program. "Applicants for training posts appear before a group of trainers and their supervisors, who pepper them with questions about why they want the job. Once accepted, training officers go through 120 hours of instruction, triple the amount in Baltimore, and teach in the academy" (Weichselbaum, 2020). Several other forward-leaning training programs have also been developed in recent years. For example, in Washington, DC, the Metropolitan Police Department has "partnered with several local universities, including Georgetown . . . to develop programs designed to push both recruits and more experienced officers to critically engage with the history and practices of their profession. All officers now visit the Holocaust Memorial Museum and the National Museum of African American History and Culture, and spend a day discussing the role of police officers in perpetuating—or ending—atrocities and injustice" (Brooks, 2020).

In New Orleans, a fellowship program for young police officers, the Crescent City Corps, was initiated in 2019. In partnership with the New Orleans Police Department (NOPD) and Loyola Law School, the Crescent City Corps includes a cohort of new NOPD officers. The members of the group are selected for their leadership potential and commitment to working with community members. Over the course of a year, they "learn from and work with other leaders and citizens in New Orleans in pursuit of a safer, stronger, and more just city" (Crescent City Corps, 2019). In December 2020, the Corps announced that in 2021 that it was expanding their program to include 4 new cohorts due to the generous support of New Orleans Saints star player Cam Jordan of the National Football League (Crescent City Corps, 2020a, 2020b). Jordan donated $120,000 to fund the expansion of the program.

The training of police to deal with the fear and anxiety associated with perceived threats in the community is of critical concern. Significantly, the mistakes police make will likely occur in the field. "So many of these bad cases are a result of an officer incorrectly perceiving a threat," according to Sue Rahr, the former sheriff of King County, Washington and the previous executive director of the Washington State Criminal Justice Training Commission, who now serves as an adviser to police-reform organizations (qtd. in Khazan, 2021). As stated previously, "Rahr has developed a method to train recruits to be courteous, show empathy, explain their actions, and preserve everyone's dignity" (Khazan, 2021). "Rahr calls her training method 'LEED,' for 'Listen and Explain with Equity and Dignity.' Instead of an emphasis on yelling and standing at attention, her recruits are trained to engage others in courteous conversation, and are evaluated during role-play exercises on their ability to listen, show empathy, explain their actions, de-escalate tense situations, and leave everyone they encounter 'with their dignity intact'" (Brooks, 2020). Police should be trained "to be sympathetic, to be guardians, rather than warriors," according to Chuck Wexler, the executive director of the PERF. He added that while police are routinely informed by their academy instructors that the "police always have to win," it is sometimes appropriate not to win, particularly if it means saving a life (qtd. in Khazan, 2021). While progressive models exist by which police departments may reform their training and practices, hate groups remain prevalent and there exists a major legal system roadblock that currently acts against such models for decreasing a police culture that has led to violent police encounters.

The Unresolved Problem of Racism and Legal Remedies

In 1838, Frederick Douglass (1818–1895) escaped from slavery. He fought for equality and justice as a youth and for the rest of his life. In 1855, he published his second autobiography, *My Bondage and My Freedom*, which expanded on an earlier first autobiography and challenged racial segregation in the North. In 1861, the nation erupted into civil war over the issue of slavery and Douglass worked tirelessly to make sure that emancipation would be one of the war's outcomes. He recruited African American men to fight in the US Army, including two of his own sons (National Park Service, 2023). After the Civil War, Douglass's advocacy continued with fervor as he recognized "that freedom would be empty if former slaves were not guaranteed the rights and protections of American citizens (National Park Service, 2023). After nearly a week of heated debate in the US House Representatives and the Senate, both chambers reconciled their differences on April 20, 1871 and approved "An Act to enforce the Provisions of the Fourteenth Amendment to the Constitution of the United States, and for other Purposes," also known as the "Ku Klux Klan Act." Later on the same day, President Ulysses S. Grant signed the bill into law. The Ku Klux Klan Act was the third of a series of increasingly strengthened laws designed to eliminate extralegal violence and protect the civil and political rights of four million freed slaves. "The Fourteenth Amendment, ratified in 1868, defined citizenship and guaranteed due process and equal protection of the law to all. Vigilante groups like the Ku Klux Klan, however, freely threatened African Americans and their white allies in the South and undermined the Republican Party's plan for Reconstruction. The bill authorized the President to intervene in the former rebel states that attempted to deny 'any person or any class of persons of the equal protection of the laws, or of equal privileges or immunities under the laws.' To take action against this newly defined federal crime, the President could suspend habeas corpus, deploy the U.S. military, or use 'other means, as he may deem necessary' " (Office of the Historian, 2023). In October 1871, "Grant used these powers in several South Carolina counties, demonstrating the willingness of the Republican-led federal government to take decisive action to protect the civil and political rights of the freed people during Reconstruction" (Office of the Historian, 2023). But the end of Reconstruction brought with it a return to White dominance in the South and a new system of second-class citizenship was created. Various state laws restricting Black eligibility to vote, to become home-owners except in segregated areas, to work in many occupations, and to attend school with White children were adopted. But even worse, was the system put into place by White supremacists to summarily punish those who defied such laws. One hate group, the Ku Klux Klan reemerged in the 20th century and "by mid-decade, the Klan claimed over 3 million members, nearly all white native-born Protestants, mostly respectable members of their communities" (Foner, 1998, p. 188). The new Klan believed that not only Blacks, but immigrant groups were a threat to individual American freedom (see Foner, 1998, p. 188).

The legacy of slavery, racism and segregation throughout American history still places an ugly stain on American freedom. Racism has persisted and continues. It is especially destructive when engaged in by police. In recent times, police misconduct has become a matter of national debate due to instantaneous coverage by mass media outlets. In 1961, the US Supreme Court case of *Monroe v. Pape* (365 U.S. 167) had the occasion to interpret the language of R.S. § 1979, 42 U.S.C. § 1983, which was derived from § 1 of the "Ku Klux Klan Act" of April 20, 1871. The applicable section reads as follows: "Every person who, under color of any statute, ordinance, regulation, custom, or usage, of any State or Territory, subjects, or causes to be subjected, any citizen of the United States or other person within the jurisdiction thereof to the deprivation of any rights, privileges, or immunities secured by the Constitution and laws, shall be liable to the party injured in an action at law, suit in equity, or other proper proceeding for redress." The petitioners (six Black children and their parents) brought an action in a Federal District Court against the City of Chicago and 13 of its police officers for damages for violation of their rights under the Fourteenth Amendment. They alleged that, acting "under color of the statutes, ordinances, regulations,

FIGURE 8.1 Ku Klux Klan at U.S. Capitol, Washington, DC; August 1925. Harris Ewing, photographer. Retrieved from the Library of Congress, https://www.loc.gov/item/2016894347/

customs and usages" of Illinois and the City of Chicago, but without any warrant for search or arrest, the police officers broke into petitioners' home in the early morning, routed them from bed, made them stand naked in the living room, and ransacked every room, emptying drawers and ripping mattress covers; that the father was taken to the police station and detained on "open charges" for ten hours while he was interrogated about a two-day-old murder; that he was not taken before a magistrate, though one was accessible; that he was not permitted to call his family or attorney, and that he was subsequently released without criminal charges being preferred against him. The decision by the US Supreme Court had a mixed result—while the complaint was valid as to a cause of action against the police officers under § 1979, the City of Chicago was not liable under that section. Chicago was not liable under § 1979 because Congress did not intend to bring municipal corporations within the ambit of that section. Thus, the petitioners were entitled to proceed with actions against each individual police officer under tort liability that makes a person responsible for the natural consequences of his actions.

However, within a few decades the US Supreme Court in different cases determined that individual officers enjoyed a "qualified immunity" in such cases so long as they had not violated a "clearly established" statutory or constitutional right.[5] According to the Legal Information Institute (LII) at Cornell Law School, qualified immunity "is a type of legal immunity.

'Qualified immunity balances two important interests—the need to hold public officials accountable when they exercise power irresponsibly and the need to shield officials from harassment, distraction, and liability when they perform their duties reasonably.' Specifically, qualified immunity protects a government official from lawsuits alleging that the official violated a plaintiff's rights, only allowing suits where officials violated a 'clearly established' statutory or constitutional right. When determining whether a right was 'clearly established,' courts consider whether a hypothetical reasonable official would have known that the defendant's conduct violated the plaintiff's rights. Courts conducting this analysis apply the law that was in force at the time of the alleged violation, not the law in effect when the court considers the case. Qualified immunity is not immunity from having to pay money damages, but rather immunity from having to go through the costs of a trial at all. Accordingly, courts must resolve qualified immunity issues as early in a case as possible, preferably before discovery. Qualified immunity only applies to suits against government officials as individuals, not suits against the government for damages caused by the officials' actions. Although qualified immunity frequently appears in cases involving police officers, it also applies to most other executive branch officials. While judges, prosecutors, legislators, and some other government officials do not receive qualified immunity, most are protected by other immunity doctrines" (LLI, 2022).

"In 1967, when the Supreme Court created the qualified immunity defense, it shielded officers from damages liability if they were acting in 'good faith.' But today's qualified immunity doctrine has nothing to do with officers' good faith. In 1982, in a case called *Harlow v. Fitzgerald*, the Court eliminated consideration of an officer's subjective intent, and instead instructed lower courts to grant officers qualified immunity if their conduct did not violate 'clearly established law.' Current Supreme Court doctrine suggests that an officer violates clearly established law only if there is a prior court of appeals or Supreme Court decision holding virtually identical facts to be unconstitutional" (Schwartz, 2021, p. 613). According to Professor Schwartz (2020), since 2005, when John Roberts became Chief Justice, the US Supreme Court has considered "twenty qualified immunity denials, and ruled in the government's favor every time. The Court has repeatedly chastised lower courts for failing to use qualified immunity to shield government officials from damages liability. And the Court's recent decisions have further expanded qualified immunity's reach" (pp. 310–311).

The issue of "qualified immunity" has become a matter of recent debate in the halls of Congress involving the proposed *George Floyd Justice in Policing Act*. Congresswoman Bonnie Watson Coleman from New Jersey issued, in part, the following statement on the two-year anniversary of the murder of George Floyd by Minneapolis police: "Two years later, we still have not made enough progress. In many ways, our nation has moved backward, and existing while Black has become more dangerous, more painful, more terrifying. Despite widespread calls for police reform, police killings increased in the year following the murder of Mr. Floyd. To no one's surprise, a disproportionate number of the victims were Black. Two years later, police continue to evade accountability for acts of violence and remain overly involved in aspects of life that should be beyond the scope of their job. Keeping our streets safe means supporting our most vulnerable communities, not terrorizing them with impunity. To truly invest in public safety, we must end qualified immunity and reduce unnecessary contact between police and communities. For too long, police have been the default responders to situations with which they lack expertise. Mental health emergencies or drug use should be dealt with by health care professionals, not armed officers with limited to no relevant medical training" (Coleman, 2022). On February 7, 2023, New Jersey Representative Bonnie Watson Coleman and her Congressional Black Caucus colleagues wore '1870' pins to President Joe Biden's "State of the Union" address. The pins were representative of the year that Henry Truman—an unarmed, free, Black man was shot and killed by police in Philadelphia. His murder is considered to be the first instance on record of an unarmed, free, Black person being killed by the police. In a card that was passed out with the pins, Rep. Watson Coleman wrote "153 years later, nothing has changed." Amid renewed energy behind calls for police reform, House Democrats were preparing to reintroduce the *George Floyd Justice in Policing Act;* however, the issue of removing "qualified immunity" for police was opposed by most Republicans. Congresswoman Coleman continued: "I will take forward movement, But I know the job is not done unless there are consequences" (qtd. at NBCUniversal, 2023).

Thus, America's racial problems need to be confronted, especially when it concerns police conduct. Incidents involving police beatings and shootings of unarmed Black men and women continue to plague society. Someone who "too easily fears for his life or fires a weapon that he has at the ready should not be a police officer . . . and it is a problem when training organizations wittingly or unwittingly reinforce the prejudice" (Kleinig, 2016). "What seems to happen . . . is that the color of a person's skin plays a role in the perception of dangerousness or threat. Even though it may be a widespread belief that those with a dark skin color ipso facto pose a greater danger than those with a lighter skin color, we cannot tolerate that status quo on the part of those to whom we have given power over life or death. It is a problem for police departments as well as for individual officers when that larger social prejudice is not counteracted" (Kleinig, 2016).

Fortunately, there are efforts being made to promote bias-free policing through greater cultural awareness throughout the nation. Bias-free policing involves having a comprehensive policy prohibiting discrimination on the basis of demographic categories in police practices. The use of a demographic category, however, may be permitted "when engaging in appropriate suspect-specific activity to identify a particular person or persons" (EHPD Agreement, 2012, p. 13). Jeffrey A. Fletcher, a retired police officer who spent more than 20 years on the New Haven police force, is the President of African American Collections, Inc. The collection is housed at the new Ruby and Calvin Fletcher African American History Museum in Stratford, Connecticut. He is a lifelong resident of the state and one of four children whose parents migrated from the south during the "Jim Crow era." The collection was initially gathered by his mother, Ruby Fletcher. With a desire to tell his family's history, "Fletcher began going to tag sales and auctions, seeking more items to add to the collection" (Chmiel, 2020). He soon developed a program for a traveling exhibit titled "Images of America/Challenges of the Badge." It is, however, of interest to note that the initial program developed by Fletcher for police instruction, entitled the "Badge Beneath the Robe," came about in 2015 due to a specific request by Boston-based staff members in the US Department of Justice (DOJ) to partner with the East Haven (Connecticut) Police Department (EHPD). It was an outcome of the Town of East Haven's agreement to resolve a DOJ lawsuit involving the Civil Rights Division, Special Litigation Section's investigation into allegations that EHPD officers engaged in discriminatory policing, unconstitutional searches and seizures, and the use of excessive force.[6] Fletcher's program was conducted over a period of two days and was aimed at reducing police-bias, discrimination, and racism toward minority populations. There were several East Haven police officers who had been arrested and ultimately sentenced for their discriminatory actions. East Haven Chief Edward Leonard and (Ret.) Assistant Chief James Nacarrato approved of this program to be conducted at their department (Jeffrey Fletcher, personal communication, July 29, 2022).

In 2022, Bridgeport Police Academy trainees were one of the first police groups to have the opportunity to visit the new museum in Stratford and learn more about Black culture and history in America. Two virtual tours of the museum's collection are posted online.[7]

Lincoln's Experiences With America's Racial Divide

An old proverb states that "Experience is the best teacher." Its origins have been traced to various sources including the Roman leader Julius Caesar who wrote "Experience is the teacher of all things" in *De Bello Civili* (c. 52 B.C.). Over a century later, the Roman author Pliny the Elder in *Naturalis Historia* (A.D. 77) wrote: "Experience is the most efficient teacher of all things" ' and the Roman historian Tacitus plainly stated "Experience teaches" in his *Histories* (c. 209). Its first English appearance was in 1539 as "Experience is mother of prudence," which was included in Richard Taverner's *Proverbes or Adagies* (Flexner & Flexner, 1993).

A more contemporary writer has explained that when we are born the process of learning begins. "It starts out very simple and develops as we mature. The process of learning is part nature and part nurture as we develop the system of learning that we use in everyday life. Some learning comes naturally while other times it is more difficult. Sometimes we learn intentionally and sometimes it is by accident. We all make mistakes throughout our lives, and they are not always failures, but sometimes they are a learning opportunity in disguise. . . . making the best choices in every situation comes from years of learning and progression" (Brush, 2022). Thus, life is about learning from our experiences. On the other hand, while experience is very important, "it is not the greatest teacher. It is slow and highly redundant, and doesn't always take. In addition, there are many things you may need to learn that you'll never have a chance to experience directly, and many other things that you won't want to experience directly" (Kristof, 2022).

James Berger, a former history teacher with 35 years of teaching experience, has provided an additional insight. He notes that "learning by doing and teaching by experience can produce higher learning results and have a more lasting effect than lecture, passive listening, or didactic teaching. Active engaged learning like dyads, problem solving group work, simulations, role play, and experiments can be an effective learning experience" (Berger, 2022).

Actual events in history can also reveal how others have overcome the most troublesome of life's experiences and learned from them. "Lincoln kept the American experiment in self-government alive when it seemed lost. He did not do so alone. Ordinary people, Black and white, sacrificed to preserve the Union against the designs of the rebel South. But Lincoln was instrumental, and his ultimate vision of the nation—that the country should be free of slavery—was informed by a moral understanding of life. To him, America ought to seek to practice the principles of the Declaration of Independence as fully as possible, for the alternatives were so much worse" (Meacham, 2022).

Abraham Lincoln also "fought clinical depression all his life" (Shenk, 2005). Yet, he managed to cope and "the suffering he had endured lent him clarity and conviction, creative skills in the face of adversity, and a faithful humility that helped him guide the nation through its greatest peril" (Shenk, 2005). Lincoln's melancholy [fear and sadness without apparent cause] "spurred him, painfully, to examine the core of his soul; whose hard work to stay alive helped him develop crucial skills and capacities, even as his depression lingered hauntingly; and whose inimitable character took great strength from the piercing insights of depression, the creative responses to it, and a spirit of humble determination forged over decades of deep suffering and earnest longing" (Shenk, 2005).

In the spring of 1862 as Northern resolve waned in the wake of battlefield failures during the Civil War, President Lincoln "weighed the tactical advantages of striking a blow at slavery in the seceded states" (Barber, 2017). By early summer, after much deliberation, he drafted the Emancipation Proclamation, granting freedom to all slaves in Confederate-held territory. If President Lincoln had not experienced the bloody Civil War firsthand for nearly three years, this measure and other critical steps for ending slavery would not have occurred.

FIGURE 8.2 The first reading of the Emancipation Proclamation before the Cabinet was painted by Francis B. Carpenter on a 9-by-15-foot canvas at the White House in 1864; later engraved by Alexander Hay Ritchie. This engraved print from National Portrait Gallery, Smithsonian Institution (Gift of Mrs. Chester E. King) shows a reenactment of Abraham Lincoln signing the Emancipation Proclamation on July 22, 1862. Depicted, from left to right are: Edwin M. Stanton, Secretary of War, Salmon P. Chase, Secretary of the Treasury, President Lincoln, Gideon Welles, Secretary of the Navy, Caleb B. Smith, Secretary of the Interior, William H. Seward, Secretary of State, Montgomery Blair, Postmaster General, and Edward Bates, Attorney General. Simon Cameron and Andrew Jackson are featured as paintings. Reproduction Number: LC-DIG-pga-02502 (digital file from original print) LC-USZ62–2070 (b & w film copy neg.). The original painting was displayed at Lincoln's second inaugural in 1865 in the Capitol Building, where it has hung permanently since 1878. Prints of Carpenter's work proved immensely popular. For years, they decorated schoolrooms and other public places across the country.

Source: https://tile.loc.gov/storage-services/service/pnp/pga/02500/02502v.jpg

Another historic event took place on June 19, 1865 when Union General Gordon Granger marched into Galveston, Texas, announcing that the Civil War was over and that slaves were free based upon Lincoln's Executive Order—the Emancipation Proclamation of January 1, 1863. The proclamation declared "that all persons held as slaves" within the rebellious states "are, and henceforward shall be free." "Despite this expansive wording, the Emancipation Proclamation was limited in many ways. It applied only to states that had seceded from the United States, leaving slavery untouched in the loyal Border States. It also expressly exempted parts of the Confederacy (the Southern secessionist states) that had already come under Northern control. Most important, the freedom it promised depended upon Union (United States) military victory . . . After January 1, 1863, every advance of federal troops expanded the domain of freedom" (US National Archives, 2022). General Granger's announcement came two months after Lee had surrendered to Grant on April 9, 1865. Lincoln was assassinated five days later on April 14, 1865. However, it was not until the Thirteenth Amendment became effective with its ratification by the states on December 6, 1865 that slavery was abolished throughout in the United States.

Lincoln was surely stressed throughout the Civil War and at pivotal stages during his earlier career. He often coped by writing and after his death a number of angry letters he had composed were found, but never sent. Among these was one to General Meade in 1863. Lincoln had ordered Meade to capture Lee's army in order to end the war. Robert E. Lee, the General of the Confederate Army, was trapped between the Potomac River and a fast-moving Union Army behind him. Lincoln was furious, but did not forward his castigating letter to Meade (Tousley, 2017).

President Lincoln's lifelong experiences and heroic actions surely deserved a fate other than assassination. Nearly, 160 years ago presidential security was quite relaxed as it wasn't until 1902 that the US Secret Service (created in 1865 to eradicate counterfeit currency), assumed official full-time responsibility for protecting the president. However, by November 1864, a White House protection detail consisting of four officers had been organized by the Metropolitan Police Department, which had been organized three years earlier for Washington, DC. On April 14, 1865, Police Officer John Frederick Parker was assigned to protect President Lincoln beginning in the late afternoon at the White House and continuing later in the evening at Ford's Theatre. "John Parker was an unlikely candidate to guard a president—or anyone for that matter. Born in Frederick County, Virginia, in 1830, Parker moved to Washington as a young man, originally earning his living as a carpenter. He became one of the capital's first officers. . . . [but] Parker's record as a cop fell somewhere between pathetic and comical. He was hauled before the police board numerous times, facing a smorgasbord of charges that should have gotten him fired. But he received nothing more than an occasional reprimand. . . . Somehow, John Parker was named to the [White House] detail. Parker was the only one of the officers with a spotty record, so it was a tragic coincidence that he drew the assignment to guard the president that evening. . . . He was supposed to relieve Lincoln's previous bodyguard at 4 p.m. but was three hours late. Lincoln's party arrived at the theater at around 9 p.m. . . . Parker was seated outside the president's box, in the passageway beside the door. From where he sat, Parker couldn't see the stage, so after Lincoln and his guests settled in, he moved to the first gallery to enjoy the play. Later, Parker committed an even greater folly: At intermission, he joined the footman and coachman of Lincoln's carriage for drinks in the Star Saloon next door to Ford's Theatre. [When] John Wilkes Booth entered the theater around 10 p.m. [and] . . . crept up to the door to Lincoln's box, Parker's chair stood empty. . . . No one knows for sure if Parker ever returned to Ford's Theatre that night. When Booth struck, the vanishing policeman may have been sitting in his new seat with a nice view of the stage, or perhaps he had stayed put in the Star Saloon. Even if he had been at his post, it's not certain he would have stopped Booth. . . . Parker was charged with failing to protect the president, but the complaint was dismissed a month later. No local newspaper followed up on the issue of Parker's culpability. Nor was Parker mentioned in the official report on Lincoln's death. Why he was let off so easily is baffling. Perhaps, with the hot pursuit of Booth and his co-conspirators in the chaotic aftermath, he seemed like too small a fish. Or perhaps the public was unaware that a bodyguard had even been assigned to the president. Incredibly, Parker remained . . . on the Metropolitan Police Force for three more years, but his shiftlessness finally did him in. . . . He died in Washington in 1890, of pneumonia. . . . No photographs have ever been found of John Parker. He remains a faceless character, his role in the great tragedy largely forgotten" (Martin, 2010).

On the night of Lincoln's assassination, Detective James A. McDevitt was on duty and one of the first at the theatre crime scene. He was able to lead a group of detectives to Mary Surratt's boardinghouse within four hours of President Lincoln's assassination. The boarding house was later discovered as a meeting spot for John Wilkes Booth and his co-conspirator. Detective McDevitt's role in helping to solve one of the most notorious crimes in American history stands out in stark contrast to Parker's infamous conduct. Perhaps, the story of Parker's dereliction of duty might be the tragic lesson that can deter future examples of police failures, while the work of Detective McDevitt might serve in some way to inspire others to become better officers (Ouellette, 2022).

Lessons From Experience

There are both limitations and opportunities involved in the current state of police training. As Lincoln did "not waver from a morally informed insistence that slavery be put on a path to 'ultimate extinction'" (Meacham, 2022), today's police training must not waver in its efforts to promote decency and equity. The need for upgrading police training has become apparent given the complex nature of crime and the realities of everyday police work. The past and more present incidents involving abject failures in police response are useful for police training purposes, including the history of Lincoln's life. It was a momentous tragedy that after preserving the union, Lincoln's demise came about, in part, due to the callousness and neglect of a policeman's duty. In that national tragedy, Metropolitan Police Officer John Parker was temporarily named to the White House protective detail. Parker had a mixed record prior to his assignment to guard the president and was clearly derelict in his duties on the day and night of his guard duty. With respect to carrying out actual police duties, the crises overcome by Abraham Lincoln should encourage all police officers to seek available assistance when coping with stress. Since police work may involve whether a person lives or dies, learning by doing and teaching by experience can produce either heartbreak or joy. Moreover, the memory of the crises faced by Abraham Lincoln to preserve the union and abolish slavery may remind officers to keep their eyes focused on their role to act as guardians as they go about their daily patrols protecting the people in the frontlines of American democracy.

Surely, new ideas are needed in the field of police training. Training and experience can be combined, but community input is essential. Policing practices in our era will remain stagnant, unless concerned citizens are also willing to do their parts in promoting decency and equity. A major thesis of the present work is that police training in the future may be enhanced by placing it substantially in the community through decentralization; thereby enabling new trainees to obtain a better understanding of the nature and needs of the population they have been recruited to work for and with—all in pursuit of safer, stronger, and more just communities, towns, and cities. While challenges will always exist with respect to determining the best combination of topics and instructional methods, it should not be considered a hindrance for police academies to tap into the vast array of available community resources. Every community possesses some people with sufficient expertise to qualify as training specialists. Such talent should not be wasted. In fact, the guidance of well qualified training specialists from local communities may help overcome many of the pitfalls associated with current training methods.

In order to help accomplish some of these goals, one key recommendation of the President's Task Force on 21st Century Policing (2015) was to "engage youth and communities in joint training with law enforcement, citizen academies, ride-alongs, problem solving teams, community action teams, and quality of life teams" (p. 93). In this way, properly trained police in cooperation with a variety of community-based groups may bolster the level of social capital in communities. Robert Putnam (1993) has explained that "social capital refers to features of social organization, such as networks, norms, and trust, that facilitate cooperation for mutual benefit" (p. 35). "It is most typically used to measure social cohesion within a given area" (Gurren, 2015, p. 33)." "Social cohesion refers to positive social relationships—it is the bond or 'glue' that binds people. A socially cohesive society is one which works towards the wellbeing of all its members, fights exclusion and marginalization, creates a sense of belonging, promotes trust and offers its members the opportunity of upward mobility" (Australian Human Rights Commission, 2015, p. 2). Chapter 12 provides further details about re-envisioning police training through a decentralization approach in order to build social capital and promote social cohesiveness.

The following chapter highlights a variety of citizens' academies. The citizens' academy was created to offer insights into how police, first responders, and other essential government workers perform their duties and how these agencies are vital to the communities they serve. Well planned community-based educational programs may expand community-based crime prevention efforts and offer police departments the prospect of learning about the concerns of their jurisdiction's inhabitants. Moreover, such citizen academies, especially those organized and implemented by everyday community members can provide almost limitless opportunities for creating the necessary social bonds for safer communities.

Notes

1 State police agencies have traditionally held much longer basic training schools and appointments are often highly sought after. For example, in 1921 when the New Jersey State Police agency was approved by the state legislature, "Sixteen hundred men, between the ages of twenty-two and forty, made application for the one hundred and twenty positions allowed by the law. Out of the total number of applicants, only two hundred and twenty-seven received a passing mark. From this number, one hundred and sixteen men reported to Sea Girt on September 1, 1921. Of this number, eighty-one officers and troopers completed the rigorous three-month training program. On December 1, 1921, the new troopers were administered the oath of office and on December 5, 1921, in a blinding snowstorm, started out on horseback and motorcycle to their posts throughout the state" (NJ State Police, 2022).

2 Overall, "the Federal Bureau of Investigation (FBI) assumed a prominent leadership role in disseminating ideas and best practices concerning law enforcement, which was crucial to amplifying the goal of professionalization" (Schrader, 2021). Nonfederal law enforcement personnel have received top level training at the FBI's National Academy (NA) since 1935. In its first 60 years of existence the NA has produced about 27,000 graduates who came from every state and 98 different countries. The current FBI Academy is located on the U.S. Marine Corps Base in Quantico, Virginia. In addition to the NA, the FBI offers numerous separate specialized training courses offered to State and local law enforcement agencies, all of which can be delivered in the field by FBI special agents and professional support personnel trained as police instructors (Nowicki, 1994).

3 Dean Brooks served as a reserve police officer in Washington, DC and has authored the following book about volunteer police experiences: *Tangled Up in Blue: Policing the American City* (New York: Penguin Press, 2021). "Brooks did not simply observe policing in America. This highly educated, tenured professor became the police. In her 40s, she successfully applied to D.C.'s Metropolitan Police Department, completed training at the police academy and became a reserve police officer—a part-time position but one with all the rights of a full-time officer. She was assigned to 7-D, the D.C. police district with the highest concentration of Black residents, the highest concentration of poverty and the highest concentration of reported crime" (Sullivan, 2021). In 2015, against the advice of everyone she knew, Brooks applied to become a sworn, armed reserve police officer with the Washington, DC, Metropolitan Police Department. The Black Lives Matter movement was gaining momentum, protests wracked America's cities, and each day brought more stories of cruel, corrupt cops, police violence, and the racial disparities that tarnish America's criminal justice system. In the poorest, most crime-ridden neighborhoods of the nation's capital, Brooks found a reality far more complex than the headlines suggested. In a nation increasingly divided by race, class, ethnicity, geography, and ideology, she argues that a truly transformative approach to policing requires us to move beyond sound bites, slogans, and stereotypes (adapted from the book's jacket). There's an excellent interview of the author on the NPR radio show, Fresh Air, available online at: https://www.npr.org/programs/fresh-air/.

4 On November 19, 2021, an incident involving a female police officer and her sergeant took place in Sunrise, Florida, a community located northwest of Fort Lauderdale. According to Anthony Rosa, the police chief in Sunrise, the incident began when police placed a man under arrest for a "violent felony." The man was being "verbally and physically resistive" as officers tried to put him into the vehicle. The sergeant at the scene then approached the suspect in an "inappropriate and unprofessional" manner and proceeded to escalate the situation. The suspect was already handcuffed and getting into the back of a police car when the sergeant approached the suspect with a can of pepper spray in one hand. According to body-camera footage, the sergeant yelled "Look at me." In response, the suspect said from the car's back seat if "you are going to mace me, mace me." Leaning in, the sergeant screamed that he would "remove" the suspect's "soul" from his body. Concerned that escalation was unnecessary, the female officer pulled the sergeant away by his belt. The sergeant then placed his hand at the throat of the female officer while pushing her backwards, according to Chief Rosa. Moments after releasing the officer, the sergeant pointed to her and yelled that he'd see her in "about five minutes" and told the officers on the scene a short time later, using an expletive, "everybody turn off their . . . cameras," the footage shows. The sergeant was placed on administrative leave and has been charged with assault and battery on an officer, as well as assault on a civilian and tampering with evidence, according to the Broward County state attorney. Rosa praised the female officer for following the department's policies by intervene immediately, saying her actions demonstrated "good leadership during a tense situation" (Mark, 2022).

5 Qualified immunity shields LEOs and other executive officials from damages liability so long as they have not violated "clearly established law," see *Harlow v. Fitzgerald*, 457 U.S. 800, 818 (1982). For an overview of qualified immunity, what constitutes clearly established law, and the ways in which the doctrine has developed, see generally Joanna C. Schwartz, *The Case Against Qualified Immunity*, 93 Notre Dame L. Rev. 1797 (2018). Professor Schwartz has also addressed the legal aspects of qualified immunity in her 2021 *University of Chicago Law Review* article entitled "Qualified Immunities Boldest Lie." In recent opinions, Justices Thomas and Sotomayor have criticized the broad scope of qualified immunity. Justice Thomas expressed concern about the lack of a historical basis for qualified immunity, and has called for the Court to reconsider its approach to qualified immunity in "an appropriate case, see *Ziglar v. Abbasi*, 137 S. Ct. 1843, 1871 (2017). Justice Sotomayor notes that qualified immunity does not adequately deter police

misconduct, see *Kisela v. Hughes,* 138 S. Ct. 1148, 1162 (2018). Justices Thomas and Sotomayor are joined in their critiques of qualified immunity by an increasing group of judges, activists, and scholars who all recognize that the Court's current immunity doctrine is overbroad.

6 "Pursuant to the Agreement, the East Haven Police Department agreed to make reforms in its general policy and training procedures. Such reforms included in the Agreement were attention to bias-free policing; modifications to practices involving stops, searches, and seizures; guidelines with respect to proper use of force; effective handling of civilian complaints, internal investigations, and disciplinary measures; and, guidelines and procedures for proper supervision and management, and implementation of community engagement. . . . Since the Agreement's effective date of December 21, 2012, many changes have occurred in East Haven and its police department" (Gurren, 2015, p. 51). The full 54-page US District Court settlement agreement and court order entitled "Agreement for Effective and Constitutional Policing" is online at: https://www.justice.gov/sites/default/files/crt/legacy/2012/10/23/ehpd_settlement_10-22-12.pdf.

7 To view a 12-minute video about the collection and museum go to: https://www.youtube.com/watch?v=-mzmhhyDRWM. In addition, a five-minute introduction to the exhibit is available at: https://www.africanamericancollections.com/media-gallery. Both programs are narrated by Jeffrey Fletcher.

References

Adams, C. (2021, April 18). *Experts stress that more training won't eradicate police violence.* Retrieved June 24, 2022, from https://www.nbcnews.com/news/nbcblk/experts-stress-more-training-won-t-eradicate-police-violence-n1264092

Australian Human Rights Commission. (2015). *Building social cohesion in our communities: A summary of the online resource for local government.* Retrieved July 30, 2022, from https://humanrights.gov.au/our-work/race- discrimination/publications/building-social-cohesion-our-communities-2015#fn2

Barber, J. G. (2017, November 15). *Remembering president Lincoln's emancipation proclamation.* Retrieved June 20, 2022, from https://www.smithsonianmag.com/blogs/national-portrait- gallery/2017/11/15/remembering-president-lincolns-emancipation-proclamation/

Berger, J. (2022). *Why is experience in life considered to be the best teacher?* Retrieved June 24, 2022, from https://www.quora.com/Why-is-experience-in-life-considered-to-be- the-best-teacher

Brooks, R. (2020, June 10). *Stop training police like they're joining the military.* Retrieved June 27, 2022, from https://www.theatlantic.com/ideas/archive/2020/06/police- academies-paramilitary/612859/

Bruggeman, L., Courts, J. W., Christie, M., Prince, H., Linehan, P., Simpson, T., Hosenball, A., & Margolin, J. (2023, February 13). 'No one took leadership': A detailed look at the failings in Uvalde school shooting. *ABC News.* Retrieved May 22, 2023, from https://abcnews.go.com/US/uvalde-investigators-probe-law-enforcement-response-robb-shooting/story?id=97046768

Brush, E. (2022, June 18). *Life is about learning from our experiences. Letters to the editor.* Retrieved June 24, 2022, from https://dailygazette.com/2022/06/18/letters-to-the-editor- saturday-june-18/

Chappell, A. T., & Lanza-Kaduce, L. (2010). Police academy socialization: Understanding the lessons learned in a paramilitary-bureaucratic organization. *Journal of Contemporary Ethnography. 39*(2), 187–214. https://doi.org/10.1177/0891241609342230

Chappell, B. (2021, June 25). *Derek Chauvin is sentenced to 22 1/2 Years for George Floyd's murder.* Retrieved June 24, 2022, from https://www.npr.org/sections/trial-over-killing-of-george-floyd/2021/06/25/1009524284/derek-chauvin-sentencing-george-floyd-murder

Chmiel, R. (2020, March 25). *Alumnus uses collection of artifacts to teach story of African- American history.* Retrieved July 29, 2022, from https://www.newhaven.edu/news/blog/2020/jeffrey-fletcher.php

City News Service. (2020, February 26). $8.1-million award upheld for deputy who claimed harassment for reporting misconduct. https://www.latimes.com/california/story/2020-02- 26/judge-upholds-8-1-million-award-to-l-a-county-sheriffs-deputy-harassed-after- reporting-misconduct

Coleman, B. W. (2022, May 25). Rep. Watson Coleman statement on the second anniversary of the murder of George Floyd. *Press Release.* Retrieved February 11, 2023, from https://watsoncoleman.house.gov/newsroom/press-releases/rep-watson-coleman-statement-on-the-second-anniversary-of-the-murder-of-george-floyd

Crescent City Corps. (2019, October 1). *Say hello to our pilot cohort!* Retrieved June 29, 2022, from https://www.crescentcitycorps.org/new-blog/2019/10/1/say-hello-to-our-pilot- cohort

Crescent City Corps. (2020a, December 3). Retrieved June 29, 2022, from https://twitter.com/CresCityCorps/status/1334562256173064193

Crescent City Corps. (2020b, December 3). Retrieved June 29, 2022, from https://twitter.com/CresCityCorps/status/1334562257267777536

Delany, J., & Elkins, F. (2015). *President's task force on 21st century policing.* U. S. Government Printing Office.

EHPD Agreement. (2012). *US district court, district of Connecticut; Agreement for effective and constitutional policing.* Retrieved July 30, 2022, from https://www.justice.gov/sites/default/files/crt/legacy/2012/10/23/ehpd_settlement_10-22- 12.pdf

Elliott, D. (2021, April 17). *Former police officer says training methods for cops need to change.* Retrieved June 24, 2022, from https://www.npr.org/2021/04/17/988331517/former-police-officer-says-training-methods-for-cops-need-to-change

Flexner, S., & Flexner, D. (1993). *Wise words and Wives' tales: The origins, meanings and time-honored wisdom of proverbs and folk sayings olde and new.* Avon Books.

Foner, E. (1998). *The story of American freedom.* W. W. Norton & Co.

Goodman, J. D. (2022, June 22). Response to Uvalde shooting called 'abject failure'. *New York Times*, p. A13.

Gurren, A. G. (2015). *The perfect storm: An analysis of discriminatory policing in East Haven (CT)* (Bachelor of Arts Senior Theses). Trinity College, Trinity College Digital Repository. https://digitalrepository.trincoll.edu/theses/463

Harris, D. A. (2020). *A city divided: Race, fear, and the law in police confrontations.* Anthem Press.

Horton, J. (2021, May 18). *How US police training compares with the rest of the world.* Retrieved June 24, 2022, from https://www.bbc.com/news/world-us-canada-56834733

Khazan, O. (2021, April 22). *American police are inadequately trained.* Retrieved June 26, 2022, from https://www.theatlantic.com/politics/archive/2021/04/daunte-wright-and-crisis-American-police-training/618649/

Kitzerow, F. J. (2022, March 17). *What can be done to keep our children safe at school?* Retrieved May 22, 2023, from https://www.nascpc.org/post/what-can-be-done-to-keep-our-children-safe-at-school

Kleinig, J. (2016, January 18). To protect and serve: What is wrong with policing of minorities in the US? *ResearchGate.* Retrieved May 21, 2023, from https://www.researchgate.net/publication/332082678_39_To_Protect_and_Serve_What_is_Wrong_With_Policing_of_Minorities_in_The_US

Kristof, D. (2022). *Why is experience in life considered to be the best teacher?* Retrieved June 24, 2022, from https://www.quora.com/Why-is-experience-in-life-considered-to-be-the-best-teacher

LLI. (2022). *Qualified immunity.* Retrieved February 11, 2023, from https://www.law.cornell.edu/wex/qualified_immunity

MacNamara, D. E. J. (1949). Higher police training at the university level. *Journal of Criminal Law & Criminology, 40*(1949–1950), 657–665.

Mark, J. (2022, July 25). Police sergeant charged after gripping colleague's neck during arrest. *The Washington Post.* Retrieved July 28, 2022, from https://www.washingtonpost.com/nation/2022/07/25/sunrise-police-assault-charges- intervene/

Marshall Project. (2022). *About us: Mission statement.* Retrieved June 26, 2022, from https://www.themarshallproject.org/about

Martin, P. (2010, April 7). Lincoln's missing bodyguard. *Smithsonian Magazine.* Retrieved July 29, 2022, from https://www.smithsonianmag.com/history/lincolns-missing- bodyguard-12932069/

McCampbell, M. S. (1987, April). *Field training for police officers: The state of the art.* U.S. Department of Justice, National Institute of Justice.

Meacham, J. (2022, October 12). Lincoln saved American democracy. We can too. *Time.* Retrieved November 27, 2022, from https://time.com/6221209/lincoln-saved-american-democracy-we-can-too/

Moore, S. A., & Womack, A. M. (1975). *A history of the San Jose police department field training program.* Retrieved July 11, 2022, from http://michiganfto.weebly.com/uploads/3/1/9/0/31905805/a_history_of_the_san_jose_pol ice_department_field_training_program.pdf

National Park Service. (2023). *Frederick Douglass*. Retrieved February 11, 2023, from https://www.nps.gov/frdo/learn/historyculture/frederickdouglass.htm

NBCUniversal. (2023, February 11). *'1870' pins, and the ongoing effort for police reform*. Retrieved February 11, 2023, from https://www.yahoo.com/now/1870-pins-ongoing-effort-police-160733994.html

NJ State Police. (2022). *1920's - The history begins*. Retrieved July 1, 2022, from https://nj.gov/njsp/about/history/1920s.shtml

Nowicki, E. (1994, January). FBI trained. *Police: The Law Enforcement Magazine*, *18*(1), 37–41.

Office of the Historian. (2023). *The Ku Klux Klan act of 1871*. Retrieved February 11, 2023, from https://history.house.gov/Historical-Highlights/1851- 1900/hh_1871_04_20_KKK_Act/

Ouellette, S. (2022). *Who was detective James McDevitt and what did he discover about Lincoln's assassination?* Retrieved July 29, 2022, from https://www.fords.org/blog/post/who-was-detective-james-mcdevitt-and-what-did-he- discover-about-lincoln-s-assassination/

President's Commission. (1967). *The challenge of crime in a free society: A report of the president's commission on law enforcement and the administration of justice*. US Government Printing Office. https://www.ojp.gov/sites/g/files/xyckuh241/files/archives/ncjrs/42.pdf

President's Task Force on 21st Century Policing. (2015, May). *Final report of the president's task force on 21st century policing*. Office of Community Oriented Policing Services. https://cops.usdoj.gov/pdf/taskforce/taskforce_finalreport.pdf

Preston, C. (2020, June 28). *Police education is broken. Can it be fixed?* Retrieved June 24, 2022, from https://hechingerreport.org/police-education-is-broken-can-it-be-fixed/

Putnam, R. D. (1993). The prosperous community: Social capital and public life. *The American Prospect*, *13*(4), 35–42.

Rodriquez v. County of Los Angeles et al. (2018, February 26). Superior Court of California, County of Los Angeles. Retrieved June 27, 2022, from https://www.documentcloud.org/documents/6999002-Andrew-Rodriguez-Summons- First-Amended

Schrader, S. (2021). Cops at war: How world war II transformed U.S. policing. *Modern American History*, *4*(2), 159–179. doi:10.1017/mah.2021.12

Schwartz, J. C. (2020). After qualified immunity. *Columbia Law Review*, *120*, 309–388. https://columbialawreview.org/wp-content/uploads/2020/03/Schwartz- After_Qualified_Immunity.pdf

Schwartz, J. C. (2021). Qualified immunities boldest lie. *University of Chicago Law Review*, *88*, 605–684. https://chicagounbound.uchicago.edu/cgi/viewcontent.cgi?article=6236&context=uclrev

Shenk, J. W. (2005, October). Lincoln's great depression. *The Atlantic*. Retrieved June 28, 2022, from https://www.theatlantic.com/magazine/archive/2005/10/lincolns-great- depression/304247/

Sullivan, B. (2021, December 17). *Kim Potter describes officers' struggle with Daunte Wright before she shot him*. Retrieved June 24, 2022, from https://www.npr.org/2021/12/17/1065071626/potter-expected-on-stand-as-trial-in-wright- death-nears-end

Sullivan, B., & Wamsley, L. (2022, February 18). *Kim Potter, the ex-cop convicted in Daunte Wright's death, is sentenced to 2 years*. Retrieved June 24, 2022, from https://www.npr.org/2022/02/18/1081597518/kim-potter-daunte-wright-sentencing

Tousley, Scott (2017, February 1). Abraham Lincoln's unconventional technique for handling stressful conflicts. Retrieved June 22, 2022, from https://blog.hubspot.com/sales/abraham-lincoln-stress

Tucker, E. (2022, May 29). *Police failed to act quickly in Uvalde. Experts say their inaction allowed for the massacre to continue and led to catastrophic consequences*. Retrieved June 22, 2022, from https://www.cnn.com/2022/05/28/us/failure-by-uvalde- police-to-act-quickly-led-to-catastrophic-consequences/index.html

U.S. National Archives. (2022). *The emancipation proclamation*. U.S. National Archives and Records Administration. Retrieved June 21, 2022, from https://www.archives.gov/exhibits/featured-documents/emancipation-proclamation

Weichselbaum, S. (2020, July 22). *One roadblock to police reform: Veteran officers who train recruits*. Retrieved June 26, 2022, from https://www.themarshallproject.org/2020/07/22/one-roadblock-to-police-reform-veteran- officers-who-train-recruits

PART IV

Citizens, Everyday Life, and Police Training

9

RE-THINKING THE CITIZEN POLICE ACADEMY

Police-related education and training for the general public has become a standard practice across the American policing landscape. It is now recognized, just as it was centuries ago, that everyone has a role to play in safeguarding themselves, their family members, and their community. Citizen Police Academies (CPAs) have been designed, at least in part, to provide some of the knowledge needed to fulfill this role. Today, a variety of factors pose significant threats to the lives of ordinary citizens, including: climate change (leading to death causing and devastating wildfires, hurricanes, flooding, and tornados, etc.); health crises; domestic terrorism (especially when it targets houses of worship and crowded commercial facilities or gatherings); aggressive drivers; and internet scammers. According to a recent US Department of Homeland Security (DHS) advisory, the leading human threats are "posed by domestic terrorists, individuals and groups engaged in grievance-based violence, and those inspired or motivated by foreign terrorists and other malign foreign influences. These actors are increasingly exploiting online forums to influence and spread violent extremist narratives and promote violent activity. Such threats are also exacerbated by impacts of the ongoing global pandemic, including grievances over public health safety measures and perceived government restrictions" (DHS, 2021). US Attorney General Merrick Garland has warned that the January 6, 2021, attack on the US Capitol by former President Donald Trump's supporters demonstrated that White supremacists and militia groups are likely the country's greatest domestic security threat. Garland remarked that in "the FBI's view, the top domestic violent extremist threat comes from racially or ethnically motivated violent extremists, specifically those who advocated for the superiority of the white race" (qtd. in Renshaw & Wolfe, 2021).

Today, both men and women are frequently away from their homes during the day due to their employment. The necessity for two-incomes per household and the design of suburban neighborhoods contributes opportunities for residential crimes due to the absence of many homeowners. Such absentee homes "provide easy targets for criminals . . . [as] very often an intruder may find no one home and . . . there are few passers-by who can spot intruders" (Sherman, 1988, p. 1). Today, the prospect of knowing "a local police officer" in either urban or suburban areas is practically unthinkable due to police budgetary restraints.

DOI: 10.4324/9781003307396-13

Very few police walk a beat. According to Sherman (1988, pp. 1–2), "The most efficient allocation of patrol cars over a large low-density jurisdiction makes it difficult to assign officers consistently to the same neighborhood." Similarly, "this low density reduces informal 'watching' by neighbors even when they are home, since there is so much more territory for each 'watcher' to cover" (Sherman, 1988, p. 1). These problems can also occur in more populated areas where neighbors are on unfamiliar terms and informal rules associated with privacy are observed. In America's largest cities, the frequency of abnormal behavior may also contribute to bystander apathy and/or the belief that others will surely intervene.

The citizens' academy was created to offer insights into how police, first responders, and other essential government workers perform their duties and how their agencies are vital to the communities they serve. The success of any program first depends upon program content. Ideally, a few academy participants may become sufficiently motivated to want to engage in one or more volunteer community support activities (e.g., assisting in a Neighborhood Improvement Task Force, serving as Explorer Post supporters and advisors, as a volunteer language interpreter).

This chapter provides an overview of the organization of several different types of citizen academies. In all, 16 programs are highlighted. The programs were selected for inclusion because of their variety, geographic diversity, and readily accessible information on the internet. However, it should be acknowledged that the curriculums of most citizen police academies are remarkably similar. Nevertheless, their overall advantages and disadvantages are discussed. A concluding section deals with recommendations for directing current CPA resources toward a new direction. Namely, having auxiliary and reserve police officers become active participants in a new public safety initiative by training them to become "Community Police Academy" instructors.

The new volunteer instructors would serve as role models for future CPA participants. Their classroom presence can perform an important function in the delivery of quality police services when they assist with educating the public to perform roles in furtherance of the needs of safer communities. Consistently, law enforcement agencies state that community involvement is the most powerful force a law enforcement agency has in the fight against crime. More than one police agency has found that its citizen education programs are most effective in gaining understanding and support from the community. By having qualified citizens train citizens, these programs can provide the means for more citizens to achieve safer living and working environments (see Greenberg, 1977, 1985).

Traditional CPA Origins and Purposes

A variety of 'junior police programs' were established during the first quarter of the 20th century most often out of concern for safety from motor vehicles and the need for organized activities to divert youth from at-risk behavior (Greenberg, 2008). In various respects they resemble today's 'citizen police academies' (CPAs), especially with regard to their inclusion of orientations to the crime prevention role of police. Youth programs, such as the Police Athletic League, often combined training and recreational activities and commenced their operations during the first two decades of the 20th century.[1] Breen and Johnson (2007) have defined CPAs as being "a planned program created by law enforcement agencies to educate . . . citizens on police operations and management" (p. 246). At the end of the 20th century, the CPAs were determined to be one of the fastest-growing community policing initiatives in the United States (Jordan, 2000).

The three main goals of Lansing (Michigan) Police Department's CPA were (1) to create a network of citizens who would benefit from a basic understanding about the work and complexity of policing; (2) to share information needed to better evaluate media reports about police performance; and (3) to increase the likelihood that CPA graduates would be willing to work with officers to identify and solve neighborhood problems. Generally, the Lansing Police Department hoped that its CPA graduates "would be sympathetic and supportive toward the agency. . . . [and] would vocalize their experiences and share the knowledge they gained with others in the community" (Bonello & Schafer, 2002, p. 20).

The earliest reported adult version of a CPA program was conducted in the United Kingdom in 1977 and was advertised as the "Police Night School." It was sponsored by the Devon and Cornwall Constabulary in Exeter, England. The plan to conduct a "Police Night School" was announced to allow citizens to gain knowledge about police functions, police operations, and the organization of the police system in England. Its organization received a positive response from the public and the program was soon overwhelmed with applicants who wished to learn about their police force. The project was so successful that it was permanently adopted as part of an ongoing police public relations program. In 1985, the Orlando (Florida) Police Department adopted the concept of the "Police Night School" for their agency and created the first known adult Citizen Police Academy (CPA) in the United States. The ultimate goal of Orlando's Citizen Police Academy was to reduce crime through a stronger citizen commitment to the police department and the community. Word of its initial success quickly reached other agencies. Missouri City in Texas soon adopted the program (Ferguson, 1985).

In the United States, the main focus of subsequent versions has been to acquaint citizens with law enforcement's role in the criminal justice system. Ideally, participants after learning about the tasks and duties that police officers face in their daily work may be able to assist in finding realistic solutions to community or neighborhood problems. At the very least, graduates of these programs should be able to share their new-found knowledge and experiences with other community members. In publicity statements, most citizen academies are careful to avoid misstating that their CPAs represent a condensed version of a regular police academy. Given their short duration, they only present a general and selective amount of law enforcement information in an informal manner.[2] Eligibility for attendance will vary from "first-come, first-served" to more stringent requirements involving the satisfactory completion of a background investigation.

Municipal and state level training academies for regular police were formed beginning in the first half of the 20th century and they now exist in every state and also at the federal level. In addition, all states have an agency that certifies its academies with respect to meeting minimum training standards. Hawaii was the last state to create a Law Enforcement Standards Board (LESB) in 2018, but has yet to announce any standards (LESB, 2020, 2021). Although Hawaii is the only state without a set of standardized requirements for law enforcement, it is working towards this goal. In addition, most states have minimum physical and academic requirements to be completed prior to entry into a basic training academy. While some states allow open enrollment in police academies, many require cadets or trainees to be hired by a police department in order to attend training. Departments and/or the state certification agencies may also require individuals to pass background checks, psychological evaluations, polygraph exams, drug screenings, firearms qualifications and demonstrations of driving skills as prerequisites for obtaining police officer/certification. "There are around 18,000 police agencies in the US, but with no national standards on training, procedures and timescales vary across the country. On average . . . [the trainees] spend around 21 weeks training before they are qualified to go on patrol" (Horton, 2021). That is far less than in most other developed countries (ICJTR, 2021).[3]

On the other hand, the length of a Citizen Police Academy usually varies from anywhere from six to 12 sessions. During the COVID-19 pandemic, some programs were conducted through Zoom Cloud Meetings, a proprietary video teleconferencing software program developed by Zoom Video Communications (commonly referred to as "Zoom"). For example, in 2021, the eight weekly sessions of the Yolo County (California) District Attorney Citizens Academy was conducted using the Zoom meeting app. The program was open only to persons 18 or older who resided in Yolo County. It was sponsored by the Yolo County District Attorney's Office in cooperation with the Yolo County Sheriff's Office, the California Highway Patrol, the Davis Police Department, the University of California, Davis Police Department, the West Sacramento Police Department, the Winters Police Department, the Woodland Police Department, and the Yolo County Probation Department (Yolo County DA, 2021).

Augmentation of Police Resources

Police agency budgets have been affected by the worldwide pandemic and general economic downturn. The Major Cities Chiefs Association (MCCA) is a professional organization of police executives representing the largest cities in the United States and Canada. The cities represented are spread across North America from Vancouver, British Columbia to Miami, Florida.[4] More than a decade ago, the MCCA found that 52 percent of agencies surveyed had furloughed sworn officers (McFarland, 2010). Police agencies have used a number of techniques to reduce their personnel costs—layoffs, mandatory furloughs, and attrition. The loss of revenues due to the coronavirus pandemic have now forced local governments to make additional cuts in their public safety operating budgets. While budget cuts continue to threaten the jobs of LEOs, the duties and responsibilities of police to ensure public safety remain. Consequently, cost reductions achieved through modifications in police training involving greater participation and revised roles for ordinary citizens could prove to be an important new agenda item for many local governments.

In a much earlier era, when communities were small and composed of close-knit families, a form of "morality policing" existed involving both formal and informal social controls mostly regulated by the family, local clergy, and nearby neighbors. In modern times, the advent of micro technology, overcrowded cities, and privacy concerns have led to the development of substitute surveillance devices. For the most part, the new tools are controlled by unfamiliar police agencies and related officials. New camera surveillance equipment and various other technological breakthroughs are being used to increase officer effectiveness and efficiency by reducing police response times to emergency calls. The widespread use of street cameras is especially effective when used with facial recognition software to help identify or locate victims or bring offenders to justice. In combination, these impersonal arrangements can watch for any deviance from societal customs.

In September 2021, in recognition of the importance of transparency and accountability in its law enforcement operations, the US Department of Justice (DOJ) announced the launch of the first phase of its "Body-Worn Camera Program" that requires department law enforcement personnel to use body-worn cameras (BWCs) during pre-planned law enforcement operations (i.e., the execution of a search or seizure warrant or order). According to Attorney General Merrick B. Garland, "keeping our communities safe is a top priority for the Justice Department. Law enforcement is at its most effective when there is accountability and trust between law enforcement and the community. That is why we have expanded our body worn camera program" (DOJ, 2021). The Drug Enforcement Administration (DEA), the Federal Bureau of Investigation (FBI) and the US Marshals Service (USMS) have begun to implement the BWC program. The new policy also applied to state, local and Tribal law enforcement who work alongside federal agents in special task force groups (DOJ, 2021).

In addition, alternative human resources are also being used by more police agencies due to budget limitations. In many agencies, responsibilities that were once performed by sworn staff have been shifted to civilian personnel and agencies also have engaged citizen volunteers to help alleviate the strain on police work loads. Such approaches can provide sworn staff with more time to focus on pressing and time-sensitive issues that can only be successfully managed by a LEO. Moreover, "Volunteers in Police Service" (VIPS) is a program within the International Association of Police Chiefs. It has become a common practice among many of the nation's law enforcement agencies to have civilians volunteering their time in a variety of roles inside and outside of station houses. For example, the Pasadena (California) Police Department volunteer activities include patrolling streets and parklands; providing pastoral care for officers, staff and related family; leading volunteer programs; assisting in the investigation of identity theft and missing persons; assisting with security for the annual Tournament of Roses Parade; participating in Police Activities League programs; providing clerical assistance; providing guidance and support to first-time juvenile offenders; and working side-by-side with sworn and non-sworn staff whenever and however needed (Pasadena PD, 2013). Significantly, some CPA graduates become interested in volunteering and may subsequently receive the necessary specialized training for such positions.[5]

University of Illinois Police Training Institute CPA

The University of Illinois is one of the 37 public land-grant institutions established after the *Morrill Land-Grant Colleges Act* was signed by Abraham Lincoln on July 2, 1862. In 1867, the state legislature passed the necessary law so the state could become eligible to receive the many acres of public land promised by the new federal statute for the purpose of fostering access to higher education for the common man. According to Brichford (1983), the University, located primarily in east-central Illinois, was first led by John Milton Gregory who "came to Illinois in 1867 to organize the Illinois Industrial University as the 'West Point for the working world.' A student of a master educational innovator, Eliphalet Nott of Union College [in Schenectady, NY], Gregory devoted 13 years to fashioning a university on the muddy prairie. . . . In 1885, the Illinois Industrial University became the University of Illinois to indicate the aspirations of faculty and alumni and to avoid confusion with schools for delinquents." The first campus building was located on a muddy field between the Illinois Central train station in Champaign and the courthouse in Urbana. The new school's first class consisted of 50 male students. Today, more than 48,000 students are enrolled on the University of Illinois Urbana-Champaign (UIUC) 785-acre campus (UIUC History, 2021).

Established in 1955 by state statute, the University of Illinois Police Training Institute (PTI) is located at the University of Illinois' Urbana-Champaign campus. It is one of the largest and longest running police academies in the United States. The institute has trained tens of thousands of police and correctional officers since its inception. It provides a 14-week 560-hour Basic Law Enforcement Academy, five-week 200-hour Basic Correctional Officer Academy, and advanced specialty courses in firearms and arrest and control tactics (PTI, 2021a). Attendees at PTI cannot enroll themselves. They must first be hired by a police department on a full-time basis and their registration may be made only by departmental personnel. "Students come from more than 300 client agencies across Illinois" (PTI, 2021b).

According to the current web pages of the Police Training Institute (PTI), it has for some time shifted away from the military-style of police training to one based on adult learning principles. "Historically, police academies have based their training concepts on those typical of boot camps, where police recruits are subjugated by instructors' strict and often demeaning methods. Adult learners resent and resist circumstances in which they feel others are imposing their will on them. . . . [However,] not following a military-style ideology does not mean that the PTI is without structure, rules, and discipline. . . . The PTI is a residential academy to provide a greater structure as well as help build the important bond between students. There is a 7 pm curfew for the first two weeks of the academy, and the class can earn a 9 pm curfew thereafter. Intense physical training also takes place every morning at 5:50 am" (PTI, 2021a).

The training institute uses a learning model that includes progressive training, interconnected training, and scenario-based training. At PTI the police trainees practice their skills during 21 four-hour blocks of scenario-based training. Its basic academy covers such topics as: "de-escalation skills, critical thinking, proper decision making, community-oriented policing, laws, strategy and tactics, arrest and control tactics, and firearms training" (PTI, 2021a).

The University of Illinois Police Training Institute (PTI) has held its Champaign County Citizen Police Academy for community members to learn about law enforcement and neighborhood safety since 1994. It is usually offered once a year and consists of three-hour blocks of instruction conducted weekly over a 10-week period on Thursday evenings from 6 to 9 pm. As has happened throughout the United States, the coronavirus pandemic interrupted the scheduling of the free course. When available, tours of local jails and a ride-a-long with police are provided to participants. Typical topics of instruction are offered such as: use of force; drug enforcement; neighborhood crime watch; firearms, and crime scene investigation. Classes are taught by instructors from PTI as well as officers and trainers from participating agencies. Graduates of the program receive a certificate of completion (PTI, 2021c).

When in session, PTI's Citizen Police Academy covers an overview of the issues that concern the delivery of police services throughout Champaign County. "This program is offered in cooperation with the Champaign County Sheriff's Office, University of Illinois Police Department, Urbana Police Department, Champaign Police Department, Rantoul Police Department, the Mahomet Police Department, Parkland Public Safety, and District 10 of the Illinois State Police" (PTI, 2021c). Its aims include: providing stronger citizen/police relationships; enhancing lines of communication; and reducing crime. Several of its overall stated benefits include: increasing citizen awareness of the problems involved in police work; providing citizens and police officers with opportunities to work together; building lines of communication between community residents and their police; enabling citizens to make informed decisions regarding controversial issues faced by their communities; encouraging greater citizen involvement with their local communities and police departments; and offering "citizens a better understanding of how their police departments work and . . . ways in which the community can better reduce crime" (PTI, 2021c).

Pasadena (California) CPA

Pasadena is located ten miles northeast of downtown Los Angeles. It is a richly diverse community. About 56% of Pasadena's approximately 140,000 residents are White, 33% are Latino, 13.4% are African-American, and 12.7% are Asian. The word Pasadena literally means "valley" in the Ojibwa (Chippewa) Indian language (Pasadena Facts, 2014). In addition to the deployment of reserve police officers (sworn positions), the Pasadena Police Department has recruited citizen volunteers since 1984. The use of volunteers is viewed as an integral part of the department's efforts to utilize the community policing model. The Pasadena PD has attempted to integrate volunteers into the department's overall operations. A "Volunteer Services" office coordinates the various opportunities for service with the Department (Pasadena PD, 2013).

The Pasadena Police Department volunteers contribute their time and efforts through the following areas of service: Chaplains; Citizens Assisting Pasadena Police (CAPP Patrol); Equestrians; Community Response to Eradicate and Deter Identity Theft (CREDIT); Missing Persons Unit (MPU); Pawn Detail; Criminal Investigations Division's Victim Assistance; Records and Traffic Sections; General Volunteers; and Youth Accountability Board (YAB). The agency also sponsors a Law Enforcement Explorer unit which includes a 22-week Explorer Academy (Pasadena PD, 2013).

In Pasadena, the Citizen Police Academy (CPA) is an informative classroom series that gives an inside look at Pasadena police operations while discussing the principles of community policing. Its stated purpose is to promote a greater awareness and better understanding of local law enforcement's continuously changing role in the community. Accordingly, the classes cover a wide variety of subject areas including: police communications; criminal law and procedures (laws of arrest); street crime enforcement; investigations; field identification, weaponless defense training; youth programs; firearms training; and the citizen complaint process and more. The course concludes with a graduation dinner, where students receive a certificate of completion. Requirements for participation include: minimum age of 18; live, work, or own property in Pasadena; no felony convictions; and no misdemeanor convictions within one year of application (Pasadena CPA, 2013).

As the second decade of the 21st century drew to a close, the Pasadena Police Department renamed its CPA to stand for "Community Police Academy (CPA). The new title was reflective. of the department's overall adoption of the concept of "community policing" and its desire to fully acquaint the participants attending the academy with its principles, especially how this form of policing can help build partnership and solve problems that arise in the community. Other curriculum topics have been consistent since the academy's inception, although there has been a reduction in the number of weekly class sessions. Each academy course currently runs for about eight sessions with classes meeting every Thursday evening from 5:30 to 9 pm. Instruction is carried out by leading police officials from all the levels of the police department as well as other professionals involved in the administration of justice. The graduates of the academy are offered opportunities to volunteer with the department in a variety of ways (see above). There is also a Spanish language version of the Community Police Academy (Pasadena PD, 2021).

The academy's revised selection process requires participants to be recommended by police staff and other citizens. The names of the selected candidates are then placed on a waiting list until the academy begins. Enrollment is limited to 50 students per academy course. The requirements for the revised academy have remained the same during its recent history (Pasadena PD, 2021).

University of Kentucky CPA

The University of Kentucky (UK) has a current enrollment of more than 29,000 students. However, during peak daytime business hours, the total campus population is around 60,000 people, making it one of the three largest communities in the state. Currently, its campus police force has an authorized strength of 64 sworn officers (UK Police Dept., 2021a). The mission of its police force is to promote a safe and secure campus environment for students, faculty, staff and visitors at the University.

The school was chartered in 1865 by the Kentucky legislature as a land-grant institution as a department within Kentucky University (a private, sectarian institution organized at the same time). This division was established pursuant to the terms of *the Morrill Land-Grant Act of 1862* as the Agricultural and Mechanical (A&M) College of Kentucky. The state legislature acted to separate the College from Kentucky University in 1878 due to denominational and theological controversies, as well as financial difficulties. By 1880, the A&M College began development as an independent institution of higher education on the site of a municipal park and fairgrounds donated by the city of Lexington. During this period the institution was often referred to as State College. The College was elevated to university status in 1908, acquiring its final name, University of Kentucky in 1916 as a result of a new state statute. Today, the campus sits on 784 acres of land in Lexington, Kentucky and is composed of 16 colleges. Students can choose from four professional degrees, nearly 100 undergraduate degrees, nearly 100 master's degrees, and many doctorate degrees. There are over 250 student-operated organizations and 23 residential halls on the campus. The University has 21 varsity teams and over 140,000 alumni currently living in Kentucky. There are many famous graduates including, Ashley Judd, actress; Thomas Hunt Morgan, Nobel Prize recipient in Philosophy of Medicine; Steven Beshear, Kentucky governor from 2007 to 2015 (the current governor of the state is his son Andy Beshear); Mitch McConnell, the current Senate Minority Leader; Paul Chellgren, CEO and Chairman of Ashland Inc.; and William Lipscomb, Nobel Peace Prize winner in Chemistry (stateuniversity.com 2021).

Like many colleges and universities, the University of Kentucky maintained an in-house security guard unit beginning in the early 1900s. By the early 1970s, the Kentucky legislature had authorized all state public universities with "the power to create campus police agencies and also set out standards for being a campus police officer. Some of the standards at that time were more stringent than what was required by law for a city police department" (UK Police Dept., 2021a). However, it was not until the mid-1980s that all campus police officers were required to attend a ten-week police academy that had been previously established in the state's capital city of Richmond. The current academy is 23 weeks in duration (UK Police Dept., 2021a).

The University of Kentucky's Police Department began its Citizens Police Academy courses in 2007 (Saylor, 2021). The course seeks to reduce the "mystery that often surrounds law enforcement" (UK Police Dept., 2021b). Its CPA provides opportunities for citizens to gain insights into the daily functions and responsibilities of law enforcement in order to foster "more cohesive relationships between law enforcement officers and the community. The goal is for graduates to share knowledge gained with others in the community, thereby helping others become more familiar with police practices" (UK Police Dept., 2021b). Graduates can become members of the Citizen Police Academy Alumni Association and help UK Police in community projects. Topics presented include: University Policing Overview & History; Criminal Procedure; Polygraph; K-9 Operations; Firearms; Use of Force; DUI Investigation; Dignitary Protection Team; Crisis Management and Preparedness; Joint Terrorism Task Force; Traffic Stops; and Support Services. Course materials are presented through lecture, audio-visual aids, and interactive scenarios. Generally, the free course is held twice a year with each session taking place one evening a week from 6 to 8 pm for ten weeks (UK Police Dept., 2021b).

The CPA is open to all faculty, staff, students, and members of the community who are 18 years or older and pass a background investigation. Prospective participants must also complete a course application (UK Police Dept., 2021b).

St. Louis County (Missouri) CPA

In 1876, St. Louis City and St. Louis County separated. With a population of just over one million, the 524 square miles of St. Louis County is located in the eastern-central portion of Missouri. It is bounded by the city of St. Louis and the Mississippi River to the east, the Missouri River to the north, and the Meramec River to the south. "The mission of the St. Louis County Police Department is to work cooperatively with the public, and within the framework of the Constitution to enforce the laws, preserve the peace, reduce fear and provide a safe environment in our neighborhoods" (St. Louis County PD, 2021a). A separate St. Louis County Department of Justice Services (St. Louis County DJS) provides for the custody, supervision and guidance of those individuals who have been incarcerated by order of the local courts within the jurisdiction. New corrections officer cadets for the county jail receive eight weeks of training consisting of four weeks of classroom instruction and four weeks of on-the-job training (St. Louis County DJS, 2019, p. 9).

During the decade of the 1960s, the St. Louis County Police Department (SLCPD) increased its basic training course from two to four weeks of academy classroom training that was supplemented with additional firearms and on-the-job training. A St. Louis County and Municipal Training Academy was organized in January of 1964, as a cooperative effort between the County and municipal police chiefs. In 1968, the training period for new officers was extended to six hundred hours and by the 1990s, the length of training had increased to 800 hours. The department also became one of the first in the nation to include college credit hours as part of the training program. During the 1970s, the SLCPD instituted a ride-along program "which allowed citizens to observe officers at work by accompanying them on patrol. In the same decade, the department began its "Law Enforcement Explorer Program," which allows young men and women to explore career opportunities in the field of law enforcement by receiving training and working with officers on patrol. In 1980, The department had 562 commissioned officers and 189 civilian employees, providing more effective coverage for the County's growing number of residents. This number represented more than a fivefold increase in personnel from the late 1950s. The department was officially founded in 1955. By the 1980s, the training of the department's newly appointed officers consisted of a 16-week academy, which was followed by a ten-week assignment with a Field Training Officer (St. Louis County PD, 2021b).

During the 1990s, the St. Louis County Police Department initiated a "Neighborhood Watch Program" whereby "Community Service Officers" worked with groups of residents from neighborhoods who became the "eyes and ears" within their neighborhoods, helping to reduce crime. By 1993, the department had managed more than 450 neighborhood watch groups. A "Neighborhood Policing" philosophy was instituted and patrol officers were assigned to a specific area so that they could better resolve problems within the community. In addition, these officers (one for each precinct) made public appearances at schools, businesses and community organizations. In the same decade, a Citizen Police Academy was developed. Because of the overall success of the Citizen Police Academy the department created a Teen Academy (St. Louis County PD, 2021b).

The web pages of the St. Louis County PD state: "The role of Police Officers has always been of interest to the average citizen. Police action is widely publicized through the news, reality TV shows and fictional movies. This Academy allows citizens a chance to learn more about their community police officers and how the Department operates. Additionally, it allows Police Officers the opportunity to receive input from citizens as well as their assistance and support. The St. Louis County Police Department encourages its citizens to become actively involved in their neighborhoods, provide information that can form a partnership with police to aid in solving community problems" (St. Louis County PD, 2021c).

The department's CPA course includes presentations on: patrol procedure; crime scene processing; tactical operations (e.g., K-9 Unit and Air Support); computer crime; fraud; domestic and child abuse; and homicide. Participants receive tours of the agency's Emergency Management Operations Center; the St. Louis County and Municipal Police Academy; and the firing range. Such field trips are scheduled on a different day or evening depending on the availability of staff. The average academy lasts 6 weeks and classes are approximately two hours per evening, once a week. After graduation, citizens have the opportunity to join the Citizen Police Academy Alumni Association. At the end of the training, each participant receives a certificate of completion during a graduation ceremony (St. Louis County PD, 2021c).

Buffalo Grove (Illinois) CPA

The Village of Buffalo Grove (10 square miles, population 41,500) is located 30 miles outside of downtown Chicago, in its northwest suburbs. O'Hare International Airport, one of the world's busiest, is a 25-minute drive from the village. In 2012, its residents had a median household income of $88,272 (Buffalo Grove, 2012). The Buffalo Grove Police Department began its Citizen Police Academy program in 1997, conducting an eight-week program. The program recently expanded and its current list of topics includes: the use of RADAR and LIDAR units in speed enforcement; traffic accident investigations; crime scene processing; crimes against property and persons; and public information sharing. Individuals attending also receive instruction in defensive tactics, CPR certification, firearms safety, and tour the Emergency Dispatch Center. The rendition of its 2020 CPA course was held for ten weeks from February 12 to April 15. Each weekly class began at 6:30 pm and lasted approximately three hours. Program participants had to be 21 or over. As is the common practice with most CPAs in the United States, potential attendees are required to complete a participant liability waiver agreement along with their application materials (Buffalo Grove, 2021).

Ponca City (Oklahoma) CPA

Ponca City, founded in 1893, is situated along a major Burlington Northern Santa Fe rail corridor linking Chicago, Illinois, to Houston, Texas. However, this corridor has been identified as a major gap in the Amtrak nationwide passenger rail service and there is no stop in Ponca City. Although the city recently celebrated a newly reconstructed modern 7,200-foot runway at the Ponca City Regional Airport, it has yet to attract a carrier for routine passenger service (McKinley, 2021).[6] Ponca City was named after the Native American members of the Ponca nation. The city is just over 18 square miles and has a population just under 25,000.

In response to COVID-19, the city's Emergency Management Department coordinated with the Federal Emergency Management Agency (FEMA). It used grant funds and state allocations to purchase and distribute personal protective equipment and worked with the Oklahoma Department of Health and Ponca City Police Department to establish safe and efficient logistics to vaccinate citizens for COVID-19 at a community vaccination pod (McKinley, 2021).

The Ponca City Police Department (PCPD) has 55 sworn officers, 11 civilian employees, and 26 "Extra Eyes volunteers." The volunteers come from graduating classes of the Citizens' Police Academy who may after extra training perform work that enables regular police officers to get back to the street more quickly, saving the taxpayers' money. Members of the Extra Eyes Program perform duties such as: records entry; fingerprint analysis; traffic control; crime stoppers; juvenile court; special patrols; parade duty; and crime scene assistance (McKinley, 2021). The citizen's academy is held annually for 13 weeks to acquaint participants with all aspects of the work of their police department. Class size is limited to 20 participants and instruction is carried out by members of the PCPD. Members of the class have opportunities to fire departmental weapons and experience the "Use-of-Force Simulator" (Ponca City, 2021). It receives support from the Ponca City Police Foundation Trust, which was organized in 2000 to financially supplement and benefit the entire community and to help keep Ponca City safe and secure (Ponca City, 2021). In 2021, the department began cultural competence/implicit bias training for all police employees (McKinley, 2021).

The history of Ponca City is tied to the history of local American Indian communities, particularly its namesake, the Ponca Tribe of American Indians. They came to the area in 1877 from their traditional homelands in Nebraska and South Dakota. The experience of the Poncas reached a national audience in 1879 when Chief Standing Bear and 66 followers returned to Nebraska to bury his son. In the landmark decision *U.S. ex Rel. Standing Bear v. Crook*, Judge Elmer S. Dundy ruled that Indians were entitled to the rights guaranteed to citizens by the United States Constitution. This case had important repercussions because it opened the judicial system to Native Americans. The full opinion of Judge Dundy is available online at: https://casetext.com/case/us-ex-rel-standing-bear-v-crook.

Texas CPA Survey

In 1994, a survey was conducted to determine the number and nature of the citizen academies being conducted in Texas. The earliest academy implemented in Texas was in 1985. The survey indicated that by the spring of 1994, more than 4,000 Texas citizens had attended such programs throughout the state and that departmental classes were generally offered two times per year, with 27 students per class. The average academy met once each week for 11 weeks, three hours each session. The purpose most widely cited by 22 agencies for conducting a CPA was to educate the public about the operations, policies, and procedures of the police department. Another often cited reason was the promotion of communication between the citizens and members of the police agency in an effort to improve relations. Other reasons included: dispelling myths and preconceptions that the public may have concerning police work; enlisting the aid of the citizens in the prevention of crime; and promoting support of the police department and the city. Topics taught at the Texas CPAs ranged from traditional police activities, such as accident investigation and crime scene investigation to newer, less traditional areas such as victim services, cults, gangs, and police stress and trauma counseling. Some of the agencies in the survey recommended that every police division or unit be discussed and reviewed (Blackwood, 1994).

The Texas survey also gathered data about the amount spent annually by police agencies for conducting each citizen academy. This amount ranged from no departmental funds to $6,000. The one agency that did not spend departmental money charged tuition. The average amount spent by agencies that did not include personnel costs was $1,600. The agencies that included personnel costs averaged $3,500 per year. These agencies reported that personnel costs consumed the largest portion of the program's budget. Several agencies used alternative sources of funding. These sources included alumni associations, citizen contributions, grants, and asset forfeitures (Blackwood, 1994).

In addition, the Texas study revealed that police departments used a variety of methods to both recruit and screen participants. The most popular method for recruitment was by word of mouth, including alumni. Other methods for recruitment included: announcements at community service clubs; neighborhood or city newsletters; flyers at the station or substations; utility billing supplements; and speaking engagements by agency personnel. Requirements for attendance at the academies also varied. Some agencies allowed high school students to attend, while others had a minimum age of 21. A criminal history check was required by some of the agencies (Blackwood, 1994). A major finding of this survey was that "all responding agencies surveyed recommended that other agencies should implement a Citizen Police Academy, if they haven't already done so" (Blackwood, 1994, p. 7). Today, the internet and newspaper announcements appear to be the most widely used methods for advertising purposes. Most interested individuals probably submit their applications using their agency's web pages.

Philadelphia CPA

The Philadelphia Police Department (PPD) is the nation's fourth largest police department, with over 6,300 sworn members and 800 civilian personnel. The PPD is the primary law enforcement agency responsible for serving Philadelphia County, extending over 140 square-miles with approximately 1.5 million inhabitants. Geographically, the department is divided into 21 police districts (each headed by a captain), comprising six police divisions (Northwest, Northeast, East, Central, Southwest, South (each headed by a Divisional Inspector). In addition, for the purposes of administration, the city has a Regional Operations Command North (ROC North) and a Regional Operations Command South (ROC South), each headed by one Chief Inspector under Patrol Operations. Personnel are assigned to work in 55 different locations throughout Philadelphia, with Police Headquarters located in the 6th Police District, in Center City, at 750 Race Street (PPD, 2021).

The Philadelphia Police Department's Civilian Police Academy (its official name) originated in 1992. The program is held over 13 weekly sessions at the PPD's training center, located at 2838 Woodhaven Road. The Civilian Police Academy motto is "Understanding through education and training." The academy is open to anyone aged 18 or older (Ravina, 2016). "The Civilian Police Academy (CPA) was formed as a special program to welcome and include all Philadelphians in the operation of their police department. . . . The overall purpose of the CPA is to produce informed graduates who will return to their neighborhoods with a more positive view of the police function, and assist them in recognizing the varied problems facing today's urban police officer. . . . The CPA is NOT designed to teach civilians to patrol the streets of Philadelphia, but to aid the trained Police Officer in the performance of their duties by creating an educated citizen who is more aware of the policies, laws and procedures that guide an officer's actions in the community" (Pauley, 2020). Some of the topics covered are: laws of arrest and high-risk car stops; controlled substances and gangs; safe operations of police vehicles; report writing and note taking; crime scene investigation; urban disorder management; the training and uses of police K-9 teams; terrorism; arrest and search warrants; history and principles of law enforcement; and crime prevention and fear reduction. There is a graduation ceremony held at the Police Academy at the end of the program (week 13). Classes are normally held on Wednesday nights from 7:00 to 9:00 pm (Pauley, 2020).

Metropolitan Washington Airports Authority CPA

While CPAs are a very common feature of many large and medium size police departments, it is unusual for specialized law enforcement jurisdictions such as airports to sponsor them. Perhaps, the first two agencies to have them were the Tampa International Airport Police Department and the Metropolitan Washington Airports Authority Police Department. The agencies desired to maintain and build up positive relations with the communities they serve.

On June 7, 1987, Washington Dulles International and Washington National Airports were transferred to the Airports Authority under a 50-year lease authorized by the *Metropolitan Washington Airports Act of 1986*, Title VI of Public Law 99–500. In 1998, the name of Washington National Airport was changed to Ronald Reagan Washington National Airport. All property was transferred to the Airports Authority, and the Federal government holds title to the lease. Prior to the transfer, the airports were owned and operated by the Federal Aviation Administration in the US Department of Transportation. The Metropolitan Washington Airports Authority (MWAA) operates a two-airport system that provides domestic and international air service for the mid-Atlantic region. The organization consists of more than 1,500 employees in a structure that includes central administration, airports management and operations, and police and fire departments (MWAA, 2021).

The Metropolitan Washington Airports Authority Police Department (MWAAPD) hosted its fourth Airport Community Police Academy for nine weekly sessions beginning in

April 2020 and concluding on June 8, 2020. The training sessions took place on Monday evenings (except for holidays) from 6 to 9 pm at the Ronald Reagan Washington National Airport. The MWAAPD's LEOs covered: K-9 Explosive Detection; Internal Affairs; Criminal Investigations; Special Response; Evidence Collection; and many other subjects. Like almost all CPAs, the Airport Community Police Academy was free to the public, but limited to 25 participants who had to be at least 18 years old, pass a background check, and agree to attend the full 9-week program. However, participants were allowed to miss three classes during the length of the Academy course (MWAAPD, 2020).

Tampa International Airport CPA

Tampa International Airport covers an area of over 3,300 acres. The airport has four passenger terminals and two cargo terminals. The existing passenger terminal complex (landside terminal) was opened in April 1971. The passenger facilities at the terminals include 60 check-in desks, 60 gates, five aircraft stands and 20 baggage claim belts. Other facilities include more than 23,000 parking spaces, a bank, restaurants, cafeterias, bars, a VIP lounge, duty free shop, gift shop, a business center, car rental offices, and disabled access/ facilities. A 296-room Marriott hotel is close to the landside terminal. A master plan for the international airport was updated in 2013. The expansions proposed under the master plan are expected to be completed by 2028 (Projects, 2021). The Tampa International Airport Police Department (TIAPD) is the agency responsible for the safety and security of the airport, as well as the employees, tenants, visitors, and the 21 million passengers who now use the airport every year. However, passenger traffic was reduced during the COVID-19 pandemic.

In the fall of 2018, the Tampa International Airport Police Department initiated its first Citizen Police Academy program "to offer insights into how police officers perform their duties and how the department serves the community. . . . The Citizen Police Academy is seven weeks long with a session held once a week. The class size is determined by citizen interest and the available staff to conduct the Citizen Police Academy" (TIAPD, 2019, p. 23). Generally, there are two sessions held per year; one in the Spring and one in the Fall. The inaugural session was held with 16 individuals participating. They received a "behind the scenes" look at the rigorous training of the airport police. "During the inaugural session, participants experienced scenario based training, viewed a K-9 demonstration, competed in the physical abilities test (PAT), trained to shoot firearms, and rode a shift with a TIAPD officer, just to name a few activities. A graduation ceremony was held once the participants completed the weekly sessions. Graduates were recognized with a CPA pin and graduation certificate and were treated to a fabulous buffet and cake" (TIAPD, 2019, p. 23). There have been three additional academy programs held since 2018, the 2020 programs had to be suspended due to COVID-19 (TPACPA@tampaairport.com, 2021).

The success of these initial classes has resulted in their adoption as a regular feature of the agency's outreach programs. The TIAPD concluded that the provision of such an educational opportunity "has been most effective in gaining understanding and support from the community (TIAPD, 2019, p. 23). The fall 2021 CPA session was held, but due to COVID-19 the class size was reduced to follow social distancing and other protocols. Participants were scheduled to: meet the command staff of TIAPD; go behind the scenes of patrol operations; experience scenario based training; tour facilities and operational areas of the airport and police department; experience hands on firearms familiarization and weapon safety with a certified firearms instructor; view a K9 demonstration and participate with a K9 handler; tackle the agency's agility obstacle course; learn about the Emergency Operation Center, Airport Operations Center, TIAPD crime prevention initiatives; and observe specialty team demonstrations (TIAPD, 2021a).

In order to qualify for attendance at the CPA, applicants had: to be at least 18 years of age; to sign an indemnity release; to pass a background check; to submit a completed application; to agree to participate in all scheduled academy sessions; and had to be a resident of the greater Tampa Bay area (TIAPD, 2021a). In addition, the Tampa International Airport Police Department has designed a separate "Citizen Ride-A-long Program" to educate citizens about police duties and allow them limited participation in the day-to-day activities of an officer at the airport. "Interested members of the community, including students, may participate in this program to promote education, awareness and communication about police department operations. Applicants must be 18 years of age . . . [and] may only apply to participate in the program once a year unless otherwise approved by the Director of Public Safety and Security" (TIAPD, 2021b). The agency also has established a "Reserve Officer program" for state-certified individuals to perform unpaid volunteer law enforcement duties at Tampa International Airport. Working under the direction of the police captain for special operations, reserve officer duties include the protection of Aviation Authority property, facilities, personnel and the general public. Along with a stated list of specific qualifications, candidates for the part-time reserve officer position must satisfy one of the following: "Three years of experience as a federal, state, county, city or airport authority law enforcement officer. Or, an associate's degree; and two years of experience as a federal, state, county, city or airport law enforcement officer. Or, an associate's degree; and successful completion of a State of Florida Criminal Justice Standards and Training Commission certified Police Academy" (TIAPD, 2021c).[7]

Tennessee Citizens' Correctional Academy

While not as common as Citizen Police Academies, various state correctional systems have begun to offer their own programs. The Tennessee Department of Correction (TDOC) employs 6,000 personnel in its correctional system. It began offering its Citizens' Correctional Academy program in 2014 to give members of the public a behind the scenes look at the department's operations. It is conducted during four sessions held one night each week from 6 to 9 pm. A fifth session involves a graduation event. Participants generally tour two facilities and visit a community supervision field office in order to gain a better understanding of how the agency functions. All applicants to the Citizens Correctional Academy will undergo a background check and are subject to the approval of the department. There are five specific eligibility requirements: (1) 18 years of age or older; (2) no criminal history other than minor traffic violations; (3) attend all sessions, including the graduation ceremony; (4) not currently have a family member or loved one incarcerated in TDOC custody or on community supervision; and (5) complete, sign, and return all required forms, waivers, and agreements before the deadline (TDOC, 2021).

Delaware Correction Citizens Academy

In the State of Delaware, more than 4,000 individuals are currently incarcerated and more than 10,000 individuals are currently on probation or court-ordered pretrial supervision (DDOC, 2021b). The Delaware Department of Correction (DDOC) began its first Citizens Academy programs in 2021. The very first program was held at three locations: the Department of Correction Administration Building in Dover, the James T. Vaughn Correctional Center in Smyrna, and the Probation & Parole Regional Office in Dover. At that time, Deputy Bureau Chief of Prisons Paul Shavack stated we wanted to be as transparent as possible, and give people a look at what the day-to-day life of both correctional officers and offenders is like. According to Shavack, "There's different perspectives out there on what the Department of Corrections is. You see it from the media perspective, you see it from what you see in the movies. But we want to give that true perspective of what goes on in the inner workings of the Department of Corrections" (qtd. in Cechini, 2021).

The first academy was conducted over a period of five weeks, one evening a week from 6 to 8 pm. The second program held in 2021 took place over six evenings. Background checks and COVID-related precautions, including social distancing and mask-wearing were required of all participants (DDOC, 2021a). The program was designed to give community members a look inside the operations and programs of Delaware's largest law enforcement agency and provide firsthand insight into how the Department of Correction (DOC) achieves its dual mission of public safety and offender rehabilitation. Its sessions provided an opportunity for participants to engage with the DOC leadership, uniformed officers, treatment and program providers, and a wide range of additional professional staff. The Citizens Academy goal is to strengthen public engagement with the DOC through information-sharing, access, and dialogue, and to build strong partnerships with local residents (DDOC, 2021b).

The academy's sessions involved informational presentations, demonstrations, class discussions and tours. Its sessions focused on a variety of topics, including: organizational structure; officer and staff training; prison operations; community supervision methods; medical and behavioral health treatment; vocational training and education as well as the DOC's role in coordinating Delaware's statewide reentry initiative. Participants learned "how DOC assesses offender needs and risks, and leverages technology, training, communication, and collaboration to meet their needs, mitigate those risks, support reentry success and reduce Delaware's recidivism rate" (DDOC, 2021b). In a statement released to the public, DOC Commissioner Monroe B. Hudson Jr., who had a distinguished 31-year career at the Delaware State Police where he attained the rank of Lieutenant Colonel, said: "Whether you are considering a career in law enforcement, want to partner with the DOC, learn more about the various programs and educational opportunities available to offenders, or have a loved one who has been supervised by us, we encourage you to apply to participate in our Citizens Academy" (DDOC, 2021b).

Mobile (Alabama) Junior Police Academy

Like their adult counterparts, junior police academies can be quite varied. Some may emphasize recreation and learning for any youth on a first-come, first-served basis, while others may seek out at-risk youth for a more specialized experience. However, their most common features are that such camps are operated and mostly sponsored by law enforcement agencies and held during times when schools are not in session. During the summer of 2021, the Mobile Police Department (MPD) offered a typical example of a recreation centered program for a week-long learning experience involving "team-building challenges and specialty unit field trips to spend some quality time with real-world law enforcement officers" (Mobile PD, 2021a). The junior academy was limited to 20 participants ages 9 to 12 and was conducted during daylight hours until 4:30 pm. Other cities have programs that are residential, especially when intended for at-risk youth. Moreover, oftentimes jurisdictions combine their resources to offer these types of programs (see Greenberg, 2015). In Mobile's program there was an enrollment fee of $85 for each camper and selection was based on students having at least a "C" average as well as the timely completion of both an application and an essay (Mobile PD, 2021a).

The Mobile Police Department sponsors a number of other types of community outreach programs including: an adult CPA; Speakers Bureau; CrimeStoppers rewards program; city-wide "Citizen Advisory Panel"; volunteer Chaplain Corps of ministers from local churches; and Project CARE (Concerns and Resources for the Elderly). Project CARE was created by the police chief in 2009 in an effort for the senior citizen community and law enforcement personnel to connect and collaborate. Mobile's "Citizen Advisory Panel" advises the police chief on matters of public concern, reviews incidents related to police-community relations at the discretion of the police chief, and acts as a sounding board on issues related to current and proposed community-oriented policing programs by providing feedback and direction (Mobile PD, 2021b).

San Juan's Homeland Security Investigations (HSI) Citizens Academy

Not unsurprisingly, the widespread creation of the traditional types of CPAs has led to the initiation of other specific types of citizen-involved academies. According to the public outreach web pages of the US ICE agency, the agency was created in 2003 through a merger of the investigative and interior enforcement elements of the former US Customs Service and the Immigration and Naturalization Service. It is housed within the US Department of Homeland Security (DHS).

> ICE now has more than 20,000 law enforcement and support personnel in more than 400 offices in the United States and around the world. The agency has an annual budget of approximately $8 billion, primarily devoted to three operational directorates—Homeland Security Investigations (HSI), Enforcement and Removal Operations (ERO) and Office of the Principal Legal Advisor (OPLA). A fourth directorate—Management and Administration—supports the three operational branches to advance the ICE mission.
>
> *(ICE, 2021a)*

Through its outreach programs, HSI seeks to enhance its ability to combat transnational crime by establishing and developing relationships with key stakeholders across industry and academia and throughout local communities. "HSI utilizes its outreach programs to initiate and foster these relationships, familiarize the public with the HSI mission and equip stakeholders with important information, tools and resources that can be used to identify, prevent and report criminal activity" (ICE, 2021b).

One of ICE's outreach programs is the "HSI Citizens Academy program" that enables HSI special agents and managers to "invite participants from local communities to learn more about the HSI mission through direct interaction and discussion with agency offices and personnel. Through the Citizens Academy program, HSI strives to enhance public awareness and understanding of HSI and its critical national security and public safety missions, and to build positive community involvement and interaction with the agency. HSI Citizens Academy programs are developed by participating HSI field offices and are tailored to address specific topics of interest and unique needs of the respective communities they serve. The program typically entails three-hour sessions held after business hours one night a week over the course of seven to ten weeks. They do not confer any type of authority, benefit or entitlement, but do allow members of the community to gain a greater understanding of HSI's mission through hands-on activities and direct interaction with HSI special agents and managers. The national roll-out of the HSI Citizens Academy program occurred in April 2019 based on earlier HSI Citizens Academy models conducted in prior years in San Juan, New York, Tampa and Los Angeles. Candidates are nominated by HSI employees, former Citizens Academy graduates and community leaders. Participants are selected by the Special Agent in Charge of the local HSI SAC office" (ICE, 2021c).[8]

ICE's first Citizens Academy program began in 2013, when ICE's HSI sponsored the first class in San Juan, Puerto Rico. The program, a project of ICE's Office of Public Affairs, was described by ICE as "a unique opportunity to receive an inside look at HSI's organizational and operational structure" for "selected community leaders" chosen by ICE agents to participate. The HSI San Juan Citizens Academy had a graduating "class" of 10 in 2014, 13 in March 2015, and 14 in April 2016 (ICE, 2016). The 14 community leaders who attended the third cohort underwent a ten-week program, meeting once a week for at least two hours. Their program's curriculum included instruction about: the "HSI San Juan communications center, airport operations, illicit trade, human smuggling and trafficking, gangs, Coast Guard interdiction, transportation of evidence, child exploitation, surveillance, seaport operations, controlled deliveries, financial investigations, pre-trial and judicial proceedings, clearing a room, special response team operations, firearms training and team building. They also had the opportunity to visit the HSI San Juan Computer Forensics Laboratory, the only laboratory of its kind in the Caribbean, and learn how HSI special agents retrieve information and evidence from electronic/digital devices and conduct child exploitation investigations" (ICE, 2016). This sounds like ICE was using the common CPA script that municipal agencies had followed for the past 30 years. However, in 2020 when the Chicago Field Office of ICE tried to hold a shorter version of the citizen's academy with "ICE" in its title, the result became mired in politics (see below). Immigrant-rights advocates "decried the academy as an example of white supremacy, saying it would lead to more fear among the immigrant community" (Malagón, 2020).

Chicago ICE CPA

In 2019, a bipartisan research group ranked Chicago as the most immigrant-friendly city in the United States (Hauck, 2020). However, before the 2020 presidential election and during the Trump Administration in the summer of that year, the US ICE announced its plans to hold its first-ever "citizens academy" in Chicago for one session each week for six weeks starting in September for the purpose of educating the public on the role of ICE officers. However, almost immediately a number of lawmakers, various elected officials, and community groups protested that the program represented a threat to immigrant communities (Hauck, 2020).

According to ICE's announcement, the program was to be modeled after other law enforcement academies—such as those by the FBI and local police departments. The ICE program was to include classroom instruction, scenario-based training and exercises, defensive tactics, firearms familiarization, arrest practices, visiting an immigration detention center, learning more about the health care ICE provides to those in its custody and "examining ICE's role in ensuring dignity, respect and due process of an immigration case from start to finish" (qtd. in Hauck, 2020). In a contemporaneous interview, ICE Public Affairs Officer Nicole Alberico noted that the program was not intended to train members of the public to do the work of certified ICE officers. She indicated that the program was hoping to have key leaders from the community apply, regardless of their stance on ICE (Hauck, 2020).

On the other hand, almost immediately after ICE's announcement, Chicago's mayor as well as federal and local lawmakers began to express deep concerns about the program's mission. Mayor Lori Lightfoot stated: "In this welcoming city, vigilantes are NOT welcome,. . . . ICE's plan to train civilians to surveil and intimidate immigrant and refugee communities is vile. We will always stand up for and protect all of our residents, no matter who this administration tries to scapegoat' " (qtd. in Hauck, 2020). At the same time, Rep. Jesus "Chuy" Garcia, (D-Illinois), joined by Reps. Ayanna Pressley (D-Massachusetts), Alexandria Ocasio-Cortez (D-New York), and Jan Schakowsky (D-Illinois) wrote to the House Appropriations Committee requesting that the committee prohibit the use of federal funds for citizen academies within the Department of Homeland Security. On the same day, Rep. Mike Quigley, D-Illinois, presented an amendment to the Homeland Security funding bill for the 2021 fiscal year to deny funding for the program. The amendment passed. Rep. Mike Quigley also stated that the "The United States is not a police state where ordinary men and women are deputized to carry out immigration enforcement based on discriminatory racial-profiling practices. . . . The so-called Citizens Academy program would do nothing less than train Americans to suspect their friends and neighbors of being dangerous criminals, regardless of their actual immigration status"(qtd. in Hauck, 2020). Moreover, the members of the Latino Caucus of the Chicago City Council sent a letter to the director of the Chicago ICE field office requesting that the agency cancel the event complaining, in part, that ICE's announcement contained very "troublesome language" about possible scenario-based training and exercises, including firearms and arrest tactics. In addition, US Senator Tammy Duckworth from Illinois stated: "This PR move by ICE is remarkably misguided, will do nothing to make communities any safer and should never have been proposed in the first place, much less while ICE is claiming they do not have sufficient funding for essential functions" (Duckworth, 2020).

The outcry over ICE's planned citizens' academy may have led to its postponement in Chicago. However, the official reason given two weeks before the planned start of Chicago's fall 2020 Citizens Academy was that it was due to the coronavirus pandemic and that the program had been rescheduled for the spring of 2021 (Malagón, 2020). There was no program held during the spring and as this book was in preparation, it was not known whether ICE had any plans to hold any additional citizen academies. A 21-page lawsuit under the *Freedom of Information Act* (FOIA), 5 U.S.C. §§ 552 et seq., seeking declaratory, injunctive, and other appropriate relief to compel ICE to produce relevant agency records concerning the planning for such citizens academies was filed in May 2021 by several concerned groups (see Organized Communities, 2021).

Other Types of Citizen Academies

Much less controversial than any federal CPA programs sponsored by ICE are those conducted by the Federal Bureau of Investigation (FBI). It has been conducting citizen academy programs since 1993.[9] This is a fact, despite the knowledge that "the FBI has either been glorified or demeaned throughout the years in movies, TV shows and in the news media" (Pilcher, 2015). The FBI's citizen academies are held in a course lasting between six and eight weeks (one evening a week) in order to provide business, religious, civic, and community leaders an inside look at the FBI. Classes meet in the evenings at the 56 FBI field offices around the country. The mission of the FBI Citizens Academies is to foster a greater understanding of the role of federal law enforcement in the community through frank discussion and education. Candidates are nominated by FBI employees, former Citizens Academy graduates, community leaders, or anyone who self-nominates. Participants are selected by the special agent in charge of the local FBI field office. Candidates must meet certain criteria: being in good standing in the community; a recognized business, religious, or community leader; living or working within the division's jurisdiction; 21 or older; consent to background investigation and fingerprint checks; and must attend all sessions (FBI, 2021a).

During a summer 2021 media interview announcing Albany, New York's FBI Citizens Academy, Sarah Ruane, FBI public affairs specialist, said: "It's such an incredible program/opportunity and we're thrilled to have it back up and running after having to hit pause during the pandemic" (qtd. in Nexstar Media Inc., 2021). Kathleen Burnett (2019) found that "in order to become more transparent and open with the community," the FBI adopted the citizens' academy program in the mid-1990s and it now exists in nearly all of the FBI field offices (pp. 42–43). Burnett is the Community Outreach Specialist (COS) for the Sacramento Field Office and all surrounding Resident Agencies. As part of her master's degree project for the California State University at Sacramento, she created an "FBI Citizens Academy Training Manual" for the Sacramento Field Office of the FBI. According to Burnett (2019), "this manual details every step taken in the process of planning and executing a Citizens Academy" (p. 44). A copy of her project report and the manual she wrote is available online at: https://scholarworks.calstate.edu/downloads/7w62f8501.

Local field offices of the FBI offer a variety of other public programs, including the "Community Awareness Presentation (CAP)," a shorter, more focused version of the FBI Citizens Academy program that is conducted in partnership and at the request of a specific community group, generally at an offsite location. The program is designed to build trust and strengthen relationships between the FBI and the communities they serve. "Community groups are encouraged to identify topics that are of concern or relevant to their group or organization for the FBI to discuss. Classes are taught by FBI subject matter experts. Generally the participants are selected by members of their organizations or community and there is no restriction on audience size" (FBI, 2021b). Many law enforcement agencies at the local level will also provide similar programs upon request about the work of their agencies. For example, the citizens of Martin County (Florida) Sheriff's Office have the option of attending a one-day condensed version of its eight to ten week citizen's academy. The same topics are covered except in an abbreviated format (Martin County, 2021a).[10]

The Idaho State Bar created a "Citizen's Law Academy" to educate the public on the law and the role of attorneys. Other agencies have created Business Police Academies (BPAs) in order to gain the support of the leaders of the business community. In Denver, Colorado, CPAs were held for their ethnic Russian population and universities have created CPAs for their students as a form of community outreach (see University of Kentucky above). Washington, DC, has created a senior citizen police academy and in 1999, the Cilmore, Arizona CPA utilized its version of the program to help train the members of its volunteer police officers (see Breen & Johnson, 2007, p. 248).

Ricardo S. Morse, an associate professor of public administration and government from the University of North Carolina at Chapel Hill, has developed web pages as well as co-authored a book[11] regarding the "citizens academy," also known as a city/county 101 program or neighborhood college, which he defines as "usually, a seven-to-eight week program where 20–25 residents are given the opportunity to meet with various local government staff and elected leaders and gain insight into local government services and operations" (Morse, 2021a). He notes that unlike citizen police and fire academies, the citizen's academy "looks comprehensively at the role and structure of local government in the community, which may include public safety. Alumni often become informal ambassadors for the local government, share information with their neighborhoods, and often go on to serve on advisory boards. Some even run for elected office" (Morse, 2021a). While the reasons for creating and sustaining this type of citizens' academy vary from community to community, Morse has described three broad goals which he found present in most programs: knowledge, involvement, and public relations. By attending this type of civic activity, participants attain a close-up look at how services and programs are carried out. Both participants and staff members have the chance to learn from one another about local concerns and the realities of governmental operations. In addition, participants may choose to become more involved in civic affairs and opportunities may occur for greater understandings between community members and officials (Morse, 2021a).

One of the ten citizen academies highlighted by Morse (2021b) and presented as a "case study" was established as a collaboration between the City of Durham and Durham County in North Carolina in 2003. They named their program "the Durham Neighborhood College" (DNC). The program has been held annually each fall for 30 residents. It was designed to permit Durham citizens to learn about governmental services, community development, and both governments' budget processes. Only Durham area residents are eligible to apply, and they must submit an application, which is used to verify residency and determine if any property or vehicle taxes are owed. Once cleared, applicants are selected to make up a class that represents a diversity of geographic residencies within Durham. The City and County of Durham budget $6,000 for each program, split evenly between the two governments." Each applicant must pay a registration fee of $30 to support the program, but some scholarships are available. A further demonstration of collaboration is exhibited through site selection for each session: the City and County equally divide the number of total sessions at each one's venues" (Morse, 2021b). In recent years, the program has been reduced from nine to seven fall evenings for two and a half hour classes and its website states that "area high school students ages 15 and up as well as Latino residents are encouraged to apply" (DNC, 2021). In addition, a light meal is served prior to the start of each class. Due to the impact of COVID-19, Durham Neighborhood College was not offered in 2021. The PowerPoints used in presentations at each of the classes held in 2019 are available online at https://durhamnc.gov/3929/Durham-Neighborhood-College-2019.

Advantages of CPAs

In recent years, the advent of police body worn cameras and citizen carried cell phone cameras have shed new light on police behavior in the streets, but there are many parts of the criminal justice system that remain hidden. According to the optimistic opinion of Aryani and his associates (2000), "citizen police academies represent a vital part of community-oriented policing. CPAs keep the public involved by making them part of the police family. . . [and] provide a productive outlet for the mutual sharing of information and concerns in order to further common goals of communities and law enforcement agencies" (p. 21). Generally, citizen academies provide: (1) citizens a better understanding of how their police department works; and (2) the graduates interested in continuing their involvement in police related activities may have the option of joining various law enforcement-related volunteer programs such as: the Citizen Police Academy Alumni Association, Citizens on Patrol, Community Emergency Response Team (CERT), Neighborhood Watch, and Volunteers in Police Service.

In one study of the effect of a citizen police academy in a large city in Texas, 25 graduates (experimental subjects) and 30 students entering the program (the control group) were compared. Overall, compared to the controls, the experimental group held more positive opinions of and demonstrated higher levels of satisfaction with the police department in all areas, including response to specific neighborhood problems, overall performance at combating and preventing crime, police image, and police services. The graduates also appeared to have a broader understanding of police work, as well as a greater appreciation and respect for officers. Furthermore, they reported significantly higher levels of involvement in crime-prevention efforts than the comparative control group (Stone & Champeny, 2001). Positive findings were also obtained in a study involving the attitudes of 48 attendees who completed a 12-week/36-hour program at a sheriff's department in the state of Michigan. Based on the analysis of pre and post-test responses, this study found that this particular citizen police academy had a positive impact on the attendees' attitudes towards the police, and their understanding of police operations, crime, and quality-of-life issues in their community (Breen & Johnson, 2007). The attendees gained a realistic overview of police work and saw firsthand that the agency's "deputies did not have enough time to perform preventive/proactive types of police work" (Breen & Johnson, 2007, p. 261). On the other hand, the authors of this study pointed out that their "sample population was quite homogeneous in the context of race and the fact that the attendees were primarily in support of the police prior to their CPA experience" (Breen & Johnson, 2007, p. 262). There were also positive outcomes in a study that compared attitudes using pre- and post-tests in a comparison involving citizen academies in two different cities (Brewster et al., 2005).

Interested citizens may bring into an academy's classroom a wealth of knowledge about their community and the problems in their neighborhoods. It is then up to agency personnel whether or not to listen and respond to their firsthand concerns. Moreover, the expression of concerns may extend to issues beyond the control of local police. This is a pivotal moment in the history of policing. Many citizens are concerned about not only local matters, but also the threats of terrorism, the coronavirus pandemic, and even the global effects of climate change. Some participants may want to address these larger issues as well as bring about more accountability in police conduct. Any discussions centered on these types of matters will extend the content of most contemporary academy curriculums.

Another advantage applies to the planning of CPAs and the use of online materials. For example, the Institute for Local Government (ILG) in Sacramento, California, founded in 1955, has posted a 14-page "Resource List of Citizen and Leadership Academies." It contains agency links under the following headings: City Citizen Academies; County Citizens Academies; Police, Sherriff, and Criminal Justice Citizens Academy; County Sheriff and Criminal Justice Citizen Academies; Community Non-Profit Leadership Academies; Other Leadership Programs (see ILG, 2021). In addition, the Florida League of Cities, Inc., based in Tallahassee, has posted a 27-page guide involving various Florida citizen academies. Several documents, useful for organizing a CPA are included in the guide as well as brief reviews of the programs in Delray Beach, Gainesville, Lakeland, Lauderdale Lakes, Port Orange and Sanford (see Florida League, 2018). In addition, a 44-page curriculum guide is available entitled "American Police Officer: A Course in Character" (see Junior Police Academy, 2021).

Furthermore, from the standpoint of the concerned police departments it is possible that greater cooperation among law enforcement agencies may be achieved. This could occur when a particular CPA coordinator invites neighboring agencies to participate in or co-sponsor a citizen's academy. New mutual aid agreements concerning emergencies or other matters may be entered into in order to advance the development of positive relationships.

The theory of the "social contract" is the view that individuals' moral and/or political obligations are dependent upon a contract or agreement among them to form the society in which they live. Thomas Hobbes, John Locke, and Jean-Jacques Rousseau are its best-known proponents. The most classic American example of this theory in actual practice was the self-government established by the Pilgrims in The Mayflower Compact of 1620. John Kleinig, one of the world's leading experts on ethics and police education, has addressed many of the issues involved in the teaching of police ethics to not only the police but also the wisdom of sharing its ethical insights with the general public. He points out that there is a strong reason for engaging the public in this topic. Since the public has delegated its law enforcement and peacekeeping functions to police authorities, "it will be important for the citizenry to have a 'feel' for 'the police role'—for the kinds of decisions that police have to make and the circumstances under which they are made" (Kleinig, 1990, p. 6). In other words, the public's interest in-keeping safe, should include concern about the nature and extent of the exercise of police power. Kleinig (1990) indicates that this concern is based on "the dominant theory of police authority, that authority is vested ultimately in the citizenry and has been 'contracted' to police in return for the protection of rights, maintenance of order, and whatever other functions are deemed to belong to the police" (p. 6). A useful forum for sharing knowledge about various aspects of police ethical decision-making is the CPA. It would be of benefit to the public to learn more about their police force at CPA sessions and for the police to provide the public "with a better understanding of what might reasonably be expected of police by way of results and regulative constraints" (Kleinig, 1990, p. 6).

Disadvantages of CPAs

The full potential of CPAs for instilling greater community safety has not yet been realized. While it is now surely recognized that everyone has a role to play in safeguarding themselves, their family members, and their community, the temptation and reality of having citizen academies serve primarily as agency showplaces has been greatly in evidence for more than 30 years. When the public relations aspects are overplayed, participants will fail to learn about the details involving the inability of the criminal justice system to contend with crime and the many ways private citizens may engage in crime prevention activities.

The planning for each academy, such as curriculum preparation and the screening of applicants, may detract from the time and resources devoted to essential police work. In some instances, liability considerations may limit or eliminate such high-interest activities as firearms instruction and ride-a-long fieldtrips. Although the expenditures needed to maintain a citizen police academy are generally quite minimal, the cost for delivering actual instruction may need to consider personnel overtime expenses. Individual attention is usually needed for each student receiving first-time firing range instruction.

Prior to the coronavirus pandemic, the programs only reached a small number of residents and local academies were only being held once or twice a year. The use and availability of Zoom technology has demonstrated that all sessions of a citizen academy need not be held in-person. Zoom technology has made it possible to reach more than 30 attendees at a time. In addition, several studies conducted on CPAs have referred to the fact that there has been little diversity among the attendees (e.g., see Bonello & Schafer, 2002; Breen & Johnson, 2007). The new technology may make it possible to reach out to those individuals who may have been overlooked in the past and may, in fact, have been critical of police practices.

Police departments have created alumni groups to address the need to maintain citizen interest after the academy ends. However, this is difficult unless follow-up activities are planned. A few months after completing the academy, some participants may be disappointed if all they have to show for their efforts are a cap or T-shirt, a certificate, and memories. Consequently, police departments or other agencies planning citizen academies will need to develop meaningful activities after the academy has ended and this will incur a continuation of personnel costs.

Academies could also turn into victims of their own success. Participants could become so overzealous in their concern for justice that they engage in conduct that undermines departmental policies and programs, for example, establishing a vigilante-type neighborhood patrol organization or the possibility that a graduate will use the information in some other inappropriate manner. Another area of concern is the number of requests for crime prevention speakers and home and business security surveys that academy participation may generate. While this is not a disadvantage, per se, such requests could overburden officers by increasing their workloads. Of course, an agency may lack the necessary financial and/or personnel resources to sponsor an academy in the first place (Maffe & Burke, 1999).

It has been recommended that citizen academy "sessions should focus on being as interactive and hands-on as possible. Usually, city employees make the presentations and/or demonstrate equipment. The residents enjoy seeing the pride that employees take in their daily tasks, their equipment and work areas. However, it is also impressive to the residents when commissioners and top administrators attend the sessions each week" (Florida League, 2018, p. 8). Clearly, such arrangements require planning and must involve officials making the necessary time commitments in their weekly schedules.

The issue of vigilantism arose in the city of Chicago when ICE sought to schedule a citizen's academy in order to address the law enforcement role of ICE officers and included such hands-on activities as firearms familiarization and arrest tactics in its initial announcement to all news media outlets. Chicago had been touted as a "sanctuary city" for undocumented persons and various community leaders and elected public officials appeared to have been "blindsided" by the announcement. The case illustrates the need for researching potential issues of local concern prior to such announcements, especially when the offering of an academy is being contemplated by a federal law enforcement agency around a highly politicized issue, such as immigration.

Although these disadvantages are quite real and there may exist a few agency personnel who may be resistant to the idea of sharing information or enlisting the aid of citizens in the prevention of crime, the weight of the arguments appear to favor the use of citizen academies (see Cohn, 1996; Blackwood, 1994; Breen & Johnson, 2007; Brewster et al., 2005; Stone & Champeny, 2001). Moreover, the availability and assistance of already trained and screened volunteer police (auxiliary or reserve) can help eliminate several of the foregoing disadvantages.

Overcoming the Disadvantages of CPAs

The Lansing (Michigan) Police Department held its first citizen's academy in the spring of 1996. Since then, they have usually held two CPA sessions each year. A Lansing police officer recruited the initial academy class from a group of "Neighborhood Watch" coordinators. Based on a survey of Lansing's program, Bonello and Schafer (2002) concluded: "Reaching out to citizens who are distrustful or skeptical of law enforcement and inviting them to take a closer look at police operations can prove intimidating and even unpleasant, but the rewards for doing so may be worth the effort. For agencies hoping to strengthen community alliances, the challenge for the future is to begin including a broader range of the public in their citizen police academy programs. Every department can identify groups within their community with which they have a history of misunderstandings and conflict. Departments should seek to draw academy participants from this portion of the community." The Lansing Police Department has begun to take steps to recruit their detractors to join the CPA. This agency has provided CPA applications to individuals who have contacted their Internal Affairs Unit about minor complaints or misunderstandings and discussed the CPA on talk radio shows that have a large minority audience. In addition, greater participation in CPAs may be achieved by conducting a "mini-academy" for leaders in minority communities and encouraging them to invite others to attend the full CPA. Other steps include hosting a youth academy for at-risk teenagers and encouraging officers to promote the CPA while on patrol (Bonello & Schafer, 2002).

The time commitments required can be a huge obstacle for agencies interested in holding a CPA. The problem of prioritizing police operations and the delivery of services can certainly weigh heavily on departmental administrators (see Breen & Johnson, 2007, p. 261). Yet, hundreds of police agencies across the United States continue to invest in the time and energy to organize them. However, the weight of the evidence shows that the reach of these classes is limited. Citizen police academies can now be presented, at least in part, using Zoom in order to reach ever-greater numbers of citizens. Such a mode of instruction can bring informative safety information to the masses and encourage police–citizen cooperation. On the other hand, the hybrid academy courses will likely need more personnel resources and some monitoring to ensure that confidential police codes and other critical "insider" information are not shared. Agencies with limited resources should be able to offer this new format by using their limited resources to first train and certify classes of citizen volunteer police instructors who would then, in turn, become qualified to offer the citizen academy courses to the public in any format.

Moreover, since graduates of the proposed instruction certification program are expected to become future teachers of citizen police academies, concern about follow-up activities should be diminished. If a "train the trainer" course (for auxiliary or reserve police) is substituted for just one or two of the traditional annual citizen academies, the reach of the citizen academies may be multiplied. Furthermore, by offering this instructional training to existing members of volunteer police units, police departments will be able to maintain close supervision over the content that will be delivered. In particular, there should now be sufficient class time during academy sessions to share advanced concepts and procedures involving crime prevention. Major reforms on a society-wide scale are needed to deal with the root causes of crime, but in the meantime individuals can make a start by making their homes secure and then their neighborhoods (see Lee, 1974, pp. 204–209).

The qualified volunteer police instructors should be able to extend the reach of the existing academies in such a way, that a new term, such as the "Community Police Academy" may come into usage. This term emphasizes the importance of people working together for the betterment of the community and seems to be a more accurate designation for the new and broader type of program envisioned here. The Pasadena Police Department changed the name from "Citizen Police Academy" to "Community Police Academy" in 2017 after the implementation of a Spanish language format of the course. According to Yadira Sanchez (2021), the program's coordinator, "the word 'Citizen' caused some confusion amongst interested participants as to the requirements for joining the class, therefore, in an effort to be more inclusive, the department decided to change the name to Community Police Academy."

By converting just one or two existing citizen police academies into "train the trainer" courses for qualifying volunteer police officers, many of the current disadvantages would be reduced. For example, the newly certified volunteer instructors would be highly motivated to concentrate on crime prevention and other relevant contemporary topics and less likely to overemphasize public relations. In addition, their services can be used to develop new curriculum, expanding and revising current materials for diverse populations. They could also serve to augment the department's personnel resources needed for conducting youth academies, sponsoring Law Enforcement Explorer Units, leading agency tours, and providing security surveys for more homes and businesses. Moreover, the training provided to these auxiliary or reserve police officers could include the qualifications necessary to handle non-moving traffic violations and mental health crises. By prioritizing these types of activities and initiatives, instead of solely relying on full-time LEOs, communities may improve overall public safety, promote racial justice, protect vulnerable community members, and allocate public resources more efficiently. In time, even the root causes associated with crime might be addressed.

Conclusion

In the United States, at the start of the 20th century, the proliferation of police sponsored junior police training and recreational programming served as the forerunners to the formation of the later adult program known as the Citizen Police Academy (CPA). Decades later, the Police Night School was established by the United Kingdom's Devon and Cornwall

Constabulary in 1977. In 1985, the Orlando (Florida) Police Department borrowed the night school idea and established the first adult CPA in the United States. Subsequently, the practice became a regular and featured program for educating citizens about police work throughout the nation (Ferguson, 1985).

Currently, some of the graduates of CPAs are able to volunteer their services to police agencies and they can join alumni groups in order to engage in further service-related activities. If police departments are interested in reaching out to more community members, a program involving certifying volunteer police to instruct "Community Police Academies" is recommended. "Agencies need to improve relationships with those citizens who mistrust or feel alienated from their police, which is especially important if an agency hopes to succeed in carrying out community policing" (Bonello & Schafer, 2002, p. 23).

Citizen Police Academies (CPAs) are an educational and informative program that allows citizens the opportunity to learn about the issues that face law enforcement efforts in their community. The programs help local residents better understand police work in their community, and it is also thought that they promote stronger ties between communities and their respective police agencies. Most CPA programs do not train individuals to be reserve or auxiliary police officers, but to produce better informed citizens. Auxiliary and reserve units pre-date by many years the existence of the CPAs. Thus far, their services with respect to expanding or making available CPAs in any format have gone unused. In today's climate of widespread dissatisfaction with police due to incidents of overt police violence directed at minority group members, especially Black individuals, CPAs could provide a forum in which community members and police officers are able to meet with one another to share mutual concerns. In such a setting, it may be possible to forge stronger citizen–police relationships and open new lines of communication. Information from citizens about crime problems and suspects are necessary in order to reduce crime. "CPAs can further community policing goals by increasing understanding, trust, and dialogue with members of the community who historically have been at odds with the police" (Bonello & Schafer, 2002, p. 23).

Well planned CPAs may expand community-based crime prevention efforts and offer police departments the opportunity to learn about the concerns of their communities (Breen & Johnson, 2007; Brewster et al., 2005). On the other hand, if CPAs are organized merely to provide a one-sided image-building view of local police operations, opportunities will be lost to enlist members of the public as concerned volunteers as well as future reserves and auxiliaries. Significantly, more than a dozen years prior to the introduction of the inaugural CPA course by the Orlando Police Department, Shidel and Komara (1974) pointed out that "a police department can become more effective, at a nominal cost, by instituting an auxiliary police force. A well-managed, well-trained auxiliary unit can greatly assist an already burdened police department" (p. 55). These volunteers, in turn, can be trained to reach a greater segment of the citizenry with important information about crime control as instructors and coordinators for CPAs.

During the summer of 2020, the murders of George Floyd, Breonna Taylor, and too many other Black Americans sparked a national dialogue around the failings of the US criminal justice system. People nationwide joined together to protest police violence, demanding local governments examine police operations and seek out new approaches to public safety and justice. One way to make significant changes in policing practices is to harness the spirit and energies of concerned community members in order to improve overall public safety.

This chapter has presented the origins of citizen police academies and descriptions of the key components of contemporary academy programs, including their inherent strengths and weaknesses. Citizen Police Academies are unique because they provide an opportunity for average citizens to look inside the organization of a traditionally closed institution in order to gain a first-hand look at the activities and operations of law enforcement agencies. Agencies at the local, state, and federal levels currently present their own versions of citizen academies. However, thus far, the academies have been primarily focused on better image building. This chapter has also shown how these programs can be transformed so that existing resources can be used to qualify auxiliaries and reserves in order to extend the number and reach of CPAs. In this way, many more members of the public will be able to actually engage in crime prevention initiatives and ultimately contribute to the development of new police training and operational strategies. The coronavirus is changing everyday life in the United States. If public education programs, such as citizen academies, are to advance community safety, a new mode of delivery is vital.

More than 85 years ago, George H. Brereton, the undersheriff of the county of San Diego, California, addressed the importance of law enforcement training for police, declaring: "There is no branch of public service where a man is so dependent upon his own initiative and resources as in the police department. When the police officer is sent out on patrol he must be ready to meet practically any situation at a moment's notice. He does not have anyone at hand to assist or advise him and he must often make an immediate decision which may bring discredit upon himself or upon the department" (Brereton, 1935, p. 248). The same sentiments can apply to active members of the public. In today's complex world, the need for ordinary citizens to learn as much practical law as possible has never been greater.

A consistent goal indicated by the CPAs was for graduates to share knowledge gained with others. The next chapter addresses the development of the Law-Related Education (LRE) movement for all age groups. As police and the public encounter individuals with wide ranging problems, this type of education can prove to be invaluable. It is also in keeping with the idea that police business is everybody's business (see Greenberg, 2021).

Notes

1 Taking place within the first two decades of the 20th century, these youth programs were sponsored mainly by local police departments or schools. A few of the first "junior" or "boy police" programs were established in Berkeley, California; Council Bluffs, Iowa; Cincinnati, Ohio; and New York City. The programs usually included instruction in good citizenship and offered recreational opportunities. Subsequently, safety concerns about automobile traffic gave rise to the first junior school safety patrols. For example, the City of Berkeley Junior Police evolved into one of the nation's first junior traffic patrols. These patrols typically involved older elementary school children who carried signs to stop traffic in order to safely escort classmates crossing streets. A few of the earliest safety patrols were located in Berkeley; Newark, New Jersey; and Milwaukee, Wisconsin (Greenberg, 2008).

2 Current anecdotal information about CPAs can be readily obtained by reviewing the hundreds of CPA-based websites on the internet. While such websites are primarily concerned with recruiting future attendees for the next CPA session, they also contain useful content regarding program length, purposes, and eligibility requirements.

3 According to a report that used data from the Bureau of Justice Statistics' (BJS) 2013 Census of Law Enforcement Training Academies, "Excluding field training, basic training programs lasted an average of about 840 hours, or 21 weeks. Major training areas included operations (an average of 213 hours per recruit); firearms, self-defense, and use of force (168 hours); self-improvement

(89 hours); and legal education (86 hours). Nearly all academies required basic training on community policing, with an average of more than 40 hours of instruction per recruit. Nearly all basic training programs addressed social issues such as domestic violence (an average of 13 hours per recruit) and mental illness (10 hours)" (Reaves, 2016, p. 1).

4 "An important Major Cities Chiefs Association (MCCA) strategic goal is to develop current and future leaders. MCCA has developed a leadership program aimed at high-level police executives who have a strong desire to become a police chief or sheriff. The Police Executive Leadership Institute (PELI) has completed seven classes, comprised of 135 participants. Nearly one third have become Police Chiefs in MCCA and other law enforcement agencies" (PELI Classes, 2021).

5 For a robust list of actual and potential roles for volunteers in police work see Appendix C in Martin Greenberg's *Everyone a Sheriff: The Democratization of Crime Prevention in America* (Lexington Books, 2021).

6 "In January 1938, Ponca City's airport was sod, a half-mile square. Later that year, a 3,600-foot concrete runway opened. The United States Army Air Forces took over the facility in the summer of 1941 and used it as part of the British Flying Training School Program until 1944. Airline service to Ponca City began in the late 1920s, with the final carrier in 2006" (McKinley, 2021).

7 The other minimum qualifications and a comprehensive list of responsibilities for the part-time reserve officer position at the Tampa Airport can be found at: https://www.tampaairport.com/sites/default/master/files/Reserve%20officer%20position%20overview.pdf

8 In 2002, the Department of Homeland Security (DHS) was created through the integration of all or part of 22 different federal departments and agencies into a unified, integrated Department. DHS's primary tool for involving the US population in terrorism prevention efforts has been the "If You See Something, Say Something®" campaign. Its purpose is to educate the American public about how to recognize and report the signs of suspicious activity. In order to reach everyone, this message has been translated into ten languages. Various campaign outreach materials have been developed for state, local, tribal, territorial, and private sector parties and organizations. The campaign offers this package of pre-developed translated materials to provide meaningful access for individuals with limited English proficiency. Since June 2021, these materials have become available at the following website page: https://www.dhs.gov/publication/seesay-translated-materials. Moreover, DHS has begun posting a huge number of relevant publications under 22 categories dating from the present time with some dating back to the year 2006. A selection of these categories are: border security; critical infrastructure security; cybersecurity; economic security; election security; human trafficking; science and technology; and transportation security. The DHS Publication Library contains guidance and policy papers, reports, strategies, program regulations, guidelines, brochures and more. It can be accessed and searched online at: https://www.dhs.gov/publications. In addition, a 96-second YouTube video prepared by the ICE Office of Public Affairs about the HSI Tampa Citizens Academy and posted on February 19, 2019, can be viewed at https://www.youtube.com/watch?v=tANH3zyXZzI.

9 According to an undated FBI 5-page document posted on the internet by the ACLU (2021), "In 1993, the Phoenix Division began a Citizens' Academy to develop and/or enhance the relationship between the FBI and the citizens of Phoenix. They solicited the input of various community leaders and visited local police agencies to discuss the ongoing program" (ACLU, 2021). In addition, the web page of the FBI Phoenix Citizens Academy Alumni Association (FBIPCAAA), a nonprofit organization separate and apart from the FBI, states that the "FBI Phoenix Citizens Academy program was launched in 1993 at the FBI's Phoenix Division by then-Special Agent in Charge (SAC) Jim Ahearn. Ahearn decided on the "Citizens Academy" model based on his experience with a local police agency with the hope of strengthening the field office's relationship with the community. Since inception, over 1,800 community, civic business, labor, media, minority, law enforcement, government, and religious leaders in Arizona have been educated about federal law enforcement issues and challenges. Nationally, over 10,000 citizens have participated in Citizens Academies offered at Field Offices across the United States and at the FBI Academy Quantico, VA" (FBIPCAAA, 2019).

10 Like many law enforcement agencies in the south, southwestern, and western sections of the United States, the Martin County Sheriff's Office includes an active "Reserve Unit." It comprises volunteer deputy sheriffs who assist and augment full-time sworn deputies. Reserve deputies are dedicated adult members of the community who are trained to act in a limited capacity as a deputy sheriff. Their duties include: assisting uniform patrol officers during regular shift patrol; helping specialized units (such as Community Policing, the Marine Unit, Traffic Enforcement Unit,

Community Operations); and working at county athletic events. The reserve deputies are certified through the Florida Department of Law Enforcement (FDLE) Criminal Justice Standards and Training Commission (CJSTC) and have completed a shortened version of the police academy. They receive ongoing training in all aspects of law enforcement functions and work alongside full-time sworn deputies. They wear the same uniform and drive the same vehicles as full-time sworn deputies (Martin County, 2021b).

11 The 178-page book, *The Citizens Academy Handbook: Building Capacity for Local Civic Engagement*, was co-authored by Ricardo S. Morse, Sabrina M. Willard, and Michelle Y. Holder and published in 2017; and is priced at $45. It provides practical guidance for the staff that runs citizens academies as well as insights to interested readers and public officials who are considering starting such a program. Its "pages are filled with nuts-and-bolts advice on all aspects of program planning and delivery, profiles of successful programs, sample materials, and spotlights on innovative practices" (Morse, 2021c).

References

ACLU. (2021). *Federal bureau of investigation: FBI citizens' academy*. Retrieved September 4, 2021, from https://www.aclu.org/sites/default/files/field_document/ACLURM000534.pdf

Aryani, G. A., Garrett, T. D., & Alsabrook, C. L. (2000). The citizen police academy. *The FBI Law Enforcement Bulletin*, *69*(5), 16–21.

Blackwood, B. (1994). Citizen police academies. *TELEMASP Monthly Bulletin*, *1*(2), 1–8. Retrieved May 4, 2009, from http://www.lemitonline.org/telemasp/Pdf/volume%201/vol1no2.pdf

Bonello, E. M., & Schafer, J. A. (2002). Citizen police academies: Do they just entertain. *FBI Law Enforcement Bulletin*, *71*(11), 19–23.

Breen, M. E., & Johnson, B. R. (2007). Citizen police academies: An analysis of enhanced police–community relations among citizen attendees. *The Police Journal: Theory, Practice and Principles*, *80*(3), 246–266.

Brereton, G. H. (1935). Police training-Its needs and problems. *Journal of Criminal Law & Criminology*, *26*(2), 247–254. Retrieved August 30, 2021, from https://scholarlycommons.law.northwestern.edu/cgi/viewcontent.cgi?article=2557&conte xt=jclc

Brewster, J., Stoloff, M., & Sanders, N. (2005). Effectiveness of citizen police academies in changing the attitudes, beliefs, and behavior of citizen participants. *The American Journal of Criminal Justice*, *30*(1), 21–34.

Brichford, M. (1983). *A brief history of the University of Illinois*. Retrieved September 2, 2021, from https://archives.library.illinois.edu/features/history.php

Buffalo Grove. (2012). *Demographics*. Retrieved May 18, 2012, from http://www.vbg.org/index.aspx?nid=142

Buffalo Grove. (2021). *Citizen police academy*. Retrieved September 1, 2021, from https://www.vbg.org/your_government/village_services/police_services/citizen_police_a cademy.php

Burnett, K. J. (2019, Spring). *Federal bureau of investigation citizens academy training manual*. Master of Science in Criminal Justice Project, California State University, Sacramento. Retrieved September 4, 2021, from https://scholarworks.calstate.edu/downloads/7w62f8501

Cechini, H. (2021, April 7). *Del. Dept. of Corrections launching citizens' academy, aim for transparency*. Retrieved September 5, 2021, from https://www.wmdt.com/2021/04/del- dept-of-corrections-launching-citizens-academy-aim-for-transparency/

Cohn, E. G. (1996). The citizen police academy: A recipe for improving police-community relations. *Journal of Criminal Justice, 24*(3), 265–271.

DDOC. (2021a). *DOC Citizens Academy to give residents a look inside correctional system*. https://www.coastalpoint.com/news/police_fire/doc-citizens-academy-to-give-residents-a-look-inside-cor rectional-system/article_3e3bf75e-90c1–11eb-b3d1-af337b4146fe.html

DDOC. (2021b). *Citizens academy to give insider perspective of correctional system*. Retrieved September 5, 2021, from https://www.capegazette.com/article/citizens-academy-give-insider-perspec tive-correctional-system/226026

DHS. (2021, August 13). *Summary of terrorism threat to the U.S. Homeland.* Retrieved September 5, 2021, from https://www.dhs.gov/ntas/advisory/national-terrorism-advisory-system-bulletin-august-13-2021
DNC. (2021). *Durham neighborhood college.* Retrieved September 4, 2021, from https://durhamnc.gov/1159/Durham-Neighborhood-College
DOJ. (2021). *Justice department announces first federal agents to use body-worn cameras.* Department of Justice, Office of Public Affairs, Press Release Number: 21–821.
Duckworth, T. (2020, July 17). Duckworth responds to ICE's Citizens Academy pilot program in Chicago. *Press Release.* Retrieved September 12, 2021, from https://www.duckworth.senate.gov/news/press-releases/duckworth-responds-to-ices- citizens-academy-pilot-program-in-Chicago
FBI. (2021a). *About: Community outreach.* Retrieved September 3, 2021, from https://www.fbi.gov/about/community-outreach#Citizens-Academies
FBI. (2021b). *Community outreach: Community awareness presentation.* Retrieved September 4, 2021, from https://www.fbi.gov/contact-us/field-offices/albany/community-outreach
FBIPCAAA. (2019). *FBI phoenix citizens academy alumni association.* Retrieved September 4, 2021, from https://www.fbipcaaa.org/FBI-Phoenix-Citizens-Academy
Ferguson, R. E. (1985). The citizen police academy. *FBI Law Enforcement Bulletin, 54*(9), 5–7.
Florida League. (2018, December). *A guide for creating a citizens' academy.* Retrieved September 6, 2021, from https://www.floridaleagueofcities.com/docs/default- source/civic-education/a-guide-for-creating-a-citizen%27s-academy-12- 2018.pdf?sfvrsn=4ce0dad5_0
Greenberg, M. A. (1977). Volunteer crime prevention program. *The Police Chief, 44*(4), 60–61.
Greenberg, M. A. (1985, April 22). The neighborhood police academy. *Law Enforcement News,* pp. 5 & 7.
Greenberg, M. A. (2008). A short history of junior police; *The Police Chief, 75*(4), 172–180.
Greenberg, M. A. (2015). *American volunteer police: Mobilizing for security.* CRC Press.
Greenberg, M. A. (2021). *Everyone a sheriff: The democratization of crime prevention in America.* Lexington Books.
Hauck, G. (2020, July 16–17). *ICE is holding a citizens academy in Chicago. Mayor, lawmakers say 'vigilantes' aren't welcome.* Retrieved September 10, 2021, from https://www.usatoday.com/story/news/nation/2020/07/16/chicago-ice-citizen-academy- mayor-says-vigilantes-not-welcome/5453758002/
Horton, J. (2021, May 18). *How US police training compares with the rest of the world.* Retrieved August 18, 2021, from https://www.bbc.com/news/world-us-canada-56834733
ICE. (2016, April 13). *Puerto Rico community leaders graduate from third nationwide HSI- sponsored citizens academy.* Retrieved September 12, 2021, from https://www.ice.gov/news/releases/puerto-rico-community-leaders-graduate-third- nationwide-hsi-sponsored-citizens
ICE. (2021a). *History of ICE.* Retrieved September 4, 2021, from https://www.ice.gov/history
ICE. (2021b). *Outreach programs.* Retrieved September 4, 2021, from https://www.ice.gov/outreach-programs
ICE. (2021c). *Citizens academy.* Retrieved September 4, 2021, from https://www.ice.gov/outreach-programs/citizens-academy#
ICJTR. (2021). *Not enough training.* Retrieved August 28, 2021, from https://www.trainingreform.org/not-enough-training
ILG. (2021). *Resource list of citizen and leadership academies* (Updated as of 2/12/2015). https://www.ca-ilg.org/sites/main/files/file- attachments/resources_list_of_citizens_and_leadership_academies_2014_2.pdf?1423777 391
Jordan, W. T. (2000). Citizen police academies: Community policing or community politics? *American Journal of Criminal Justice, 25*(1), 93–105.
Junior Police Academy. (2021). *American police officer: A course in character.* Retrieved September 12, 2021, from https://juniorpoliceacademy.dropmark.com/343848/7839777
Kleinig, J. (1990). Teaching and learning police ethics; Competing and complimentary approaches. *Journal of Criminal Justice, 18*(1), 1–18.

Lee, A. (1974). *Crime-free: How to protect your property and yourself.* Baltimore, MD; Penguin Books.
LESB. (2020, December 3). *Hawaii law enforcement standards board law enforcement standards board meeting minutes.* Retrieved September 3, 2021, from https://ag.hawaii.gov/wp-content/uploads/2021/05/LESB-Minutes-120320.pdf
LESB. (2021, April 9). *Hawaii law enforcement standards board meeting minutes.* Retrieved September 3, 2021, from https://ag.hawaii.gov/wp- content/uploads/2021/05/Unapproved-Draft-Minutes-for-Meeting-040921.pdf
Maffe, S. R., & Burke, T. W. (1999). Citizen police academies. *Law and Order, 47*(10), 77–80.
Malagón, E. (2020, September 3). ICE postpones controversial 'citizens academy' in Chicago. *Chicago Sun Times.* Retrieved September 12, 2021, from https://chicago.suntimes.com/2020/9/3/21421321/chicago-immigration-ice-citizens- academy-postponed
Martin County. (2021a). *Citizen's academy.* Retrieved September 5, 2021, from https://www.mcsofl.org/164/Citizens-Academy
Martin County. (2021b). *Reserve unit.* Retrieved September 5, 2021, from https://www.mcsofl.org/171/Reserve-Unit
McFarland, C. (2010). *State of America's cities survey on jobs and the economy.* National League of Cities, Center for Research and Innovation.
McKinley, T. (2021, August 31). *Special report: State of the city.* Retrieved September 2, 2021, from https://poncacitymonthly.com/articles/special-report-state-of-the-city/9064/
Mobile PD. (2021a). *Junior police academy.* Retrieved September 8, 2021, from https://www.mobilepd.org/juniorpoliceacademy/
Mobile PD. (2021b). *Community.* Retrieved September 8, 2021, from https://www.mobilepd.org/community/
Morse, R. S. (2021a). *About citizens academies.* Retrieved September 3, 2021, from https://www.sog.unc.edu/resources/microsites/citizens-academies/about-citizens- academies
Morse, R. S. (2021b). *Citizen academies: City-county of Durham, NC.* Retrieved September 4, 2021, from https://www.sog.unc.edu/resources/microsites/citizens-academies/city-county- durham-nc
Morse, R. S. (2021c). *The citizens academy handbook: Building capacity for local civic engagement.* Retrieved September 15, 2021, from https://www.sog.unc.edu/publications/books/citizens-academy-handbook-building- capacity-local-civic-engagement
MWAA. (2021). *MWAA history and facts.* Retrieved September 8, 2021, from https://www.mwaa.com/about-authority/mwaa-history-and-facts
MWAAPD. (2020). *Airport community police academy.* Retrieved September 8, 2021, from https://www.mwaa.com/airport-community-police-academy
Nexstar Media Inc. (2021, July 3). *Albany FBI seeks citizens academy nominees.* Retrieved September 4, 2021, from https://www.news10.com/news/albany-county/albany-fbi-seeks-citizens-academy-nominees/
Organized Communities. (2021). *Organized communities against deportations, immigrant defense project, and the center for constitutional rights v. United States immigration and customs enforcement.* US District Court, Northern District of Illinois. CASE NO. 1:21-cv-02519; filed May 11, 2021. Retrieved September 11, 2021, from https://ccrjustice.org/sites/default/files/attach/2021/05/ICE_Citizens_Academy_FOIA_C omplaint_051121.pdf
Pasadena CPA. (2013). *Citizen police academy.* Retrieved September 26, 2013, from http://www.ci.pasadena.ca.us/police/citizen_police_academy/
Pasadena Facts. (2014). Retrieved January 22, 2014, from http://www.ci.pasadena.ca.us/Pasadena_Facts_and_Statistics/
Pasadena PD. (2021). *Community police academy.* Retrieved September 1, 2021, from https://www.cityofpasadena.net/police/divisions-and-sections/community-relations/community-outreach/community-police-academy/
Pauley, J. (2020, June 18). *Civilian police academy overview: Class #52.* Retrieved September 2, 2021, from https://www.eastmountairy.org/news/civilian-police-academy-overview- class-52

PELI Classes. (2021). *PELI classes*. Retrieved August 30, 2021, from https://majorcitieschiefs.com/police-executive-leadership-institute/
Pilcher, J. (2015, July 7). *5 Surprising things I learned about the FBI*. Retrieved September 14, 2021, from https://www.cincinnati.com/story/news/2015/07/06/surprising-things-learned- fbi/29761911/
Ponca City. (2021). *Citizens police academy*. Retrieved September 2, 2021, from http://www.poncacityok.gov/193/Citizen-Police-Academy
PPD. (2021). *About the department*. Retrieved September 2, 2021, from http://www.phillypolice.com/about/index.html
Projects. (2021). *Projects: Tampa international airport*. Retrieved September 6, 2021, from https://www.airport-technology.com/projects/tampa-international-airport/
PTI. (2021a). *About*. Retrieved September 2, 2021, from http://pti.illinois.edu/about/index.html
PTI. (2021b). *Training*. Retrieved September 2, 2021, from http://pti.illinois.edu/training/index.html
PTI. (2021c). *Citizen police academy*. Retrieved September 2, 2021, from http://pti.illinois.edu/community/citizen-police-academy.html
Ravina, R. (2016, August 11). *Philadelphia police department to offer civilian police academy*. Retrieved September 2, 2021, from https://www.montgomerynews.com/roxreview/news/philadelphia-police-department-to-offer-civilian-police-academy/article_9c478af4-d662-5680–9192–29a9b9a70484.html
Reaves, B. A. (2016, July). *State and local law enforcement training academies, 2013*. U.S. Department of Justice, Office of Justice Programs, Bureau of Justice Statistics Bulletin. Retrieved August 28, 2021, from https://bjs.ojp.gov/content/pub/pdf/slleta13.pdf
Renshaw, J., & Wolfe, J. (2021, June 15). *U.S. lays out plan to confront white supremacist violence*. Retrieved September 5, 2021, from https://www.reuters.com/world/us/biden-administration-unveils-plan-tackle-domestic-terrorism-2021-06-15/
Sanchez, Y. (2021, September 9). *Yadira Sanchez, program coordinator, Pasadena police department, community relations section*. Personal communication.
Saylor, A. L. (2021, September 1). *Alan L. Saylor, senior officer, Univ. of Kentucky PD*. Personal communication.
Sherman, L. W. (1988). *Neighborhood safety; Crime file study guide*. U.S. Dept. of Justice, National Institute of Justice. Retrieved September 6, 2021, from https://babel.hathitrust.org/cgi/pt?id=mdp.39015043702912&view=1up&seq=1
Shidel, T. J., & Komara, D. F. (1974). Orientation and training programs for auxiliary police. *The Police Chief*, *41*(2), 55–58.
St. Louis County DJS. (2019). *St. Louis county department of justice services 2019 annual report*. Retrieved September 1, 2021, from https://stlouiscountymo.gov/st-louis-county- departments/justice-services/annual-reports/2019-annual-report/
St. Louis County PD. (2021a). *Who we are*. Retrieved September 1, 2021, from https://www.stlouiscountypolice.com/who-we-are/
St. Louis County PD. (2021b). *Our history*. Retrieved September 1, 2021, from https://www.stlouiscountypolice.com/who-we-are/our-history/
St. Louis County PD. (2021c). *Citizens police academy*. Retrieved September 1, 2021, from https://www.stlouiscountypolice.com/citizen-resources/citizens-police-academy/
stateuniversity.com. (2021). *University of Kentucky*. Retrieved August 30, 2021, from https://www.stateuniversity.com/universities/KY/University_of_Kentucky.html
Stone, W. E., & Champeny, S. (2001). Assessing a citizen police academy. *Police Practice and Research*, *2*(3), 219–241.
TDOC. (2021). *Citizens' correctional academy*. Retrieved September 5, 2021, from https://www.tn.gov/correction/about-us/citizens-correctional-academy.html
TIAPD. (2019). *2019 Annual report Tampa international airport police department*. Retrieved September 6, 2021, from https://www.tampaairport.co https://www.tampaairport.com/sites/default/master/files/2019%20TPA%20Police%20An nual%20Report.pdf m/sites/default/master/files/2019%20TPA%20Police%20An nual%20Report.pdf

TIAPD. (2021a). *TIAPD citizen police academy*. Retrieved September 6, 2021, from https://www.tampaairport.com/tiapd-citizen-police-academy

TIAPD. (2021b). *TIAPD citizen ride-along program*. Retrieved September 6, 2021, from https://www.tampaairport.com/tiapd-citizen-ride-along-program

TIAPD. (2021c). *TIAPD reserve officer program*. Retrieved September 6, 2021, from https://www.tampaairport.com/reserve-officer

TPACPA@tampaairport.com. (2021). Personal communication. Retrieved September 13, 2021, from anonymous at TPACPA@tampaairport.com

UIUC History. (2021). *History of the Universities system*. Retrieved September 2, 2021, from https://www.uillinois.edu/president/history/history_of_the_university

UK Police Dept. (2021a). *About UKPD: History*. Retrieved August 31, 2021, from https://www.uky.edu/police/history

UK Police Dept. (2021b). *Citizens police academy*. Retrieved August 30, 2021, from https://www.uky.edu/police/citizens-police-academy-1

U.S. ex Rel. Standing Bear v. Crook, 25 F. Cas. 695, 5 Dill. 453 (D. Neb. 1879).

Yolo County DA. (2021). *Citizen's academy*. Retrieved September 8, 2021, from https://yoloda.org/progressive-programs/citizens-academy/

10

THE ROLE OF POLICE IN LAW-RELATED EDUCATION

Incidents in which police officers use overly aggressive arrest tactics or engage in outright misconduct should always be matters of critical importance and urgency, but it has been only in recent times that the media's omnipresence has become a key factor in generating police accountability reform efforts. Aided by the advent of cellular technology (such as mobile phones and body-cameras) and the growth of social media platforms, incidents of police violence can no longer be hidden from the public.[1] Many of the reform proposals have centered upon the professional training and education of police. According to Vicky Wilkins, Dean of American University's School of Public Affairs, the way "police officers are trained is the most important factor that dictates how successfully the 800,000 sworn officers across the U.S. serve their communities" (qtd. in Firman, 2021). Moreover, according to Wilkins, "policing in America is at a transformative juncture when all aspects of policy, practice, and mission are being examined by the very communities they serve" (qtd. in Firman, 2021). Many police leaders now realize that "community members, watching benign events turn into tragedies, have every right to question how police think and act, and how training influences performance" (see American University, 2021, p. 5).

Presently, hundreds of law school students throughout the United States and in over 25 countries are instructing youth in LRE programs (Greenberg, 2021, p. 153). This chapter focuses on the importance and availability of materials regarding LRE for the police and the general public. In the pursuit of LRE, both police officers and citizens alike may first become "receivers," but subsequently, they can come to serve as "givers." They can first spend time learning about the justice system, i.e., as receivers of information. Later, they can also spend time as teachers about the justice system, i.e., willing to share their knowledge with others. In this chapter special emphasis is given to what the police need to know about the law beyond their initial academy training as well as how the police have and may continue to extend knowledge about the law to others. A good example of how police may move from "warrior" to "guardian" status is for police to become qualified as LRE instructors. Over several recent decades, thousands of police have become certified to act as school resource officers and/or D.A.R.E. (Drug Abuse Resistance Education) and G.R.E.A.T. (Gang Resistance Education and Training) instructors and many officers have

DOI: 10.4324/9781003307396-14

engaged in the presentation of a variety of other safety education classes. In this way, they have already undertaken law-related educator functions. Typically, post-academy training has been available for such roles and these positions are described below.

The nature of our times, perhaps, more than ever before requires innovations in order to deal with both present and projected existential concerns. The delay of police to confront the perpetrator of the massacre at Robb Elementary School in Uvalde, Texas is just one example, out of many, which has caused the public to mistrust their police. People are asking why the response protocols established after the massacre at Columbine High School on April 20, 1999, were not followed?[2] On the other hand, police training and educational programs are useful and oftentimes vital to contend with the stresses of modern society, including the protection of at-risk children and older individuals with substance use issues, victims of crime (especially victims of domestic violence), the vulnerable (such as the elderly who are subject to identity theft as well as healthcare, wire, and mail fraud), mentally ill persons, extremist targets, and displaced persons. The continuation of police education in such critical subjects can create the specialists needed to address such problems. Their training can be sustained through app-based lessons, webinars, podcasts, games, videos, and live classes with real instructors. Given "our increasingly interconnected world which faces complex global problems, effective citizenship education is imperative" for all persons (Berry, 2020).

Civic Engagement in America

Concern about the education of all young Americans was of particular interest to reformers in the mid-19th century. It was in the late 1840s when Horace Mann, often referred to as the "father of American education," undertook an active role to achieve universal schooling in order that the American experiment of self-governance might be preserved (Winthrop, 2020). From 1850 to 1900, about 55% of all 5- to 19-year-olds were enrolled in school, mostly on the elementary grade levels. During that time period enrollment rates for White males and females were roughly similar throughout the period, but rates for Blacks were much lower than for Whites. Prior to the emancipation of Southern Blacks, school enrollment for Blacks largely was limited to only a small number in Northern states. Still, the proportion of young people enrolled in school remained relatively low during the last half of the 19th century (Snyder, 1993, p. 6). While universal public-school education has been largely achieved, today there remains concern over the declining levels of civic engagement across the country, a trend that started several decades ago. Studies have revealed that there is limited civic knowledge by a large segment of the American public as well as divisiveness among all party groups within the country. For example, according to a 2016 survey by the Annenberg Public Policy Center, one out four individuals are unable to name the three branches of government (Winthrop, 2020). In addition, a Gallup poll conducted in January 2021 found that the nation's top problem was a lack of unity involving government-related issues. The Gallup poll was conducted in the aftermath of the violent breach of the US Capitol by pro-Trump rioters on January 6, 2021 (Saad, 2021). In the summer of 2022, America's continuing political divide, caused President Joe Biden to declare that: "for a long time, we've reassured ourselves that American democracy is guaranteed. But it is not. We have to defend it. Protect it. Stand up for it. Each and every one of us" (qtd. in Liptak et al., 2022).

The RAND Corporation report entitled "Strategic Choices for a Turbulent World: In Pursuit of Security and Opportunity" found that political dysfunction is "the greatest obstacle to effective U.S. global leadership" (RAND, 2017). This challenge is also complicated by Americans' lack of engagement in civic behaviors as evidenced by their limited participation in community organizations and generally reduced participation in elections, especially among young voters (Putnam, 1995). Although youth voter turnout varied widely in 2020, half of Americans ages 18–29 cast a ballot in the general election, one of the highest youth voting rates in recent history and an 11-point increase from 2016 (from 39% to 50%). However, the turnout among new voters was still at lower rates than their slightly older peers (McAndrew & Smyton, 2021). When the contemporary calls for police training and educational reforms are uttered due to officer misconduct, there is little mention of the general decline in civic engagement among the general public. The two matters may seem unrelated; yet, they are intertwined.

History of Law-Related and Citizenship Education

Law-Related Education was defined in the federal statute known as the *Law-Related Education Act of 1978* as "education to equip non-lawyers with knowledge and skills pertaining to the law, the legal process, and the legal system, and fundamental principles and values on which these are based." In addition to helping students understand the law and legal issues in our complex and changing society, LRE, according to the Washington State Administrative Office of the Courts (2022): increases understanding of the role of the justice system in our society in the settlement of disputes; provides a foundation for improving civic skills; and affords opportunities to learn about the basis for government and its rules. Through the use of case studies, role playing, mock trials, and other active learning techniques, LRE may make a difference in participants' lives by (1) demonstrating real issues as they affect real people; (2) teaching students to reason through hard questions and to grapple with realistic problems; (3) encouraging active participation in civic activities; and (4) improving students' self-image, attitudes, and their knowledge of law and government (Washington Courts, 2022). When Isidore Starr (1911–2018), who is considered the "father of LRE" was nearly 101-years old, he reflected upon how the law is alive and constantly changing—"From the moment you get up in the morning until the moment you go to sleep at night, the law is with you" (qtd. in Samuels, 2012).

Feinstein and Wood (1995) have provided a comprehensive narrative regarding the history of LRE. They noted several differences between LRE and citizenship education (its forerunner) and described the motivations for the creation of LRE programs in the early 1960s. In particular, they pointed out that citizenship education was traditionally focused on the structure, functions, and history of the government with lessons "centered around the United States Constitution, specifically the Bill of Rights" (Feinstein & Wood, 1995, p. 1). An early leader of the field was the YMCA. It "has been involved in nonpartisan civics education since 1936. Over 55,000 students in 42 states and the District of Columbia participate in its model government program, Youth and Government" (Vasilogambros, 2021).

According to Feinstein and Wood (1995), three developmental periods in LRE have taken place from 1962 to mid-1990s. The three periods are distinguished by material content, instructional approaches, and patterns in funding. During the period 1962–1968 the focus of LRE was the Bill of Rights. At first, case studies were used "as the primary instructional technique, an innovation from traditional textbook based education. During the second period [from 1968 to 1978], the emphasis in LRE shifted somewhat away from the Bill of Rights toward students' understanding the responsibilities of a citizen and knowledge of law in everyday life. Major content areas included conceptual law, street law, and community action. Funding for LRE during the second period came mostly from the federal government and legal organizations" (Feinstein & Wood, 1995). In the generations following, LRE shifted its emphasis to delinquency prevention, citizenship, and local community involvement.

Citizenship education was thought to be an essential goal for building up both the patriotic and moral fiber of young students, but several major social and geopolitically events of the 1950s and 60s began to erode these two purposes and a need for innovation in the field of social studies education arose. In essence, societal changes called for an updated version of citizenship education. The most impactful events included the fallout over the McCarthy era, the Cold War, US involvement in the "race for space," and the various landmarks cases dealing with civil rights, such as *Brown v. the Board of Education* (1954). But, the most important change contributing to the shift for LRE was the willingness of the federal government to foster its growth through grants to states that then passed the funds to local school districts. It became understood by many educators that that law was an integral part of the field of social studies. The federal government wanted "to utilize knowledge gained from various local programs and then disseminate this information nationally. It was believed that local school districts were the best place for curriculum and material development. Ideas that were suitable for replication from these local districts would then be circulated on a national basis" (Feinstein & Wood, 1995, p. 4). Thus, curriculums were developed for helping with the specific legal questions the students would likely encounter in their current and future lives. There was emphasis placed on lesson plans designed to help students develop the analytical skills for addressing moral and ethical dilemmas and for coming to understand that "there are not simple answers to complex problems" (Feinstein & Wood, 1995, p. 5). Today, the field is still evolving and there is a renewed interest in "civic education," a more generalized term for the field of citizenship education. Like LRE, a variety of frameworks "for high-quality civics education have been set forth by leading scholars and organizations in the field, but without national implementation of these frameworks, many student citizens are not receiving an effective or adequate civics education" (Kaplan et al., 2022).

Since 1972, perhaps, the most well-known program in the field of LRE has been the Georgetown University Law Center Street Law Program. It provides law-related educational services in the District of Columbia and has served as a model for "Street Law" programs both nationally and internationally. The program's purpose is to provide legal education to laypersons while also aiding in the professional development of the University's law students. The law students, as law teachers to District of Columbia high school students and community members, are an integral part of these efforts (Street Law, 2009). As noted above, hundreds of law students throughout the United States and in over 25 countries now participate in this type of LRE. Regular certified social studies teachers also teach this subject as there exists specific textbooks containing this curriculum, such as *Street Law: A Course in Practical Law, 10th Edition* published by McGraw Hill in 2021. In the United States, "Street Law" is typically a semester long high school social studies elective that serves as an introductory course to law and the legal system. Instructional units include: Introduction to Law; Constitutional Law; Criminal Law and the Criminal Justice Process; Civil Law (Torts, Contracts and Family Law); and a Mock Court exercise (Portland Schools, 2020). Law students may receive academic credit, receive a financial stipend, or participate as part of a volunteer *pro bono* or public service requirement (Street Law, 2009).

Advancing Police–Citizen Civic Education Initiatives

A major theme of the present book is that the public has a stake in police training and education. The public may and should be involved when police are participating at their basic police school and fieldwork experiences just as they are already involved as professors during their completion of college degree programs. At the very least, the eligible voters need to take active roles before and on Election Day when the nation's lawmakers are chosen. The involvement of the public in policing is longstanding and predates the advent of most police departments in the United States. Policing in Colonial America was carried out in a rather informal and inefficient manner involving both paid and unpaid watchmen. In some instances, it was "a for-profit, privately funded system that employed people part-time. Towns also commonly relied on a 'night watch' in which volunteers signed up for a certain day and time, mostly to look out for fellow colonists engaging in prostitution or gambling" (Waxman, 2017). In 1636, a night watch started in Boston. New York began one in 1658 and Philadelphia created one in 1700 (Waxman, 2017). In the rural South before and concurrently with events in the urban North, from 1704 through the period before the Civil War, slave patrols, hardly informal, consisting of citizens "regulated the activity of slaves as their civic obligation for pay, rewards, or exemption from other duties. Unlike the watches, constables, and sheriffs who had some nonpolicing duties, the slave patrols operated solely for the enforcement of colonial and State laws" (Reichel, 1988, p. 51). It is also an interesting fact that the San Francisco Vigilance Committee of 1856 had enormous impact on the evolution of the government and society in that city—"the Vigilantes changed everything. By literally driving the Democratic party out of town and installing their own chiefs through a 'front' party, they established a grace period of stability during which the service ideal could take root" (Ethington, 1987, p. 199). "Professionalism, meaning the long-term commitment to a career in accordance with the 'service ideal,' requires a stable bureaucratic environment within which to operate" (Ethington, 1987, p. 199).

A better understanding of the historical connection between the police and public may contribute to the re-envisioning of the police role. "To police is to maintain law and order, but the word derives from *polis*—the Greek for 'city,' or 'polity'—by way of *politia*, the Latin for 'citizenship,' and it entered English from the Middle French *police*, which meant not constables but government. 'The police,' as a civil force charged with deterring crime, came to the United States from England and is generally associated with monarchy—'keeping the king's peace'" (Lepore, 2020). It took several decades for the English Parliament to be convinced to establish the first modern police force in western society—the London Metropolitan Police Force. Its seventh guiding principle states: "To maintain at all times a relationship with the public that gives reality to the historic tradition that the police are the public and that the public are the police, the police being only members of the public who are paid to give full-time attention to duties which are incumbent on every citizen in the interests of community welfare and existence" (Policing Principles, 2022, p. 3). A corollary to this principle is that police must not only enforce the laws that reflect the values of the nation, but they must also embody those values in the performance of their duties. A study by the Siena College Research Institute identified three major value areas: Equality, Liberty and Progress. The poll found that "Americans, across regions, political outlooks, the current partisan divide as well as by gender, race, ethnicity and age, all report believing in and embodying [such] core American values" (Levy, 2021). Moreover, many participants in the study said that Americans "are held together by our Constitution, Bill of Rights, Declaration of Independence—our values" (Levy, 2021). The commonality of interests and values suggests that the police and the public are in need of a similar range of teaching and learning experiences in order to preserve American democracy and the best possible civic behaviors.

LRE Can Uplift Police Professionalism

The nation's polarization over government-related issues should not interfere with the need to raise the level of police professionalism. Additionally, with increasing frequency during the opening decades of the 21st century, a cycle of overreactions by police responding to calls has led to the deaths of Black men. Alice George (2018), an independent historian with a special interest in America during the 1960s has noted that "Since the arrival of the first African slaves in North America early in the 17th-century, prejudice, often supported by law, has circumscribed the experiences of African-Americans." A greater emphasis on the study of law by police as well as the general public could help alleviate some of the crises due to these on-going patterns of behavior. A national licensing plan for police might deter future misconduct and provide some relief to Americans' distrust of their government and its leadership.

The licensing of police, an indication of having met certain professional standards, has lagged behind most other professions. For example, it was in1761 that licensing to become a lawyer in the colony of Massachusetts was adopted with such requirements as seven years of apprenticeship and adherence to a code of professional ethics and regulations (Debry, 2022). Other significant steps towards the professionalization of the practice of law did not become standardized until after the Civil War (Blaustein, 1968). These developments reached a highpoint in the early 20th century when many local bar associations required graduation from an accredited law school before a candidate could take the bar exam and begin the practice of law. In 1921, the American Bar Association (ABA) began to publish a list of ABA-approved law schools that met its standards for legal education (ABA, 2022a). Today, lawyers need an undergraduate degree, a Juris Doctor (JD) degree (with some exceptions), and a passing score on the bar examination (Debry, 2022; ABA, 2022b).[3] The JD degree was introduced in the late 1960s. National standards for police practice have yet to be required. Concerned members of the public as well as police should undertake initiatives to rectify this oversight.

There was a time near the end of the 1960s during which it was thought that a turning point had been reached in efforts to advance police professionalism. Its genesis, unfortunately, was the gross misconduct of some police officers during urban riots and other forms of domestic unrest. Calls for revisions in the basic training and education provided to police raised hope for significant reforms. While there had been efforts to raise standards since the days of August Vollmer, the era gave rise to the establishment of several new "blue ribbon commissions" to address the breakdowns in the justice system. The well-known President's Commission on Law Enforcement and the Administration of Justice was established in

1967. It recommended "that all police personnel with general enforcement powers have baccalaureate degrees" (President' Commission, 1967). The following year, President Lyndon Johnson's Kerner Commission issued its report regarding the factors contributing to the 1967 riots that killed 43 in Detroit and 26 in Newark along with hundreds of other casualties in 23 different African American neighborhoods in other American cities. The causes for the riots found by the Kerner Commission includes "bad policing practices, a flawed justice system, unscrupulous consumer credit practices, poor or inadequate housing, high unemployment, voter suppression, and other culturally embedded forms of racial discrimination" (George, 2018). "The report became big news. 'Johnson Unit Assails Whites in Negro Riots,' read a headline in the *New York Times*. Rushed into print by Bantam Books, the 708-page report became a best-seller, with 740,000 copies sold in a few weeks. *The Times* featured front-page articles about the report every day in the first week following its release. Within a few days, both CBS and NBC aired documentaries about the ties between race and poverty" (George, 2018).

Subsequently, a variety of studies were conducted to ascertain the efficacy of police training and higher education. One study, for example, which compared junior ranking college-educated police officers and non-graduate police officers before and after basic training with senior police ranking college graduates and non-graduates. The findings suggested that a university education prevents the development of an authoritarian, conservative, and rigid attitude. The findings also suggested that experience in police work does something to the police officer to make him authoritarian, conservative, and rigid (Dalley, 1975). An evaluation of an Indiana University Police Academy cadet program providing on-the-job law enforcement training to students as a part-time supplement to their full-time college studies was determined to have been a success since its graduates were found to be enthusiastic and qualified police recruits (Delaney, 1973). Yet, by the 1990s, only about 14% of police departments surveyed required more than a high school diploma or equivalent for entry (Travis, 1995). A report prepared by American University in 2021 found that "the instructional models that are used to train police officers across the U.S. at the academy, in-service, mid-rank, and leadership levels are, in many cases antiquated, inadequate, and in critical need of immediate transformation" (Firman, 2021). More than ever, the need to elevate the status of police through better training and education is still critical for the fulfillment of significant police reforms. One way to encourage higher education among police is to foster the idea that police have a role to play in the delivery of LRE.

Police as Educators

As the decades of America's 21st century progressed, police reform proposals were being announced almost weekly. Many of the reform measures came about after the widespread showing of the video footage of a Minneapolis police officer pressing his knee into the neck of George Floyd in 2020, leading to his death. This incident and a series of other police abuses are serving to spread interest in police reform in local communities as well as at the state and federal levels. However, many of the reforms approved or pending have focused on short-term impacts. A large number of the bills pending in Congress deal with greater police accountability as did President Biden's Executive Order 14074 establishing a National Law Enforcement Accountability Database (see Appendix C).[4] Some of the common reforms being instituted involve bans on chokeholds and no-knock warrants as well as improvements to police data collection procedures. One city government, San Francisco, has adopted plans for police to stop responding to non-criminal activities such as neighbor disputes, reports on homeless people, and school discipline interventions. Under the proposal, the police are to be replaced with trained and unarmed professionals. "As part of the reform plan, military-style weapons would also be banned in an effort to demilitarize the San Francisco Police Department. This would include weapons like tear gas, bayonets and tanks. Other reform priorities include addressing bias in the police department, strengthening accountability and promoting economic justice, according to the mayor" (ABC7 Eyewitness News, 2020).

Significantly, none of the reforms being adopted involve new efforts to raise the civic knowledge of the public. Yet, LRE can promote good citizenship in a constitutional democracy by bringing law to life. Citizens need to be able to resolve disputes, discuss and analyze public issues, and think critically. LRE can foster interest in society and encourage active participation in community affairs. "Since . . . the 1960s, LRE has emphasized the use of expert resource people—including lawyers, judges and law enforcement officers—in the classroom. In the early 1980s, researchers established that the use of resource people drawn from the community was one of the factors that defined LRE programs that had a demonstrably positive impact on students" (Fraser, 2004). At a past annual meeting of the American Bar Association, former US Supreme Court Justice Stephen G. Breyer observed "that more and more people are seeing those in the other county as the enemy. To keep the country functioning, kids need to understand that the Constitution allows people of opposing views to work out their differences" (qtd. in Weiss, 2011).

Police forces can be found in communities across America, and they should play an important role in catalyzing increased civic engagement. Along with the schools found in most communities, police can assist both young people and adults "develop and practice the knowledge, beliefs, and behaviors needed to participate in civic life. Schools can also directly provide opportunities for civic engagement as a local institution that can connect young and old people alike across the community. . . . Many in the civics education community are advocating for more time devoted to civics from the elementary grades through high school and the corresponding teacher professional development and support required to make this a reality" (Winthrop, 2020).

In particular, police acting as school resource officers (SROs) may be invited to enter school classrooms in order to present instruction, including discussing current events and helping students develop their media literacy skills. Some of their lessons may include "experiential learning approaches, such as service learning where students work on a community project alongside organizations or extracurricular activities where students learn to work together in teams. Experiential learning can also include simulations of democratic procedures or, better yet, direct engagement in school governance and school climate initiatives. In communities where there is limited opportunities for civic engagement, schools [and police departments] can themselves model civic values by becoming the place where community members gather and connect with each other" (Winthrop, 2020).

School resource officers are certified LEOs who are most often assigned to middle schools and high schools (Finn et al., 2005, p. 7). However, SROs may be on call for the elementary schools in a school district (Finn et al., 2005, p. 298). It is commonplace for SROs to teach law-related classes (such as D.A.R.E.), coach or supervise extracurricular activities, and advise administrators on crisis intervention (Finn et al., 2005, p. 241). The goals of the Pensacola (Florida) School Resource Officer Program are: (1) to help reduce crime in the school system and the community by assisting students in understanding benefits of a freedom-bearing democracy; (2) to foster a better understanding of the law enforcement function and to create a positive concept of the legal system; (3) to develop an appreciation of citizen rights, obligations and responsibilities; and (4) to promote student behavior in accordance with the law that is mutually beneficial to the student and to society. In addition, SROs often attend various functions within and outside a school. In the city of Pensacola, "SROs are often invited to teach law-related education classes such as driver's education, civics, life management skills, and criminal justice . . . [and] often attend various functions within and outside a school" (Pensacola, 2022). On occasion, in other communities it has been reported that SROs have had opportunities to work with teachers to integrate LRE into their lesson plans whenever possible (Finn et al., 2005, p. 245). A site assessment of SROs found that "SROs periodically teach or give presentations, although the frequency varies widely among sites and SROs. The most common classes in which SROs speak are driver education, health, or biology (usually speaking about the effects of illicit drugs and alcohol on health, motor skills, and perception), and social studies or civics (usually speaking about criminal due process, search and seizure, or Miranda rights). SROs are also occasionally brought into nearly any type of class to offer 'stand-alone' presentations and to answer questions about police work in general or their role as SROs in particular" (Finn et al., 2005, p. 364). Generally, for each of these topics, "the SRO has developed a curriculum outline and handouts, preparing most of them himself but using other resources at times, such as materials available on the [National Association of School Resource Officers] NASRO website" (Finn et al., 2005, p. 30).

"Past research by the North Carolina Department of Juvenile Justice and Delinquency Prevention's Center for the Prevention of School Violence has shown that SROs typically spend approximately half their time performing the law enforcement role, one-third of their time performing the counseling role, and the remainder of their time as an educator. Over time, the role emphasis shifts from the law enforcement role to the law-related counseling and educator role; however, law enforcement typically remains the highest priority" (Finn et al., 2005, p. 321). In one school district in the study conducted by Finn and his colleagues (2005), some students had opportunities to "attend a challenge camp during the summer hosted by the SROs and designed to help keep the youth off the streets during the summer and teach them life skills. These activities also help the SROs build rapport with students, which improves the officers' effectiveness as counselors" (p. 303). In another district, "as a result of the SROs' increased involvement with school activities, students voluntarily go to them for law-related counseling. During the summer, the SROs frequent student hangouts in order to stay in contact" (Finn et al., 2005, p. 311).

Due to a teacher shortage and a rise in daily COVID infections, in January 2022, Kevin Stitt, the governor of Oklahoma, signed into law a temporary executive order that allowed state employees with no formal educational training to step in and serve as substitute teachers in order to keep in-person classes going. Consequently, police officers in a few Oklahoma communities began acting as substitute teachers because the regular classroom teachers were sick or quarantining due to COVID. The Moore Police Department in the small city of Moore, Oklahoma, posted photos on Facebook showing some of its members stepping in to serve as substitutes since the school district's actual teachers were quarantining at home with coronavirus infections. Governor Stitt said it is the responsibility of the state to ensure that students can receive an in-person education. It was a highly unusual policy decision, and it received national news coverage at the time (Schnell, 2022; Dellinger, 2022). There was criticism that such substitutes would only be capable of rolling out a cart with a television monitor on it and therefore students would be spending most of their days watching movies (see Dellinger, 2022). Surely, that would not have to be the case if qualified police LRE instructors were available.

Police officers can also present courses or serve as guest lecturers in post-secondary schools. In such roles, qualified officers will prepare and deliver lectures to undergraduate or graduate students on topics such as criminal law, defensive policing, and investigation techniques. Furthermore, they can initiate, facilitate, and moderate classroom discussions. Similarly, qualified police may also coordinate and supervise a wide range of internship programs for college students.

The police role in LRE is also displayed when qualified officers serve as community educators. "In many parts of the United States, crime prevention is primarily addressed by local law enforcement agencies with a focus on the specific types of crime that are most significant in their localities. Innovative crime prevention programs are born from necessity and shaped by available resources and local partnerships" (Arrington et al., 2020). Police undertake the role of community educators when conducting neighborhood watch workshops, citizen police academies, and similar community-based programs such as: senior citizen police academies; youth police academies; and safe driving programs for youth and chronic offenders. Much briefer public education takes place during encounters associated with: Coffee with a Cop; National Night Out, home and business security surveys; senior welfare and vacation property checks. Of course, being let go with a warning during a traffic stop is the most common type of "educational" police–citizen encounter.

Citizen police academies and other public relations style events are most often conducted by police or other practitioners or volunteers working in the criminal justice system. When such program solely focus on police operations, crime scene investigation, courts and other activities related to crime control, they differ from the general movement known as "law-related education." However, there is no standard curriculum so program content varies from jurisdiction to jurisdiction.

A study reviewing the extent and effectiveness of the use of courses in the secondary schools designed and taught by police within the jurisdiction of the Lancashire Constabulary (England) determined that improvements were needed in the training of participating officers and in the development of course materials (Lenton, 1982). The importance of appropriate training for LRE police instructors and the selection of appropriate educational materials cannot be overemphasized.

In the United States, a national survey of schools and law enforcement's involvement in public school safety was conducted during the first half decade of the 21st century. The survey's final 219-page report contained data regarding the range of roles performed by the police assigned to various school districts. Almost half of all respondents reported that they had school resource officers (Travis & Coon, 2005, p. 6). In addition to law enforcement–related activities, advising/mentoring, and presence at school events, various questions about the teaching activities of police were included. Police agencies and school principals were asked the same series of questions. Slightly more than half of the principals reported that police taught D.A.R.E. at their schools. About one third reported that police taught some other anti-drug class. Alcohol awareness or DUI prevention classes were fairly common, followed by crime awareness or prevention, and safety education classes. Firearm safety courses were the least likely to be taught by the police (Travis & Coon, 2005, p. 40). On the other hand, the teaching activities reported by police departments indicated that teaching classes was a fairly common activity. Slightly more than half of the police departments reported that officers taught anti-drug classes and safety education. The least commonly taught class was firearm safety (Travis & Coon, 2005, p. 63). An interesting finding was that the police reported significantly more teaching activity in schools than did school principals. Moreover, a higher percentage of police respondents than school principals perceived that police were more involved in law enforcement, advising/mentoring with staff, advising/mentoring with groups, advising/mentoring with students or families, and presence at school events (Travis & Coon, 2005, p. 7). The researchers concluded that "it is unclear whether members of the community could as effectively perform some of the duties of school resource officers. It is also unknown precisely how much schools influence the role of the police. It may be that the more involved the school is in suggesting officer activities, the broader the role of the police. Many schools seem to benefit from the range of police involvement in their schools" (Travis & Coon, 2005, p. 216).

In-Service Training

The Street Law course may assist youths by providing them with "practical, relevant content that they can use in their daily lives, while developing skills that are important for civic and workplace success" (Street Law, Inc., 2022). Its foundational text and supplementary resources can be used by post-academy police instructors and others to prepare police officers for the delivery of LRE classes. For example, according to Don Bridges, a former NASRO president, "I have served as a school resource officer (SRO) since the inception of the SRO Program in the Baltimore County Public Schools in 1998. Baltimore County has one of the largest SRO programs in the country. Since 1998, SROs in our district have used the Street Law curriculum to teach thousands of students. Its user-friendly approach to law-related education allows SROs the ability to teach students the law, and the importance of obeying the law, while building positive relationships with students and community members" (qtd. in Johnson & Hanson, 2017, p. 1). Various resources are available for the purposes of presenting LRE to students (see below).

In-service training regarding preparation for LRE instructor roles can be conducted for all ranks of police from new officers to those in advanced leadership and management positions. The Police Academy at Rowan College of South Jersey offers a number of tangentially related LRE courses of a technical nature, including: Mountain Bike Patrol; Crash Investigation; Crime Scene Processing; Defensive Tactics; Field Training Officer Training; Firearms Instructor; High Technology Investigations; Methods of Instruction; Report Writing; etc. The costs for these courses range from zero to $100 for New Jersey law enforcements officers. New Jersey officers are given preference over out-of-state officers in the registration process in some classes and course lengths vary from a couple of days to several weeks (Rowan College, 2022). However, this type of advanced training could help qualify police to teach these subjects to private citizens who may volunteer for auxiliary or reserve police units.

The newly recruited and qualified volunteer police officers would then be eligible to register for many of the in-service courses only available to regular police officers. Significantly, the volunteer officers could represent an additional pool of qualified candidates who would be able to present more specific LRE classes to citizens as well as regular police. For example, the qualified members of both regular police and volunteer units would then be able to complete a new series of police ethics programs known as the "ABLE Project." The Georgetown University Law Center for Innovations in Community Safety (previously known as the Innovative Policing Program) has partnered with the global law firm Sheppard Mullin, for the creation of the Active Bystandership for Law Enforcement (ABLE) Project. The project's main goal is to create a law enforcement culture that supports peer intervention by promoting "an organizational culture where officers are empowered to intervene when noticing their colleagues are—or are about to—engage in dangerous, unwanted, or inappropriate behavior. It focuses on direct intervention in an informal capacity rather than formalized reporting" (Justice Clearinghouse, 2022). The ABLE Project provides a wide array of resources to communities and law enforcement agencies across the country interested in adopting ABLE." There is a core, eight-hour ABLE curriculum and yearly updates to the curriculum are provided to ensure it reflects the latest learning on active bystandership in law enforcement contexts (Georgetown Law, 2022a). In addition, the project provides either monthly or annual subscription options to have unlimited access to more than a thousand hours of previously recorded webinars, access to speaker presentation materials, and other benefits (Georgetown Law, 2022b). Such efforts to improve the ethical standards of behavior within police departments may help alleviate prevailing levels of citizen mistrust of police.

An LRE program originally founded by R. Fred Lewis is now the Justice Teaching Center for Civic Learning at Florida Southern College. Justice Lewis served on the Florida Supreme Court from 1999 to January 2019 and serves as the Eminent Professor of Law and Letters at Florida Southern College. As Chief Justice in 2006, Justice Lewis "created Justice Teaching which partners lawyers and judges in Florida with schools throughout the state. Upon his constitutionally required retirement in 2019, Justice Lewis returned to his undergraduate alma mater to teach constitutional law, civil liberties, and other classes. He also brought the Justice Teaching program with him for continued statewide implementation" (Annette Pitts, personal communication, September 7, 2022). The program provides a wide variety of interactive programs and instructional resources such as: law-focused lessons and activities aligned with Florida state standards in civics and government for elementary and secondary students; Justice Teaching™ training courses to prepare attorneys and judges to engage with students of all ages; civic and LRE resources for use with college students and adult education programs; high school and middle school mock trial programs; and the Florida Law Honor Society (Florida Southern, 2022a). Overall, a broad range of law-focused civics programs, academic competitions, simulations, and showcases are provided for students and teachers in Florida's elementary, middle, and high schools (Florida Southern, 2022b).

The online resources for learning about American law, history and government are practically unlimited. The Gilder Lehrman Institute of American History has available 50 separate low-cost self-paced courses involving video lectures present by renowned and award-winning scholars and a one-year subscription to hundreds of online reading and visual materials useful for providing civic education costs only $25. Current and prospective LRE instructors should also browse the websites of such notable institutions as: National Archives, Smithsonian, Library of Congress, Mount Vernon, Monticello, the Huntington Library, the National Constitution Center, the Gettysburg Battlefield National Park and Museum, the New York Historical Society, the Morgan Library & Museum, the American Library Association, the National Endowment for the Humanities, and many universities.

These leading American centers of education typically provide free online exhibits relating to such topics America's Founding Principles, African American History, Voting Rights, Nuremberg Trials, etc. (see, e.g., https://www.archives.gov/exhibits; https://www.gilderlehrman.org/collection/exhibitions; https://www.si.edu/exhibitions/online; https://www.loc.gov/exhibits/; https://exhibits.law.harvard.edu/full-online-exhibits, etc.).

Law-Related Education for All

While the materials covered in this chapter have addressed the trend for police themselves to serve as law-related educators for members of the public, particularly children, everyone can benefit from citizenship education. "We are not born knowing how to be great citizens, how democracy works, or what is required to ensure it serves everyone. We have to be taught how to be an effective member of a democratic society" (Berry, 2020). Ali Berry (2020) has observed that "we are living in a historical moment—with a variety of interconnected global issues: a pandemic, widespread inequality, and climate change. . . . The spread of COVID-19 and the fight for racial justice require collective action, and meeting this call for collective work requires a citizenry that's empathetic, empowered, and motivated." Furthermore, she notes that "citizenship education brings education's institutional function of creating an informed electorate to the forefront in an interdisciplinary and holistic way. It seeks to cut across all subject areas, integrating many skills and competencies that will benefit students throughout their lives as individuals, community members, citizens, and professionals. Citizenship education can transform society; more thoughtful and engaged citizens lead to a stronger and more just society" (Berry, 2020).

Charles Higginbotham (1980) urged that proper in-service training upgrades officer performance and decreases the likelihood of complaints and potential litigation.[5] He noted that officers are often asked questions about their in-service training when they called to testify in cases involving injuries. It is at these times when the nature and quality of training becomes of paramount concern. Officers who have had the benefit of LRE should be able to approach such appearances with greater confidence and hopefully, there will be less need for such testimony because of the nature of the training provided.

Conclusions

In the future, the steps needed to build public trust in policing will be collaboratively focused and will represent a distinctive organizational philosophy for many departments. In some respects, this model is already being tested as departments seek to engage community groups through community partnerships and educational awareness programs, such as those which include a range of roles for police to perform in local schools. These projects also involve business and residential associations as well as obtaining corporate funding through the creation of police foundations. At the same time, it is becoming more and more apparent that the central focus of police work is moving towards the protection of children, individuals with substance use issues, victims of crime (especially victims of domestic violence), the elderly, mentally ill persons, extremist targets, and displaced persons—often classified as society's most vulnerable groups.

Illustrative of the movement away from a warrior approach to policing, are the thousands of local law enforcement agencies providing one or more of the following community partnerships: the virtual neighborhood watch program (E-Watch), Citizens and Youth

Police Academies, Law Enforcement Explorer Programs, National Night Out, Coffee with a Cop, Vacation Watch, and RU-OK? (a senior citizen welfare check program). In addition, hundreds of law enforcement agencies at the federal and state levels also have begun to engage in information sharing and have community outreach programs, but true collaborations must also involve information coming from community groups and individuals. The establishment of the National Law Enforcement Accountability Database (Accountability Database) by President Biden's Executive Order as a centralized repository of official records documenting instances of LEO misconduct as well as commendations and awards is but one example the new information sharing approach being undertaken to further reduce citizen mistrust of their police, in this case, at the federal level of law enforcement. Among other things, the Accountability Database is to include "records of criminal convictions; suspension of a law enforcement officer's enforcement authorities, such as de-certification; terminations; civil judgments, including amounts (if publicly available), related to official duties; and resignations or retirements while under investigation for serious misconduct or sustained complaints or records of disciplinary action based on findings of serious misconduct" (Biden, 2022). On the other hand, much remains to be done in the field of police accountability. "State, local, and tribal police departments should expand upon the executive order, which only governs federal officers. The vast majority of peoples' interactions with police are with state, local, and tribal law enforcement" (Eisenberg et al., 2022).

In the same way that active and successful crime prevention programs can reduce crime and save lives, LRE courses and workshops for both police and the public may reduce workload for patrol officers and detectives due to the occurrence of more positive interactions, both with the communities and by individual members of the public. "Americans' participation in civic life is essential to sustaining our democratic form of government. Without it, a government of the people, by the people, and for the people will not last" (Winthrop, 2020). Education, as Isidore Starr once explained, is "a slow, laborious process, which in a sense holds the key to the future. People have to be educated that humanity is a many-splendored thing, many colors and many views, many opinions, many ideas (qtd. in Samuels, 2012).[6] This chapter has set forth a number of ways for police to advance the continuation of the "arc of justice" through LRE in our times. The main consideration is for more qualified officers to work directly in public school classrooms on a regular basis with teachers and students to present LRE lessons. Involvement in the classroom through well-planned activities and lessons can provide opportunities for knowledge and skill building as well as attitudinal changes. The changes in attitude apply to the police, the students, and the general public.

In one of his annual reports on the federal judiciary, Chief Justice of the United States John G. Roberts, Jr. focused on the urgent need for more and better civic education, stating "we have come to take democracy for granted and civic education has fallen by the wayside" (p. 2). He concluded: "Civic education, like all education, is a continuing enterprise and conversation. Each generation has an obligation to pass on to the next, not only a fully functioning government responsive to the needs of the people, but the tools to understand and improve it" (Roberts, 2019, p. 4).

Members of the police world and others with special expertise can be of great assistance in augmenting reforms in police training and education. According to the recommendations of 12 diverse and nationally respected police and educational experts, contained in a report released by American University's School of Public Affairs in 2021 "visionary trainers look to other disciplines, particularly the education field, to find and adopt teaching methods that enhance learning. For example, a complete understanding of learning theory is essential to any successful police training model. Instructors must also make clear to students that police cannot and must not work in isolation. Police working alongside health care experts, psychologists, counselors, and victim advocates are positioned to achieve a much greater level of success—modeling that behavior in the classroom is an essential step" (American University, 2021, p. 9).

According to several of America's leading advocates in the field of justice policy and research, "Reforming the institution of policing and reimagining safety remains an urgent priority that will require brave and sustained commitment across all levels of government as well as collaboration with communities that have been most harmed by police violence" (Eisenberg et al., 2022). The tension between freedom and equality forms the context for the struggle of all Americans—to exercise their rights as citizens. LRE can provide a critical evaluation of the leading events and thinkers in American government and history. Police who would enter schools as guardians as well as necessary first responders may help future generations understand what it means to be both an American citizen and a civilized human being.

There is every reason to believe that the popular media could play a much greater role in sharing LRE. C-SPAN, the cable industry's main public service network as well as local PBS television and radio affiliated stations are the current "go-to" media outlets in the United States for LRE programs. There are also several major network and cable television channels which cover the news cycle around the clock and feature expert commentators. The following chapter addresses how the police academy theme and institution is presented in popular media. The chapter focuses on how media outlets cover and portray police trainees and working police officers in news formats, podcasts, television, and feature films.

Notes

1 A 29-minute documentary and a transcript of its contents entitled "Echoes of Columbine" are available online. The documentary explores the issue of school shootings and what schools, parents, and law enforcement can do to help prevent these attacks. In the video, John McDonald, Executive Director, Security and Emergency Management, Jefferson County Schools, Colorado, states: "I'd say this to cops: If you don't have good relationships with your educators, fix it. Schools: If you don't have good relationships with your cops, fix it. Fix it right now before it's too late." It is found at: https://www.fbi.gov/video-repository/echoes-of-columbine-2019a.mp4/view.

2 However, "seventy-five percent of states restrict access to police disciplinary records," according to Rebecca Brown, the director of policy at the Innocence Project, which works to exonerate people who've been wrongfully convicted (nbcnews.com, 2022). She was interviewed during a special edition of *Meet the Press*, televised on NBC-TV on September 4, 2022. This is the case despite the efforts of a number of study groups to provide useful guidelines, such as the report entitled *Standards and Guidelines for Internal Affairs: Recommendations from a Community of Practice*, developed by the National Internal Affairs Community of Practice group, a collaborative partnership of the Los Angeles (California) Police Department and 11 other major city and county law enforcement agencies (US Dept. of Justice, 2005, p. 6). In addition, the establishment of a National Law Enforcement Accountability Database in 2022 applies only to federal LEOs and indicates strict limitations on the release of information to the public.

3 Another area of inquiry by bar examiners "involves the character and fitness of applicants for a law license. Bar examiners seek background information concerning each applicant that is relevant to the appropriateness of granting a professional credential. Because law is a public profession, and because the degree of harm a lawyer, once licensed, can inflict is substantial, decisions about who should be admitted to practice law are made carefully by bar examining boards" (ABA, 2022b).

4 President Biden's EO No. 14074 of May 25, 2022 revoked the June 16, 2020 EO No. 13929 of President Donald Trump which directed the Attorney General to establish best practices for law enforcement agencies and condition federal grants on compliance with those standards. Specifically, the Trump EO directed the Attorney General to certify independent credentialing bodies that can assess agencies' policies in areas such as use of force, de-escalation, and identifying officers who may require intervention. Of particular note, the credentialing bodies had to confirm that state and local use-of-force policies prohibited the use of chokeholds (Lampe, 2020, p. 4). President Biden's EO went a step further declaring in section 7 that "(a) The heads of Federal LEAs shall, as soon as practicable, but no later than 90 days from the date of this order, ensure that their respective agencies issue policies with requirements that are equivalent to, or exceed, the requirements of the policy issued by the DOJ on September 13, 2021, which generally prohibits the use of chokeholds and carotid restraints except where the use of deadly force is authorized by law. (b) The head of every Federal LEA shall incorporate training consistent with this section." However, various aspects of the standards that were originally put forward in President Trump's various EOs were given attention in President Biden's new order. An important section deals with the accreditation of State, Tribal, local, and territorial law enforcement agencies (LEAs). In particular, Biden's executive order establishes a national registry of federal LEOs fired for misconduct. It mandates that all officers wear body cameras, and restricts transfers of military equipment to law enforcement agencies. It also includes incentives for state and local agencies to employ these same protections and encourages them to follow the Justice Department's restrictions on chokeholds and "no knock" warrants. See the full 19-page order of President Biden at: https://www.govinfo.gov/content/pkg/FR-2022-05-31/pdf/2022-11810.pdf.

5 Charles Edwin Higginbotham (1943–2020), a former member of the Marine Corps and Fairfax (VA) Police Department, was the second editor of the *The Police Chief* magazine, as well as the second editor of the *Journal of Police Science and Administration*. His career with the International Association of Chiefs of Police (IACP) spanned 45 years. He was a writer of the Training Key and for over 20 years was the director of the Information Services Division, overseeing the association's magazine and annual conference. The IACP's annual conference could attract thousands of police leaders from around the world. Another of his many duties was acting as liaison for Law Enforcement Exploring (Obituary, 2020). John Firman, professor of practice, American University and former director of research for the IACP wrote that when he arrived at IACP in 1994, "Charlie was one of the first senior staff to take me under his wing . . . he . . . treated me like family! I am forever in his debt for helping me over the rough spots so I could put in my many (ok, not so many in comparison to Charlie!) years at IACP as a contributing member of the organization he helped build" (Firman, 2020, p. 24).

6 Isidore Starr was interviewed by Anna Samuels, a volunteer with the Washington State Legacy Project on July 29, 2012. A 68-page transcript of her interview with Starr at his home in Seattle is available online at: https://www.sos.wa.gov/legacy/stories/isidore-starr/pdf/complete.pdf.

References

ABA. (2022a). *Standards archives: History*. Retrieved September 1, 2022, from https://www.americanbar.org/groups/legal_education/resources/standards/standards_archi ves/

ABA. (2022b). *Bar exams*. Retrieved September 1, 2022, from, from https://www.americanbar.org/groups/legal_education/resources/bar-admissions/bar- exams./

ABC7 Eyewitness News. (2020, June 12). *San Francisco police will no longer respond to non-criminal calls*. Retrieved August 15, 2022, from https://abc7.com/police-reform-london-breed-san-francisco-department-sfpd-use-of-force/6244540/

American University. (2021). *Re-envisioning police training in the US.: Rejecting the status quo, speeding the pace of progress toward a true 21st century model*. American University, School of Public Affairs. Retrieved September 3, 2022, from https://www.american.edu/spa/jlc/upload/policing-report_web_final.pdf

Arrington, Rick, Schultz, P. D., Crampton, J., & Long, R. T. (2020). Crime prevention in the 21st century. *Police Chief Online*. Retrieved August 22, 2022, from https://www.policechiefmagazine.org/crime-prevention-in-the-21st- century/?ref=965172fd6e730489ca570c63cc1a8655

Berry, A. (2020, October 9). *What is citizenship education and why is it important?* Retrieved August 5, 2022, from https://xqsuperschool.org/rethinktogether/what-is-citizenship-education-and-why-is-it-important/

Biden, Jr., J. R. (2022, May 25). *Executive order on advancing effective, accountable policing and criminal justice practices to enhance public trust and public safety.* Retrieved September 7, 2022, from https://www.whitehouse.gov/briefing-room/presidential-actions/2022/05/25/executive-order-on-advancing-effective-accountable-policing-and-criminal-justice-practices-to-enhance-public-trust-and-public- safety/

Blaustein, A. P. (1968). New York bar associations prior to 1870. *American Journal of Legal History, 12*(1), 50–57.

Dalley, A. F. (1975). University vs non-university graduated policeman: A study of police attitudes. *Journal of Police Science and Administration, 3*(4), 458–468.

Debry, R. (2020). *A history of lawyers.* Retrieved September 1, 2022, from https://robertdebry.com/a-history-of-lawyers/

Delaney, M. J. (1973). *Indiana University police academy cadet program evaluation; Police technical assistance report.* Westinghouse Justice Institute; U.S. Dept. of Justice.

Dellinger, A J. (2022, January 19). *Cops are teachers now, I guess.* Retrieved August 1, 2022, from https://www.mic.com/impact/police-substitute-teachers-oklahoma-schools-covid

Eisenberg, R., Kahan, K., Ndumele, N. L., & Ofer, U. (2022, June 1). *The Biden administration's executive order on policing is a foundation to build upon.* Retrieved September 7, 2022, from https://www.aclu.org/news/criminal-law-reform/the-biden-administrations-executive-order-on-policing-is-a-foundation-to-build-upon

Ethington, P. J. (1987). Vigilantes and the police: The creation of a professional police bureaucracy in San Francisco, 1847–1900. *Journal of Social History, 21*(2), 197–227. doi:10.1353/jsh/21.2.197

Feinstein, S., & Wood, R. W. (1995, May). *History of law-related education.* US Department of Education, Educational Resources Information Center (ERIC). Retrieved August 6, 2022, from https://files.eric.ed.gov/fulltext/ED401163.pdf

Finn, P., McDevitt, J., Lassiter, W., Shively, M., & Rich, T. (2005, March). *Case studies of 19 school resource officer(SRO) programs.* Abt Associates Inc. Retrieved August 16, 2022, from https://www.ojp.gov/pdffiles1/nij/grants/209271.pdf

Firman,J.(2020).*Tributebook:HonoringthelifeofCharlesEdwinHigginbotham.*RetrievedSeptember7, 2022, from https://www.tributebook.com/domains/a673f575- d623-4a76-8d57-a2f80084c9c0/obituaries/19519664/book

Firman, J. (2021, October 21). *Police training needs urgent reforms, new report from American University reveals.* Retrieved September 3, 2022, from https://www.theiacp.org/news/blog-post/police-training-needs-urgent-reforms-new- report-from-American-university-reveals

Florida Southern. (2022a). *Justice teaching center for civic learning.* Retrieved September 6, 2022, from https://www.flsouthern.edu/academic-life/centers-institutes/justice-teaching-center/home.aspx

Florida Southern. (2022b). *Justice Teaching™ history and model.* Retrieved September 6, 2022, from https://www.flsouthern.edu/academic-life/centers-institutes/justice-teaching- center/about.aspx

Fraser, K. (2004). *The role of the resource person in law-related education.* Retrieved August 15, 2022, from https://www.miciviced.org/wp-content/uploads/2018/04/The-Role-of-the- Resource Person-in-Law-RelatedEducation.pdf

George, A. (2018, March 1). The 1968 Kerner Commission got it right, but nobody listened. *Smithsonian Magazine.* Retrieved September 2, 2022, from https://www.smithsonianmag.com/smithsonian-institution/1968-kerner-commission-got- it-right-nobody-listened-180968318/

Georgetown Law, Center for Innovations in Community Safety. (2022a). *About Us: The ABLE project.* Retrieved August 3, 2022, from https://www.law.georgetown.edu/cics/able/about-us/

Georgetown Law, Center for Innovations in Community Safety. (2022b). *Resource hub.* Retrieved August 3, 2022, from https://www.law.georgetown.edu/cics/able/resource- hub/

Greenberg, M. A. (2021). *Everyone a sheriff: The democratization of crime prevention in America.* Lexington Books.

Higginbotham, C. E. (1980, September). In-service training: How to organize a program and overcome the problem of costs, labor, standardization, scheduling, and content. *Police Chief*, *67*(9), 16–19.

Johnson, Y., & Hanson, M. (2017, February). Street law for police & teens: Advancing justice through classroom education programs. *Community Policing Dispatch: The e- newsletter of the COPS Office*, *10*(2), 1. https://cops.usdoj.gov/html/dispatch/02- 2017/street_law_for_police_and_teens.asp

Justice Clearinghouse. (2022, May 3). *Active bystandership: Applications for criminal Justice agencies, a recorded webinar.* https://www.justiceclearinghouse.com/resource/active-bystandership-applications-for- criminal-justice-agencies/

Kaplan, L., Bamberg, N., Shah, P., Okolo, N., Pepper, J., & Morscher, K. (2022). *History of civics education in the United States.* Retrieved August 8, 2022, from https://research4sc.org/history-of-civics-education-in-the-united-states/

Lampe, J. R. (2020, June 25). Congress and police reform: Current law and recent proposals. *Congressional Research Service.* Retrieved August 15, 2022, from https://crsreports.congress.gov/product/pdf/LSB/LSB10486

Lenton, R. (1982). *Police in secondary schools: An account of the debate concerning the involvement of the police in secondary schools and the material that should be included in the police-schools package.* Police Staff College 19th Senior Command Course, Bramshill Police College.

Lepore, J. (2020, July 13), The invention of the police. *The New Yorker.* Retrieved September 2, 2022, from https://www.newyorker.com/magazine/2020/07/20/the-invention-of-the- police

Levy, D. (2021, October 25). *Americans, deeply divided, yet share core values of equality, liberty & progress.* Retrieved September 2, 2022, from https://scri.siena.edu/2021/10/25/americans-deeply-divided-yet-share-core-values-of- equality-liberty-progress/

Liptak, K., Mattingly, P., & Collins, K. (2022, September 1). *Biden to issue a warning over American democracy in rare prime-time speech: 'We have to defend it'.* Retrieved September 1, 2022, from-https://www.cnn.com/2022/09/01/politics/joe-biden-democracy- speech/index.html

McAndrew, J., & Smyton, R. (2021, April 29). *Half of young people voted in 2020, major increase from 2016.* Retrieved September 2, 2022, from https://now.tufts.edu/2021/04/29/half-young-people-voted-2020-major-increase-2016

nbcnews.com. (2022). *Meet the Press—September 4, 2022.* Retrieved September 2, 2022, from https://www.nbcnews.com/meet-the-press/meet-press-september-4-2022-n1298632

Obituary. (2020). *Obituary: Charles Edwin Higginbotham October 15, 1943-December 29, 2020.* Retrieved September 7, 2022, from https://www.raynesfuneralhome.com/obituaries/Charles-Edwin-Higginbotham?obId=19519664

Pensacola. (2022). *School resource officers.* Retrieved August 15, 2022, from https://www.cityofpensacola.com/2468/School-Resource-Officers

Policing Principles. (2022). *Policing principles: Transition to modern day policing, slide outline* (pp. 1–6). Retrieved August 8, 2022, from https://police.stanford.edu/pdf/PolicingPrinciplesOutline_013020.pdf

Portland Schools. (2020). *Street law class syllabus: Ms. Doane.* Retrieved October 20, 2020, from https://www.streetlaw.org/assets/site_18/files/our%20work/high%20school%20law%20course/doane_street%20law%20syllabus.pdf

President' Commission. (1967). *President's commission on law enforcement and the administration of justice, the challenge of crime in a free society.* US Gov't. Printing Office.

Putnam, R. D. (1995). Bowling alone: America's declining social capital. *Journal of Democracy*, *6*(1), 65–78. doi:10.1353/jod.1995.0002

RAND. (2017, January 18). *Domestic political discord now the greatest threat to U.S. global leadership.* Retrieved September 5, 2022, from https://www.rand.org/news/press/2017/01/18.html

Reichel, P. L. (1988). Southern slave patrols as a transitional police type. *American Journal of Police*, *7*(2), 51–77.

Roberts, Jr., J. G. (2019, December 31). *2019 year-end report on the federal judiciary.* Retrieved August 30, 2022, from https://www.supremecourt.gov/publicinfo/year- end/2019year-endreport.pdf

Rowan College. (2022). *Police academy: In-service training courses 2022*. Retrieved August 3, 2022, from https://www.rcsj.edu/policeacademy/training-2022
Saad, L. (2021, January 25). *Americans' concern grows about government, national discord*. Retrieved September 5, 2022, from https://news.gallup.com/poll/328754/americans- concern-grows-govern ment-national-discord.aspx
Samuels, A. (2012). *Isidore Starr and the law studies movement*. Retrieved September 5, 2022, from https://www.sos.wa.gov/legacy/stories/isidore-starr/
Schnell, M. (2022, January 18). *Oklahoma calls on state employees to substitute amid teacher shortage*. Retrieved September 5, 2022, from https://thehill.com/homenews/state-watch/590302-oklahoma-calls-on- state-employees-to-substitute-amid-teacher- shortage/
Snyder, T. D. (Ed.). (1993, January). *120 years of American education: A statistical portrait*. U.S. Department of Education, Office of Educational Research and Improvement. Retrieved August 30, 2022, from https://nces.ed.gov/pubs93/93442.pdf
Street Law. (2009). *Overview of street law programs*. Retrieved May 22, 2009, from http://law.hofstra.edu/studentlife/StudentOrganizations/StreetLaw/strl aw_overview.html
Street Law, Inc. (2022). *Starting a high school law course*. Retrieved September 6, 2022, from https://streetlaw.org/our-work/strategic-initiatives/high-school-law-course/
Travis, J. (1995, February 10). *Education in law enforcement: Beyond the college degree*. Retrieved July 3, 2022, from https://nij.ojp.gov/speech/education-law-enforcement- beyond-college-degree
Travis III, L. F., & Coon, J. K. (2005, July 10). *The role of law enforcement in public school safety: A national survey; Final report for the national institute of justice*. Retrieved August 1, 2022, from https://www.ojp.gov/pdffiles1/nij/grants/211676.pdf
US Dept. of Justice. (2005). *Standards and guidelines for internal affairs: Recommendations from a community of practice*. US Dept. of Justice, Office of Community Oriented Policing Services. Retrieved September 4, 2022, from https://cops.usdoj.gov/ric/Publications/cops-p164-pub.pdf
Vasilogambros, M. (2021, May 19). *After Capitol riot, some states turn to civics education*. Retrieved August 6, 2022, from https://www.pewtrusts.org/en/research-and- analysis/blogs/stateline/2021/05/19/after-capitol-riot-some-states-turn-to-civics- education
Washington Courts. (2022). *Law-related education*. Washington State Administrative Office of the Courts. Retrieved September 5, 202, from https://www.courts.wa.gov/education/?fa=education.geninfo
Waxman, O. B. (2017, May 18). How the U.S. got its police force. *Time*. Retrieved September 3, 202, from https://time.com/4779112/police-history-origins/
Weiss, D. C. (2011, August 6). *For Justice Breyer, the need for civic education is as clear as blue and red*. Retrieved August 16, 2022, from https://www.abajournal.com/news/article/for_justice_breyer_the_need_for_civic_education_is_as _clear_as_blue_and_red
Winthrop, R. (2020, June 4). *The need for civic education in 21st-century schools*. Retrieved August 30, 2022, from https://www.brookings.edu/policy2020/bigideas/the-need-for-civic-educa tion-in-21st-century-schools/

11

POLICE ACADEMIES IN POPULAR CULTURE

Popular culture can spur discussion, dictate relationships, and influence political opinions and participation among the general public. The concept of popular culture is widely studied and defining it can be difficult and controversial (Dolby, 2003). "Popular culture (or 'pop culture') refers in general to the traditions and material culture of a particular society. In the modern West, pop culture refers to cultural products such as music, art, literature, fashion, dance, film, cyberculture, television, and radio that are consumed by the majority of a society's population" (Crossman, 2019). For the purposes of this chapter, popular culture is broadly considered "the set of practices, beliefs, and objects that embody the most broadly shared meanings of a social system" (Kidd, 2021). Citizens experience the world of the criminal justice system not only through individual interactions with criminal justice officials, but also vicariously through the dissemination of popular culture's messages about police, courts, and corrections. Most people routinely consume media in various forms and can construct their subjective realities through the lens of popular culture, at least in part, through this consumption (Asimow & Mader, 2004).

Examining the types and content of media (e.g., movies, television) of a certain era can help better understand social issues (Strinati, 2000). Studying popular culture overall provides insight into how people get information, what they do with that information, and how that information influences opinions and even behaviors. This chapter explores the representation of police academies and police activities in general in popular culture, primarily through media outlets. "As recently as 2000, 'mass media' [the way pop culture is delivered] meant only print (newspapers and books), broadcast (televisions and radio), and cinema (movies and documentaries). Today, it embraces an enormous variety of social media and forms" (Crossman, 2019). Outside of some movie franchises and niche shows, police academies are not generally the main subject of popular culture activities. Consequently, a more general discussion of police in society is given primary attention. While the police academies themselves are not always specifically portrayed, they are still intimately connected to policing more generally. By default, offering opinions or perpetuating stereotypes involving police officers or their activities through popular culture outlets aligns with widely held perceptions of police training. The actions of police, theoretically, are learned through training and education, which depend on experiences in academies as well as other

DOI: 10.4324/9781003307396-15

training opportunities. Moreover, some of what popular culture media disseminates to the general public may find its way into academy or post-academy training, and thereafter into the behaviors of police officers on the job.

What people watch on television or in movies, listen to, and/or read can help shape their ideas, opinions, and behaviors–including people who are or will become police officers. The mass media is a large force in covertly educating (and often "miseducating") the public, particularly when individuals are passively taking in information without much critical thinking about the subject matter (Tisdell, 2008). Social media is, perhaps, the largest producer of "news" in the United States. The Pew Research Center (Shearer, 2021) estimates that over 80 percent of Americans get their news digitally, with over half finding that news via social media. While older adults tend to get their news directly from news websites, over half of adults under the age of 30 are most likely to get their news from social media outlets or digital podcasts (Shearer, 2021).

Police-media relationships have evolved, with many ups and downs over the course of the 20th and 21st centuries. Social media can be a useful tool for law enforcement to share information about crime and safety, but these platforms can also be a place for the public to share negative encounters (including excessive use of force) with countless people. Furthermore, the increasing popularity and changing tone of police shows can also encourage negative perspectives of police officers (see McGovern & Phillips, 2017). While positive examples exist, the negative stories are often what receive the most attention on social media. Whatever is trending at a given moment in time can find its way into the homes (and minds) of media consumers on a wide scale.

Popular culture as disseminated and shared through media outlets influences everyday life in America; the public often learns about policing through these outlets. Stories in the media can have a large influence on the public opinion of police officers and the citizens with whom they interact as a result. Media outlets can help perpetuate stereotypes and racism, both of which have implications for police training and police–citizen encounters and interactions. Exploring the ways that various sources of media describe and present police (and police training) helps to illuminate the strength of influence popular culture can have in the minds and daily lives of citizens. At times, popular culture as presented in various media outlets has encouraged bias and perpetuated stereotypes—even ultimately resulting in violence. The circumstances leading to such developments are augmented due to the public's interest in reality television and true crime as entertainment. On the other hand, it is also possible for media outlets to better educate the public by encouraging critical thinking and providing opportunities for transparency at police academies and departments. However, this type of constructive information sharing is rare and is dependent on program producers and media executives. The Public Broadcasting Service (PBS) programs created and directed by Ken Burns and the PBS NewsHour are superior examples of quality media content.

One example of a well-balanced presentation of police work in the media is Netflix's original documentary series *Flint Town* which first aired in 2018. Over a two-year period, filmmakers embedded with local police in Flint, Michigan, revealing a department grappling with volatile issues in untenable conditions. The series focused "on a town of 100,000 people and only 98 officers. The town has high rates of poverty and crime, making it particularly difficult for the officers that work the streets. . . . [It] shows both sides of the story; the marginalized people of a community that feel hatred towards the very people who protect them and the fear those officers have in trying to do their jobs" (in Time.com, 2022).[1]

The fictional crime drama *Training Day* (Fuqua, 2001) is a discussion-generating film, which earned Denzel Washington his second Oscar. Denzel's character is an undercover detective who runs a narcotics squad in west Los Angeles. In a corrupt world one officer says no—this is the new officer played by the actor Ethan Hawke. "At times, the realism of the film might lead a viewer to thinking it's based off of a real event" (Schuhart, 2022); however, it is not. "*Training Day's* realistic qualities are brought to fruition through director Antoine Fuqua's upbringing in the rougher areas of Pittsburgh. Likewise, Fuqua went out of his way to use real-world L.A. gang members as extras throughout the film (Schuhart, 2022). According to Denzel Washington, in " '*Training Day*,' I ad-libbed, like, 50% of what you hear. We had a lot of real folks that had done real things, so I used those people. I learned from those people" (qtd. in Dowd, 2021). "The film . . . manages to pose difficult questions about whether it is possible to protect and serve without getting your hands dirty in the process" (Kinsley, 2021).

Media's Role in Creating Stereotypes and Bias

A stereotype can be defined as "a standardized mental picture that is held in common by members of a group and that represents an oversimplified opinion, prejudiced attitude, or uncritical judgment" (Merriam-Webster, 2022). Stereotypes are often presented or disseminated through various media outlets. The "Thomas Theorem" (Thomas & Thomas, 1928) notes that situations defined as real are real in their consequences. Racial stereotypes that result in actual actions that include prejudice, bias, and/or violence are prime examples of the "Thomas Theorem" in action. In other words, stereotypes that are created from definitions of race have real-world consequences (Henricks, 2017). The criminalization of the Black male has arguably contributed to high-profile uses of force by White officers against unarmed Black men, some incidents ending in death. The news media perpetuates these stereotypes (Smiley & Fakunle, 2016), often (though perhaps unintentionally) using race as a variable in their reporting (Dowler, 2004). In fact, the news media has long been held responsible for perpetuating stereotypes that Black men are dangerous, which has been argued to influence violent encounters among police officers and young, Black males (Oliver, 2003). When racial stereotypes have been widely spread, they have profound and negative impacts on members of society, particularly African Americans.

Racial profiling continues to be a burden to minority groups in society, and ongoing stereotypes continue to contribute to unofficial policies criminalizing Black males (Welch, 2007). Research suggests that media portrayals promote bias against minority groups, particularly Black males, even when they are the victims of violence. A type of victim-blaming via racial stereotypes may occur after death (particularly in interracial shootings), suggesting that information released by the media on both victim and shooter can impact public opinion about the individuals involved. For example, the media often portray victims of police violence in negative (or positive, depending on the source) light after their deaths (Dukes & Gaither, 2017). Dukes and Gaither's (2017) study does not look specifically at police shootings, but they note that their findings can plausibly be applied in such scenarios. Black victims of police shootings as well as Black LEOs can be targets of negative media spinning that can influence public opinion. More research on the impact of the media's influence on stereotypes of police officers (in addition to citizens interacting with police officers) is warranted.

A variety of studies (including Stelter et al., 2022) find that prejudiced attitudes (of community members, not only police officers) can result in more traffic stops of Black drivers.

"Driving while Black" is a popular culture phrase (a play on the term driving while intoxicated) that signifies the racial profiling of Black people during traffic stops. It has spurred discussion in many college courses as well as a television special on PBS funded by multiple foundations (PBS, 2020), books (Meeks, 2000; Sorin, 2020), and countless articles. According to labeling theory (Bernburg, 2019), stereotypes can encourage individuals to internalize external labels and behave accordingly. Profiling has the potential to damage individuals and groups in society, and can even become a self-fulfilling prophecy, continuing to perpetuate stereotypes and bias.

Implicit bias can result from being constantly inundated with stereotypes about groups in society and police training has sought to reverse the effects of this in recent years. Implicit bias training has become popular among police departments as a result. The New York City Police Department implemented such training in 2018 and has been studying its impacts. Post-training, officers are more aware and willing to use tactics to manage implicit bias, according to surveys. However, post-training behavior shows little change when looking at outcomes. The trainers and proponents of the training still suggest the importance and success of the training and promote its continuance (Kaste, 2020). Identifying shortcomings and negative encounters in police practice spurs modifications to training. Citing a problem is a starting point, and training and education must be responsive and adaptive to ongoing issues of bias. Digging deeper into training and outcomes can create new responses to address such problems. In the long run, continuous anti-bias training should be helpful in bringing about the necessary cultural changes for decreasing the amount of police violence.

Thanks to social media and the internet, a lot of what used to be private or closely guarded information among agencies has increasingly become public knowledge. Citizens now have more information about what happens in government, including police agencies. In Austin, Texas, where police academies have been underfunded in recent years, reports indicated that training videos for new police officers included evidence of racial bias. The videos showed officers acting more violently with people of color as compared to White people. The report by the city of Austin's Equity Office found that many of the videos were outdated, should be removed from training, and that future training needed to be done correctly. A group of (compensated) community members tasked with responding to these issues recommended "having trainers explicitly acknowledge race, class, and gender dynamics in officers' interactions with people in the videos. The group also wants the training academy to introduce a course addressing the history of police and race in the U.S." (Autullo, 2021).[2]

Stereotypes spread by media outlets are not limited to those directed at citizens who encounter law enforcement officials. Police officers are also subjects of stereotyping and bias in popular culture. At least one study (Morrow, 2019) even suggests that falsehoods spread by media outlets about law enforcement can influence people's behavior to act negatively toward police, including making negative comments within the digital world and creating more violence and negative interactions with police officers. As the "Thomas Theorem" helps to explain, ideas that are defined as real become real in their consequences. Media stories and portrayals of police officers as biased can serve to perpetuate stereotypes. It is a vicious circle of stereotyping of citizens and police officers, all of which have negative consequences. Research suggests that portrayals of police officers (of all races) as racist are correlated with behavior that leads to excessive force, largely due to the "theory of stereotype threat" (see Richardson & Goff, 2014; Trinkner et al., 2019). The "theory of stereotype threat" suggests that "individuals do not actually have to enforce the stereotype to experience threat from it" and "officers concerned about appearing racist are also more likely to engage in behaviors that confirm the stereotype" (Trinkner et al., 2019, pp. 422–423). As both the public and the police internalize stereotypes and biased representations, negative opinions and actions can be perpetuated, creating a negative cycle of interactions.

Not all stereotypes are exclusively negative, and some can even spark humor in the appropriate context. The ever-present image of a cop eating a doughnut is one many will recognize from a variety of television shows, movies, and even songs. One can even find articles showcasing "hilarious crime busts involving donuts" in popular police publications (see Police 1, 2016). Police snacking on a doughnut, potentially with a cup of coffee, is a pop culture staple (Giaimo, 2015). This stereotype likely emerged because police officers work long hours, including overnight shifts (times when options for food are limited), when all-night coffee (and doughnut) shops have historically been the only available options. Late night diners can also provide air conditioning and/or heat as well as tables to take a "lunch" break (Smallwood, 2013). The presence of police in all-night shops also made the workers feel safe (Giaimo, 2015). Some younger police officers note this stereotypical activity is more of a generational phenomenon, although the stereotype persists. Such stereotypes also find their way into police academies' popular culture. For example, the Houston Police Department has been known to give doughnuts to academy graduates as a humorous gift (Smallwood, 2013). Various police departments and officers across the nation lightheartedly embrace the stereotype, having doughnuts for special events or to lighten stressful situations (Giaimo, 2015). Some police departments even make videos to share as they participate in celebrations on National Donut Day (Edwards, 2022).[3]

Police on Television[4]

While overnight shift officers may or may not spend some of their early morning break time in coffee shops, Americans definitely spend a significant amount of their leisure time watching television and movies (Bureau of Labor Statistics, 2019). The continuing conversation of how media, such as movies, impact individuals' behaviors, attitudes, and overall public opinion began long ago (Fearing, 1947). Findings are mixed on exactly how much influence fictional television shows and movies have on public opinion, including thoughts on public policy (Mutz & Nir, 2010). Research is also complicated by individual personalities and emotions, which are difficult to study at the macro level. Ongoing television series create followings where viewers become deeply invested in the storylines and lives of the fictional characters (Zillerman & Bryant, 2002). One small study (Mutz & Nir, 2010) suggests that crime dramas have the ability to influence views on public policy, due at least in part to the emotional involvement of viewers who may have become deeply invested in various television shows. Fictional shows have become a primary source of "information" influencing the public's perceptions of crime (Dowler et al., 2006), which can be dangerous when consumers translate fiction to fact.

Theoretical explanations can help contextualize the influence television can have on viewers. Cultivation theory posits that watching television can sway people's personal beliefs in a manner consistent with the television they watch; this impact grows with the amount of time people spend watching television. Specifically, watching more television does not necessarily change the attitudes of viewers, but it can strengthen people's ideas and/or sway them toward the "mainstream" ideas portrayed on the shows they watch (see Gerbner,

1970; Williams & Fedorowicz, 2019). If viewers gravitate toward shows that align with their preconceived ideas and beliefs, shows can reinforce their personal values. This may hold additional relevance when choosing a television news outlet based on one's political ideology (Hsu, 2009).

Fictional television has long been a place to find actors portraying police characters. The history of the relationship between police and the media, particularly television shows, is long and complicated (Rosenberg, 2016). Movies and shows about police officers have been changing in scope and tone over the years. "During the 1960s, police dramas on television meant *Dragnet* and '*The FBI*'—shows that were largely divorced from the reality of what was taking place on the street as the decade spilled into turbulence" (Lopez & Johnson, 2017). By the 1980s, *Hill Street Blues* was "groundbreaking in that it ventured into the personal lives of the police force, not the neatly solved detective whodunits that had dominated the landscape" (Lopez & Johnson, 2017). Generally, however, "for the generations growing up in the 70s and 80s, whatever their private views, the actual police force as depicted by mainstream . . . popular culture was almost exclusively either comical or the bad guys, or both" (Pinfold, 2020). More recent portrayals have had negative connotations. Yet, these shows have also dealt with more complex issue due, at least, in part to "the increasing visibility of criminal justice groups led by young and vocal activists [who] . . . demand a much more complex look at how the system is portrayed" (Lopez & Johnson, 2017). This shift has created discontent as well as outrage among police officers and those supportive of the profession (Marcou, 2019). Literature continues to emerge on the extent of and the mechanism by which media portrayals of police officers impacts public opinion, especially on the problem of police use of excessive force (Donovan & Klahm, 2015). Additionally, the depictions of LEOs may vary among different demographic groups in society (Franklin et al., 2019; Miller et al., 2004).

Reality television shows are a popular genre that can allow viewers to (supposedly) obtain an insider view about various aspects of life in America, including professions such as police officers (Ranker TV, 2022). With the national interest in crime as entertainment, police shows have been a part of the reality television movement. "Reality TV programs have extremely low productions costs when compared to other popular programs and are highly versatile due to the lack of temporal references [such as dates]. For example: reality programs cost somewhere between $150,000 and $250,000 per week to produce, while one episode of *Star Trek: Next Generation* costs approximately $1.5–1.7 million to produce" (Cotter et al., 2008, p. 289, note 5). Due to its low production costs, this type of popular programming has a lengthy shelf life and flexibility. "The flexibility of such programs has been seen as advantageous to TV executives who can move the program to time slots that require filling" (Cotter et al., 2008, p. 280).

The show *COPS* premiered in 1989 and ran until 2021, making it one of the longest running and highly watched television shows. *COPS* depicts police officers on actual calls, allowing viewers a glimpse into the world of policing. Watched for entertainment, individuals often developed qualitative conclusions about policing from the show. Viewers' opinions have varied depending on the content of a particular episode. Tactics carried out in some of the shows were questionable even though they were portrayed as "good policing" by the officers. Moreover, due to the shows perceived authenticity and its flexible scheduling, "the episodes' images allows their continuous re-telling, inviting viewers not only to recover what they already know, but also what they want to know" (Cotter et al., 2008, p. 280). For better or worse, the show has helped shape viewers perceptions about policing for over three decades (Molofsky, 2020).

A podcast series, *Running from COPS,* recently emerged in response to viewer interest. The podcasts focus on the many ways in which *COPS* culturally impacts the nation's conceptions about policing (Taberski, 2019). "In the podcast series 'Running from Cops', host Dan Taberski and his team watched nearly 850 episodes of the show and tallied what they saw: roughly four times the amount of violent crime than there is in real life, three times as many drug crimes, and ten times the amount of prostitution. 'Cops' . . . makes the world seem more crime-ridden than in reality. It has also inspired copy-cat shows, like the popular 'Live PD,' that also warp depictions of what's appropriate (and legal) in policing" (WNYC Studios, 2019).

John Langley, creator of the reality series *COPS*, has indicated that his series must be considered from a broad perspective without rushing to any one critical assessment about police work. "It's easy to judge when you're seeing one video clip. You see a picture but not necessarily the big picture" (qtd. in Lopez & Johnson, 2017). "Langley says that in the decades his show has been on the air, policing has become more transparent, noting that among other things, police officers now wear body cameras. He says that one of the primary achievements of *COPS* has been to 'humanize police officers, so you don't just witness a uniform' " (qtd. in Lopez & Johnson, 2017).

Another genre of reality shows and videos (posted on social media outlets like YouTube) that has gained popularity involves an inside look at places and institutions that "regular citizens" would not regularly have access to. Michelle Khare is a widely watched YouTube personality. She undertakes unusual experiences from training as if she were becoming a member of an elite military force to training like a pageant queen. One of her most popular videos (with over 11.7 million views as of mid-2022) is about training with the San Diego Police Academy (Khare, 2019). The overlap between social media and reality programming coupled with the interest in policing illustrate the interplay between police training (and policing more generally) and popular culture. Viewers want to get the experience of a difficult subject from the comforts of their homes, and these popular media outlets offer many ways for citizens to explore policing and potentially develop or reinforce opinions about the law enforcement profession.

Fascination With True Crime

The "True Crime" genre has taken off as one of the most popular topics for podcasts, television shows, documentaries, and books (Dukes, 2022). Netflix routinely has true crime shows in their "Top 10" list (Sayles, 2021). Podcasts about crimes are abundant, and books about true crime line the shelves of bookstores and have been popular throughout most the 20th century (Dukes, 2022; Persaud, 2022). In 2018, *TIME's* website featured a list of the 16 best true crime books of all time. Among this list was the national bestseller—*In Cold Blood* by Truman Capote. The first edition of *In Cold Blood* was published by Random House in 1965. "In 1959, four members of the Clutter family, who owned a farm in Kansas, were shot to death in their home. *In Cold Blood* weaves together the stories of the murderers and the investigators hunting them with interviews with those who knew the victims and the killers" (Raymond, 2018). When Capote learned of the quadruple murder before the killers were captured, he decided to travel to Kansas and write about the crime. "The novel is a true crime classic—it was researched by award-winning novelists Truman Capote and Harper Lee, and its ability to bring every detail of the crime to life revolutionized the true crime novel genre when it was released" (Raymond, 2018). Magazines featuring true crime stories were most popular from the early 1920s through the 1970s. The first true crime magazine, *True Detective,* was published in 1924. It featured basic accounts of crimes and how they were solved.[5] "A fully stocked newsstand could feature perhaps as many as two dozen different titles every month (Marr, 2015).

More recent forms of true crime entertainment provide people with a problem to solve, a puzzle to put together, which allows them to experience something that feels exciting,

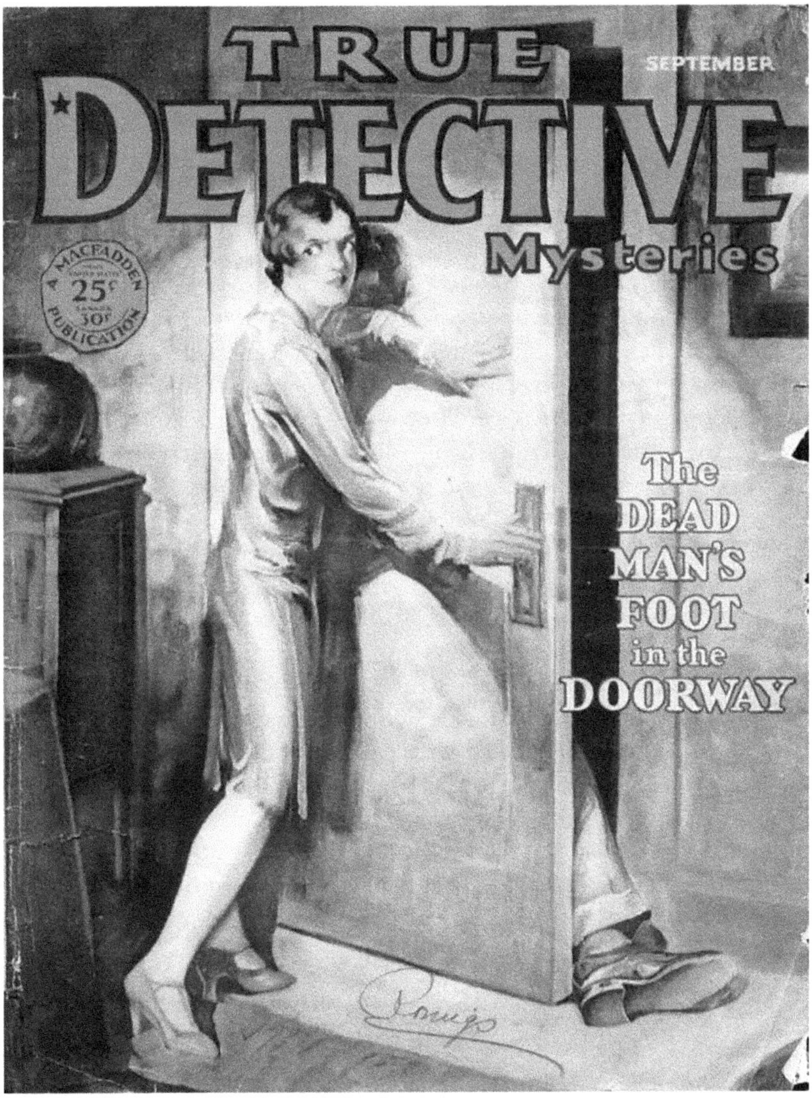

FIGURE 11.1 Cover photo of True Detective Mysteries, September 1929, Vol. XI, No. 6 (116 pages). This was the first pulp crime magazine that had tons of imitators over the years. Publisher: New Metropolitan Fiction, Dunellen, New Jersey. Cover art: Edgar McGraw. One of the featured stories is entitled: "How Pinkerton Solved the Rock Island Express Robbery by Cleveland Moffett. Public Domain. Complete issue available online at: https://archive.org/details/true-detective-sept-1929/mode/2up.

even dangerous, in the safety of their own homes (University of Derby, 2022). There is a bit of disconnect from the real world when immersing in a true crime experience. The fact that there are real victims, or real people out there charged with solving the case can be lost on the listener, the viewer, or the reader. Some even blur the lines between true (or even fictionalized) crime dramas and police television shows, using such media for "infotainment" purposes instead of exclusively entertainment.

True crime shows offer a variety of angles from which to view crime. Sometimes the focus is on the people committing the crime and other times the focus is on the investigation and policing aspect of criminal activity. The public fascination with true crime is connected with police academies, even though most of these shows are occurring after police academies have been completed. Consequently, in both true crime and fiction drama shows and movies, viewers will see mere glimpses of what takes place in police training academies or at other times.

The *Police Academy* Movies

Hollywood has taken artistic liberties to fictionally explore the police academy life for decades, particularly from a comedic perspective. Quite possibly the most memorable pop culture reference to police academies would be the *Police Academy* movie franchise. The first *Police Academy* movie, released in 1984, grossed over $148 million in profits worldwide. While the subsequent movies were not as successful, the franchise has grossed over $573 million over the years (Box Office Mojo, 2022). The characters in these comedies were portrayed as incompetent and unqualified, to say the least. Based on the idea that it is hard to get enough police officers to work in large cities, the premise of the original movie was to spark hilarity by bringing together a bunch of individuals who would not fit the typical profile of LEOs. The "Police Academy brand" took on a life of its own within pop culture, as the initial movie spawned six sequels and other spin-offs, including an animated series (Boone, 2022).

According to Gur Tirosh (2023), the original idea for the *Police Academy* movies came from Hollywood producer Paul Maslansky. While he was working on the movie set for the film *The Right Stuff*, "a police bus filled with cadets drove up to help with crowd control. Maslansky noticed that these diverse groups of cadets that came off the bus were terrible at their jobs. Maslansky, who asked the sergeant in charge if these individuals would be the future of San Francisco's finest, was told that they accepted all those who applied but could get flunked out, eventually. This experience brought up the initial idea for the movie, and the next day he already had a two-page treatment written and presented to Alan Ladd Jr., who loved the idea."

Today, various websites and forums continue the discussion about the *Police Academy* movies (see Boone, 2022; Jacobs, 2020; Ryan, 2020; Sage, 2021). This movie franchise also led to the creation of a crowd-funded, not wildly successful, documentary—*What an Institution: The Story of Police Academy* (see Campbell, 2018; Milano, 2018). More than a few podcast episodes have also been dedicated to discussing the significance of the *Police Academy* movies in popular culture. According to William Pinfold (2020), "it's not an enlightened franchise by any means; the whole series essentially runs on stereotypes and bad taste and therefore has the capacity to offend . . . [but] the series is so determined to make fun of every possible point of view that. . . . it remains largely watchable where many similar films do not, while also feeling significantly less reactionary than, say the previous year's Dirty Harry opus, *Sudden Impact.*"

Podcasts: News and Entertainment on Policing[6]

With most Americans owning a cell phone allowing for constant access to the internet, the popularity of podcasts continues to grow. Figures vary depending on source and methodology, but it is estimated that there are currently over two million podcasts (Wise, 2022) with about 80 million teenagers and adults listening to podcasts weekly (Edison Research, 2021). Podcasts have become an influential source of media (including news and investigative reporting) in popular culture, providing listeners with information and entertainment while becoming an important revenue-producing market in popular culture.

A casual search for podcasts on policing quickly reveals a huge number, and some of these include police academy training or experience as part of their storyline (Go Law Enforcement, 2022). A handful of podcasts are dedicated specifically to issues of police training, and many more are related to crime and policing more generally. The public's fascination with all things crime-related continues to make podcasts on the topic popular. According to Edison Research (2022), "True Crime" is one of the most listened-to genres. With the renewed interest in police reforms, many podcasts dealing with news, society, and culture have included discussions about police training.

Social Media

Social media refers to internet-based virtual locations where information is shared and includes platforms including Facebook, Twitter, Instagram, TikTok, and YouTube; over 4.5 billion individuals worldwide regularly use social media (Dollarhide, 2021). With the advent and huge popularity of social media, people often get their news and other information from electronic sources, versus traditional television or print media. Many people also find their information about policing through social media sources (Khare, 2019). With the technological revolution and increased popularity of social media, police departments often turn to various social media outlets to disseminate information and communicate with the public (Manzoor, 2019). Social media can be the quickest way to reach a large number of people in a community. The reach of such information can be greatly extended depending upon whether or not the message is shared by its original receivers.

YouTube is a popular social media outlet (Shepherd, 2022), providing a variety of videos about police academies. Videos range from lay citizens experiencing police academy training (see Khare, 2019) to police academies across the United States showcasing what happens during academy life, including the common practice of sharing the images of graduation ceremonies. Other topics include: showing what happens when a recruit is tasered or pepper sprayed (Frederick News Post, 2017); how to be successful in a police academy (Officer401, 2020); and how some recruits fail (Officer401, 2018). Such videos may be targeted at potential recruits and their families, but are available for anyone to see.

A word search for "police academy" on Facebook produces a variety of hits, including: fan pages for the *Police Academy* movies; local and state police academy pages; advertisements for documentaries; congratulatory posts to friends and family members completing academy training; and news stories about mishaps at police academies. However, one can certainly question the good judgment of making a Facebook post about a police recruit shooting himself at the Massachusetts State Police Academy (Boston 25 News Staff, 2022). Police departments, particularly with the shift toward community policing, use social media to engage citizens and promote their departments and disseminate their own information to connect with citizens as well as to ward off false claims and incorrect news by other outlets. Applying and expanding cultivation theory to this relatively new interactive way of reaching the public, Williams and Fedorowicz (2019) found mixed results, as have other scholars researching similar topics. While people who engaged most often with the social media accounts of police departments were more likely to be satisfied with police officers, some discrepancies were highlighted. The study showed that "liking" police self-promotion was correlated with higher satisfaction and "disliking" such posts was correlated with lower levels of satisfaction. Also, as other scholars have found, minority groups were overall more dissatisfied with police than Whites (Williams & Fedorowicz, 2019). A small study (Campbell & Valera, 2020) of college students, mostly persons of color, finds that social media is often used to view incidents of police brutality which produce strong, negative emotions. Findings also suggest that viewing such encounters encouraged the participants to fear their own, personal interactions with police in the future. In short, social media stories on policing can have positive or negative impacts on the audience, depending on various social and personal characteristics of those consuming the stories, as well as their previously held opinions.

The "News"

The news media is probably the most universal outlet by which information is passed to citizens. In operation for 24 hours each day, the news media can assist in the development of beliefs as well as the stereotyping of groups of people within society. Law enforcement is no exception. Stories of excessive use of force by police officers have become more common in recent years, and media outlets are eager and in competition with one another to present any details about the most shocking cases. For individuals who do not have personal interaction with police officers, these images may serve to define what it means to be a police officer (see Schultz, 2019). News reports and videos about police use of force play significant roles in shaping attitudes about police officers engaging in unjustifiable violence (Miethe et al., 2018). Their influence on police-community relations is enormous.

The fact that high-profile negative interactions with police are widely viewed via media outlets by the general population can greatly impact public opinion. Political polarization reflected in the news media has the potential to skew viewers' perceptions and shape opinions, theoretically shifting them farther toward the ideological camp with which they already most agree. Wozniak et al. (2021) have studied public opinions regarding military-style weapons used by police officers; typically finding that the public does not support the use of such weapons. Wozniak and colleagues (2021) found that "militarized" versus "routine" weapons are not easily classified by citizens. The analyses of such topics do not tease out nuances, such as what police officers may be responding to when they deploy certain weapons.

The perceptions of police officers in particularly dangerous situations can easily be overlooked. The fear factor appears to be seldom given the serious attention it deserves in news media accounts of shootings. In 1989, the US Supreme Court ruled in *Graham v. Connor*

(490 U.S. 386) that "a particular use of force must be judged from the perspective of a reasonable officer on the scene, rather than with the 20/20 vision of hindsight." Jury instructions for both civil and criminal cases involving the excessive use of force by police can be found online at: https://www.ce9.uscourts.gov/jury-instructions/node/163. "Tracie Keesee, the senior vice president of justice initiatives at the Center for Policing Equity, said in an interview that most officers begin to realize in the academy how dangerous policing can be—that there is a lot to be afraid of" (Harkins & Ellis, 2021).

It has also been reported that political affiliation is correlated with opinions about law enforcement (Wozniak et al., 2021). Moreover, people often choose social media outlets (and the content within them) based on already-held views. With the increasing polarization on political topics, including policing, social media has become a powerful determinate of the status of community-police relations.

Popular Culture and Public Opinion of Police

The public's opinion of police officers varies over time and place. Polls suggest that confidence in police officers in the United States is reaching historic lows (Ortiz, 2020). How community members perceive police officers can have an impact on interactions between police and citizens, and even whether or not residents will call police officers in the case of an emergency. Some police departments will go to great lengths to find out what the public thinks about them (see Weichselbaum, 2018). Various types of social media have been used to find out what community members think about their local police. Social media can be a double-edged sword when the role of policing in society gets excessive press attention. It is essential that police officers and community members fully understand the impact of their current and future interactions, in person and virtually. Social media provides a platform for indirect interaction among such groups in society. As mentioned, efforts have been made to determine how police are viewed through social media outlets, such as Twitter, where, for example researchers can see how many posts about police officers are positive versus negative, and how that data changes over time and the occurrence of certain events (see Oglesby-Neal et al., 2019). Problems can arise when social media shows police officers in a negative light, highlighting and quickly spreading information about excessive use of force, other violent encounters, or inaction. Justifiably, any incidents demonstrating poor training and/or planning are highlighted in the media. The police response to the school shooting at Robb Elementary School in Uvalde, Texas is a case in point. Nineteen students and two teachers died. The first extensive report on the May 24, 2022, mass shooting at the elementary school placed blame across every law enforcement agency responding to the attack, faulting local police for mistakes and more experienced agencies for failing to take charge (Hernández & Bailey, 2021).

The Media's Role in Public Safety

According to Valerie Jarrett, who served as a senior adviser to former President Barack Obama, "Pop culture has a significant impact on the lens through which people view the relationship between police and communities of color, and of criminal justice more broadly. They humanize stories in a way that doesn't come across in the 24-hour news cycle. They bring people closer to issues they may not experience in their own life—and that's where the empathy begins. . . . The humanization of criminal justice is essential to reform a broken system" (qtd. in Lopez & Johnson, 2017). Empathy must be a two-way street. The public must learn about the feelings of the police and the police must reciprocate by learning about the needs and concerns of the public. Jerome Skolnick,[7] a preeminent scholar in the field of law and society, long ago wrote about this essential problem from the police perspective, stating that "The citizen prefers to see the police officers as an automaton, because once the police officer's humanity is recognized, the citizen necessarily becomes implicated in the officer's work, which is, after all, sometimes dirty and dangerous" (Skolnick, 1965, p. 54).

Social media, the news media, and various mass entertainment formats can help promote the public's safety. Popular culture entertainment and news outlets routinely include stories related to policing, and sometimes police training. In the social media age, information spreads rapidly, whether it is about a new "True Crime" show or an excessive use of force case by police officers. Training materials for police officers that would have been seen only by those going through the academy now find their way into sources accessible by the public. Information (and sometimes misinformation) about policing is abundant in popular culture even when people are not interacting with the police themselves. The fascination with crime-related news and shows continues to grow. This inundation of information does more than just provide entertainment for viewers, readers, and listeners; it is integral in terms of creating opinions and influencing behavior. The simple act of taking in information (fact or fiction) about policing and crime can have real-world implications for how people live their daily lives. Research from the early 2000s suggests that watching police reality shows has increased the likelihood of endorsing capital punishment as well as owning a handgun. Watching television has also raised the level of the public's fear of crime (see Holbert et al., 2004).

"The depictions of police on TV do more than influence what the public thinks—they also motivate people to become officers. In a study asking 42 officers why they applied for the job, just under a third said shows like *Law & Order* influenced them, a percentage supported by a consulting firm survey of over 1,600 officers. These might be low numbers . . . as it can seem embarrassing or silly to admit that a TV show encouraged you to pursue a career" (Nemo, 2020).

Popular culture moves information quickly in the digital age. Stories of excessive use of force and discriminatory or violent encounters become widely shared, which can widen the divide between police officers and civilians through the various mediums of popular culture. Numerous calls for reform specifically suggest additional training (or education)[8] as a necessary precondition for positive change in the field of policing. Although the stories and problems allow for communal discussions with citizens, for example, a police training director might hold a virtual "town hall" session specifically to address community concerns about police training. However, it will take effort to rebuild severed ties—or build ties when and where they have been absent. Significantly, there is a need for the public to be engaged, in some way, in the process of police training and education. The use of various media and popular culture outlets can help the field of policing become more transparent and augment necessary reforms.

The public also needs to be better educated on issues of stereotypes perpetuated by popular culture, about both citizens and police officers. While social media is often the source of negative information sharing, it can have positive, educational uses, as well. The digital age allows for a change in content and direction of the discussion. Government officials, police chiefs, and police academy directors can use the power of the media in the interest of public safety education. They can spread more facts (versus drama and fiction), helping the public to receive correct information, whether it is positive or negative. Police specialists may even engage the public interest by explicitly noting the differences between the various forms and purposes of cultural transmission. Citizens may be interested in learning how their police are being trained and greater use of the "citizen police academy" model can be encouraged. Such efforts could even better prepare future police officers by providing a more accurate picture of what training and police work is like. While it is plausible to assume that future generations will continue to laugh at the goofy characters in the *Police Academy* movies and be entertained by depictions of true or embellished crime stories, it is time to shift the discussion of police training beyond stereotypes and popular culture references. The resources provided by popular culture have made it easier to educate the public regarding police and police training. Ultimately, the goal must be to encourage critical thinking about the administration of justice, rather than leaving vast segments of the public to be only entertained, mildly amused, or at times horrified by the existing content of popular cultural outlets.[9]

This discussion has centered in large part about how Americans obtain their news and entertainment through electronic means. It is hypothesized that a large segment of the American public would prefer to see a return of the "the friendly neighborhood beat cop" or "community guardian" on their community's streets. They would prefer to have officers who do not resemble an "urban warrior, trained for battle and equipped with the accouterments and weaponry of modern warfare" (see Harkins & Ellis, 2021). The next and final chapter proposes a training model to help turn this sentiment into a reality.

Notes

1 An official trailer for this docuseries is available at: https://www.youtube.com/watch?v=EfNURrdgWTU.
2 See Chapter 7 for a discussion on the importance of education in human relations for violence prevention.
3 It has been reported that the option by police officers to pick up a doughnut dates to the years after World War II. "Graveyard cops in the forties and fifties had few choices. They could pack lunch, pray for an all-night diner on their route or fill up on doughnuts . . . They were cheap and convenient. . . . Former Baltimore City police detective Dick Ellwood . . . recalled being allowed to just eat doughnuts off the assembly line shortly after the shops opened in the wee hours of the morning. . . . As late-night food options expanded, police came to be able to eat other things, but the joke stuck" (Waxman, 2017).
4 See Appendix A for a list of television shows and movies on the topic of police training.
5 During the genre's heyday, before WWII, 200 different true crime magazines were sold on newsstands, with six million magazines sold every month. By itself, *True Detective* had two million in circulation. The lurid covers of the magazines generally featured women being menaced in some way by a potential criminal perpetrator, with the scenarios being more intense in the 1960s. Public interest in the magazines began declining in the 1970s, and by 1996, almost none were being published, including *True Detective*, which had been bought and shut down by a new owner (Marr, 2015).
6 See Appendix B for a list of podcasts on police training.
7 Jerome Skolnick, Claire Sanders Clements Dean's Chair Professor of Law (Emeritus), joined the University of California at Berkeley faculty in 1962 and became part of the Berkeley Law faculty in 1977. From 1972 to 1984 he chaired the Center for the Study of Law and Society. He has also taught at UC San Diego, the University of Chicago and Yale University, and has been a visiting fellow at Oxford. Skolnick's books include *Society and the Legal Order: A Reader in Sociology of Law* (edited with R.D. Schwartz); *Justice Without Trial: Law Enforcement in Democratic Society;*

House of Cards: Legalization and Control of Casino Gambling; The New Blue Line: A Study of Police Innovation in Six American Cities (with D. Bayley); and *Above the Law: Police and The Excessive Use of Force* (with J. Fyfe). He is also coeditor (with J. Kaplan and M. Feeley) of the fifth edition of the text *Criminal Justice*. His awards include Carnegie, Guggenheim and National Science Foundation fellowships as well as prizes for distinguished scholarship from the American Society of Criminology, the Academy of Criminal Justice Sciences and the Western Society of Criminology (Berkeley Law, 2023).

8 See Chapter 7 for a discussion on the nuances between training and education for police officers.

References

Asimow, M., & Mader, S. (2004). *Law and popular culture: A course book*. Peter Lang.

Autullo, R. (2021, January 20). New report: Austin police training videos reinforce racial stereotypes, bias. *Austin-American Statesman*. Retrieved July 20, 2022, from https://www.statesman.com/story/news/2021/01/20/austin-police-report-training-videos-reinforce-racial-stereotypes-bias/4230355001/

Berkeley Law. (2023). *Jerome Skolnick: Profile*. Retrieved February 5, 2023, from https://www.law.berkeley.edu/our-faculty/faculty-profiles/jerome-skolnick/#tab_profile

Bernburg, J. G. (2019). Labeling theory. In M. D. Krohn, N. Hendrix, G. P. Hall, & A. J. Lizotte (Eds.), *Handbook of crime and deviance* (2nd ed.). Springer Nature Switzerland.

Boone, B. (2022, May). The untold truth of police academy. *Looper*. https://www.looper.com/224576/the-untold-truth-of-police-academy/

Boston 25 News Staff. (2022, July). Trainee at state police academy accidentally shoots himself. *Boston 25 News*. https://www.boston25news.com/news/local/trainee-state-police-academy-accidentally-shoots-himself/CRVSQYODURB6FPFBFHVHEEZKOQ/?utm_campaign=trueAnthem_manual&utm_medium=trueAnthem&utm_source=facebook&fbclid=IwAR2CLt1qg10G1ygAcEc_OAmj4QrHkBiCT5KqeVStcRqwl-mgCaM1kczs5s0

Box Office Mojo. (2022). Retrieved November 12, 2022, from https://www.boxofficemojo.com/search/?q=Police+academy

Bureau of Labor Statistics. (2019). *American time use survey*. https://www.bls.gov/tus/

Campbell, C. (2018, May). The story of the comedy franchise is subject of a new crowd-funded documentary. *FSR*. https://filmschoolrejects.com/time-to-put-your-money-where-your-police-academy-nostalgia-is/

Campbell, F., & Valera, C. (2020). "The only thing new is the cameras:" A study of U.S. college students' perceptions of police violence on social media. *Journal of Black Studies, 51*(7), 654–670. https://doi.org/10.1177/0021934720935600s

Cotter, R. S., O'Connor, D., & Lint, W. B. (2008). Ordered images: Cooking reality in Cops. *Journal of Criminal Justice and Popular Culture, 15*(3), 277–290.

Crossman, A. (2019, December 9). *Sociological definition of popular culture*. Retrieved February 5, 2023, from https://www.thoughtco.com/popular-culture-definition-3026453

Dolby, N. (2003). Popular culture and democratic practice. *Harvard Educational Review, 73*(3), 258–284.

Dollarhide, M. (2021, August). Social media. *Investopedia*. https://www.investopedia.com/terms/s/social-media.asp

Donovan, K. M., & Klahm, C. (2015). The role of entertainment media in perceptions of the police use of force. *Criminal Justice and Behavior, 42*(12), 1–21. https://doi.org/10.1177/0093854815604180

Dowd, M. (2021, December 4). Denzel Washington, man on fire. *The New York Times*.

Dowler, K. (2004). Dual realities? Criminality, victimization, and the presentation of race on local television news. *Journal of Crime and Justice, 27*(2), 79–99. NCJ 208306.

Dowler, K., Fleming, T., & Muzzatti, S. L. (2006). Constructing crime: Media, crime, and popular culture. *Canadian Journal of Crime and Criminal Justice, 48*(6), 837–850.

Dukes, J. (2022). *What is true crime?* Retrieved July 18, 2022, from https://celadonbooks.com/what-is-true-crime/

Dukes, K. N., & Gaither, S. E. (2017). Black racial stereotypes and victim blaming: Implications for media coverage and criminal proceedings in cases of violence against racial and ethnic minorities. *Journal of Social Issues, 73*(4), 789–807. doi:10.1111/josi.12248
Edison Research. (2021, March). *The infinite dial of 2021.* https://www.edisonresearch.com/the-infinite-dial-2021-2/
Edison Research. (2022, May). *Comedy is top podcast genre in U.S.* https://www.edisonresearch.com/comedy-is-top-podcast-genre-in-u-s/
Edwards, J. (2022, June). See: State police celebrate Donut Day with a passion. *Patch.* https://patch.com/new-york/bedford/see-state-police-celebrate-donut-day-special-passion
Fearing, F. (1947). Influence of movies on attitudes and behavior. *The ANNALS of the American Academy of Political and Social Science, 254*(1), 70–79. https://doi.org/10.1177/000271624725400112
Franklin, A. S., Perkins, R. K., Kirby, M. D., & Richmond, K. P. (2019, September). The influence of police related media, victimization, and satisfaction of African American college students' perceptions of police. *Frontiers in Sociology.* https://doi.org/10.3389/fsoc.2019.00065
Frederick News Post. (2017, November 18). *Police academy taser and pepper spray.* [Video]. YouTube. https://www.youtube.com/watch?v=spkzY8QhHw0
Fuqua, A. (2001). *Training day.* Warner Bros.
Giaimo, C. (2015, September). The long, sweet love affair between cops and doughnuts. *Atlas Obscura.* https://www.atlasobscura.com/articles/the-long-sweet-love-affair-between-cops-and-doughnuts
Gerbner, G. (1970). Cultural indicators: The case of violence in television drama. *Annals of the American Academy of Political and Social Science, 388,* 69–81.
Go Law Enforcement. (2022). *The best police podcasts of 2022.* https://golawenforcement.com/articles/best-police-podcasts-of-2020/
Harkins, P., & Ellis, A. (2021, November 22). Is the fear factor overblown in police shootings? Retrieved February 6, 2023, from https://www.pbs.org/wgbh/frontline/article/police- shootings-fear-factor/
Henricks, T. (2017). Race: The reality of the imagined. *Psychology Today.* https://www.psychologytoday.com/us/blog/the-pathways-experience/201702/race-the-reality-the-imagined
Hernández, A. R., & Bailey, H. (2021, July 17). Texas House report on Uvalde shooting blames all agencies at scene. *The Washington Post.* Retrieved July 18, 2021, from https://www.washingtonpost.com/nation/2022/07/17/uvalde-school-shooting-report/
Holbert, L., Shah, D. V., & Kwak, N. (2004). Fear, authority, and justice: Crime-related TV viewing and endorsements of capital punishment and handgun ownership. *Journalism and Mass Communication Quarterly, 81*(2), 343–363. https://doi.org/10.1177/107769900408100208
Hsu, J. (2009, June). People choose news that fits their views. *Live Science.* https://www.livescience.com/3640-people-choose-news-fits-views.html
Jacobs, E. (2020, March). Police Academy facts you never knew you needed. *Movieweb.* https://movieweb.com/police-academy-movies-classic/
Kaste, M. (2020, September). NYPD study: Implicit bias training changes minds, not necessarily behavior. *NPR.* https://www.npr.org/2020/09/10/909380525/nypd-study-implicit-bias-training-changes-minds-not-necessarily-behavior
Khare, M. [Michelle Khare]. (2019, September 29). *I tried police academy.* [Video]. YouTube. https://www.youtube.com/watch?v=ZJGirITl6sE
Kidd, D. (2021). Popular culture. In *Oxford bibliographies.* https://www.oxfordbibliographies.com/view/document/obo-9780199756384/obo 9780199756384–0193.xml. doi:10.1093/OBO/9780199756384–0193
Kinsley, D. (2021, September 28). *'Training Day' at 20: Welcome back to the jungle.* Retrieved July 18, 2022, from https://awardswatch.com/training-day-at-20-welcome-back-to-the-jungle-retrospective/
Lopez, R., & Johnson, T. (2017, August). Movies, tv shows evolve to reflect a changing, more complex view of police. *Variety.* https://variety.com/2017/film/features/police-in-movies-tv-shows-1202511299/
Manzoor, A. (2019). Use of social media for policing. In Information Resources Management Information (Ed.), *Police science: Breakthroughs in research and practice* (pp. 259–289). IGI Global. doi:10.4018/978-1-5225-7672–3.ch013

Marcou, D. (2019). Are cops being harmed by Hollywood depictions of LE? *Police 1*. https://www.police1.com/community-policing/articles/are-cops-being-harmed-by-hollywood-depictions-of-le-ueb6tmqm0yvTdNHf/

Marr, J. (2015, August 19). The long life and quiet death of *True Detective* magazine. Retrieved July 18, 2022, from https://gizmodo.com/the-long-life-and-quiet-death-of-true-detective-magazin-1725094095

McGovern, A., & Phillips, N. D. (2017). Police, media, and popular culture. *Oxford Research Encyclopedias*. https://oxfordre.com/view/10.1093/acrefore/9780190264079.001.0001/acrefore-9780190264079-e-279. https://doi.org/10.1093/acrefore/9780190264079.013.279

Meeks, K. (2000). *Driving while Black: Highways, shopping malls, taxi cabs, sidewalks: How to fight back if you are a victim of racial profiling*. Crown/Archetype.

Merriam-Webster. (2022). *Stereotype*. Retrieved July 6, 2022, from https://www.merriam-webster.com/dictionary/stereotype

Miethe, T. D., Venger, O., & Lieberman, J. D. (2018). Police use of force and its video coverage: An experimental study of the impact of media source and content on public perceptions. *Journal of Criminal Justice, 60*, 35–46. http://dx.doi.org/10.1016/j.jcrimjus.2018.10.006

Milano, V. (2018, October). Check out this sneak peek of "what an institution: The story of police academy." *The Hollywood Times*. https://thehollywoodtimes.today/check-out-this-sneak-peek-of-what-an-institution-the-story-of-police-academy/

Miller, J., Davis, R. C., Henderson, N. J., Markovic, J., & Ortiz, C. W. (2004). *Public opinions of the police: The influence of friends, family, and news media*. Vera Institute of Justice.

Molofsky, H. (2020, June). Cops: The violent legacy of a TV show that sculpted America's view of police. *The Guardian*. https://www.theguardian.com/tv-and-radio/2020/jun/11/cops-american-police-tv-show

Morrow, S. (2019). Social and news media's effects on law enforcement. *Global Journal of Forensic Science and Medicine, 1*(4). https://irispublishers.com/gjfsm/fulltext/social-news-medias-effects-on-law-enforcement.ID.000516.php

Mutz, D. C., & Nir, L. (2010). Not necessarily the news: Does fictional television influence real-world policy preferences? *Mass Communication and Society, 13*, 196–217. https://doi.org/10.1080/15205430902813856

Nemo, L. (2020, June 11). How do police dramas shape what we think of real-life officers? *Discover Magazine*. Retrieved February 5, 2023, from https://www.discovermagazine.com/mind/how-do-police-dramas-shape-what-we-think- of-real-life-officers

Officer401. (2018, July 15). *5 ways people fail the police academy*. [Video]. YouTube. https://www.youtube.com/watch?v=OoFXQMF-2Fs

Officer401. (2020, August 5). *How to pass the police academy*. [Video]. YouTube. https://www.youtube.com/watch?v=mUi0rA12Pp0

Oglesby-Neal A., Tiry, E., & Kim, K. (2019, February). Public perceptions of police on social media: A big-data approach to understanding sentiment toward the police. *The Urban Institute*. https://www.urban.org/sites/default/files/publication/99789/public_perceptions_of_police_on_social_media_0.pdf

Oliver, M. B. (2003). African American men as "criminal and dangerous": Implications of media portrayals of crime on the "criminalization" of African American men. *Journal of African American Studies*, 7(2), 3–18. http://www.jstor.org/stable/41819017

Ortiz, A. (2020, August 12). Confidence in police is at record low, Gallup survey finds. *The New York Times*. https://www.nytimes.com/2020/08/12/us/gallup-poll-police.html

PBS. (2020). Driving while Black. https://www.pbs.org/show/driving-while-black/

Persaud, C. (2022, January). Why is America so obsessed with true crime? *Digital Trends*. https://www.digitaltrends.com/movies/true-crime-obsession/

Pinfold, W. (2020, November 25). *The law won—police academy and 80s pop culture*. Retrieved February 5, 2023, from http://williampinfold.com/the-law-won-police-academy-and-80s- pop-culture/

Police 1. (2016, June). 5 hilarious crime busts involving donuts. *Police 1*. https://www.police1.com/police-humor/articles/5-hilarious-crime-busts-involving-donuts-Gnt5uhEligMxEn1q/

Ranker TV. (2022, June). From the police to fishermen, these are the best reality shows about professionals. *Ranker*. https://www.ranker.com/list/best-profession-reality-shows/ranker-tv

Raymond, G. (2018, August 10). The 16 best true crime books of all time. *TIME*. Retrieved February 5, 2023, from https://time.com/5355643/best-true-crime-books-of-all-time/

Richardson, L. S., & Goff, P. A. (2014). Interrogating racial violence. *Ohio State Journal of Criminal Law, 12,* 115–152.

Rosenberg, A. (2016, October 24). Dragnets, dirty Harrys, and dying hard: 100 years of the police in pop culture–How police censorship shaped Hollywood. *The Washington Post*. Retrieved July 16, 2022, from https://www.washingtonpost.com/sf/opinions/2016/10/24/how-police-censorship-shaped-hollywood/

Ryan, M. (2020, April). What effect did the 'police academy' sequels have on the original films legacy? *Uproxx*. https://uproxx.com/movies/police-academy-legacy/

Sage, T. (2021, August). The doom of a franchise: 'Police academy: Mission to Moscow'. *UCR Classic Rock and Culture*. https://ultimateclassicrock.com/police-academy-mission-to-moscow/

Sayles, J. (2021, July). The bloody bubble. *The Ringer.* https://www.theringer.com/tv/2021/7/9/22567381/true-crime-documentaries-boom-bubble-netflix-hbo

Schuhart, J. (2022, September 21). Is training day based on a true story? Retrieved February 2, 2023, from https://www.looper.com/347725/is-training-day-based-on-a-true-story/

Schultz, J. (2019). *Media coverage of law enforcement and effects of the image created* (Unpublished senior thesis). Dominican University of California

Shearer, E. (2021, January). More than eight-in-ten Americans get their news from digital devices. *Pew Research Center*. https://www.pewresearch.org/fact-tank/2021/01/12/more-than-eight-in-ten-americans-get-news-from-digital-devices/

Shepherd, J. (2022). *What are the different types of social media platforms and which is best for your business?* Retrieved July 11, 2022, from https://www.titangrowth.com/blog/types-of-social-media-platforms/

Skolnick, J. H. (1965). *Justice without trial: Law enforcement in democratic society*. John Wiley & Son, Inc.

Smallwood, K. (2013, September). What started the "cops eating doughnuts" stereotype? *Today I Found Out*. http://www.todayifoundout.com/index.php/2013/09/started-cops-eating-donuts-stereotype/

Smiley, C., & Fakunle, D. (2016). From "brute" to "thug:" The demonization and criminalization unarmed Black male victims in America. *Journal of Human Behavior in the Social Environment, 26*(3–4), 350–366. doi:10.1080/10911359.2015.1129256

Sorin, G. (2020). *Driving while Black: African American travel and the road to civil rights*. Liveright.

Stelter, M., Essien, I., Sander, C., & Danger, J. (2022). Racial bias in police traffic stops: White residents' county-level prejudice and stereotypes are related to disproportionate stopping of Black drivers. *Psychological Science, 33*(4), 483–496. https://doi.org/10.1177/09567976211051272

Strinati, D. (2000). *An introduction to studying popular culture*. Routledge.

Taberski, D. (2019). *Running from COPS*. Topic Podcasts. https://www.topic.com/runningfromcops

Thomas, W. I., & Thomas, D. S. (1928). *The child in America*. Knopf.

Time.com. (2022). *5 police documentaries you should watch right away*. Retrieved July 17, 2022, from https://intime.com/industries/police/top-police-documentaries/

Tirosh, G. (2023). *The story of police academy, the movie*. Retrieved February 5, 2023, from https://nostalgicreads.com/movies/the-story-of-police-academy-the-movie/

Tisdell, E. J. (2008). Critical media literacy and transformative learning: Drawing on pop culture and entertainment media in teaching for diversity in adult higher education. *Journal of Transformative Education, 6*(1), 48–67. https://doi.org/10.1177/1541344608318970

Trinkner, R., Kerrison, E. M., & Goff, P. A. (2019). The force of fear: Police stereotype threat, self-legitimacy, and support for excessive force. *Law and Human Behavior, 43*(5), 421–435. https://doi.apa.org/fulltext/2019-36698-001.html

University of Derby. (2022). *Why are we so obsessed with true crime?* https://www.derby.ac.uk/magazine/issue-11/why-are-we-so-obsessed-with-true-crime/

Waxman, O. B. (2017, June 2). This is why doughnuts are associated with police officers. Retrieved July 17, 202, from https://time.com/4800386/donuts-doughnuts-police-cops/

Weichselbaum, S. (2018). Yelp for the cops. How am I doing? Check the sentiment meter. *The Marshall Project*. Retrieved July 17, 2022, from https://www.themarshallproject.org/2018/07/16/yelp-for-cops

Welch, K. (2007). Black criminal stereotypes and racial profiling. *Journal of Contemporary Criminal Justice, 23*(3), 276–288. doi:10.1177/1043986207306870

Williams, C. B., & Fedorowicz, J. (2019). *Does social media promote the public's perception of the police: Survey results on trust cultivation*. Proceedings of the 52nd Hawaii International Conference on System Sciences, 3109–3118. Retrieved July 17, 2022, from https://scholarspace.manoa.hawaii.edu/items/9e68500a-12dd-40b5-bbaa-4d266dcdeaac

Wise, J. (2022, July). Podcast statistics 2022: How many podcasts are there? *Earthweb*. Retrieved July 5, 2022, from https://earthweb.com/podcast-statistics/

WNYC Studios. (2019, June 12). *What 'running from cops' learned from 'cops'*. Retrieved February 5, 2023, from https://www.wnycstudios.org/podcasts/otm/episodes/onthemedia- what-running-cops-learned-cops

Wozniak, K. H., Drakulick, K. M., & Calfano, B. R. (2021). Public opinion about police weapons and equipment: An exploratory analysis. *Criminal Justice Policy Review, 32*(9), 960–991. https://doi.org/10.1177/08874034211005005

Zillerman, D., & Bryant, J. (2002). Entertainment as media effects. In J. Bryant & D. Zillerman (Eds.), *Media effects: Advances in theory and research* (2nd ed., pp. 473–462). Erlbaum.

PART V

Looking Towards the Future

A Call to Action

12

A MODEL FOR DECENTRALIZED POLICE EDUCATION AND TRAINING

Studies by the PERF and other groups have concluded that police retention has suffered in recent years. According to PERF (2021), police agencies reported an overall 18% increase in the resignation rate in 2020–2021, compared to 2019–2020. Police officers not only have to confront the occurrences of major and minor crimes but also have to deal with citizens experiencing mental health problems, addiction, and homelessness, as well as a myriad of service calls, such as noise complaints, other quality-of-life concerns, and lower-risk neighborhood conflicts. "Yet because police often lack the tools and training to address such concerns, these calls for service can result in unnecessary uses of force, justice system involvement, and other adverse outcomes for civilians, as well as put a strain on public safety resources" (Irwin & Pearl, 2020). At the same time, body cameras and bystanders' cell phones have placed a media spotlight on many officers at a level never experienced before.

In America, primarily due to the widespread availability of video technology, several police departments have received scathing criticism due to their officers' aggressive tactics as well as the outright misconduct committed by rogue cops. At the same time, an increase in police militarization has taken place, which has been accompanied by a lack of transparency and accountability. Nowhere is this more noticeable and painful than in African American and other minority communities. Moreover, the police who engage in misconduct seem to exercise undue influence, infecting other police with their negative attitudes toward minorities and even citizens with mental illness (Stamper, 2016). This pattern of behavior may have contributed to the death of George Floyd on May 25, 2020, when Minneapolis police officer Derek Chauvin knelt on Mr. Floyd's neck for more than nine minutes and less senior officers failed to react in time (Bogel-Burroughs, 2021). The incident reignited sustained "Black Lives Matter" protests across the country and globally, as well as widespread calls for reforming and even defunding police forces.

In an effort to counter brutality by police as well as encourage the recruitment of qualified minority applicants into the field of law enforcement, a more decentralized model for police training is proposed. The proposed training model would help accomplish a more

DOI: 10.4324/9781003307396-17

democratic and humane police system by involving community members and institutions of higher education as integral components in the (ongoing) training process of police officers. Its hallmarks would include: community participation and cooperation, accountability, transparency, mutual responsibility for effective safety management, open communication, increasing synergy between the police and other local institutions, respect for victims and witnesses, and flexibility in developing strategies to solve problems and meeting local priorities.

The United States' 18,000 police forces need sweeping law enforcement reforms regarding how best to qualify and monitor police officers; this can also help with recruiting and retention of those who meet and exceed expectations. While no standardized model of training or monitoring police officers across jurisdictions is currently in use, college education and even advanced degrees are no longer rarities (Roberg & Bonn, 2004). Yet, in parts of the United States, some smaller communities sponsor academies that barely meet state minimum police training hourly standards, while others cannot even afford to sponsor their own police officers' basic training. By comparison, many larger departments may have adequate resources to devote to their police academies and therefore can greatly exceed minimum hourly standards. Furthermore, those larger jurisdictions may require a college degree as a preliminary requirement for merely taking a police officer civil service exam, whereas smaller departments often do not have this hiring prerequisite.

Nationwide, these issues have led agency administrators to seek better methods for monitoring and uplifting the integrity and professionalism of their police officers. In this chapter, we propose the revision of police partnerships with area colleges and universities in order to provide a more meaningful way to educate future LEOs. As such, the program has the potential to encourage more positive relationships between police officers and community members, partially by helping diversify police forces nationwide.

Earlier Reform Efforts

Every good story usually has a hero and the field of criminal justice education and police training has one as well. The hero in this case was August Vollmer. After a number of years of planning, in the summer of 1916, Berkeley, California's Police Chief August Vollmer, "in coordination with the University of California, created a baccalaureate degree granting program for his police officers. . . . The program was titled Criminology and consisted of courses on police practices, criminal law, and many of the natural science classes including biology, chemistry, and toxicology. This program continued through the summer of 1932, when a university-wide program was developed and overseen by then Professor August Vollmer. The summer program, begun in 1916, developed into both the modern criminology and criminal justice programs of today" (Oliver, 2016, p. 455). However, it should be noted that "not all scholars trace the development of criminal justice as an academic field back to August Vollmer. One scholar traces the field back to Supreme Court Justice Robert Jackson and the American Bar Foundation's Research conducted in the 1950s . . . while Stephens (1976) commences with the establishment of the American Institute of Criminal Law and Criminology in 1909 and the initiation of the *Journal of Criminal Law and Criminology* one year later. It should also be noted here that many scholars outside of the United States have a very different perspective on the development of criminal justice education" (Oliver, 2016, p. 456n1).

In New York City, perhaps the most important early reform in police training took place in 1915 when the period of training for recruits was extended from six weeks to 12 weeks. In addition to physical training, the major topics covered were: laws and ordinances; court procedure and evidence; cooperation with other departments; and discipline in the department. Physical training was increased by adding walking exercises "to prevent falling arches and flat feet; boxing; Indian club swinging and bag punching. The course formerly consisted of training in calisthenics, humans handling of prisoners and wrestling" (Commissioner Woods, 1915).

The hours devoted to the basic training of police officers have risen steadily, especially since the 1960s. An important feature of modern-day police training is the opportunity for recruits to ride with a field instructor, "who monitors their movements and helps them apply principles learned in rookie school. . . . After completing training, they continue to ride with one or more training officers who continue to evaluate their street performance" (Wrobleski & Hess, 1979, p. 463). The additional field training usually continues during a probationary period of employment. Nonetheless, a college degree requirement for police candidates has been met with slow progress since the President's Commission on Law Enforcement and Administration of Justice (1967) recommended "that all personnel with general enforcement powers have baccalaureate degrees" (p. ix).

In 1978, Warren Bennis, chairman of the National Advisory Commission of Higher Education for Police Officers and the former president of the University of Cincinnati, declared: "It's sad and ironic, but a large part of police education is a rip-off. The field needs important universities like Harvard and Northwestern, to offer programs. If there is to be any improvement, the faculty that teaches police officers must be independent of police departments" (qtd. in McGrath, 1978, p. 3). The commission's report, entitled *The Quality of Police Education*, contained 43 recommendations; in general, these recommendations emphasized the need to upgrade course content and the credentials of police educators. According to Norval Morris, a commission member and dean of the University of Chicago Law School, "We want police officers to find through education new methods for coping with crime and providing social justice" (qtd. in McGrath, 1978, p. 3). The commission took notice of the great expansion in the number of colleges offering programs for police and other peace officers since funding had become available through the US Justice Department's Law Enforcement Assistance Administration. However, despite the bulk of the funds aiding in-service police attendance in courses in higher education, there had been little change in the overall practices of policing in the United States (McGrath, 1978).

A dozen years later, a proposal for new police to be hired with baccalaureate degrees that had been germinating for seven years reached Congressional attention in the form of the *Police Corps Act of 1989*. Yet, it was not until 1994 that the *Police Corps Act* was finally authorized to address violent crime and disorder by increasing the number of patrol officers with advanced education to serve in communities throughout the United States. The plan was supported by both liberal and conservative lawmakers, but when first introduced, it received a lukewarm reception from the head of the National Association of Police Organizations (NAPO), which represents 90,000 police officers. The initial idea was to add 100,000 new officers to the existing 480,000 already employed by having participating students obtain federally guaranteed loans for their education and then having up to $40,000 ($10,000-a-year scholarships) repaid by the government once they completed four years of police service (Barker, 1989). Significantly, the plan called for the federal government to not only make these student awards, but also fund the basic training for these new officers. In the 1996 legislative version of the plan, student scholarship assistance was limited to a maximum of $30,000 in educational assistance, but the federal government was to provide local and state agencies that hire Police Corps officers $10,000 a year for each of an officer's first four years of service (Police Corps Annual Report, 2000, p. 2). Rules for the program were subsequently developed requiring the submission of state plans for participation. The state plans had to demonstrate that the standards for applicant selection were "at least as demanding as the most rigorous hiring standards utilized by law enforcement agencies within the state" (Police Corps Annual Report, 2000, p. 6).

When the Police Corps plan was first introduced, the *New York Times,* in a supportive editorial, stated: "Benefits of the idea go way beyond such savings. The college-educated cops would likely bring more motivation to community patrolling than civil service recruits. And the four-year cycle of officers through a department could ventilate an inbred squad-room subculture, even as it expanded public understanding of police work" (Editorial, 1990). On the other hand, Robert Scully, the president of NAPO, pointed out in his Congressional testimony that it is usually only after at least four years that novice police officers have obtained sufficient experience that they are not prone to errors. His organization would prefer that educational benefits go to in-service personnel who have already demonstrated their commitment to police work, instead of to pre-college entrants who would be forced to make early decisions with respect to their career plans. President Scully also noted that the best way to attract qualified police candidates is to increase police salary levels and permit collective bargaining (Scully, 1989). One letter writer attacked the proposal and newspaper's support for it more directly: "What you eloquently refer to as the 'squad-room subculture' will not be penetrated by federally dispatched students, whatever they are called. And if it is, they will become integrated into the squad room and adopt its values. People whose work entails unpredictable dangers tend to develop a comradeship and brotherhood, which is what makes that work bearable" (Rowe, 1990, p. A24).

The critics of the Police Corps plan who may have been worried about police morale and related matters may have overreacted. By December 1999, only a total of 434 men and women had participated in the program. Of the total number of participants, 169 were attending college as undergraduates, 34 participants were in Police Corps training, and only 231 Police Corps participants had completed their undergraduate degrees and Police Corps training and had begun their service as Police Corps officers. The serving officers were located in 120 local police departments, 17 sheriff's offices, and 12 state police agencies (Police Corps Annual Report, 2000, p. 7).

According to the *Police Corps Annual Report* (2000), Police Corps training typically included "far more training hours than required by the minimum standards set by state POST boards. Michigan's first Police Corps training, for example, nearly doubled the typical number of basic training hours. The additional time was used, among other things, to add firearms simulation training to range training, add a number of intense scenarios and practicums, introduce readings on social context from the Police Corps Readings for Training Programs, and bring in outside speakers who ordinarily would not be available in basic recruit training" (p. 17). The entire program was phased out by 2012. It should not be confused with President Clinton's 1994 crime bill initiative, which led to the hiring of not quite 100,000 more police officers across the country by paying for two-thirds of the new officers' salaries in participating cities (see Kessler, 2014; Keneally, 2016). This funding program has been ongoing since the Clinton presidency, and it allocated $304 million to state, local, and tribal law enforcement agencies in 2019. It is commonly known as the Community Oriented Policing Services (COPS) program (Lee, 2020). The Police Corps only received modest funding beginning in 1996 with an initial $10 million appropriation (Police Corps Annual Report, 2000, p. 3).

In 1985, when Benjamin Ward, New York City's Police Commissioner, was informed about the Police Corps proposal, he viewed the idea as "impractical, not well thought out" and "simplistic" (qtd. in Oreskes, 1985, p. 42). "He said the program would be expensive and that he preferred a plan, put forth by the John Jay College of Criminal Justice, to create a police academy in which college students would serve internships in police departments before joining full-time after graduation" (Oreskes, 1985, p. 42). Within a year, the college's plan was adopted by the New York City Police Department. Participants received grants totaling $3,000 toward the expenses of their last two years of a bachelor's degree, which could be earned at any college in the city or in neighboring Westchester and Nassau Counties. The loans were forgiven if the student served as an officer for two years after graduation. The first duty of the cadets after graduation would be to attend the full five-and-one-half-month program of the city's police academy, although they could be excused from driver training if they took it as cadets. All the cadets had to be residents of New York City and have successfully completed the initial police recruit qualifications, including passing the examination given for regular police officers. The cadets were also paid seven dollars an hour for two summers of full-time work and three days a month during their college years. They wore police style uniforms but without weapons and were assigned to the police department's existing Community Patrol Officer Program (CPOP) in 45 of the city's 75 precincts. The CPOP officers served in small units of seven to ten officers, under the command of a sergeant. The CPOP officers patrolled neighborhoods to prevent crime and to address quality of life issues with an emphasis on making a closer connection with the public. The cadets were permitted to join these patrols, but were instructed to avoid dangerous situations and provide assistance of a service nature (e.g., comforting crime victims or other persons in distress). In subsequent years, the cadets were offered opportunities to work in other specialized units of the department (Burden, 1988). The current program is similar, but cadets now receive up to $20,000 in tuition assistance ($2,500 to $5,000 per semester, up to four semesters) and the current hourly wage is $16.31 (NYPD, 2021).

Decentralized Precinct Training

Building on some of the concepts of these prior reform efforts, the envisioned decentralized precinct training involves harnessing the energies and talents of outstanding and experienced LEOs, social service professionals, and college educators in order to prepare candidates for police officer work. When appropriate, the latest available technology for video and audio conferencing, chat, and webinars would be used to offer training content. Significantly, local police and related facilities would serve as an extension of the college campus. Police personnel, social service professionals, and college faculty would collaborate on the coproduction of the types of police training that would be added to enhance basic training beyond the scope of the minimum state standards of traditional training academies.

Overall, the new enhanced decentralized precinct training would include: an intensive fieldwork experience; a college degree course of study; the initial completion of a volunteer police training course (auxiliary or reserve) in conformity with state standards; and the completion of the state mandated basic police school. This model permits a unique collaboration between police agencies and colleges for the purpose of designing an appropriate curriculum that fulfills public safety objectives. In particular, this approach can help ensure that all training courses place emphasis on eliminating the unnecessary use of force and building stronger community relationships.

The concept of the decentralized precinct training model takes inspiration from the formation of the new Camden, NJ police department (see Bauman & Chakrabarti, 2020; Zernike, 2014) and the achievements of the Sheriff's Academy in Chautauqua County, New York, which "has saved the taxpayers of western New York hundreds of thousands of dollars in training costs" (Dyment, 1997). The design begins with students pursuing a degree at a local college in a field related to criminal justice. College administrators would assign students to a cooperating precinct as police interns during the entire length of their study after declaring their intent to complete the program (most likely, this would occur during the first or second years of undergraduate coursework). Thus, the extended college campus would consist of a police department's physical buildings but also the surrounding public streets, schools, community centers, and parks within its jurisdiction. It could also include special assignments at related social control agencies, local government (e.g., code enforcement), schools, hospitals, civic clubs, recreational facilities (public and nonprofit), jails and courts. Such collaboration encourages partnerships not only between the participating colleges and police departments, but also among various local community organizations.

Police departments would carefully screen all participants to ensure they satisfy the basic requirements for peace officer selection (for positions in police departments as well as courts or correctional facilities). The program is especially well-suited for areas that currently lack the resources to conduct adequate recruit training or offer academies that only satisfy minimum standards. Though it would not be imperative that a graduate join the police department in which he or she completed the program, it will provide a pool of potential employees for the criminal justice agencies in geographic areas while also providing well-educated and uniquely trained peace officers for departments and agencies across the nation. The program is viable for those jurisdictions that lack a preliminary college degree requirement for officers and may lack sufficient minority representation. The community collaboration at the center of the model will assist in recruiting diverse groups of individuals to fill roles as criminal justice professionals. The program coincides with the views of those police education experts and other scholars who advocate that police officer candidates should acquire a sound educational background prior to beginning their police service (see Bilek, 1995; Burkhalter, 2020; Carter & Sapp, 1990; Kelderman, 2020; Michelson, 2016). However, the program differs from the general type of criminal justice degree programs commonly offered at colleges and universities in the United States as it would require students to involve themselves in day-to-day law enforcement operations as police interns and include satisfying basic mandated state peace officer/police training requirements. Thus, the combination of mandatory field work alongside of an academic program will offer participants unique experiences to blend these two aspects of a criminal justice education.

The proposed new program would fill a distinct void in the field of police training found in many parts of the country by centering police training at the grass-roots levels of community life—local college campuses and local neighborhoods. Thus, unlike some police academies where completion of a college degree merely represents an option for participants, the program would require the completion of a college degree as well as significant periods of fieldwork spread out during the length of an academic degree educational experience, allowing for a deeper understanding of research and theory by applying classroom knowledge to real-life experiences. This would allow for the bridging of theory and practice through daily civic engagement of all participants.

A significant amount of the program's academic course requirements could take place at the campus of a local college or through remote viewing and learning formats. Members of sponsoring police agencies would serve as instructors on the college campus along with traditional college professors. Local police and college instructors would develop the academy's curriculum, which must be approved by college and state authorities, while allowing for the tailoring of the program for the unique needs based on the geographic areas and cultural communities in which the program's participants are located.

College officials would select an advisory council of knowledgeable community members for oversight purposes. The program would require students to work as police interns for a minimum of four hours per week, depending upon the requirements set forth for their degree and stage in the program. All students would need to stay in good standing with their program's requirements in order to remain eligible for police training and to serve as police interns. As required by state law, the sponsoring police agency would register its recruit school and members of the recruit class with appropriate state authorities, such as each state's POST division. Furthermore, if available, police departments would advance police interns to auxiliary or reserve police status to mark their progress. In this way, students could begin to perform selective duties while still completing their academic work and eventually the required basic police school prior to graduation. The enhanced curriculum planners would decide upon the type of internships that can best be used to complement their community's needs.

More specifically, the structure of the internship would be designed as a long-term field experience alongside of the acquisition of academic knowledge. The experience should provide participating students with important information that will be useful in their careers. In addition, combining the two types of experiences (practical and academic) synchronously versus having them occur separately allows for a deeper understanding of the profession and the duties of a police officer (or other peace officer professions). The ultimate goal of the model is to improve relationships among police officers and the communities they serve. To achieve this goal, police officers must better *understand* and work *with* the communities they serve. The field experience and academic courses will complement each other by providing context to one another. Individuals will see real-world examples of policing at the same time they are learning about the social, psychological, and cultural aspects of their communities. Officers who complete a program based on the model will be better poised to interact with community members respectfully and effectively, presumably bringing about more positive relationships between police departments and community citizens.

Types of Internships

For better or worse, the field of academia is filled with a variety of different terminology when it comes to the provision of real-world work experiences for students. A basic internship is a work-related learning experience for individuals who wish to develop practical experience in a certain occupational field. While most internships are temporary assignments, lasting for only a few weeks or months, some may last a lot longer. College-level internships typically last approximately three months, or one semester. The decentralized precinct program would allow for variation in the type of internship a participant experiences, based largely upon the structure of the college the student is attending and can include multiple internship experiences at various times during the duration of the program. Again, with a focus on community, individual programs have the flexibility to determine which type(s) of internships is most beneficial to their locations.

Generally, an internship helps students gain valuable experience to increase their marketability after graduation. The experience is expected to help them narrow down their career choices. Students usually earn a minimum of three college credits for part-time internship work or may be eligible for 12 to 15 credits for the completion of a full-time semester internship. The granting of college credits is typically contingent on having a faculty member who will be responsible for supervising the completion of an academic project that is related to the internship focus in addition to their on-the-job supervisor. In order to facilitate the placement of interns, many colleges maintain the services of at least one full-time career advisor who assists students with their internship applications.

One type of brief internship experience is known as an "externship." Generally, externships are not for credit and exist to provide students opportunities to explore fields of potential interest for a brief period. In such a program a student volunteer engages in a short "job shadowing" experience, often appealing to college freshmen and sophomores. For example, students would spend one week during school recess breaks (e.g., in March or late December) observing and working in an agency. These types of programs offer the chance to investigate the nature of a career opportunity without risk and without a semester-long commitment. Of course, this can benefit some students by enabling them to get their "feet in the door" for such an internship at a later date.

On the other hand, some internships may involve full-time work as well as a salary and other benefits. These types of internships are often categorized as "cooperative education," since they involve a three-way partnership between a college, an employer, and a student. Furthermore, students can get college credit for this type of real-world work experience.

Still another internship format is known as the practicum experience. Practicums are used when students apply their academic experience to a real-world project. For the most part, students work in teams or individually with an employer and academic supervisor.

The common term "apprenticeship" is most often applied when students are assigned to an agency or employer for the specific purpose of learning a skilled trade to get practical experience and in-school training at the same time. Sometimes internships may be referred to as "doing fieldwork" or "service learning." Service learning takes place when students work in an organized service within a community in order to fulfill specific course requirements. Such interns might work at a school, university, or community service program. On the other hand, the term "fieldwork" is often associated with the fulfillment of specific programmatic requirements such as the need for students in the sciences to develop skills observing, recording, and interpreting data. It is also commonly used to refer to applied work requirements in the fields of social work, counseling, and teaching.

Fellowships are yet another type of internship, but these are typically not connected with formal undergraduate degree work, but rather are undertaken after obtaining a graduate degree or as part of a program of graduate education (on the doctoral or post-doctoral level). Most fellowships are restricted to recent graduates (within five years of graduation).

The primary goal of such a program is to provide advanced professional training and/or opportunities for early-career entry. Fellowship positions are usually for one year and may sometimes be renewed or extended for up to one additional year on a case-by-case basis. Fellows usually receive financial compensation and even some fringe benefits.

While the specifics of an internship experience, as well as what it would be called, would be flexible dependent on location, need, and program, overall the proposed experience would be long-term and during the time students are engaged in college coursework. It is also possible that different types of internships will be completed at different times or levels of study to allow students to build on their practical experiences as their educational knowledge builds. The idea is that the internship compliments the academic work being done by future police officers, and that both practical training and academic education are happening simultaneously. Community involvement of the application of classroom studies is key; the incorporation of an auxiliary status component in the process can also assist in this pursuit.

Importance of Auxiliary or Reserve Status

The inclusion of part-time peace officer training leading to auxiliary or reserve status for student interns is ideal because it combines the best aspects of a practicum and apprenticeship, namely, real world experiences. In an era with so much of the public interested in serious police reform (while formal, civics education is declining), a useful way to reduce or deter overly aggressive regular police behavior is to ensure an adequate presence of well qualified citizens in close proximity to regular police officers. Thus, a key component of the program should be to recruit, train, and deploy "Auxiliary Police Officers." Auxiliaries are the civilians whose duties and training most closely approximate the police and whose activities blur the lines between civilian and cop, volunteer, and worker. Often referred to as "the eyes and ears of the police," auxiliary police officers patrol on foot or in a patrol car, wearing uniforms nearly indistinguishable from those of sworn police officers. They may train and operate out of police stations and police departments fund them. Auxiliaries' primary purpose is to observe and report suspicious activities. In New York City, they carry no guns, only nightsticks. Auxiliary officers also help crime victims and work "details," public events at which they provide crowd control and assistance. In order to join the ranks of the auxiliary police, recruits must enroll in various training courses and pass written and physical examinations. Auxiliaries are expected to serve a specific number of unpaid hours each month. As civilians, in most jurisdictions, auxiliary police officers are empowered to make arrests for crimes that occur in their presence, but are usually discouraged by departmental policies from doing so.

Each police agency can decide on the actual duties of its volunteer police and, if sufficient personnel are available, offer the opportunity for qualified interns to complete the requirements of the jurisdiction's basic police school. For example, in addition to adding an element of transparency to police work, incorporating an auxiliary program or unit within the proposed decentralized precinct program would enable community centers to be better staffed, neighborhood watch programs given more attention, school safety patrols enhanced, DARE and anti-bullying programs reinstated or expanded, traffic patrols expanded, pedestrian safety increased, homeless people better cared for, and more coaches available for youth sport leagues. College interns serving as volunteer police officers after their certification would be required to adhere to the same standards and hold the same qualifications as any other auxiliary or reserve officer in the jurisdiction. Moreover, they would be subject to the rules and discipline as specified by the sponsoring law enforcement agency.

About 200 years ago, Sir Robert Peel introduced the idea and achieved the implementation of a uniformed municipal police force based on democratic principles. Public support was essential for its success and its mission included: crime prevention, community trust and engagement, reasonable force as a last resort, impartiality without favor, never above the law, and that "the police are the public and the public are the police." The lattermost theme is especially critical for understanding the need for such police/citizen partnerships as an auxiliary police corps. The inclusion of such an experience within the program model is to further expand participants' knowledge and experiences of and with local communities to offer them a strong foundation as a paid officer upon completion of the program.

Recommended College Courses

Colleges have flexibility in developing revised curricula based on their institutional guidelines and missions to augment the envisioned program of merged academic work and preservice training. At its core, this model is flexible, providing a blueprint to assist individual jurisdictions to create programming to meet unique needs of their communities. Moreover, the changes would not depend on any new local, state, or national laws. There is no need for more state or federal aid. Administrators could freely adjust their curricula as needed, as long as they ensured that it satisfied their state's higher educational standards and involved stakeholders (citizens, colleges, and police agencies) in their discussions. In revising curriculums for the proposed program, colleges might consider the inclusion of such courses as: crisis intervention, psychology, sociology, anthropology, history, social work, and communication. Each of these subjects would allow for students to explore areas of policing beyond the "technical" skills and the law as it is written. Doing so will better prepare officers for communicating with citizens in the communities where they work by better understanding larger social contexts, individual characteristics, and variance in cultural practices.

A course in crisis intervention would recognize that during recent decades, law enforcement has "moved away from a traditional reactive model to one based on a concept called community-oriented policing. . . . Its key elements, problem-solving and the creation of partnerships with local stakeholders, provide the theoretical and practical underpinnings for the development of atypical techniques for handling potentially dangerous confrontations with those suffering from mental illness. This population is commonly known to law enforcement as EDPs or Emotionally Disturbed Persons" (Nislow, 2008). The proposed program can enhance law enforcement's response to people who are in a state of confusion, crisis, or mental illness. The overuse of deadly force by police in recent times, especially those involving people of color, has caused major public concern throughout the United States. Both college student interns and sworn police officers should complete one or more courses involving the methods of crisis intervention because discretionary arrest situations have led to the deaths of Black civilians. "Traditionally, law enforcement officers are the first to respond to crisis situations involving individuals with mental illnesses and, therefore, must receive training on how to resolve these situations more efficiently and with greater sensitivity" (Klein, 2002).

The subjects of psychology, sociology, anthropology, and history are all part of a rounded liberal arts education. The intellectual development that occurs through a liberal arts program has benefits in helping students become more well-rounded citizens, leaders, and critical thinkers while learning effective communication (see Goodwin, 2019; Rose, 2017). Such courses expose students to a broad range of topics that are important for police officers to explore, including social institutions, race, and culture, as well as issues related to intersectionality. An inclusion of humanities courses can also expose students to thinking deeply about culture, language, and interacting with people of different backgrounds. Such courses challenge students to think beyond the lens of their individual experiences and biases to better understand differences among people. They provide a vocabulary for students to use alongside of theoretical frameworks with which to discuss social problems and potential solutions. To move toward positive, qualitative change in police-community relations, it is imperative that police officers better *understand* and *respect* all community members and groups, without bias. A future police force that embraces and encourages diversity will be helpful in recruiting officers from underrepresented groups, with further potentials for building stronger bonds and trust within communities.

Beyond these liberal arts traditions, the program would also encourage courses in victimology, social work, and communication. Police officers are often called upon to do social worker-type duties, for example, when working with victims and their families. A basic understanding of how to handle these situations from an academic perspective (which would include best practices, theory, and case studies) will broaden students' viewpoints and allow them to practice real-world scenarios before being alone on a call where they must use social worker-type skills. Further, courses in communication (in conjunction with the other liberal arts subjects) will expose future police officers to a deeper level of understanding of how individuals communicate, including differences in modes of communication from varying languages, cultures, and socioeconomic backgrounds, as well as individuals with disabilities. The combination of these academic courses with constant real-world and real-time exposure to police work through internships will allow participants the opportunity to see the overlap between theory and practice, academics, and techniques.

Key Elements of the Model Precinct: Civilian Oversight

There are a number of additional key elements to be considered about the nature of the proposed "Model Precinct." The steps to be undertaken begin with existing or updated screening processes involving intellectual, physical, mental, and legal selection considerations. However, instead of new recruits reporting to a local, zone, or municipal police academy for a generally uninterrupted four- to six-month program of instruction, they immediately report to a police precinct or other location where police are routinely assigned to patrol areas in their home jurisdiction. In some small towns or other types of municipalities, this location may be a central police headquarters building or office. The locations become the focal point of all basic training instruction and activities. Whenever possible, this instruction is supplemented by an academic educational program conducted at a nearby campus. The lack of a nearby college campus is compensated for through Zoom and other hybrid computer-assisted methods of instruction. The need to have expert instruction in such fields as self-defense, firearms, crisis intervention/de-escalation techniques, substance abuse, emergency vehicle operation, and related areas can be addressed by intermittent course attendance at state police and/or correctional academies.

New recruits who already possess significant academic and professional credentials may have parts of their training program waived through appropriate testing. If new recruits possess prior experience as volunteers or peace officers, they would also have the opportunity to have portions of their training waived through testing procedures. All new trainees will be provided with supervisory instructor/mentors for the length of their training program. Such mentor/instructors must be qualified through the relevant peace officer and training (POST) state agency or board as well as vetted by a community civilian oversight panel. Their qualifications and supervisory performance will be reviewed on a quarterly schedule by the local panel. During daily assignments, the new trainees will engage in a progressive series of field exercises from basic traffic enforcement and the delivery of mental health first aid to responding to the crises and other emergencies expected of sworn officers. Significantly, at each stage of the program trainees will be expected to work closely with community members and organizations in order to become familiar with resources and needs of their jurisdictions. Appropriate orientations and other guidance are to be provided by the supervisory instructor/mentors. Program curriculums are also to be evaluated periodically by the civilian oversight panel and all recruit performance records as an auxiliary officer will be similarly evaluated before a new recruit can be fully sworn-in to serve as a full-time police officer. Such community engagement is a two-way street, holding agencies accountable and encouraging citizen involvement in and knowledge of policing activities in their communities.

The participation of community and faculty members in all phases of the proposed model program is essential. They must routinely engage with police trainers and should serve on advisory boards and be engaged to implement, evaluate, and improve these collaborative efforts. The voice of the citizens must be heard for the continuous, qualitative advancement of police training and education to bolster community acceptance and support for local police.

Student Benefits From the Model Precinct Internship Program

Micro-level benefits are those that would directly impact individuals who would participate in or partner with the decentralized training program. College students concerned about community safety will have an important competitive edge in the occupational marketplace. The opportunity to gain work experience is the most beneficial advantage that can be acquired by completing any internship. Both traditional and non-traditional college students can benefit. Obviously, having this work experience on a resume may result in more job offers as compared to individuals who lack such work experience. For adult career changers, an internship is often a method to bridge past career history to a new career objective, often without having to complete lengthy additional schooling. The program allows for various groups of students from different educational and occupational backgrounds to gain the education and experience necessary to work as a peace officer and better serve their communities from their respective positions.

In particular, participation in the internship component of the program can help students: (1) learn about a career field from the inside; (2) decide if this is the right career field; (3) gain new skills and add to their knowledge base; (4) gain confidence in their own abilities; (5) apply some of the concepts learned in other areas of their schooling and afterwards; (6) practice their communication and teamwork skills; (7) meet new people and practice networking skills; (8) demonstrate their initiative and their sense of responsibility; (9) bridge the gap between school and the professional world; (10) gain sufficient information to make a more knowledgeable career decision; (11) enhance their applications for graduate school; (12) stimulate new interest in their own academic course work; (13) investigate organizational cultures; (14) obtain a mentor who can help with career goals: and (15) receive a job offer or a recommendation about the next step(s) to take on their career path.

Generally, students will gain a richer understanding of the relationship between theory and practical application. The experience may test a career objective on the basis of a real-world encounter. Students have the opportunity to develop good professional work habits and to become acquainted with people employed in professional occupations. The relationships may grow into a network of contacts for future career pursuits. Such an internship should also enhance the self-confidence of interns, particularly young/traditional undergraduates, as they learn self-reliance and independence and develop skills necessary to interact with more diverse populations. At the very least, they can refer to their experience during job and graduate school interviews in other fields and reflect on these experiences for future educational and/or career endeavors—and the knowledge and experiences gained will certainly be beneficial for civic and community life.

Students would gain vital police experience by participating in the program and have the opportunity to earn a variety of police training certifications during their academic years. By obtaining firsthand knowledge of police work, students would better determine whether they wish to embark on a career in law enforcement. Upon graduation, students would not only possess a college degree in a field related to criminal justice but also have the appropriate qualifications to begin working as police officers in many communities without the need for additional formal training. However, students seeking full-time careers would be required to take the desired career civil service exams. This significant requirement is a major feature of the New York City Police Cadet program and frequently is included in other police cadet programs. Students' participation in the program would better prepare them for exams, which historically have been an obstacle for some police candidates. Moreover, police departments often pay the cadets for their precinct work, but students in the proposed program would not need to be paid. The students still would usually have the benefit of insurance protection provided by the college for interns as well as a state's workmen's compensation law upon achieving auxiliary or reserve status.

Additional Benefits for Agency Personnel and Beyond

Significantly, in return for their supervisory work, local police officers or others should receive the opportunity to return for any educational credits still needed for degree completion at the cooperating college. In this way, full-time employees who serve as intern mentors and field supervisors may receive tuition credits for their efforts from the participating college. Colleges typically use this benefit to reward agency field personnel who volunteer to supervise student interns.

During the course of the students' enrollment in the program, local police and other participating agencies would monitor the progress of each intern. When openings become available, the agencies would have the advantage of being familiar with the candidates, and the students would possess at least an introductory knowledge required for the job. The sponsoring departments also would benefit from the program by having the additional personnel available throughout the year and building bridges with their communities. Also, by supervising and instructing the interns, agency personnel would gain useful leadership experience.

Police officers assigned to supervise interns may also benefit by having the opportunity to engage in professional activities that they might not otherwise be able to do, for example, serving as role models and mentors to interns. As such, individual-level benefits are expanded to the meso-level within police agencies and communities. The meso-level refers to the connection, interaction and ongoing coordination of numerous different social roles simultaneously. The proliferation of relevant degree programs provides police departments with unparalleled opportunities to recruit college and university students to the field of law enforcement. For agencies, criminal justice or other majors can provide the labor and skill needed to complete special projects that would otherwise not be finished or undertaken. Moreover, schools and police agencies involved in training interns may find that their own employees experience professional growth as a result of their necessary supervisory roles. In turn, such efforts can help establish a pool of potential employees who have demonstrated their abilities. Additionally, these agencies may benefit from an introduction of fresh, new ideas. At the same time, they have an opportunity to send goodwill ambassadors back to campus. Colleges benefit by the enrichment to its educational programs that results from a strong internship program. Both school administrators and department heads have the opportunity to reinforce positive relationships within the community and hopefully, gain community support for their programs.

The community would benefit from the services of the additional uniformed personnel for crime deterrence. And with direct citizen involvement and oversight, the voices of community members will be heard, hopefully building more trust between communities and the police officers that serve them. Moreover, because of the availability of these police interns, departments could establish a variety of community policing programs. One of the most unique features of the proposed Model Precinct program is that it can result in a substantial savings in regular police training costs, which become a shared undertaking with a local college.

Societal-level benefits are also possible through the program on a macro level. Better educated police officers can provide a myriad of benefits to the communities they serve—if this program is adopted on a national level, we can see even more widespread benefits. Further, expanding opportunities for higher education in general can have societal benefits that can be derived from the increasing synergy between the police and other local institutions. Such an education should further respect for victims and witnesses, develop strategies to solve problems, and meet local priorities. Even if participants do not spend any or all of their careers in policing or even the criminal justice system, there will still be benefits to increasing numbers of individuals completing the program, including but not limited to citizens having a better understanding of the justice system and how it influences and is influenced by other social institutions. Further, graduates will be better poised to engage in any type of work as concerned and involved citizens of their own communities.

Limitations of the Program

The occurrence of police corruption, even in small doses through highly publicized cases, can seriously undermine the public's faith in its police force and weaken the bonds necessary for successful community policing initiatives. The program might be a factor in convincing bad officers to leave their agencies because of the presence of "too many" civilian volunteers, especially members of minority groups. On the other hand, this new model cannot stop agencies from hiring such personnel in the first place. Police departments must still put into place better practices to screen applicants to weed out those with racist, violent, or simply bullying tendencies—people who only make their able colleagues' jobs harder by alienating whole swaths of the communities they serve. Further, the implementation of the program would only apply to NEW officers. This does little to immediately change the culture of policing. Nonetheless, this program opens the door for long-term qualitative improvement across the country.

Police forces will also still need to seek diversity in their ranks by holding public campaigns, job fairs, and school outreach. The ability to attract minorities to law enforcement careers requires a devoted effort to help police agencies reflect the communities they serve. On the other hand, the recruitment of college student interns to serve as auxiliaries should decrease the apparent sense of alienation, suspicion, tension, or outright hostility between many minority groups and police departments. Nonetheless, more uniform "use of force" policies may still be needed and police conduct monitored. The proposed national police misconduct database should help in this regard.

It might be argued that a better solution for lessening community tensions and obviating the need for such a new program is to rely on the idea of "community policing." However, this must not remain a mere pronouncement on a department's website; rather it requires a whole network of police-community partnerships involving continual maintenance. Moreover, all such efforts must contend with the history of inequity between privileged Whites and the working poor dating back hundreds of years. Currently, easing tensions between the police and the public must not only contend with harsh economic conditions but also address the racial health disparities exposed by the COVID-19 pandemic. Bridging connections with law enforcement agencies and educational institutions is a step toward this goal.

A statement by a former New York City police commissioner may indicate a new trend in police reform. Commissioner Dermot Shea stated: "I think it's time to move forward and change how we police in this city. We can . . . move away from brute force." Officers in anti-crime units were reassigned in efforts to focus America's largest police department on "community policing. Shea indicated that crime-fighting efforts will shift more toward using technology, intelligence, data and video, and do away with targeted raids. "This is 21st-century policing, . . . What we always struggle with, I believe, as police executives, is not keeping crime down, it's keeping crime down and keeping the community with us and I think those two things, at times, have been at odds" (tad. in Togo, 2020).

The establishment of a decentralized training program will require extraordinary leadership. One recent editorial asked: "Where are the leaders who would not merely promise such an agenda, as so many politicians do, but who will follow through on those promises? Many of the . . . people protesting on America's streets are no doubt there not only because of broken promises of equal justice, but broken promises of equal opportunity" (Times Union, 2020, p. D1). Though it will be a large task, efforts to identify and utilize the appropriate parties to move this model program forward is imperative. This time in history opens a window of opportunity. Hopefully, criminal justice educators in law enforcement agencies and within colleges and universities will seize this opportunity and to move ahead.

As with any new program, funding may be a limitation and community support is not guaranteed. Though the potential to *save* money exists through the proposed Model Precinct program, financial and time costs will always be present, particularly to launch a new program in any new area. Gaining public support and securing the resources necessary may be a barrier to getting started. Appropriate education of communities, colleges, and police departments about the long-term benefits of the program should help elicit support to move forward.

Conclusion

Ultimately, direct participants and communities should overwhelmingly benefit from the program. Agencies would gain a pool of applicants as well as members of society who have successfully completed volunteer police officer (e.g., part-time peace officer status) or all police training requirements, or both. Governments would benefit from the financial relief that comes from reducing the cost of training prospective police officers. The participating college would profit from increased enrollment, potentially recruiting a more diverse student body, and better relationships with community partners. The students themselves would benefit by becoming pre-certified and thus more marketable. Additionally, intrinsic values that come from a well-rounded education and job satisfaction are likely to be experienced by graduates of this program.

The proposed program would do more than merely take an existing training program and link it with an existing college program. The relationship envisioned between police agencies and colleges demands more than a typical cooperative agreement might require, and community volunteers will also need to be secured. The personnel within the colleges and the police agencies must commit to the goals of the model program, and work collaboratively, step by step, to create their own local program that is meaningful and relevant in their respective locations. On a continuing basis, college leaders must be prepared to acknowledge the major role performed by local law enforcement professionals in the program, and likewise, police leadership must be willing to accept input from the college community, as well as from citizens at large. This proposal allows for flexibility in structure and implementation to fit the needs of individual areas and the communities served by different police forces.

The adoption of the proposed Model Precinct program for the delivery of modern police education can make a well-educated and accountable police force a reality for many agencies. The adoption of the program could begin a new era of police-citizen partnership and simultaneously lead to greater public safety and better police-citizen relationships in neighborhoods throughout the United States. Time is of the essence; many police departments are continuing to struggle with how to train and cope with crime in their jurisdictions. As the authors were working on the book's final draft, the brutal death of Tyre Nichols, a 29-year-old Black man, at the hands of Memphis officers in the first month of 2023, had renewed questions around police accountability, training, and use-of-force policies. Yet, the everyday work of police must continue, and there is a continuing need for good people to enter the field of law enforcement. "Few police officers, however, are unaffected by the sheer intensity of their work, which brings them face-to-face with chaos, depravity, fear, and a depressing repetition of human suffering and injustice" (Nicholl, 1999, p. 39).

This concluding and final chapter has sought to reimagine the manner in which public safety can be advanced in a democracy. It seems that the long-ago statement of Thomas Paine in his famous work entitled *The American Crisis*, begun in late 1776, is still applicable: "These are the times that try men's souls." Paine, seeking to stir up revolutionary spirit in the American colonies, continued, "The summer soldier and the sunshine patriot may, in this crisis, shrink from the service of his country; but he that stands deserves the love and thanks of man and woman." Today, words and deeds matter more than ever before. For so many, the proliferation and mistaken use of firearms in American society have meant the difference between living and dying! Surely, an approach to training based on a "guardian style" can do much to alleviate such suffering. The police can be aided in their work by promoting citizen participation and police training in LRE. The Citizen Police Academy, better organized by qualified volunteer officers, can further enhance this goal. The many challenges of our day "require us to think broadly and even more creatively about the future" (Nicholl, 1999, p. viii). The police must be aided by the public to cope with community safety. At the same time, they must always be accountable because of the overriding need to preserve the integrity, meaning, and purpose of law in a democratic society.

References

Barker, J. (1989, July 12). Police corps plan: Scholarships for service. *Cortland Standard*, p. 26.

Bauman, A., & Chakrabarti, M. (2020, June 11). *Portrait of police reform: How Camden, New Jersey rebuilt its police*. Retrieved July 23, 2020, from https://www.wbur.org/onpoint/2020/06/11/police-reform-camden-new-jersey-rebuilt-its-police-department

Bilek, A. J. (1995). *Winning back the support of the public by stopping police corruption and misconduct before it starts with pre-service police education*. Paper presented at the Conference on Criminal Justice Education, John Jay College of Criminal Justice, New York City.

Bogel-Burroughs, N. (2021, March 30). Prosecutors say Derek Chauvin knelt on George Floyd for 9 minutes 29 seconds, longer than initially reported. *The New York Times*. Retrieved April 5, 2021, from https://www.nytimes.com/2021/03/30/us/derek-chauvin-george-floyd- kneel-9-minutes-29-seconds.html

Burden, O. P. (1988, March). Recruiting police from college. *FBI Law Enforcement Bulletin, 57*(3), 1–6.

Burkhalter, K. (2020, June 11). Retired officer: Give police a real education before putting them on the streets. *USA Today*. Retrieved June 22, 2020, from https://www.usatoday.com/story/opinion/policing/2020/06/11/ex-cop-academy-training-falls-short-police-need-extensive-education/5342917002/

Carter, D. L., & Sapp, A. D. (1990). The evolution of higher education in law enforcement: Preliminary findings from a national study. *Journal of Criminal Justice Education, 1*(1), 59–85.

Commissioner Woods. (1915, Sunday, October 17). Commissioner Woods tells what the police are doing. *The Brooklyn Daily Eagle*, p. 5.

Dyment, R. (1997, July). A successful training program: Police academy thrives in cooperation with local college. *Law and Order*, pp. 93–97.

Editorial. (1990, February 11). Support your local police corps. *The New York Times*, p. 24.

Goodwin, A. N. (2019). The future of liberal arts in higher education: A policy Delphi study. *Educational Perspectives, 51*(1), 13–17.

Irwin, A., & Pearl, B. (2020, October 28). *The community responder model*. Retrieved November 24, 2022, from https://www.americanprogress.org/article/community-responder-model/

Kelderman, E. (2020, July 1). Can higher education help fix America's policing problem? *The Chronicle of Higher Education*. Retrieved July 6, 2020, from www.chronicle.com

Keneally, M. (2016, April 11). *What's inside the controversial 1994 crime bill that's plaguing Hillary Clinton on the campaign trail?* Retrieved April 4, 2021, from https://abcnews.go.com/Politics/inside-controversial-1994-crime-bill-plaguing-clinton- campaign/story?id=38313757

Kessler, G. (2014, September 26). Bill Clinton's claim that 100,000 cops sent the crime rate 'way down.' *The Washington Post*. Retrieved April 4, 2021, from https://www.washingtonpost.com/news/fact- checker/wp/2014/09/26/bill-clintons-claim- that-100000-cops-sent-the-crime-rate-way-down/

Klein, M. (2002, February 1). Law enforcement's response to people with mental illness. *FBI Law Enforcement Bulletin*, *71*(2), 11–14.
Lee, N. (2020, June 25). *Here's how two federal programs helped expand police funding by over 200% since 1980*. Retrieved April 4, 2021, from https://www.cnbc.com/2020/06/25/two- federal-programs-helped-expand-police-funding-by-over-200percent.html
McGrath, N. (1978, November). National commission calls for major changes in college-level training for police officers. *The Chronicle of Higher Education*, p. 3.
Michelson, R. (2016, March 8). Why cops should pursue higher education. *PoliceOne*. Retrieved June 22, 2020, from www.policeone.com
Nicholl, C. G. (1999). *Community policing, Community justice, and restorative justice: Exploring the links for the delivery of a balanced approach to public safety*. US Department of Justice, Office of Community Oriented Policing Services.
Nislow, J. (2008). *Law enforcement and the mentally ill: A pathfinder*. Retrieved June 15, 2020, from https://www.lib.jjay.cuny.edu/research/mentallyill.pdf
NYPD. (2021). *Cadet corps requirements & benefits*. Retrieved April 5, 2021, from https://www1.nyc.gov/site/nypd/careers/cadets/police-cadets-program.page
Oliver, W. M. (2016). Celebrating 100 years of criminal justice education, 1916–2016. *Journal of Criminal Justice Education*, 27(4), 455–472. https://www.tandfonline.com/doi/full/10.1080/10511253.2016.1186992
Oreskes, M. (1985, Sunday, June 9). Study advocates college tuition aid for recruits in a police corps. *The New York Times*, p. 42.
PERF. (2021, June 11). *Survey on police workforce trends*. Retrieved November 29, 2021, November 24, 2022, from https://www.policeforum.org/workforcesurveyjune2021
Police Corps Annual Report. (2000, April). *The police corps: A report to the president, the attorney general and the congress*. U.S. Department of Justice, Office of Justice Programs, Office of the Police Corps and Law Enforcement Education. https://www.ojp.gov/pdffiles1/Photocopy/183680NCJRS.pdf
President's Commission on Law Enforcement and Administration of Justice. (1967). *The challenge of crime in a free society*. U.S. Government Printing Office.
Roberg, R., & Bonn, S. (2004). Higher education and policing: Where are we now? *Policing: An International Journal of Police Strategies and Management*, 27(4), 469–486.
Rose, C. (2017, August 30). Why we need liberal arts now more than ever. *Time Magazine*. Retrieved July 8, 2020, from https://time.com/4920389/bowdoin-college-liberal-arts-education/
Rowe, P. M. (1990, March 8). National junior police force wouldn't work (Letter to the editor). *The New York Times*, p. A24.
Scully, R. (1989, November 15). The police corps: Agreeing on aims, but disagreeing on approaches. *Law Enforcement News*, pp. 1 & 13.
Stamper, N. (2016). *To protect and serve: How to fix America's police*. Nation Books.
Stephens, G. (1976). Criminal justice education: Past, present and future. *Criminal Justice Review*, *1*(1), 91–120.
Times Union. (2020, June 7). Editorial: Where do we go from here? *Times Union*, p. D1.
Togoh, I. (2020, June 16). *'Seismic shift': NYPD disbands controversial anti-crime unit involved in many shootings*. Retrieved June 17, 2020, from https://www.forbes.com/sites/isabeltogoh/2020/06/16/seismic-shift-nypd-disbands-controversial-anti-crime-unit-involved-in-many-shootings/#2f9186236607
Wrobleski, H. M., & Hess, K. M. (1979). *Introduction to law enforcement and criminal justice*. West Publishing Co.
Zernike, K. (2014, August 31). Camden turns around with new police force. *New York Times*. Retrieved July 23, 2020, from https://www.nytimes.com/2014/09/01/nyregion/camden-turns-around-with-new-police-force.html

APPENDIX A

Police Academy TV and Movies

A selection of movies and television series showcasing police academies, in alphabetical order:

21 Jump Street (2012)
CHIPS (2017)
Code Two (1953)
Cop and a Half (New Recruit) (2017)
Crime Busters (1977)
The Delicate Delinquent (1957)
Gen X Cops (1999)
A Gun in His Hand (1945, short)
Highway Patrolman (1991)
I Take This Oath (1940)
Internal Affairs (2002)
Little Nellie Kelly (1940)
Mobs, Inc (1956)
Police Academy (1–7) (1984–1994)
Police Academy, the series (1988–1989)
The Recruit (2003)
Ride Along (2014)
TJ Hooker (1982–1985)
Vice Academy (1989)

APPENDIX B

Police Training in Various Entertainment Formats

A selection of podcasts with episodes about police academies (including the *Police Academy* movies), in alphabetical order:

Barnes Boys (Season 1, Episode 2; December 18, 2020)
The Bitter End (Season 6, Episode 1, May 1, 2017)
Citizen's Arrest: Rapid City Police Academy
Clash of the Titles (Episode 152, Parts 1 and 2; June 27 and 30, 2022)
Darren and Matt's 1980s Adventures (September 6, 2020)
Frank and Eric (Season 1, Episode 2; October 23, 2019)
Film Snuff (Episode 48; August 15, 2017)
The GR80s—1980's Movie Show (April 21, 2020)
Hey, Do You Remember? (March 6, 2020)
Movie Muggin (November 17, 2019)
The Number One Movie in America (November 23, 2020)
The Old Time Dragnet Show with Adam Graham (May 14, 2007)
Podstalgic: A Film Podcast (February 3, 2015)
Police Academy
The Police Applicant Podcast
Ruined Childhoods (May 9, 2019)
Street Cop Training Podcast
This Silicon Valley Beat (Season 1, Episode 7; June 25, 2019)
Trysto Film Commentaries (March 8, 2015)
The Villain Was Right (Episode 47, August 15, 2019)

INDEX

Note: Page numbers in *italics* indicate a figure on the corresponding page.

For Product Safety Concerns and Information please contact our EU
representative GPSR@taylorandfrancis.com
Taylor & Francis Verlag GmbH, Kaufingerstraße 24, 80331 München, Germany

www.ingramcontent.com/pod-product-compliance
Ingram Content Group UK Ltd.
Pitfield, Milton Keynes, MK11 3LW, UK
UKHW050234200926
475702UK00020B/3027
9781032308739